WITHDRAWN

# Providence and Love

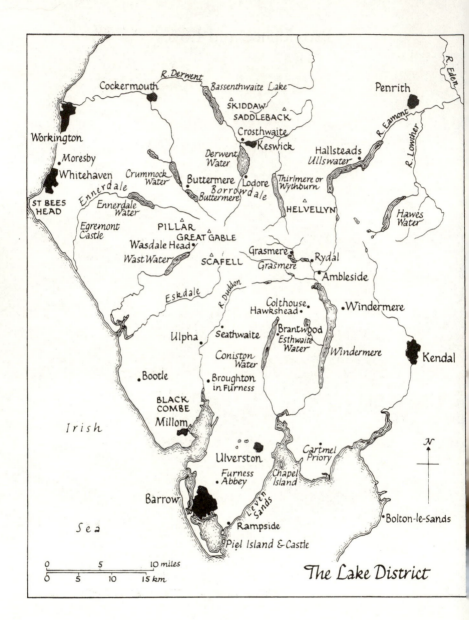

The Lake District

# PROVIDENCE AND LOVE

## Studies in Wordsworth, Channing, Myers, George Eliot, and Ruskin

JOHN BEER

CLARENDON PRESS · OXFORD
1998

Oxford University Press, Great Clarendon Street, Oxford OX2 6DP

Oxford New York

Athens Auckland Bangkok Bogotá Buenos Aires Calcutta
Cape Town Chennai Dar es Salaam Delhi Florence Hong Kong Istanbul
Karachi Kuala Lumpur Madrid Melbourne Mexico City Mumbai
Nairobi Paris São Paulo Singapore Taipei Tokyo Toronto Warsaw
and associated companies in
Berlin Ibadan

Oxford is a registered trade mark of Oxford University Press

Published in the United States
by Oxford University Press Inc., New York

British Library Cataloguing in Publication Data
Data available

Library of Congress Cataloging in Publication Data
Beer, John B.
Providence and love: studies in Wordsworth, Channing, Myers, George Eliot, and
Ruskin / John Beer.
Includes bibliographical references and index.
1. English literature—19th century–History and criticism. 2. Love in
literature. 3. Ruskin, John, 1819–1900—Criticism and interpretation. 4. Cambridge
(England)—Intellectual life—19th century. 5. Providence and government of god in
literature. 6. Wordsworth, William, 1770–1850—Characters—Lucy. 7. Channing,
William Ellery, 1780–1842—Influence. 8. Myers, Frederic William Henry,
1843–1901. 9. Romanticism—England. 10. Parapsychology. I. Title.
PR468.L68B44 1998 820.9'008—dc21 98-29841
ISBN 0-19-818436-0

1 3 5 7 9 10 8 6 4 2

Typeset by Best-set Typesetter Ltd., Hong Kong
Printed in Great Britain
on acid-free paper by
Bookcraft Ltd
Midsomer Norton, Somerset

*For*
A. S. BYATT

# Preface

FOR my research on the background to Wordsworth's 'Lucy' poems I wish to acknowledge the assistance of the staffs of the County Record Offices at Barrow-in-Furness and at Carlisle, and of the church of Latterday Saints, whose microfilms of sections from English parish registers much facilitate the researcher's task. The work has also benefited from discussions with members of the Wordsworth Summer Conference and of the 1995 conference of the British Association for Romantic Studies at Bangor at which I was able to present a part of the chapter. I am particularly grateful in addition to the Librarian and staff of the Dove Cottage Library at Grasmere for giving me ready access to manuscripts there and acknowledge the kindness of the Wordsworth Trust in allowing me to quote a few passages from them, some of which have not been previously reproduced, and to include a photograph of one page.

In connection with my chapter on William Ellery Channing, I am greatly indebted to Katherine H. Griffin of the Massachusetts Historical Society, who came across his manuscript journal when searching unsuccessfully at my request for Channing's account of his visit to Coleridge (see Chapter 3, note 26 below) and very kindly made a xerox available to me. I am most grateful both to her and to the Society, which has allowed me to reproduce the extracts which appear in this article. The accounts of the conversations with Wordsworth and Southey there are given in full in my text. My account first appeared in a slightly different form in an article for the *Review of English Studies*, and I am happy to thank the Editors and publisher for permission to use it again here.

In dealing with the work of F. W. H. Myers I owe a particular debt to the work of Alan Gauld. Although my work on the manuscripts was carried out in independence from his, I quote some of the same passages in my section on Myers as appeared in his excellent book, *The Founders of Psychical Research*. Although his work contains apt and shrewd comments on

Myers's writing from a literary point of view his focus is always on the significance of Myers as an initial worker in the field of psychical research rather than on the literary matters that are my concern here. I am particularly grateful to Dr Gauld for having spared the time for a brief conversation in which he told me about some matters that had come to light since he wrote his study, including Charlotte Mackenzie's book on Victorian psychiatry and the availability of the papers concerning Walter Marshall's stay at Ticehurst. He also drew my attention to the misleading diagnosis of Walter's condition by the doctors there. I also wish to acknowledge the help from the staff of the Wellcome Institute and the permission of the Trustees of Ticehurst Hospital to draw on information from their archives.

A visit to the Ruskin Seminar at the University of Lancaster prompted several conversations, particularly with Michael Wheeler, Robert Hewison, and David Carroll, which were most helpful in the last stages of my work. I should also like to thank the librarians and staff of the John Rylands Library in Manchester and of the Bodleian Library for their ready co-operation.

My greatest debt is to the librarians and staff of Trinity College, Cambridge, who have untiringly assisted me in my use of their Myers and Sidgwick archives. I wish to acknowledge my gratitude to the Master and Fellows of Trinity, and to the Curator of the Special Collections in the Beinecke Rare Book and Manuscript Library at Yale University, for permission to reproduce a number of these manuscripts. Dr Pegram Harrison gave me invaluable help in locating the letters at Yale.

I should also record my pleasure that the organizers of the annual Wordsworth Summer Conference at Grasmere have so often given me opportunities to present early versions of the views expressed here, and thank the participants for their successive discussions. Other debts are recorded in the footnotes, but I must mention the kindness of Professor Margaret Harris, editor of the George Eliot Diaries, in showing me the relevant brief extracts, attending to my account of George Eliot's relationship with Myers and offering further encouragement. I am also grateful to Kevin Taylor of Cambridge University Press for informing me, from the CD-ROM disk of Ruskin's *Works*, about his many uses of the word 'Providence', while further thanks are due to the Master and Fellows of Trinity College, Cambridge, for permission to reproduce the sketches in the letter on page 145. The staff at Hallsteads, now an Outward Bound school, were very helpful when I visited the house and grounds as they are today.

## Additional Note

Since this book went to press Kenneth Johnston's new study of Wordsworth, *The Hidden Wordsworth: Poet, Lover, Rebel, Spy*, has appeared, in which he firmly identifies Dorothy Wordsworth with 'Lucy' throughout, reading 'Ah! what a crash was that . . . ' (see p. 40 below) as a direct reproach to her (as 'Lucy') for the greed of sexual feelings which make her want to ravish him violently in the way that he had plundered hazel nut clusters during his own boyhood. This poem does not read to me as if it was originally addressed to Dorothy, though as mentioned below parts of it were certainly taken up into their relationship later. Similarly, he develops a reading of 'The Waterfall and the Eglantine' by which William identifies himself with the eglantine as he tries desperately to stand in the path of the overpowering waterfall of Dorothy's erotic passion for him. Although there was a clear element of ardent intimacy in the relationship, as witnessed by his tendency to speak of her as 'my Love' in poems of 1800–2 and she of him as 'my Beloved' and 'the Darling!' in one or two journal-entries of the same period, such extreme readings strike me as far-fetched to the point of absurdity: Dorothy Wordsworth's 'wildness' was hardly of that kind. Any sexual undertones in their love are, in my view, best understood (following the interpretation developed in my *Wordsworth and the Human Heart* (1978), especially chapter 6) in the context of an intensity of feeling accompanied by strong and unquestioning mutual restraint, Professor Johnston's comment on Dorothy Wordsworth's wearing her future sister-in law's wedding-ring on her forefinger during the night before the wedding seems to me, by contrast, more apt: '[Her] behaviour was not so strange in that era of Sensibility as it seems today.' My own interpretation of the relationship between Dorothy and 'Lucy', similarly, as developed in recent years (see below pp. 63–9) is that it was both complex and subtle—not a matter of simple identification. If 'Ah! what a crash was that . . .' *was* addressed to her, it may then be read as an early instance of the shift I posit there.

# Contents

# Illustrations

## PLATES

### (*between pages 160 and 161*)

# Abbreviations

Place of publication is given only when outside London.

| | |
|---|---|
| Abse, *Ruskin* | Joan Abse, *John Ruskin: The Passionate Moralist* (1980) |
| Bateson, *Wordsworth* | F. W. Bateson, *Wordsworth: A Reinterpretation* (1954; 2nd edn., 1956) |
| Bobbitt, *Dearest Love* | Mary Anne Bobbitt, *With Dearest Love to All: The Life and Letters of Lady Jebb* (1960) |
| Bradbrook, *Infidel Place* | M. C. Bradbrook, *That Infidel Place* (1969) |
| Burd, *Christmas Story* | *Christmas Story: John Ruskin's Venetian letters of 1876–1877*, ed. Van Akin Burd (Newark, 1990) |
| Burd, *RLT* | Van Akin Burd, *John Ruskin and Rose La Touche: Her Unpublished Diaries of 1861 and 1867* (Oxford, 1979) |
| *CBL* | Coleridge, *Biographia Literaria*, ed J. Engell and W. J. Bate, (CC vii) (2 vols. 1983) |
| *CC* | *The Collected Works of Samuel Taylor Coleridge*, general ed. Kathleen Coburn, associate ed. Bart Winer (in progress, Princeton NJ and London, 1969– ) |
| *CC&S* | Coleridge, *On the Constitution of the Church and State*, ed. J. Colmer (CC x) (1972) |
| *Channing Memoir* | *Memoir of William Ellery Channing*, ed. W. Channing (2 vols. 1848) |
| *CL* | Coleridge, *Collected Letters*, ed. E. L. Griggs (6 vols. Oxford, 1956–71) |
| *CLS* | Coleridge, *A Lay Sermon*, ed. R. J. White (CC vi) (1976) |
| *CM* | Coleridge, *Marginalia* (CC xii), ed. ed. George Whalley (in progress, 1980– ) |

CN

*The Notebooks of Samuel Taylor Coleridge*, ed. Kathleen Coburn (4 vols. pub. out of 5 projected, Princeton NJ and London, 1959– )

Committee Report

'Report from the Select Committee on Lunacy Laws, together with the proceedings of the Committee, Minutes of Evidence, and Appendix': *Reports of Committees* xiii (London: House of Commons 1877), Evidence from Walter Marshall: pp. 419–27

*CPW* (EHC)

Coleridge, *Poetical Works*, ed. E. H. Coleridge (2 vols. Oxford, 1912)

DC MS

Manuscript in Wordsworth Library at Dove Cottage, Grasmere

*DQ Recollections*

Thomas De Quincey, *Recollections of the Lakes and the Lake Poets*, ed. David Wright (Harmondsworth, 1970)

*DQW*

*The Collected Writings of Thomas De Quincey*, ed. D. Masson (14 vols., Edinburgh, 1889– )

*DWJ* (Woof)

Dorothy Wordsworth, *The Grasmere Journals*, ed. Pamela Woof (Oxford, 1991)

Gauld, *Founders*

Alan Gauld, *The Founders of Psychical Research* (1968)

*GEL*

*The George Eliot Letters*, ed. Gordon Haight (9 vols. New Haven, 1954–78)

Haight, *Eliot*

Gordon Haight, *George Eliot: A Biography* (Oxford, 1968)

Hilton *R Early Years*

Tim Hilton, *Ruskin: The Early Years* (New Haven, 1985)

Kermode, *Secrecy*

Frank Kermode, *The Genesis of Secrecy: On the Interpretation of Narrative* (Norton lectures) (Cambridge, Mass., 1979)

Leon, *Ruskin*

Derrick Leon, *Ruskin: The Great Victorian* (1949)

| | |
|---|---|
| Lutyens, 'Correspondence' | M. Lutyens, 'The Millais–La Touche Correspondence' *Cornhill* 176 (1967–8), 1–18 |
| MacDonald, *Reminiscences* | G. MacDonald, *Reminiscences of a Specialist* (1932) |
| Moorman, *Wordsworth* | Mary Moorman, *William Wordsworth: A Biography* (2 vols., Oxford, 1957) |
| Myers, *CP* | F. W. H. Myers, *Collected Poems, with Autobiographical and Critical Fragments*, ed. Eveleen Myers (1921) |
| Myers, *EM* | F. W. H. Myers, *Essays–Modern* (1883, repr. 1908) |
| Myers, *FIL* | F. W. H. Myers, *Fragments of Inner Life* (London, Society for Psychical Research, 1961) |
| Myers, *FPP* | F. W. H. Myers, *Fragments of Prose and Poetry*, ed. Eveleen Myers (1904) |
| Myers, *HP* | F. W. H. Myers, *Human Personality and its Survival of Bodily Death* (1903) |
| Myers, *SFL* | F. W. H. Myers, *Science and a Future Life, with other Essays* (1893) |
| Myers, *Wordsworth* | F. W. H. Myers, *Wordsworth* (English Men of Letters) (1880) |
| Peabody, *Reminiscences* | E. M. Peabody, *Reminiscences of Rev W. E. Channing, D. D.* (Boston, 1880) |
| RCEN | *The Correspondence of John Ruskin and Charles Eliot Norton*, ed. John Lewis Bradley and Ian Ousby (Cambridge, 1987) |
| R Diaries | *The Diaries of John Ruskin, 1835–1889*, sel. and ed. Joan Evans and John Howard Whitehouse (3 vols., Oxford 1956–9) |
| RLMT | *The Letters of John Ruskin to Lord and Lady Mount-Temple*, ed. J. L. Bradley (Columbus, Oh., 1964) |

| | |
|---|---|
| *R Winnington* | *The Winnington Letters: John Ruskin's Correspondence with Margaret Alexis Bell and the Children at Winnington Hall*, ed. Van Akin Burd (1969) |
| *R Works* | *The Works of John Ruskin*, the Library Edition, ed. E. T. Cook and Alexander Wedderburn (39 vols., 1903–12) |
| *Sidgwick Memoir* | Arthur Sidgwick and Eleanor Mildred Sidgwick, *Henry Sidgwick: A Memoir* (1906) |
| *S Letters* (CCSouthey) | Robert Southey, *Life and Correspondence*, ed. C. C. Southey (1850) |
| *S Letters* (Curry) | *New Letters of Robert Southey*, ed. K. Curry (New York, 1965) |
| *S Letters* (Warter) | *Selections from the Letters of Robert Southey*, ed. J. W. Warter (1856) |
| Spence, *Talbot* | Margaret Spence, *Dearest Mama Talbot: A Selection of Letters written by John Ruskin to Mrs Fanny Talbot* (1966) |
| TCL MS | Manuscript in the Library of Trinity College, Cambridge |
| Vargish, *Providential Aesthetic* | Thomas Vargish, *The Providential Aesthetic in Victorian Fiction* (Charlottesville, Va., 1985) |
| *W Chronology EY* | Mark Reed, *Wordsworth: The Chronology of the Early Years, 1770–1799* (Cambridge, Mass., 1967) |
| *W Chronology MY* | Mark Reed, *Wordsworth: The Chronology of the Middle Years, 1800–1815* (Cambridge, Mass., 1975) |
| Wilenski, *Ruskin* | R. H. Wilenski, *John Ruskin* (1933) |
| WL (1787–1805) | *The Letters of William and Dorothy Wordsworth, The Early Years, 1787–1805*, ed. E. de Selincourt, 2nd edn., rev. C. L. Shaver (Oxford, |

|            |                                                                    |
|------------|--------------------------------------------------------------------|
|            | 1967) (*WL* dated similarly for other volumes of the 2nd edition)   |
| W *Prel*   | Wordsworth, *The Prelude*, ed. E. de Selincourt (1st edn. 1926); 2nd edn. rev. Helen Darbishire (Oxford, 1959) |
| W *Prel* (1799) | 1799 version in Wordsworth, *The Prelude*, 1799, 1805, 1850, ed. Jonathan Wordsworth, M. H. Abrahams, and Stephen Gill (New York, 1979) |
| *WPrW*     | Wordsworth, *Prose Works*, ed. W. J. B. Owen and J. W. Smyser (3 vols. Oxford, 1974) |
| *WPW*      | Wordsworth, *Poetical Works*, ed. E. de Selincourt and H. Darbishire (5 vols., Oxford, 1940–9) |

I

# Providence Displaced

'WAS she beautiful or not beautiful?' The question about Gwendolen Harleth as she played her game of chance at the opening of George Eliot's last novel remains unanswered at the end, confirming one's sense of this character's elusive significance. It might also have served for a question that lay behind that of chance and subsisted urgently though covertly in her œuvre.

It is hard to be sure about the nature of Providence, even about the origin of her deification. She is found in ancient times, predating Christianity. In Greece she was Pronoia, regarded less as a goddess than as an aspect of Athena; on coins she appears not as figure but as emblem, usually of fertility. In Christianity, on the other hand, she becomes an aspect of the divine—not necessarily with human characteristics at all. We have to unfocus attention slightly before being able to think of her again as Providentia and assign her a humanized, feminine form. When more sharply focused in Christianity she too easily becomes not figure but topic, subject to question, by Milton's devils for instance. Not that Milton himself accepted such boundlessness outside devildom, believing on the contrary that he could 'assert eternal Providence'.[1] It was a different rhetoric that led him to picture the necessary fate of those who lost themselves in the labyrinths of endless disputation.

In the century after Milton the position of providence became unexpectedly less subject to such contentions. While still a major theme for justification in moralistic writing of the seventeenth and eighteenth centuries, its presence was now being taken for granted as a motif in fiction. Defoe provided excellent examples: 'Providence' is everywhere in *Robinson Crusoe*—so much as often to be hardly more than a synonym for 'Heaven'

---

[1] *Paradise Lost*, I. 25.

or the divine ordering of things. Crusoe sometimes questions its workings, but never its existence. The new emphasis on design in the physics of the time had made the idea for the time being an even more natural one to entertain. Meanwhile Robert Leighton's discourse on the subject in his Theological Lectures of the time may be taken as typical: he quotes a classical writer such as Claudian, who matched his admiration for the divine order with a voicing of his doubts about Providence when he looked at the affairs of men and the uneven distribution of rewards and punishments, but concludes by bringing together many other classical statements about the benevolent, if mysterious, workings of the divinity which concur with the views of the Christian fathers.[2]

During subsequent years the Augustan view of the world found itself underpinned by the vision of ordered harmony that was the first effect of Newton's demonstrations, allowing writers to believe in a *concordia discors*, and to see all nature as art—even if unknown to the observer, all chance as direction— even if it could not be perceived.[3] In such a scheme any questioning of providence was otiose: indeed an age that saw works such as William Sherlock's *Discourse Concerning the Divine Providence* (1694) or Richard Kingston's *Discourse on Divine Providence* (1702) regarded such affirming discussions as commonplace. Bishop Berkeley, who shared Milton's distaste for fruitless disquisitions,[4] was content to argue for its presence simply from the existence of order and beauty in the universe.[5] Bishop Butler, meanwhile, was more intent to find in it an occasion to balance God's benevolence against his demand for moral behaviour, he being not only 'Author of Nature' but 'natural Governor of the World' and thus controller of rewards and punishments.[6] Providence was so obvious a concomitant of the natural and artistic order that it became a fixed point of

---

[2] See Lecture, viii and xiii: *Whole Works*, ed. J. N. Fraser (4 vols., 1830), iv. 236, 271–3.

[3] Pope, *Essay on Man*, I. 289–90.

[4] George Berkeley, Preface to *Three Dialogues between Hylas and Philonous* (1713): *Works*, ed. A. C. Fraser (Oxford, 1871), i. 258.

[5] Berkeley, *Alciphron, or the Minute Philosopher* (1732), III. 10–11: *Works*, ii. 124–6.

[6] See Alexander Welsh, *Strong Representations: Narrative and Circumstantial Evidence in England* (Baltimore, 1982), 168–9,

reference, the ground against which variations might be elaborated but which would remain reassuringly constant. The centrality of its position in the mid-century is clear from *Tom Jones*, where the heroine Sophia Western becomes virtually its Platonic representative. Here the variation necessary to art is created by the etymological fact that the derivation of the word brings it close to that of 'prudence'. The education of Tom Jones consists in his learning to find a way through the territory encompassed by the two concepts.

Some of these matters have been documented and discussed by Martin Battestin in his book *The Providence of Wit*. When Richardson affirmed that virtue was punished and vice rewarded in this world Fielding could remark urbanely that it was 'A very wholesome and comfortable Doctrine, and to which we have but one Objection, namely That it is not true.' Yet as Battestin points out, he quite unblinkingly introduced the workings of providence into *Tom Jones*, where he seemed to go out of his way to produce apparently coincidental happenings that could be interpreted according to its workings. In the same spirit, and acting in his alternative role as judicial commentator, he produced in 1752 a pamphlet entitled *Examples of the Interposition of Providence in the Detection and Punishment of Murder*. Interventions of the kind, to provide crucial evidence, were taken for granted at the time in the law-courts: Henry Bathurst, producing the piece of paper that sent Mary Blandy to her death for murdering her father in the same year, asked, 'what, but the hand of Providence, could have preserved the paper thrown by her into the fire, and have snatched it unburnt from the devouring flame?'[7]

There were good reasons why writers of fiction should find themselves particularly interested in the matter. The sense of a hidden working behind events that would make sense of what was otherwise incomprehensible commended itself to creators of plot. The idea that the figure of Providence might sometimes carry out its work in disguise produced the possibility of still more complicated ingenuities. Its status as a question for serious discussion subsisted alongside the novelist's sense of an audience waiting to be entertained, in terms of which it could be related

---

[7] Quoted by Welsh, ibid. 45.

to the 'happy ending'. The demand for things to turn out well
might in part reflect a need for reassurance, but this was not
the whole story. Equally important was the sense that a fiction
should have a moral dimension; that in terms of the plot good
should be seen to be rewarded and evil punished—not because
novelists believed this to be the way things happened in the
world but because they thought it good for readers to be encouraged to hope so. In this manner the need to be entertained could
march with the demand for moral improvement, with a happy
outcome to satisfy all parties.

Refinements on the theme introduced minor complexities.
*The Vicar of Wakefield* (1766) can be read as a meditation on
one of the most common topics of the time, the Book of Job
as the record of a man who questioned God's providence and
was eventually afforded the satisfaction he sought. Even this
basically pious novel was a pointer toward new explorations,
however, since it acknowledged the very possibility of such a
questioning. Elsewhere the point became more implicit. Already
*Tristram Shandy* had exhibited operations of chance so omni-
present and absurdly wanton as to undermine the whole concept, the product of a writer who could at one and the same time
accept the notion of providence yet so disport himself with the
vagaries of fortune as to provide a text subverting the basis of
order it presupposed.

The shifting emphases were part of a process given new
impetus by *Candide* (1759), its ridicule of the idea that everything was for the best in this best of all possible worlds presenting a direct challenge to those who took the providential order
for granted. Even Samuel Johnson, whose examples of the word
and its associates in his Dictionary furnish in themselves a neat
compendium of orthodox thinking on the subject, and who
indicated to Boswell on one occasion that he believed himself to
have experienced a special intervention of divine providence
during a period of illness,[8] was less amenable to complacent
ideas about an underlying order that made everything right if
one could only appreciate it more fully, as he showed when he
read Soame Jenyns's *Nature and Origin of Evil*, one of the most
important apologias for providence at the time, with its asser-

---

[8] May 1784: *Life*, ed. Arnold Glover (3 vols., 1925), iii. 293 and Boswell's note.

tion, among other things, that ignorance was 'a cordial admin-
istered by the gracious hand of Providence', the only 'opiate'
that could help the poor to endure the miseries and fatigues of
the world. Johnson's review[9] gave short shrift to such bland
optimism—as did his own novel *Rasselas*.

By the end of the century there were few outward signs of
change. Coleridge, lecturing on Revealed Religion at Bristol in
the 1790s, could assume that Providence as a concept, was a
given,[10] even if he did not lean on it heavily. It remained a part
of his linguistic furniture, not much questioned, ready for admonitory use certainly, as in his poem of 1798:

> Therefore evil days
> Are coming on us, O my countrymen!
> And what if all-avenging Providence,
> Strong and retributive, should make us know
> The meaning of our words, force us to feel
> The desolation and the agony
> Of our fierce doings?[11]

The established belief that providence worked most compre-
hensibly through a system of punishments as well as rewards
gave it this chastening force in addition to the status as agent of
Universal Benevolence that was more common in the moral
writings of the time. The severer aspect remained particularly
current in North America, where the word was sometimes used
to characterize a disaster, such as a fatal skating accident—
which must be submitted to as an 'act of God'.[12]

The dominance of the more benign aspect at the end of the
century owed much to the writings of William Paley, sustaining
the idea of nature as the work of a great Designer whose
operations must be acknowledged to be wise and beneficent. In
arguing that nature's activity fitted the confines and needs of
human beings he was aware of difficulties and awkwardnesses,
certainly, the most notable being the fact that the animal
creation which bore so many resemblances to the world of

---

[9] Soame Jenyns, *Miscellaneous Pieces in Verse and Prose* (1730), 264. Johnson's
review is reprinted in the sixth volume of the Pickering edition of his *Works* (1825).
See Basil Willey, *The Eighteenth-Century Background* (1950), 48–55.

[10] See e.g. *Lectures 1795: On Politics and Religion* (*CC* i), 225.

[11] 'Fears in Solitude', ll. 123–9: *CPW* (EHC), i. 260.

[12] See *Oxford English Dictionary*, s.v. 5(b) for examples.

human beings consisted of organisms acting on one another in ways that must sometimes seem cruel; the benevolence of the world, however, could still be rescued by regarding humans as members of a category of being under a special dispensation that enabled them to intervene morally in the whole process.

In *Biographia Literaria* Coleridge was to describe how his moral opinions were deeply disturbed (though not ultimately overthrown) by an onset of questioning during the 1790s. Wordsworth, equally, was one of the first to perceive the implications of the new thinking in upsetting the idea of a providential order: it became all the more important for him to demonstrate that the workings of nature were at their heart favourable to the aspirations of mankind. When he gave an account of his own early fostering in *The Prelude* he tried to trace from his earliest years the presence of a providential work by spirits in nature that had sought him out 'with gentle visitation':

> They guided me: one evening led by them
> I went alone into a shepherd's boat . . .[13]

Within a very short time the 'spirits' would be subsumed into 'Nature', but the sense of being 'led' remained,[14] prompting, for example (even if with less assurance) the description of the meeting with the old leech-gatherer that was pivotal for the poem 'Resolution and Independence':

> Now, whether it were by peculiar grace,
> A leading from above, a something given . . .
> I saw a Man before me unawares . . .[15]

In this case the meeting was seen as being in some fashion providential, the exact nature of the intervention being left uncertain. The old man was so closely associated with the nature where he was encountered that it was easy to mistake him for a part of it. We know from external evidence that some of the detailed elements of the meeting were fictitious: it happened not in a lonely place on the moors but on a road, and Wordsworth was not unaccompanied at the time. Yet this does

---

[13] *W Prel* (1799), I. 81–2.
[14] See *W Prel* (1805), I. 363–73; (1850), I. 352–8.
[15] 'Resolution and Independence', ll. 50–1, 55: *WPW* ii. 237.

not affect his sense of a basic providentiality, linking the conversation to those parts of *The Prelude* where such interventions were seen as experiences assisting his growth as a poet.

As Wordsworth's views became more orthodox, so his use of the term shifted. Apart from two dramatic usages in *The Borderers* he did not employ the word in the years up to completion of the 1805 version of *The Prelude*, when he had recourse to it as he meditated on his experiences in France and reflected on the favour of his preservation from being submerged in the general destruction. The indications are that the belief in the fostering work of nature that he had cultivated during the years between was being brought back into a purview which enabled it to be seen as a supervised operation of transcendental Benevolence.

Coleridge, more intent to see nature in terms of the divine dispensation, filled out the picture. Towards the beginning of his manuscript *Logic* he wrote of the wise purposes of Nature with the parenthesis '(by which we would be always understood to mean the Divine Providence in the creation)'.[16] The development of his theodicy may originally have been assisted by a reading of Berkeley's *Siris*, which formed part of the volume of his works he borrowed from the Bristol Library in the spring of 1796.[17] There Berkeley suggests, citing Plutarch and others, that 'Providence' corresponds to a soul or vital spirit that inhabits the whole world.[18] On this or a similar foundation Coleridge and Wordsworth were enabled to build the idea of a nurturing nature, a sense which in the end was sustained most coherently in theistic terms by Coleridge, as he became increasingly adept at tracing design in the processes of history by which the Christian order of revelation could be explained, the anti-commercial laws of the Hebrews being seen, for example, as part of the purposes of their becoming a separate people.[19] For him a life without providence must be the prelude to a death without hope.[20]

[16] *Logic* (CC xiii) 8.
[17] See G. Whalley, 'The Bristol Library Borrowings of Southey and Coleridge, 1793–8', *The Library* (Oxford, 1950), 5th series, 4: 114–32.
[18] Berkeley, *Siris* (1744), paras. 152–3; *Works*, ed. A. C. Fraser (Oxford, 1871) ii. 418–19.
[19] CLS 8, 223; CC&S 39.
[20] *The Friend* (CC iv) II. 45, repeated CLS 83.

But in any case, the foundations of the traditional idea of providence had been shaken by developments in the late eighteenth century. Blake, who constantly affirmed its workings, was forced into a general questioning when he pictured Urizen surveying his scheme of things:

> For he saw that life liv'd upon death
> The Ox in the slaughter house moans
> The Dog at the wintry door
> And he wept, & he called it Pity
> And his tears flowed down on the winds[21]

Keats, who described a similar glimpse into the universal preying instinct in his 'Epistle to John Hamilton Reynolds', did not address the question of providence directly, while Shelley used the word only sparingly. Even Tennyson, to whom the question was central, used it hardly at all: in 'Enoch Arden', Enoch's speech to Annie about 'providence and trust in Heaven' before his voyage, delivered 'in sailor fashion roughly sermonizing', does nothing to check her conviction that she will not see his face again.[22]

The fact that Tennyson should have placed the word on the lips of an unreflective character and set it in an honest but crude attempt at consolation was not accidental. From now on there was to be a duality of usage: a straightforward one for the pious, calling for respect but not necessarily assent, a less stable one for the thoughtful, whose adoption of it might range between a semi-casual suggestion that favourable factors were at work in the pattern of events and implied awareness of an underlying problem. It would often be as if invisible inverted commas were hanging around the word.

After the Romantic period serious thought about providence was in fact far more likely to be carried out in prose. An important point of departure lay in Scott's Waverley novels, sometimes thought of as marking the secularization of justice through the invocation of history, where the workings of providence were no longer regarded as divine.[23] The position was

---

[21] *The Book of Urizen*, ch. viii, plates 23 and 25: *The Poetry and Prose of William Blake*, ed. David V. Erdman and Harold Bloom (Garden City, NY, 1965), 80–1.

[22] 'Enoch Arden', ll. 201–12: *Poems*, ed. C. Ricks (1969), 1134–5.

[23] See Welsh, *Strong Representations*, 88–91.

further complicated by the fact that under the conditions of nineteenth-century thinking a twofold critique of the concept could be mounted. On the one hand a moral censure lurked, based on the ease with which it could be invoked as a means of describing, and to some extent therefore seeming to justify, one's own good fortune; on the other a more searching perplexity, less often allowed to surface, was provoked by the growing consciousness that recent scientific work made it harder to believe in the existence of such a guiding presence in the first place, so threatening the very basis on which moral judgements might be based.

At this time, writers of fiction virtually took over the important discussions, as Thomas Vargish has shown in an important discussion which has furnished me with some of my illustrations.[24]

The first attitude enabled a novelist to work by way of clear-cut implied judgements, assisting satire. It underlay, for example, many references by Dickens, who was aware of the larger spectrum, including the shifts of polarity that might change the reader's sense of the issues involved, but chose to focus attention rather on the side-effects—particularly if they were comic. His readiest expression lay in the representation of hypocrisy—as with Mr Pecksniff's 'Providence, perhaps I may be permitted to say a special Providence, has blessed my endeavours':

> Mr Pecksniff said grace: a short and pious grace, invoking a blessing on the appetites of those present, and committing all persons who had nothing to eat, to the care of Providence, whose business (so said the grace, in effect) it clearly was, to look after them.[25]

This, together with similar utterances by Podsnap in *Our Mutual Friend*—not to mention the parentheses of Uriah Heep ('(With the blessing of Providence, Master Copperfield) . . .')— helps establish Thomas Vargish's point that in Dickens's work 'it is the wicked and the weak who refer often to providence'.[26]

[24] Thomas Vargish, *The Providential Aesthetic in Victorian Fiction* (Charlottesville, Va., 1985).

[25] *Martin Chuzzlewit*, ch. xx, p. 393; ch. ix, p. 204; Vargish, *Providential Aesthetic*, 103.

[26] Ibid. 102.

Dickens was content to dramatize such attitudes and leave it at that, allowing his plots to take care of the poetic justice by which misfortunes and disasters, set in a fuller context, would be seen as having worked towards an ultimate good. In his own most direct comment he described the relation between the novelist's art in creating plot and the role of fiction in presenting an attempted interpretation of experience:

I think the business of art is to lay all that ground carefully, not with the care that conceals itself—to show, by a backward light, what everything has been working to—but only to *suggest*, until the fulfilment comes. These are the ways of Providence, of which all art is but a little imitation.[27]

Vargish shows how the tradition continued to be drawn on directly in the work of writers following Dickens, with little more than an uneasy suspicion that it was not to be taken for granted. Meredith's reiterated point in *The Ordeal of Richard Feverel* that the error of his hero's father, Sir Austin, was to believe in his ability to usurp the part of Providence is so explicitly made as in itself to need little further discussion. Sometimes, however, the role of providence in fiction would be questioned at a deeper level. A key writer here is Charlotte Brontë and a central text *Jane Eyre*, a work which may all too easily—almost as a commonplace of criticism, in fact—be described as a 'providential novel'. Barbara Hardy has used the term in her criticism, though with a curious disjunction in her thinking. 'When we come to the nineteenth century,' she writes, 'the concept of Providence is plainly outworn and discredited'; yet she also declares that in *Jane Eyre* 'Providence is still very much alive', 'not a dead word'. Since she further insists on the 'superior subtlety of Charlotte Brontë's psychology and imagination'[28] one is left asking how such intellectual blindness is thought to be reconciled with such insight.

So far from finding the concept outworn and discredited, a pious reader of the time might well have traced an essential providentialism in the plot of *Jane Eyre*, the coincidences contributing to the working out of a scheme in which eventually

---

[27] Letter of 6 Oct. 1859, *Letters*, iii. 125, quoted Vargish, *Providential Aesthetic*, 97–8.
[28] *The Appropriate Form* (1964), 63–4.

Rochester is chastened to recognize the validity of a religious order beyond himself.[29] Yet that too would be an oversimplification.

Contemporary reception of the novel, which in general was favourable, particularly from individual readers, shows that, pious or not, it was felt to be in tune with its time. Kathleen Tillotson cites a number of approbatory comments from memoirs of succeeding years.[30] The contemporary reviews, also, were positive, though with enough indications of protest for Charlotte Brontë to have included in her second edition, published in January 1848, a defence written for the 'timorous or carping few'. Against those who criticized the implications of her religious position she maintained the necessity of distinguishing convention and self-righteousness from morality and religion, the first being what she was attacking. The God of these orthodox people was not to be identified with the 'world-redeeming creed of Christ', to which she declared her firm adherence. That, she thought, rightly gave primacy to the power of love.

Some of the more violent attacks on the novel came *after* this defence, however, and may even, Kathleen Tillotson maintained, have been prompted by it. The *Christian Remembrancer* for April 1848 spoke of it as burning with 'moral Jacobinism', while the *North British Review* for August spoke of 'an unamiable reliance on self . . . if not positively irreligious'. The most notorious, in the *Quarterly Review*, saw it as an 'anti-Christian composition . . . a murmuring against the comforts of the rich and against the privations of the poor, which, as far as each individual is concerned, is a murmuring against God's appointment'. In other words, against providence. 'We do not hesitate,' went on that reviewer, 'to say that the tone of mind and thought which has overthrown authority and violated every code human and divine abroad, and fostered Chartism and rebellion at home, is the same which has also written Jane

---

[29] For some recent critics the central key lies rather in the liberation of the feminine, Charlotte Brontë being seen either as a proto-feminist who must castrate Mr Rochester before he can be allowed to enter into an intimate relationship with her heroine, or make her a sensible and judicious woman struggling almost against the grain before he can be subdued into being a worthy partner for her.

[30] *Novels of the Eighteen-Forties* (1954), 259.

Eyre.'[31] This tirade betrays the anxieties of the time: 1848 was after all a year of revolutions on the continent of Europe and of strong manifestations of Chartism at home. It is still striking, nevertheless, that such trends should have been detected in what seems from most points of view to be a conservative narrative, written, as we know, by an admirer of the Duke of Wellington and an Anglican churchwoman. The fact is that whatever the outcome of the plot, Jane Eyre herself was seen as showing such independence of mind throughout as to align her for many readers with the new spirit felt to be pervading society.

It can be seen that the dangers foreseen by the *Quarterly Review* were by no means absent from Charlotte Brontë's own mind. She insisted firmly on her religious beliefs, and was willing to give over the final words of the novel to St John Rivers and his urgency of belief. Her central character, however, remains Jane Eyre, whose more complex attitude impels her to refuse him. The parsonage of Haworth contained advanced literature of the day; one could not live there in innocence of what was going on in the world of intellect and of science.[32] These were, after all, the years during which Tennyson was writing *In Memoriam*: an intelligent reader of the journals would already have known of the questionings that prompted many of its stanzas and which were currently agitating the intellectual world. Chambers's *Vestiges of Creation*, published in 1844, had given further turbulence to the debate that had previously been stirred by Lyell's *Principles of Geology* in 1830–3.

During these years Charlotte neither became, nor was even drawn towards becoming, a freethinker. Her reaction to the publication by Harriet Martineau and H. G. Atkinson in 1851 of *Letters on the Laws of Man's Social Nature* shows well her reaction to such views. It was 'the first unequivocal declaration of disbelief in the existence of a God or a future life' that she had seen, and she found it difficult to put aside the 'sort of instinctive

---

[31] *Quarterly Review* (Dec. 1848), 173–4.

[32] There are many references to contemporary journals in Elizabeth Gaskell's *Life*. John Elliot Cairnes, an Irish economist, seeing Charlotte's library at Haworth some years later, noticed works such as Carlyle's *Life of Sterling* and *Sartor Resartus*, along with F. W. Newman's *The Soul: Her Sorrows and her Aspirations* (1849). See T. P. Foley, 'John Elliot Cairnes' Visit to Haworth Parsonage', *Brontë Society Transactions*, 18 (1992), 292–3. I am grateful to Dr Heather Glen for telling me of this article.

horror they awaken', and consider them in 'an impartial spirit
and collected mood'. At the same time she deplored the sneering
tone adopted by some critics towards Harriet Martineau; it was
her own wish, she said, to find the Truth, the Truth which she
believed covered itself with a veil.[33] (The image seems to recall
her recent reading of *In Memoriam*[34].) This desire would inevitably have led her to take seriously the questions raised in recent
literature. If one had a sense of the current direction of scientific
thinking in the 1840s 'providence' was not a word one would
use dogmatically or with utter assurance.

It is indeed a word of power in the novel, but far from
providing the 'ideology' that Barbara Hardy wants to trace, the
form against which the novelist could explore the humane elements she valued so deeply, it was one that Charlotte Brontë
relied on only lightly. While not so far discredited it was at this
moment a questioned concept, one to be considered carefully
before use. This may be one reason why the word appears so
rarely in her novel. At first it is assigned to the less reflective
characters. Mrs Fairfax thanks providence for the choice that
brought Jane to Thornfield Hall, the servants find it providential
that Mr Rochester thought of throwing water over himself
during the fire (which of course he did not, Jane performing
the act on that occasion).[35] It is Grace Poole who, in one of her
rare contributions to the narrative, comments, 'A deal of people,
Miss, are for trusting all to Providence; but I say Providence will
not dispense with the means, though He often blesses them
when they are used discreetly.' To Grace, Providence, inter-
changeable in her view with God and so masculine, acts subtly
in evaluating human appeals. Jane Eyre and Edward Rochester
both refer (once each) to trust in providence but the crucial
moment comes at the nadir of Jane's fortunes, when she is at her
last extremity on the moor. It is then that she utters the important speech in which she cries out 'Oh, Providence! sustain
me a little longer! Aid—direct me!'[36] Even this cry is still in line
with Grace Poole's comments; the appeal that she should be

---

[33] Elizabeth Gaskell, *Life of Charlotte Brontë*, ch. xxiii in *Life and Works* (1900),
vii. 506.

[34] Ibid. 475.

[35] *Jane Eyre*, chs. xiii, xvi; *Life and Works* (1899), i. 145, 182.

[36] Ch. xxviii, *Life and Works*, i. 402.

sustained (as opposed to being rescued) comes from one who even now preserves her independence and strives for support in it, not of someone who submits herself totally or cravenly.

The formula 'coincidence is the symbol of Providence', which Barbara Hardy ascribes to Kathleen Tillotson,[37] is, then, inadequate, ignoring the careful distinctions Charlotte made in these areas. There is, indeed, more than one realm of order in this novel. The world of nature and romance which dominates the first half is matched in the second by the world of orthodox religion and morality; and orthodoxy, despite the high respect afforded to it, does not in this plot conquer. St John Rivers, embodiment of a forceful religious will, faultless in terms of his faith, does not ultimately succeed in dominating Jane; it is her bonding with Rochester that receives apparent supernatural reinforcement. If one is to take the plot seriously the implication is that it backs a view of things under which such love is absolute—certainly powerful enough to make even suffering such as Rochester undergoes of little account at its side. Providence is not an ideology or dogma, to provide the form against which the events of the novel are to be measured; it is a mystery to be respected. In the same way the real power in the universe is not to be identified with the monolithic God revealed in the Old Testament but with the 'Mighty Spirit' sensed by Jane Eyre after her forceful rejection of St John Rivers, a spirit which is as present in the great energies of Nature as in the moral law, and as little confined by them.

*Jane Eyre*, then, was written at a particular moment, when an honest thinker was bound to take account of current scientific thinking, even if the full implications that might be discerned by someone of a more conservative cast of mind need not yet be accepted. For Charlotte Brontë the main need was for courage and resoluteness, in the faith that the difficulties she was beginning to envisage would be vanquished in the light of a fuller knowledge. But this meant that providence was already a site of inquiry, even a battleground, no longer a rock of defence. Within a short time she would read *In Memoriam*, in which the questions were laid out at length, no longer to be avoided. In the poem as printed in 1850 Tennyson does not actually use the

---

[37] *The Appropriate Form* (1964), 63. She gives no reference.

word 'providence', but the concept is pervasive below the surface of the discussion, the probings always present. In the end Christian faith is maintained, but barely.

By the time Charlotte Brontë wrote *Villette*, certainly, the providential was no longer an issue to be considered with the assurance of an anterior underlying acceptance. In this novel there is to be no traditional happy ending; she finds her own way of propitiating the moral demand for one by opening the paragraph in which we expect the denouement with an urgently imposed suspension of plot:

Here pause: pause at once. There is enough said. Trouble no quiet, kind heart; leave sunny imaginations hope. Let it be theirs to conceive the delight of joy born again fresh out of great terror, the rapture of rescue from peril, the wondrous reprieve from dread, the fruition of return. Let them picture union and a happy succeeding life.

The narrative resumes to give its darker account; it then concludes in the language of the happier providence reserved for some, shadowed by a long penumbra stretching back over the unconcluded part of the narrative: 'Madame Beck prospered all the days of her life; so did Père Silas; Madame Walravens fulfilled her ninetieth year before she died. Farewell.'

Although *Villette* may now strike us as religious in its total effect, it was not so for most readers at the time. The reviewer in the *Observer* described the novel as 'half atheistical and half religious';[38] what was perhaps the most perceptive review, in the *Spectator*, focused its comments on Lucy Snowe herself:

While her eyes turn upward with the agony that can find no resting-place on earth, she indulges no Pagan or Atheistical despair—she does not arraign God as cruel or unmindful of his creatures—she still believes that the discipline of life is merciful; but she does not pretend to solve God's providence—she rather with a certain sincerity cries aloud that her soul is crushed, and drinks the bitter cup with the full resolve not to sweeten the bitterness by delusion or fancy.[39]

This is different from the kind of thing to be looked for in standard novel criticism, either then or now: it sets Lucy's experience outside the normal considerations of

---

[38] *Observer*, 7 Feb. 1853, p. 7, cited Vargish, *Providential Aesthetic*, 71 n.
[39] *The Spectator*, 12 Feb. 1853, p. 155, cited ibid.

characterization and plot and calls rather for sympathy with her set of mind. Charlotte Brontë's authorial attitude is by now closer to that of Tennyson than to a pietistic writer such as Keble. She is willing to take her cue from the more bracing assurances and exhortations of the Old Testament; yet whenever they appear one senses the pressure on her from contemporary expressions of doubt and from her increasing consciousness of the need for consolation and resolution in the face of a world that does not answer first and foremost to human needs and in the case of some people palpably conflicts with them. She knows that their suffering cannot be subordinated to some grand design: kept at the forefront of her attention as a novelist it makes any idea of providence problematic.

At about the same time Arthur Hugh Clough was facing the same question, to be resolved neatly in his poem 'The Bothie of Tober-na-Vuolich', where the tutor contends (using an argument strangely predictive of those brought out to justify unquestioning obedience in later wars) that it is not for the soldier in the battle to choose where to station himself:

There is a great Field-Marshal, my friend, who arrays our battalions;
Let us to Providence trust, and abide and work in our stations . . .

Clough's protagonist replies,

I am sorry to say your Providence puzzles me sadly . . .
Would that the armies indeed were arrayed, O where is the battle?
Neither battle I see, nor arraying, nor King in Israel,
Only infinite jumble and mess and dislocation,
Backed by a solemn appeal, 'For God's sake do not stir, there!'[40]

Charlotte Brontë's more natural successor in this respect was George Eliot, who took her role as interpreter of providence even more intensely to heart, facing the problems involved with a seriousness that only increased with time. Thomas Vargish's discussion again bears strongly on the issue, showing that whereas at the beginning of her novel-writing career she gave prominence to protagonists whose view of the world was providential, she also took on board the first of the critiques mentioned above, her last three novels including characters (Tito Melema, Raffles, Grandcourt) whose worldly successes

[40] 'The Bothie of Tober-na-Vuolich', IX, 44–65.

were achieved by way of opportunistic nihilism and who, if they believed in a 'Providence' at all, assumed that its interventions were always favourable and began with themselves.[41] The function of poetic justice, on the occasions when it did enter her plots, was often to chastise such a belief. It was sometimes possible to suggest further depths, however. Discussing *Middlemarch*, Vargish quotes the narrator's ironic agreement with Fred Vincy's belief that if he needed money a 'providential occurrence' would always intervene to supply it: 'What can the fitness of things mean, if not their fitness to a man's expectations? Failing this, absurdity and atheism gape behind him.'[42] It is also important to note how the basis of her critique has here been abruptly switched: by allowing this vision of an abyss to open in the text, she keeps the reader's mind alert to the existence of further dimensions, of a cosmic kind, which would not be likely to cross the moral horizon of a character such as Fred Vincy but which hover, nevertheless, behind the novel as a whole.

The theme that most human beings tend to regard providence as working for their own benefit covers Mr Casaubon himself, who in his letter to Dorothea proposing marriage speaks of his growing sense of need and then of his introduction to her as having been, he trusts, 'not . . . superficially coincident with foreshadowing needs but providentially related thereto as stages towards the completion of a life's plan'. That plan is of course his own plan, and George Eliot says as much later on, just after she has remarked that Providence, 'in its kindness, had supplied him with the wife he needed':

Whether Providence had taken equal care of Miss Brooke in presenting her with Mr Casaubon was an idea which could hardly occur to him. Society never made the preposterous demand that a man should think

---

[41] One can see something of the transition from the unsophisticated to the sophisticated view in *The Mill on the Floss*, where in the early chapters Aunt Pullet can speak casually of those who try to treat themselves medically as 'flying in the face of Providence' (I, ch. ix) but later the narrator comments on Philip's sophistry in arguing for the possibility of accidental meetings with Maggie that '. . . by adopting the point of view of a Providence who arranges results . . . we shall find it possible to obtain perfect complacency in choosing to do what is most agreeable to us in the present moment.' (V, ch. iii)

[42] *Middlemarch*, ed. David Carroll (Oxford, 1986), ch. xiv, p. 132.

as much about his own qualifications for making a charming girl happy
as he thinks of hers for making him happy. As if a man could choose
not only his wife but his wife's husband!

In each case the thought of Providence assists self-deception.
During the courtship Dorothea is undisturbed by his exactness
and formality. 'She filled up all blanks with unmanifested
perfections, interpreting him as she interpreted the works of
Providence, and accounting for seeming discords by her own
deafness to the higher harmonies.' In one of the crucial chapters
of the novel, at least as far as their relationship is concerned,
she speaks to him late at night concerning Will Ladislaw's
current needs and Casaubon's previous efforts on his behalf. She
reflects that she herself has always had too much money 'and
especially the prospect of too much'. His comment, 'These, my
dear Dorothea, are providential arrangements,' provokes the
reply,

'But if one has too much in consequence of others being wronged, it
seems to me that the divine voice which tells us to set that wrong right,
must be obeyed.'[43]

The perceptiveness of the moral sensibility that speaks
through her affirmation, only to be consistently disregarded by
Casaubon, is a quality lacking also in Lydgate, the ambitious
scientist of the story. His desire to discover the key to knowledge
in the form of the 'primitive tissue' resembles Casaubon's search
for the key to all mythologies, even if it is marginally nobler,
springing from an attitude of sympathy towards human suffering and pursued with an ardour that resembles Dorothea's. His
blindness to finer considerations is linked with the 'spot of
commonness' that George Eliot traces in him.

In Nicholas Bulstrode, least worthy among these characters,
the novelist finds not simply a moral blindness but a deliberate
avoidance of moral issues, by way of belief in a kind of
predestinarianism. At first he regards the advent of Lydgate to
Middlemarch as a providential intervention, but then, when
the young doctor's financial difficulties become apparent,
'providential indications', he says, 'demand a renunciation'. As

---

[43] *Middlemarch*, ed. David Carroll (Oxford, 1986), ch. xxix, pp. 272–3; ch. ix, p.
73; ch. xxxvii, p. 365.

Vargish comments, 'He has severed in his own consciousness the essential connection between personal desire and moral action, thus permitting himself a radical latitude of behavior for which he is accountable in no human context.'[44]

Vargish's conclusions about the role of providence in this novel are convincing and illuminating. He contends that in spite of a guarded view that prevents her from any easy assent to the concept, the various references in the novel to the effects of sympathy and compassion within the social web amount to a doctrine concerning the nature of that web itself, transcending the aims pursued by the most ambitious of the male characters such as a key to all mythologies or the discovery of a primitive tissue: 'Such assertions . . . strongly suggest that an organic solidarity subsists—an elemental social mythos for which no key exists, a tissue too basic for analysis—and that despite its subtlety and resistance to systematization it remains subject to representation in narrative.'[45] Although this idea could act as a tentative resolution to the problems of mind and society, however, George Eliot's growing consciousness of the implications of Darwinism entailed awareness of the difficulties raised by any attempt to link such organic solidarity with moral affirmation. If poetic justice was achieved the reader might well be left regarding it as a concession to his or her own pleasure. A more serious analysis was likely to reveal that (as in Coleridge's world) the two elements remained obstinately separate, in a tension as yet unresolved.

There was, in other words, a degree of complexity in the fiction of the time, even George Eliot's, which meant that readers could approach it at varying levels of sophistication. Those who read simply for the story could accept the ending without questioning as they might accept the record of events that really happened and judge it by its poetic justice; those who thought more fully about its moral implications, on the other hand, would question first the plot and then the author.

The effect of the increasing play around the concept of providence was to project it into a state of instability that suspended it between abstraction and figuration. It could neither quite

---

[44] Vargish, *Providential Aesthetic*, 224.
[45] Ibid. 228.

assume human lineation, nor could it be allowed to sink into non-human theorization. There was, meanwhile, a conceivable area for exploration in the phenomenon of human love. For male writers, particularly, there was an element of the unforeseen and the gratuitous in the advent of a particular person who seemed sent to help one fulfil one's human destiny, that allowed one to treat her as providential—even like a personification of Providence herself, fit to be set in the place of the deity (or aspect of the deity) that had proved unreliable. The beloved was then looked to not only as the provided but as the provider—not just a welcome presence but potentially a complete resource.

In the case of George Eliot more will need to be said in a later chapter, when her development after *Middlemarch* comes to be discussed: the questions examined so far became even more crucial in the thinking from which *Daniel Deronda* took shape. By then belief in providence had been more decisively undermined by the widespread acceptance of Darwinism, though even so, the sense died hard. (Even Darwin himself confessed that the sense of an intelligence working through the biological processes sometimes came strongly over him.[46]) So George Eliot's hero could still look for its operations in his coincidental encounters with the heroine and with the Judaism that he discovered to be his own heritage.

For the other writers to be considered in the present study it was not enough to make the ways of the providential plausible in the creation of their novels; they needed to discover how far the workings of the providential could still be discerned in the processes of the world as they knew it to be. This was true from the very beginning of the century and just before. In the wake of the French Revolution Wordsworth's Lucy was a figure who mattered to him as guaranteeing a faith that the more benign workings of nature were sometimes found incarnate in a human being. William Ellery Channing, similarly, looked at Nature constantly for evidences of her providential workings and read

---

[46] When the Duke of Argyll told him that he found it impossible to contemplate the remarkable contrivances recorded in his books on earthworms and orchids without seeing that they were the effect and the expression of mind, Darwin replied: ' "Well, that often comes over me with overwhelming force; but at other times," and he shook his head vaguely, adding, "it seems to go away." ' Francis Darwin (ed.), *The Life and Letters of Charles Darwin* (1887), i. 316 n.

Wordsworth for the light his poetry might throw on them. Frederic Myers, even more than his poetic predecessor, believed in the transcendent value of the love he found providentially granted to him.

As the evidence for a benevolent divine presence at the heart of nature retreated, in short, stress was laid more and more heavily on the feminine itself, as possible guarantor of the providential. Romantic love could be envisaged in these very terms, embodying the advent of a woman to whom one could devote oneself absolutely, a development which, however, brought dangers of its own. Labouring under the loss of a metaphysical basis of certainty in human affairs, an ardent individual might easily lay on a particular relationship more weight than it could properly bear. The loved one might be elevated to the status of revelatory being. The resulting pressure can be seen in relationships such as those between Keats and Fanny Brawne, or in Shelley's pursuit of an 'epipsyche' in himself and in various idealized women. There was likely to be a strong Platonic element (whether openly declared as such or not) in such love, allowing it to remain unconsummated physically but at the same time putting the participants under strain.

This narrowing and intensification of the providential was usually a private matter, even if the individual protagonists might regard the enterprise they were engaged in as having more general implications. One of the earliest and more extraordinary of the relationships involved was that between Coleridge and Sara Hutchinson, Wordsworth's sister-in-law. Although not to be dealt with in detail here it deserves mention, both as a prototype of others that will be discussed and as a vivid example of the degree to which such a love could matter for the protagonist in metaphysical terms. If Coleridge's love for Sara owed much to the harmonizing affection that he responded to in his dealings with the Wordsworths and found missing from his own marriage, various of his statements, ranging from poetry to entries in notebooks, make it evident that he found in her something more, corresponding to the kind of revelation that he sensed at the heart of things and which he believed to be at the core of Wordsworth's poetry also. Wordsworth's occasional glimpses into 'something far more deeply interfused' linked with his own sense of an eternal self that was revealed in Sara. A

belief that Wordsworth appreciated this potentiality also is no
doubt reflected in his earlier description of the poem beginning
'A slumber did my spirit seal . . .' as 'a sublime epitaph', and in
his puzzlement and resentment that Wordsworth, author of the
'Lucy' poems, could show so little understanding of his own
predicament as he forsook his family in the pursuit of what was
for him a central Wordsworthian ideal. Wordsworth himself in
his most characteristic poetry, was more wary, looking for his
providence not only in occasional glimpses of an other-worldly,
or inner-worldly, illumination but in the unregarded charities
of down-to-earth everyday life. He brought the oppositions of
his philosophy to bear in the poem 'She was a phantom of
delight . . .', where he weighed his wife's elusive spirit-beauty
against her solid household virtues and tried to honour both.
This was alien to the vision of Coleridge, who could not imagine
such a combination of forces as true love. For him such
love must be an all-embracing revelation, subsuming all other
factors, just as the rising sun might seem not just to combine
with, but to *create* the landscape it released from the grip of
night.[47]

Belief in the providential nature of platonic love, which
reached its nineteenth-century apogee in the careers of figures
such as Coleridge, Shelley, and Myers, was in lesser forms a
recurrent under-theme in contemporary writing. At its most
extreme it might be believed that for each man or woman a
single ideal partner existed, and that it was vital for that one
person to be found, but given the comparatively few contacts
any individual might expect to make in the course of a lifetime
this must seem an aspiration rather than a likely expectation.
Instead the sense, if it existed at all, would be read back into
events, in the form of a subsequent belief, on the part of those
lucky enough to find a compatible love, that no other coupling
would have been conceivable. The finding supplanted the seeking; the sense of pleasurable fulfilment generalized itself into a
conviction of uniqueness and ordained necessity. It was this that
was seen as providential—and which could cause disappointment and disillusion if the light failed or if the sense of illumination was found not to be mutually shared. As already suggested,

---

[47] See below, Chapter 4, n. 134.

the finding of a providential element in romantic love could place a relationship under stronger pressure.

It was not just romantic love that was affected, for better and worse, by the decline of the sense of Providence, though that will be a major theme in the later chapters of this book. The devotion to scientific thinking that brought about that erosion threw greater stress on the status of fact, also. In that sense the whole mode of representing the world, particularly in imaginative literature, was affected: a new anxiety to get their accounts exactly right arose among novelists. It became a source of major concern for George Eliot in the planning of her later fictions, as we shall see.[48]

Attempts to rescue the sense of a general providence presiding over human fate, which continued throughout the nineteenth century, inevitably languished. But it is only in the twentieth century that the wheel has turned more fully, producing a view of the universe which for the generality of mankind in Western civilization is starkly non-providential. The providential sense continues to haunt the culture, still to be traced in phenomena such as astrology or addiction to games of chance. This is not unnatural, since gambling of any kind, like the concept of providence, represents a tribute to hope and a faith that life will develop for the better. But the disappearance of the larger concept from any serious consideration of humanity's significance has had its own cultural effects, among others that of depriving fiction of important ballast. At first the providential novel could be replaced by the anti-providential novel. If that meant that only unhappy endings were now acceptable it was obviously equally unsatisfactory, but at least plots remained weighted by an identifiable theory. As this line of fictional exploration has been played out, however, a loss of gravitational force has been experienced, bringing into larger prominence still the role of fact—an issue still surprisingly little considered as such in study of the novel. Arguments tend instead to be shunted on to a subordinate question, that of the relationship between fact and text: since all the reader can deal with in the end is a text, it is argued, that is what must be taken as central. Whether that text deals with something that did or did

[48] See her letters quoted below, Chapter 5, pp. 207–9.

not actually happen is regarded accordingly as a matter of lesser importance.

Yet it *is* important. The growing uncertainty about the nature, and purpose if any, of the universe that not only destabilized the notion of Providence but caused an impossibly high valuation to be placed by some on personal love also affected the status of so-called factual statements, thus from another point of view influencing literary issues to an extent that would, if anything, grow with the years. A good example of the issues raised could be seen some years ago in the controversy around D. M. Thomas's *The White Hotel*, a novel the content of which included a piece of documentary record concerning the Nazi death camps, related in words taken almost verbatim from an account already published. The author was able to argue that he had acknowledged his debt, however briefly, in the introductory publishing details of the book, and that in fact there was no way in which a contemporary author of fiction could feel justified in altering the actual recorded words describing so harrowing an experience.

In the case of some other novels, the question arises in a different form when it is discovered that particular characters are in some respect founded on fact. Before long certain readers will regard it as a *roman-à-clef* and treat the whole text as biographical record, ignoring the novelist's right to create complex characters based on more than one person or to manipulate incidents for the sake of dramatic effect. In this case, also, novelists can argue that if they do not draw upon their own experience in some way their treatment runs the risk of being regarded as wholly unrealistic. Such considerations can result in writs for defamation on the part of aggrieved parties and prolonged legal actions while a work is defended against such assaults. In the eyes of the law, there is in some sense such a thing as fact and the whole process rests upon a faith that it can be discovered—even if in some cases justice will have to make do with the best evidence available.

When the document under examination offers itself as something other than fiction, on the other hand, the situation changes again. George Orwell's essay 'A Hanging', for example, which describes one of his experiences when working as a police officer in Burma, is a case in point. As he watched a prisoner making his way to be hanged, he relates, he was startled to see him turn aside to avoid a puddle: the simplicity of the action brought home to him with crushing force the unnaturalness of the act that was about to be performed. It is an impressive piece of writing; yet it is possible—probable, some would maintain— that Orwell never witnessed such a hanging at all.[49] When readers' attention is drawn to this they may well feel cheated: they thought they were being confronted by a fact of human experience, brought home with unexpected intensity by its vividness, and now do not know whether as a 'recorded' fact it has any authenticity. Not only is the supposed demonstration invalidated but humanity itself seems slighted.

The importance of the point in this case has to do with the fact that Orwell appears to be offering himself as an uncompro- mising truth-teller, and adding to his moral stature in doing so. In an essay such as 'Inside the Whale',[50] indeed, it seems to be the main point he is trying to make.

But in that essay, too, further investigation raises doubts: it is, after all, an essay about fiction, in which the point of his praise for Henry Miller is not that his writing is factual but that 'you have all the while the feeling that these things are happening to *you*', the reason being that the novelist is 'owning up to every- day facts and everyday emotions'. Orwell might have claimed that in the essays of his that purported to be based on actuality it had been more important to give the *sense* of fact than to be faithful to it. The hinge between fact and fiction can after all be seen to run through the whole of Western thought. There are similar uncertainties at the heart of science also, made more complex by the difficulty of establishing just what a 'fact' might be. Where a writer is less concerned with such matters, on the other hand, the issue recedes. An incident in the work of a major

---

[49] George Orwell, 'A Hanging', *Collected Essays* (1961), 11. In *George Orwell: A Life* (1980), 85, Bernard Crick notes that there is no direct evidence of Orwell's having ever seen any of the several hundred hangings that took place while he was in Burma: it would not have been a part of his duties, though he could have done so at his own request. Since he is said to have told enquirers on two occasions that it was 'only a story' Crick concludes that it might have been a 'brilliantly crafted short story' and sets it among a group of documentary short stories 'the merit of which does not depend on [their] factual, historical veracity' (ibid. 112). Orwell claimed elsewhere to have seen a hanging, however: see his *The Road to Wigan Pier* (1937), 178.
[50] In *Inside the Whale and other Essays* (1940), 131–88.

novelist such as Tolstoy, for example, may be accepted as 'true' not because we believe that it necessarily happened, or happened in precisely that way, but because his narrative has convinced us that his people are behaving in the way that they do in real life. In that sense it is veridical.

It can still be maintained, nevertheless, that many readers would find a difference between indubitable authenticity and an irresistible sense of it, preferring the former. If what is ostensibly presented as a fact cannot after all be so trusted the writer's standing is correspondingly diminished, as in the case of Ernest Hemingway's way with facts. Here too an impression is created that truth-telling is the aim; it is not, however, directly claimed—and in this case a certain lack of sobriety makes the reader readier to ask questions.[51]

Some of the issues involved are discussed from a different point of view in Frank Kermode's *The Genesis of Secrecy*, where the interests he gained as a student of narrative fiction are brought to bear on questions of interpretation in the New Testament. At one point he turns to Mark's Gospel narrative and the episode there of a young man wearing 'a linen cloth'. Mark reports that after Jesus' arrest his disciples forsook him and fled, adding, 'And a young man followed him, with nothing but a linen cloth about his body; and they seized him, but he left the linen cloth and ran away naked.'[52] Kermode relates the appearance of this young man to other events of the same kind that he has come across in fiction—notably that of the 'rough-looking customer' in Henry Green's *Party Going* or the man in a mackintosh in Joyce's *Ulysses*, each of whom is suggested by the narrative as a whole to have an importance belied by the casualness of the narrative presentation.

Discussing the implications of this particular incident, Kermode identifies three possible ranges of interpretation. One begins with the idea that the young man was Mark himself, and therefore represents a kind of personal signature to the Gospel itself, rather like the brief appearances of Alfred Hitchcock in

---

[51] In his *Ernest Hemingway* (1985) Jeffrey Meyers gives numerous instances of his cavalier way with facts: see his index under 'Hemingway, Character: lies and tall stories'. It is indicative that his book *The Sun also Rises* should have provoked a reply (by Harold Loeb) entitled *The Way it Was* (New York, 1959).

[52] Mark 14: 51–2.

his own films; another sees it as intended to lend the whole story verisimilitude, as 'an odd incident that looks as if it belongs to a history-like fortuity rather than to a story coherently invented'; a third sees it as a piece of narrative calling for further esoteric or literary interpretations. Notable among the last are the theory that it belongs to an occult gospel, underlying the narrative; on this reading it can be related to another incident, surviving only in a rejected version, in which a rich young man was raised from the dead and later went to Jesus by night wearing a linen garment over his naked body to be instructed in the mystery of the kingdom of God. Such incidents, it is suggested, might have formed parts of a gospel narrative in which baptism played a more central part.[53] Another, more literary theory was developed by Austin Farrer:[54] it relates the incident to that in Genesis where Joseph flees away naked from Potiphar's wife and to Amos's prophecy that 'he that is courageous among the mighty shall flee away naked in that day',[55] and sees it as one of the attempts to show how events in the New Testament answer to types already present in the Old Testament, thus serving to fulfil its prophecies. Kermode also reports that Farrer's work was rejected by the establishment—and eventually by Farrer himself—because it was 'damaging to what remained of the idea that the gospel narratives were still, in some measure, transparent upon history'.[56]

The last point is particularly relevant to the present discussions. The hostility to some kinds of biblical interpretation from those who belong to organized religious institutions has indeed to do with an 'idea that the gospel narratives are transparent upon history'—and not just an idea in most cases, but a firmly held belief. Although Kermode is quite aware of this, however, it is not his central concern. His own position is made clear in a chapter entitled 'What Precisely are the Facts?': 'We are so habituated to the myth of transparency that we continue, as Jean Starobinski neatly puts it, to ignore *what is written*

---

[53] This theory is cited as having been developed particularly by Morton Smith in *Clement of Alexandria and a Secret Gospel of Mark* (Cambridge, Mass., 1973): Kermode, *Secrecy*, 58–60, 63–4.
[54] Cited Kermode, *Secrecy*, 60–4.
[55] Gen. 39: 12; Amos 2: 16: Kermode, *Secrecy*, 111–12.
[56] Kermode, *Secrecy*, 111.

in favor of *what it is written about*'.[57] Since his book is an
attempt to reverse the trend, it is not surprising if issues
relating to historical transparency are constantly deflected to the
margins.

Yet the effects on a larger scale of this approach become
evident when one considers how little is said in his study concerning the Resurrection. In his reading of the Gospel narratives
he dwells on the way in which particular Old Testament texts
are seen to bear on those of the New, so that they constantly
suggest 'the same universal plot of which the Passion is the
denouement',[58] an evaluation which can claim some support
from the disproportion between the space, five chapters, in
which the Passion is described in the New Testament, and the
single one recording the Resurrection, which, containing also
the start of the preaching of the gospel, may appear in consequence perfunctory. Yet in terms of the faith that is being
initiated there with such brevity the question will be of crucial
importance, since for many people its acceptance is intimately
associated with the question whether or not the Resurrection
narrative is 'transparent on history'. According to St Paul, traditionally regarded as pivotal interpreter of the Gospels, 'If there
be no resurrection of the dead then is Christ not risen: And if
Christ be not risen, then is our preaching vain, and your faith
is also vain.'[59] He, at least, regarded it as crucial whether the
narratives of the Resurrection were constructed round an actual
physical happening, with universal significance, as opposed to
an apparition which some people found overwhelmingly convincing, or events which were to be regarded purely as symboli-
cal. The later poetry of Arthur Hugh Clough, acutest among
those who have concerned themselves with the question of
factuality, is haunted by the refrain of a poem he found himself
composing one day in Naples, 'Christ is not risen'—a line in
which, for all its sombreness, he was disturbed to find unexpected relief.[60] The nature of the differences involved is demonstrated to this day by the strength of the controversies that
surround anyone who suggests the importance of the Resurrec-

---

[57] Kermode, *Secrecy*, 118–19.          [58] Ibid. 99.          [59] 1 Cor. 15: 13–14.
[60] 'Easter Day. Naples, 1849' and 'Dipsychus', ll. 6–33. *The Poems of
Arthur Hugh Clough*, ed. F. L. Mulhauser (2nd edn., Oxford, 1974), 199–203,
218–19.

tion to be that of a symbol rather than a physical fact.[61] And this central issue affects in turn attitudes to the other narratives in the New Testament, since their status as records of fact has a part to play in supporting claims that the culminating narrative relates something that actually happened. Among other things, the credibility of providence as a Christian concept ultimately depends on it.

In the nineteenth century the underlying anxiety betrayed by such religious debates was far more powerful, a fact that helps to account for some of the attitudes to be encountered in this book. In an oblique way it explains as well the accent on the documentary in recent secular culture. What debates about the narratives of Orwell and the New Testament have in common has to do with claims that they are not simply 'true' but factual. In Orwell's case this matters partly because he elsewhere places such stress on the fragility of truth in modern political life; in that of the Gospels, equally, there are those who need to be reassured concerning the factual validity of the event on which their faith is founded.

In the present book the question of factual record is raised most sharply by the existence of Wordsworth's 'Lucy' poems, where there is an obvious difference of scale. The narratives of the Resurrection, after all, claim to describe events that have become central to the faith of a great religion; whether an important poet did or did not meet an actual young woman in his youth may seem a trifling matter by comparison. Nor did Wordsworth in writing these poems make the direct claim for factual accuracy that is implicit in the way that Orwell's piece is presented; if anything, he seems to have wished to divert his readers from thinking about the question. If the Lucy poems are now treated as symbolic narratives nothing much might seem to have changed.

To some extent readers will no doubt judge the issue according to temperament. Some will feel that the question of factuality makes little or no difference and that a text exists to be treated simply in its own terms; others by contrast will argue that the crossing of the border from accepted fiction to assertion

---

[61] A well-known recent example is that of David Jenkins, Bishop of Durham from 1984 to 1994.

of factual truth must be a crucial transition. The lights and shadows will always change; once one is convinced that what is being described actually happened particular phrases will inevitably be weighted differently. Such readers really need to know whether they are reading a factual account or an author's fantasy.

The further reason, I suggest, why the issue has been of importance to certain writers lies in its relevance to the main question to be discussed in the chapter. Long before Darwin the relationship between Nature and the providential was seen by some as problematic, there being virtually no convincing prima facie evidence of benevolent purpose in her workings. Yet readers such as Wordsworth needed an assurance of the kind. If one were to find a simple human being who seemed to embody such a relationship, therefore, so that a spirit of natural beauty and harmony seemed to speak through him or her in accents of beneficence, one might claim to have found the looked-for key. The advent of even one such person could be regarded as, literally, providential. That, it may be submitted, was why Lucy was such a crucial figure for Wordsworth, at least at the period when he was most concerned with such issues, and why it mattered so much during the subsequent period that she should have been not an invented character of his imagination but a real, and beautiful, presence in his past. Only later, as he became less sure about the validity of any intimations suggesting the certainty of a benign link between Providence and Nature, would he feel justified in covering some of the traces of such an original relationship with her.

## 2

# Wordsworth's 'Lucy': Fiction or Fact?

'... [H]e always preserved a mysterious silence on the subject of that "Lucy", repeatedly alluded to or apostrophized in his poems.' Thomas De Quincey's remark about Wordsworth, published in 1839,[1] is one of the very few references to the matter to have survived from among his contemporaries. After a century and a half his silence still remains a puzzle, if only as uncharacteristic of his normal behaviour. Although inclined to reticence, he was ready to offer explanations of personal things in his poetry that were less than transparent; when, for example, he gave fictitious names to his friends and associates, he made the disguises very thin. Yet in the instance of the Lucy poems he offered no illumination whatever—a silence all the more puzzling in view of his marriage to Mary Hutchinson in 1802 and his constant celebrations of their mutual affection. If Lucy had been simply a creation of his own imagination one would have expected him to state the fact firmly, in order to avoid misunderstanding.

Do we need to know? Is such a matter really relevant to the way in which a reader should approach a work of literature? For the moment it is enough to say that if questions of the kind are to be put to any writer Wordsworth must be one of the first, given the striking play between the abstract and the concrete in his work. While he attempted to justify Coleridge's trust that he would be accounted 'the first & greatest philosophical Poet'[2] he always aimed to found his general statements in the particular: it was indeed one reason for the effects of bathos that were to

---

[1] See the first version of the essay 'William Wordsworth', as printed in *Tait's Edinburgh Magazine* in 1834: *DQ Recollections*, 188. The reference to Hawkshead gossip was omitted in 1854.

[2] Letter to Richard Sharp of 15 Jan. 1804: *CL* ii. 1034.

disturb many critics. In such cases it could also matter that the reader should believe the events related to have actually happened. Of the power of the imagination to produce dramatic changes in one's physical nature, as exemplified in 'Goody Blake and Harry Gill', he wrote 'The truth is an important one; the fact (for it is a *fact*) is a valuable illustration of it.'[3]

The 'Lucy poems' amount to a core of five or six lyrics, supplemented by other poems or passages in which a young woman named Lucy is mentioned or some other factor suggests a connection with her. They provide a crucial test case of this respect for the factual. If the question of their authenticity as fact has not received much attention recently, one reason is that many of the most important debates have focused on the one poem associated with the series in which no person is actually named. 'A slumber did my spirit seal . . .' is also the shortest and in many respects the best known—indeed, it has probably been more often discussed in print than any other poem of its length in the language. A recent book was devoted almost entirely to it,[4] referring in addition to a very large number of previous discussions.

This extraordinary amount of critical attention is due partly to a combination of compactness and ambiguity, coupled with a use of nouns that are almost exclusively general or abstract, creating a dispersed referentiality that offers wide scope for interpretation.

Epitaph

A Slumber did my spirit seal,
   I had no human fears:
She seem'd a Thing, that could not feel
   The touch of earthly years.

No motion has she now, no force;
   She neither hears nor sees,
Mov'd round in Earth's diurnal course
   With rocks, & stones, and trees![5]

The main issue for critical argument turns on the relationship

---

[3] Preface to *Lyrical Ballads* (1800): WPrW i. 150. See my *Wordsworth and the Human Heart* (1978), 61–2.

[4] Brian Caraher, *Wordsworth's 'Slumber' and the Problematics of Reading* (University Park, Pa., 1991).

[5] Letter from Coleridge to Poole, 6 Apr. 1799: CL i. 480.

between the first stanza and the second, about which the range of disagreement has been wide. Cleanth Brooks asserted that the latter part of the poem suggested 'agonized shock at the loved one's present lack of motion . . . her utter and horrible inertness':

Part of the effect, of course, resides in the fact that a dead lifelessness is suggested more sharply by an object's being whirled about by something else than by an image of the object in repose. But there are other matters which are at work here: the sense of the girl's falling back into the clutter of things, companioned by things chained like a tree to one particular spot, or by things completely inanimate like rocks and stones . . . [She] is caught up helplessly into the empty whirl of the earth which measures and makes time. She is touched by and held by earthly time in its most powerful and horrible image.[6]

At about the same time, by contrast, F. W. Bateson was asserting that the impression left by the poem was not of two moods, but of

a single mood amounting to a climax in the pantheistic magnificence of the last two lines. . . . We put the poem down satisfied, because its last two lines succeed in effecting a reconciliation between the two philosophies or social attitudes. Lucy is actually more alive now that she is dead, because she is now a part of the life of Nature, and not just a human 'thing'.[7]

The text itself offers no clear grounds for deciding between the two readings—both of which, it may be noted in passing, go further than the words of the text properly allow. Wordsworth does not write of Lucy being 'whirled' round, as Cleanth Brooks twice suggests, but 'rolled' round, a more stately process. Beyond the existence of that stateliness in the second stanza, equally, it is hard to trace the explicit intimations of life and joy called for by Bateson's reading.

The issue raised here may encourage the application of deconstructionist methods. J. Hillis Miller has discussed the poem on more than one occasion, arguing that the figurative

---

[6] Cleanth Brooks, 'Irony as a Principle of Structure', in M. D. Zabel (ed.), *Literary Opinion in America* (2nd edn., New York, 1951), 736. This and the following quotation are found in E. D. Hirsch Jr, *Validity in Interpretation* (New Haven, 1967), 228, where they are brought together in his discussion of the problem.

[7] F. W. Bateson, *English Poetry: A Critical Introduction* (1950), 33, 80–1.

element in the poem can be taken further. His most developed account[8] begins with an apparently straightforward construal of the poem that carries no signals of irony on his part. (He later maintained that his intentions had been ironic throughout and that he wished it were possible to mark such passages in some way so as to indicate the fact.) His interpretation pointed to an element of 'family romance' in what was being written in the poem, with Lucy playing both virgin child and missing mother. These two women between them, jumping over the male generation in the middle, 'have erased its power of logical understanding, which is the male power *par excellence*'. But this feminist triumph is overtaken in turn by a further dialectic that in turn involves both male and female elements. Lucy's name means 'light': 'to possess her would be a means of rejoining the lost source of light, the father sun as logos, as head power and fount of meaning.' The result of her death is a loss 'both of light and of the source of light. It is the loss of the logos, leaving the poet and his words groundless . . .' And so the reader is 'caught in an unstillable oscillation unsatisfying to the mind and incapable of being grounded in anything outside the activity of the poem itself'[9]—in other words the *aporia* that it is common to discover at the end of a deconstructive process.

M. H. Abrams finds this an over-reading of Wordsworth's text, maintaining that when he returns from Hillis Miller's discussion to the poem itself he finds it to be, first and foremost, not a series of 'double-binds', but rather what Coleridge called it at the time: a 'sublime elegy'.[10] With this judgement many readers will no doubt agree. Stated in such bald terms, however, it suggests simply that the poem contains a direct and ascertainable meaning, and that readers who find that and respond to it will be rewarded by a moving poem of loss corresponding to their own common human experiences. This is recognizably in line with the doctrines of the New Criticism, which maintained that critical analysis of a good poem could be relied upon to

---

[8] 'On Edge', in Morris Eaves and Michael Fischer (eds.), *Romanticism and Contemporary Criticism* (Ithaca, NY, 1986), 101–18.

[9] Ibid. 108–9.

[10] See his contribution, 'Construing and Deconstrucing', ibid. 142–58. A more hostile view has been expressed by Gertrude Himmelfarb in *Looking into the Abyss: Untimely Thoughts on Culture and Society* (New York, 1994), 10–13.

yield a publicly available meaning of strong human significance. Yet Hillis Miller's approach cannot be so swiftly dismissed, since his sense of an 'oscillation' in the reader's response to the second stanza corresponds to a reaction which may well be experienced by other readers. If, for example, we put together the two responses recorded above, from Cleanth Brooks and F. W. Bateson, and suggest ways in which *both* might be seen as valid, an oscillation will be set up in the mind which may be supposed not simply to be created by the text as such (as a deconstructionist might assume) but to correspond to one that existed in Wordsworth's own. At the time when he was writing it he was under the sway of contrary impulses. On the one hand he had been exploring with Coleridge an elevated view of nature, constantly verging on pantheism, which was expressed in, for example, the 'Lines written . . . above Tintern Abbey' when he described how be could sometimes, in moments of unusual revelation, sense the workings of

> A motion and a spirit, that impels
> All thinking things, all objects of all thought,
> And rolls through all things . . .

On the other, the bleakness of some of his experiences in Germany during the winter of 1798–9 was reminding him with equal force of a contrary tendency that he knew all too well, inducing a state in which we might find ourselves

> Viewing all objects unremittingly
> In disconnection dead and spiritless[11]

In his own states of dejection nature sometimes presented herself to the mind in just such terms. During those months in Goslar, moreover, it was urgently present to his mind that awareness of the fact of human death fed the latter tendency, all too easily creating the sense that we lived in a 'universe of death'. At this time the thought of an untimely death (real or imagined) could strike on the sense with unusual force, the thought that a young woman of beauty and liveliness might unexpectedly die casting him between alternating modes of consciousness. In this ambiguous universe the fact that a creature who had been for him

---

[11] *The Excursion* IV. 961–2.

an embodiment of life in all its sensitivity and pleasure could be transformed without warning into an equally potent emblem of death was desolating, to say the least. If there is a genuine aporia at the end of the poem, in other words, it is one that can be said to have originated in Wordsworth's own mind, registering the alternating impulses set in motion by the experience he has recorded. A state is discovered—if only by accident—that corresponds temporarily to one that deconstructionists trace everywhere.

The personal process that has just been outlined was not confined to 'A slumber . . .'. The three Lucy poems written during the winter of 1798–9 may all be seen as meditations on the contentions between the universe of life and the universe of death that followed the withdrawal to Göttingen of the life-conscious Coleridge, leaving Wordsworth a prey to more sober reflections. As a result the inward debate that informed the writing of 'A slumber did my spirit seal' came to a head, to be replicated in them.

But if this argument is accepted the question of the possible identity of Lucy again raises itself. Does it matter whether or not she once walked the earth as a physical human being? Most recently critics and scholars have tended to suggest what their answer might be by treating her—at least implicitly—as a poetic construct. In his full-length study, *The 'Lucy' Poems: A Case Study in Literary Knowledge*[12] Mark Jones treats the making of this group of poems as a piece of literary institutionalization. Jonathan Wordsworth, similarly, sees the writing of the first Lucy poems in 1798–9 as marking a move back into what he terms Wordsworth's 'border vision'—which is in his view tantamount to a transition into the world of poetic symbols. Following David Ferry, who transposed Lucy into several young women and contended that 'these girls . . . are . . . symbols for the relation with the eternal which he is always seeking',[13] he maintains that Lucy 'remains an abstraction';[14] he sees the two stanzas of 'A slumber . . .', for instance, as first describing a loss of bodily awareness and then enacting it in symbolic terms.

---

[12] (Toronto, 1995).
[13] David Ferry, *The Limits of Mortality* (Middletown, Conn., 1959), 79.
[14] Jonathan Wordsworth. *The Music of Humanity* (1969), 75.

The idea that the poems might contain centrally symbolic statements is by no means unattractive. The reflection of Wordsworthian concerns detected above in 'A slumber . . .' may also be traced in image clusters that recur elsewhere. Lucy's name, as already mentioned, suggests light, and the images of the poems associated with her form patterns that are natural polarities, with heavenly luminaries such as the stars or the moon at one extreme and organic earthly radiancies such as the violet or the glow-worm at the other. Such pairs of images can in turn be viewed as forming one term of a further polarity between visionary trance and the light of common day, with the stars and moon and flowers and glow-worms on the one hand able to exercise a trance-inducing power that may bring intimations of immortality, while on the other the universe of uncommunicating objects reminds human beings of their mortality. This is an extraordinary weight of significance for six or seven poems to bear, yet the argument that they do so is reinforced by the fact that Wordsworth explored such significances more fully in other and later works. When in 1818 (to give one example) he wrote a poem called 'The Pilgrim's Dream' he attached to it the subtitle 'The Star and the Glow-worm'.

As one reads these poems with such possibilities in mind the question of their factuality may seem to recede. The sense of patterning in Wordsworth's mind stands out increasingly, inviting one to see them as participating in a philosophical mediation that has more to do with the human experience of nature than with a love that might once have taken actual human form. Jonathan Wordsworth's summing up begins to sound persuasive: 'What put it into Wordsworth's head to write these beautiful, elegiac love-poems we shall never know,' he writes; and then, having mentioned the theory that Dorothy might be the true focus of the poems, he remarks on the danger of overstressing the sense of personal loss and passes rapidly on.[15]

---

[15] Jonathan Wordsworth, *The Borders of Vision* (Oxford, 1982), 26–7. In a note he examines critically the view put forward by Hugh Sykes Davies that the poem was not about Lucy, no one being named in this poem, but about Wordsworth's own 'Spirit', referred to by the 'She' of the poem—a view which takes the 'symbolic' interpretation of the Lucy poems to one of its possible extremes. ('Another New

A nagging doubt may still survive, nevertheless—particularly when we recall that the first of these poems were sent to Coleridge in a batch in which the others were all autobiographical. Is it not likely that such an element is present here too, the records of physical excitement in his boyhood and youth that were to form a starting-point for *The Prelude* being here matched by reminiscences of a tender affection that was equally vivid—even if it can now be viewed only as loss, actual personal loss? It is, after all, the explicit theme shared by every one of them apart from 'The Glow-worm'.

And if they relate to an actual event in Wordsworth's early life, does this not in fact mean that our reading of the poems concerned is importantly changed? That certainly is what the presentation in the poems themselves urges on the reader:

> But she is in her grave and oh!
> The difference to me.

The point of this, in its final positioning as the conclusion of the poem, is that factuality *does* make a difference; and it would be fully consonant with this that our answer to the question whether the poem in which the statement was made was based on fact or fiction should have an effect on the way in which we read it.

The question of chronology has already been touched on; it will now be best to proceed by looking at the various references by name to Lucy in their original order—and, in the case of poems addressed to her, in their earliest known versions.

To do so leads immediately to an unexpected fact. The form of the main Lucy poems and the fact that they were written in the winter of 1798–9 may provoke a natural assumption that their composition was part of an unexpected lyrical efflorescence in Wordsworth's writing at that time. Closer examination

Poem by Wordsworth', *Essays in Criticism*, 15 (1965), 135–61). Appraising this theory, he points out that it involves attributing feeling, hearing, and seeing to his spirit, which Wordsworth was unlikely to do, but then goes on to remark, 'What is interesting is that there should be so little opposition between what would appear at first to be two radically different ways of looking at the poem. . . . one's concern is merely as to whether the poet is talking directly or in some symbolic terms about his own experience.' *The Borders of Vision*, 419.

of the manuscripts of the time leads one to believe, however, that insofar as this happened it was only as part of a larger process. The writing of his contributions to the *Lyrical Ballads*, the first volume of which had just been completed, can profitably be viewed against a questioning that he had been undertaking with Coleridge and which had at its root the disillusionment that had set in once the French Revolution failed to provide the pattern for an improvement of political activity in other European states. The result was an attempt to look more closely at human nature itself, enquiring into both its potentialities and its intransigences. In *The Prelude* Wordsworth described how during his time of reaction against the Revolution he had at one stage 'yielded up moral questions in despair', to be lifted in time from his despondency by the help of his sister and Coleridge. Coleridge himself told his brother George in March 1798 that he had withdrawn himself 'almost totally from the consideration of *immediate* causes, which are infinitely complex and uncertain, to muse on fundamental & general causes . . . to the seeking with patience and a slow, very slow mind, . . . what our faculties are & what they are capable of becoming'.[16] A similar concern is evident in Wordsworth's 'Lines written . . . above Tintern Abbey', where experiences of unusual peace and harmony in nature are seen as perhaps related to 'that best portion of a good man's life, | His little, nameless, unremembered acts | Of kindness and of love' and in the poetic drafts that Wordsworth was setting down in his notebook during the same period. If the work of providence was to be located in the power of the human heart it had to be recognized that many contemporary factors conspired against its flourishing there. One example was that of the man who must accept a degree of enslavement in order to fulfil his responsibility in bringing up a family:

> For let the impediment be what it may
> His hands must clothe & nourish them & there
> From hour to hour so constantly he feels
> An obligation pressing him with weight
> Inevitable that all offices
> Which want this single tendency appear

[16] *CL* i. 397.

> Or trivial or redundant hence ~~appears~~ remains
> So little to be done which can assume
> The appearance of a voluntary act
> That his affections in their very core
> Are false, there is no freedom in his love.
> Nor would he err perhaps who should assert
> That this perceiv'd necessity creates
> The same constriction of the heart, the same
>                                in those with whom he loves
> His wife & children.

The meditation on the loss of freedom and perceptiveness created by the drudgery needed to support one's dependents continues; the passage is then followed by one of a quite different kind:

> While in the cave we sat thou didst oerflow
> With ~~the~~ love even for the unsubstantial clouds
> And silent incorporeal colours spread
> Over the surface of the earth & sky.
> ~~But now, if I had met thee here unknown~~ ⟨in this wood⟩
> ~~Thy cheeks thus rich with a tempestuous bloom~~
> ~~In truth I might have thought that I had~~ pass'd
> ~~A houseless being in a human shape.~~

The lines, including those struck out, were subsequently incorporated into a passage beginning 'Ah what a crash was that' which in turn was to form a projected introduction for the narrative that would eventually be published as 'Nutting'. It ran as follows:

> Ah! what a crash was that—with gentle hand
> Touch those fair hazels; My beloved **Maid**;
> Though tis a sight invisible to thee,
> From such rude intercourse the woods all shrink
> As at the blowing of Astolpho's horn.
> It is a fancy which will make thee smile
> Again—~~while in the cave we sat, thy face~~
> ~~Was still as water when the winds are gone~~
> ~~And no one can tell whither. Now, in truth~~
> ~~If I had~~ Yet had I met thee with those eager ~~looks~~ eyes
> And cheeks thus ~~rich~~ wild with a tempestuous bloom
> ⟨In truth⟩ I should have thought that I had seen ~~in thee~~
> A houseless wanderer ~~with~~ in a human shape,

> An enemy of nature one who comes
> From regions far beyond the Indian hills.[17]

The cancellation shows how, in the very process of writing, the description of the young woman's differing responses to nature was being modified, the direct account of her expression of love dropping out in favour of attempts to bring her back to her initial mood. First the description became more objectified. Instead of indicating her love of the appearances of nature the newly cancelled passage, as transcribed above, showed her rather as if her face itself was presenting such a peaceful appearance. In the following lines, presumably drafted subsequently, this was changed again, to a more general description of her expression and an invitation to her to join in a process of restoration:

> While in the cave we sate this      noon
> Oh! what a countenance was thine come here
> And rest on this light bed of purple heath
>                      and let me see thine eye
> As at that moment, rich with happiness
> And still as water when the winds are gone
> And no man can tell whither

Finally, the first two lines dropped out altogether, to be replaced by an immediate transition from the description of the 'houseless wanderer' to the invocation

> Come rest on this light bed of purple heath
> And let me see thee sink to a dream
> Of gentle thoughts      till ⟨once again⟩ thine eye
> Be like ⟨the⟩ heart of love & happiness
> Yet still as water when the winds are gone
> ~~When~~ And no man tell whither—

On the next page the following lines appeared:

> For seeing little worthy or sublime
> In what we blazon with the pompous names

---

[17] *WPW* ii. 504 from DC MS 15 p. 29. (The previously quoted and following extracts all appear there on pp. 28 and 29.) The use of the word 'houseless', with its apparent reminiscences of *King Lear* (III. iv. 26, 30) probably means that the drafts were composed before 'Tintern Abbey', where the development of the usage in the phrase 'vagrant dwellers in the houseless woods' took the enquiry into the relationship between nature, human nature, and moral worth and developed it further.

Of power and action I was early taught
To love those unassuming things, that find
A silent station in this beauteous world
And dearest maiden thou upon whose lap
I rest my head oh! do not dream that these
Are idle sympathies.

After a space of a page, probably left blank for possible further lines, the composition resumed with the words 'It seems a day . . .' and into an early version of the boyhood experience recorded in 'Nutting'. This concluded with alternate endings, the second of which was rather longer:

Then dearest maiden, if I have not now
The skill to ~~teach~~ be thy teacher think ~~I pray~~ of him
The ragged boy let his parting look
Instruct ~~thee how to move~~ Move sweet maid along these shades
In gentleness of heart.—With gentle hand
Touch, for there is a spirit in the woods.

The full passage was eventually rewritten in another notebook, where, again, there were slight differences:

Ah! what a crash was that! with gentle hand
Touch these fair hazels—My beloved ~~Friend~~ **Maid!**
Though 'tis a sight invisible to thee,
From such rude intercourse the woods all shrink
As at the blowing of Astolpho's horn.—
**Thou, Lucy, art a maiden 'inland bred'**
**And thou hast known 'some nurture';** but in truth
If I had met thee here with that keen look
Half cruel in its eagerness, those cheeks
Thus   flushed with a tempestuous bloom,
I might have almost deem'd that I had pass'd
A houseless being in a human shape,
An enemy of nature, hither sent
From regions far beyond the Indian hills.
Come rest on this light bed of purple heath,
And let me see thee sink into a dream
Of gentle thoughts, protracted till thine eye
Be calm as water when the winds are gone
And no one can tell whither . . .[18]

[18] *WPW* ii. 504, from DC MS 16 p. 108.

In this version the lines about his early feeling for the 'unassuming things' in nature were then expanded, but no longer followed by a reference to his lying with his head in the lap of the young woman. The 'dearest maiden', who in the earlier version showed her love for nature in the cave was now given a name, 'Lucy', which thus may have made its first appearance in Wordsworth's work, since this version seems to predate any of the well-known lyrics addressed to her. It was a little after, as already mentioned, that Wordsworth began writing autobiographical passages, some of them transcribed by Dorothy for transmission to Coleridge in December 1798, that were eventually to provide material for *The Prelude*—though even to mention that work at this date may be to anticipate his future development misleadingly. Her description of the first extract, the account of skating, as 'the conclusion of a poem of which the beginning is not written' suggests that the idea of writing the much longer poem that would become *The Prelude* existed in Wordsworth's mind at this time, if at all, only vestigially.

The last of the autobiographical passages, which in the drafts had appeared as a supplement to 'Ah, what a crash was that!' was never in fact included in *The Prelude*, but was later adapted for the 1800 *Lyrical Ballads* collection to form the poem 'Nutting', where it began with the description of himself as a boy, 'a figure quaint', equipped on the advice of his nurse, Ann Tyson, 'with wallet and with crooked stick', setting out to go nutting in the woods near Esthwaite, and continued with the well-known description of the 'merciless ravage' that ensued, followed by a subsequent sense of pain at what he had done. The continuity of this passage with the earlier address to Lucy is shown by the concluding lines of the latter version:

> —Then, dearest Maiden! move along these shades
> In gentleness of heart; with gentle hand
> Touch, for there is a spirit in the woods.

The successive revisions had been for the most part polishings, but at one point, as we have seen, they involved a more significant change: the elision from the opening of lines describing the experience that gave rise to them. The original description of their sitting in a cave at midday and a trance-like moment when

the young woman's face had expressed her overflowing love of
the nature about her had given place to one that described her
expression simply as one of calmness—a condition to which,
after her disturbing exhibition of recklessness, he wishes
through his ministrations to reclaim her. In the further revision
it is in fact only the violence and the account of the state to
which he wants her restored that survive. In this not untypical
Wordsworthian movement the final desired calmness is not
only seen as a return to an original trance-like state but
takes precedence over his giving an account of it. It is even
possible that the initial opening movement was the original
of the trance-experience described in the first stanza of 'A
slumber . . .', in which case he found in that lyric a way of
describing it in a less localized manner, the subsequent account
of her unaccustomed violence being replaced by reflections on
her death, so prompting a later reflection and a different kind of
contrast.

The observation that the final draft quoted above probably
contains the first mention of 'Lucy' in Wordsworth's surviving
writings is further complicated by the fact that the two lines
printed in bold type were a later addition, either filling a gap or
written over an excised passage. The deleted 'Friend' of line 2,
moreover, seems not to have been the word originally written
there; another had occupied that space, which may have been a
name. No part of this passage appeared in the letter version of
'Nutting' that was sent by the Wordsworths in December 1798
to Coleridge, who had by then left to study in Göttingen while
they wintered on their own in Goslar. If the lines for 'Nutting'
were those described by Dorothy as 'the conclusion of a poem
the introduction of which is not yet written', we do not have to
infer, of course, that the drafts we have been examining were
not yet in existence: she could simply have meant that they were
not yet in a condition to be transmitted. In the same letter
Wordsworth mentioned the difficulties he had recently been
experiencing:

I should have written five times as much as I have done but that I am
prevented by an uneasiness at my stomach and side, with a dull pain
about my heart. I have used the word pain, but uneasiness and heat are
words which more accurately express my feeling. At all events it
renders writing unpleasant. Reading is now become a kind of luxury to
me. When I do not read I am absolutely consumed by thinking and

feeling and bodily exertions of voice or of limbs, the consequence of those feelings.[19]

Despite the physical hindrances he described, Wordsworth had certainly not been unproductive: the transcriptions by Dorothy of recent compositions on the other side of the sheet included not only the descriptions of winter skating, the stealing of a boat, and nutting in autumn but the two shorter 'Lucy' poems already mentioned, the first of which was introduced with the words: 'In the last stanza of this little poem you will consider the words "Long time" as put in merely to fill up the measure but as injurious to the sense.'

The transcriptions themselves run as follows:

I

My hope was one, from cities far,
  Nursed on a lonesome heath;
Her lips were red as roses are,
  Her hair a woodbine wreath.

2

She lived among the untrodden ways
  Beside the springs of Dove,
A maid whom there were none to praise,
  And very few to love;

3

A violet by a mossy stone
  Half-hidden from the eye!
Fair as a star when only one
  Is shining in the sky!

4

And she was graceful as the broom
  That flowers by Carron's side;
But slow distemper checked her bloom,
  And on the Heath she died.

5

Long time before her head lay low
  Dead to the world was she:
But now she's in her grave, and Oh!
  The difference to me!

The next poem is a favorite of mine—i.e. of me Dorothy—

[19] Letter to Coleridge from William and Dorothy Wordsworth, Dec. 1798: *WL* (1787–1805), 235–43. Dated 21 or 28 Dec. by Mark Reed (*W Chronology EY* 260n.)

1

Once, when my love was strong and gay,
　　And like a rose in June,
I to her cottage bent my way,
　　Beneath the evening Moon.

2

Upon the moon I fixed my eye
　　All over the wide lea:
My horse trudg'd on, and we drew nigh
　　Those paths so dear [to] me.

3

And now I've reached the orchard-plot,
　　And as we climbed the hill,
Towards the roof of Lucy's cot
　　The moon descended still.

4

In one of those sweet dreams I slept,
　　Kind nature's gentlest boon,
And all the while my eyes I kept
　　On the descending moon.

5

My horse moved on; hoof after hoof
　　He raised and never stopped,
When down behind the cottage roof
　　At once the planet dropp'd.

6

Strange are the fancies that will slide
　　Into a lover's head,
'O mercy' to myself I cried
　　'If Lucy should be dead!'

7

I told her this; her laughter light
　　Is ringing in my ears;
And when I think upon that night
　　My eyes are dim with tears.

The two poems have in common with 'A slumber...' an exploration of the paradoxical effects set up in the mind by the death of a young woman: the difference between her being alive—even if she had latterly been 'dead to the world'—and her being truly dead; and then in conclusion the difference between the liveliness of her recollected laughter in reaction to his thought of her death and the nature of his own reaction to that thought now it is fulfilled in fact.

The next poem in chronological order is probably the one beginning 'A slumber did my spirit seal...', already quoted and discussed above. This was sent on by Coleridge to Poole in a letter of 6 April 1799, where he introduced it with the words

Some months ago Wordsworth transmitted to me a most sublime Epitaph/whether it had any reality, I cannot say.—Most probably, in some gloomier moment he had fancied the moment in which his Sister might die.[20]

In the meantime, Wordsworth had by 23 February 1799 composed another short lyric, which he entitled 'Lucy Gray', and had mentioned to Coleridge a further poem (now lost) beginning 'One day, the darling of my heart...', for which, he declared, he did not 'care a farthing'.[21]

Another and longer poem was, according to the note later dictated to Isabella Fenwick, composed about the same time (in 1799, that is) 'in the Hartz Forest':

> Three years she grew in sun and shower,
> Then Nature said, 'A lovelier flower
> On earth was never sown;
> This Child I to myself will take;
> She shall be mine, and I will make
> A Lady of my own.
>
> 'Myself will to my darling be
> Both law and impulse: and with me
> The Girl, in rock and plain,
> In earth and heaven, in glade and bower,
> Shall feel an overseeing power
> To kindle or restrain.
>
> 'She shall be sportive as the fawn
> That wild with glee across the lawn
> Or up the mountain springs;
> And hers shall be the breathing balm,
> And hers the silence and the calm
> Of mute insensate things.
>
> 'The floating clouds their state shall lend
> To her; for her the willow bend;

[20] *CL* i. 479–80.
[21] See his letter to Coleridge, 27 Feb. 1799: *WL* (1787–1805), 256.

Nor shall she fail to see
Even in the motions of the Storm
A beauty that shall mould her form
By silent sympathy.

'The stars of midnight shall be dear
To her and she shall lean her ear
In many a secret place
Where rivulets dance their wayward round,
And beauty born of murmuring sound
Shall pass into her face.

'And vital feelings of delight
Shall rear her form to stately height,
Her virgin bosom swell;
Such thoughts to Lucy I will give
While she and I together live
Here in this happy dell.'

Thus Nature spake—The work was done—
How soon my Lucy's race was run!
She died, and left to me
This heath, this calm, and quiet scene;
The memory of what has been,
And never more will be.

The various lyrical pieces so far specified can be said to constitute the original group of 'Lucy poems'. Among them, the poem 'Lucy Gray' is mentioned here only because it contains the name 'Lucy'; since the girl concerned is depicted as having died in childhood it is not fully congruent with the others. It does, however, contain important features which link it to the present discussion. It was based on an actual event, being 'founded on a circumstance told me by my Sister'—a fact which Wordsworth made a point of mentioning in his Fenwick note on the poem.[22] When he published it, also, Wordsworth gave it as an alternative title 'or, Solitude', which shows that despite his insistence on its factual basis he was also thinking of the girl in symbolic terms. Speaking about the poem many years later he told Henry Crabb Robinson that since his object in it had been 'to exhibit poetically entire *solitude*', he represented the child as 'observing the day-*moon*, which no town or village girl would

---

[22] *WPW* i. 360.

ever notice'.[23] The exact formulation should be noted, since it stresses the value of an upbringing in a solitude so extreme that it would not be found even in a village, but must be looked for in a wilder setting. The selection of this particular element in the upbringing of someone who never grew beyond childhood suggests the extent to which Wordsworth's thinking at this time was concerned with the value of growing up in isolation from the main forces of human civilization and with the finding of a symbolism for it. In this one respect at least there may well be a link with the Lucy of the other poems.

The use of the name 'Lucy' in the title of a poem where the subtitle directs the reader explicitly towards symbolic significance prompts one to look more closely at the name itself. Certainly if one thinks of her as a possible real person living in the Cumbrian countryside the name is an unlikely one. One would search the parish registers of the region for a long time before one came across a Lucy: the usual names are the more familiar Marys, Sarahs, Annes, and the like, among a host based primarily on the Bible. If a record of a Lucy having died in the area during the 1790s were to be discovered, indeed, there would be a strong prima-facie case for asking whether she might not have been the original of Wordsworth's young woman.

As a literary name, on the other hand, its status was quite different. The Lucy in a poem by Burns, 'O wat ye wha's in yon town' is by no means an isolated instance. Other poems noticed by scholars include Samuel Rogers's 'A Wish', which begins 'Mine be a cot beside the hill', and includes the lines

> Around my ivied porch shall spring
> Each fragrant flower that drinks the dew;
> And Lucy at her wheel shall sing
> In russet gown and apron blue.

This was available to Wordsworth in a collection published in 1786.[24] Before that Lucy was the name for the female protagonist in poems about tragic love in a pastoral setting.[25] The

---

[23] Diary entry for 11 Sept. 1816, in *Henry Crabb Robinson on Books and their Writers*, ed. Edith J. Morley (1938), i. 190, quoted *WPW* i. 360.

[24] See his *An Ode to Superstition with some other Poems* (1786), 22–3.

[25] In one of Edward Moore's pastoral songs Lucy goes to the churchyard to join her dead Colin by falling into his grave: Edward Moore, *Poems, Fables, and Plays* (1756), 197–9 (cf. p. 186); in Thomas Tickell's ballad, on the other hand, the Colin

content of these poems corresponds to the kind of poetry that Wordsworth was to turn out in his earliest juvenile efforts.[26]

As Herbert Hartman has noted, the name was still appearing in poetry in the late 1780s. A poem attributed to William Collins, 'Song: The Sentiments Borrowed from Shakespeare', which appeared in the *Gentleman's Magazine* for February 1788, included lines about the mourning of 'young Damon':

> Each maid was woe—but Lucy chief,
> Her grief o'er all was tried;
> Within his grave she dropped in grief,
> And o'er her loved-one died.[27]

From his survey of such poetry Hartman concluded that the name had by then become 'a neo-Arcadian commonplace, an eighteenth-century poetic fixture'.

Some at least of the poems strongly support this observation, but not all. George Lyttelton's *Works*, published in 1774, contained, by contrast, a sequence of poems addressed to a real Lucy, the Lucy Fortescue whom he married in 1742; these were followed by a monody on her death and lines from her epitaph.[28] These identifications were made in outline by H. W. Garrod,[29] but neither he nor Hartman took notice of a further poem, published in the *Gentleman's Magazine* in the year after the one quoted above, which provides a further exception to the 'neo-Arcadian' view. The poem, entitled 'Moon-light', begins as follows:

> Here on this bank, while shine the stars so clear,
> Come, Lucy, let us sit: how tranquil seems

is a faithless lover who is greeted at his wedding by the corpse of his rejected Lucy and promptly dies himself: *The Works of Thomas Tickell*, in *The Works of Celebrated Authors of whose Writings there are but small Remains* (1750), 335. 'The Happy Pair' by Chatterton (dated by his editor in 1770) consisted, similarly, of stanzas spoken alternately by 'Lucy' and 'Strephon'.

[26] See for example 'A Ballad', a poem of 1787 in which a lovelorn Mary was rejected by a William, her faithless lover and died of despair, threatening that her ghost would haunt his bed. *WPW* i. 265–7.

[27] For the history of the poem and the dispute about its authorship see *The Poems of Thomas Gray, William Collins, Oliver Goldsmith*, ed. R. Lonsdale (1969), 403–5. See also Herbert Hartman, 'Wordsworth's "Lucy" Poems, Notes and Marginalia', *PMLA* 49 (1934), 141.

[28] George, Lord Lyttelton, *Works* (1774), 623–40. (Lyttelton's second wife was also called Lucy.)

[29] *The Profession of Poetry* (Oxford, 1929), 90–1.

All Nature! with what mildness from above,
Yon regent of the night looks down on earth,
And gives to every herb, tree, plant, and field,
Of softer green; mark now her virgin front;
How calm she looks, how open, and how pure!
Nor, Lucy, on thy paler beauty dwells
Less sweet serenity; as pure art thou,
As frank and as benignant as the light
Of that fair Planet, when no vapour thin,
Flitting o'er ether, tarnishes her face
With momentary dimness: she, bright Queen
Of all those starry gems which deck this vault
Magnificently built, her silver horn
Monthly replenishes: from that strong blaze
Of unexhausted glory, whose quick heart
Invigorates the world, she still relumes
Her darken'd countenance. But, Lucy, thou,
When Time shall steal those youthful charms away,
From what full fountain of immortal grace,
What Sun of Beauty, shalt thou then repair
Thy form's diminish'd elegance? Alas,
That female lustre, fairer than all stars;
And dearer than the light which rules the day,
Should know no second rising: that, once set,
Nor months, nor years, nor ages can recall! . . .

Here the pastoral ethos common to many previous poems containing a 'Lucy' has been changed importantly. The Lucy of this poem is no longer a figure in a neo-Arcadian world, described in the third person, but a young woman of contemporary sensibility, addressed directly and treated as the equal of the young man issuing the invitation. We know beyond doubt, moreover, that Wordsworth read the *Gentleman's Magazine* for 1789, since in 1792, in a note to *Descriptive Sketches*,[30] he referred to a controversy that had been conducted in its pages from April to December of that year. It is not difficult to imagine the young man of sensibility that Wordsworth describes himself as having been during his Cambridge days visiting Cumbria during the summer vacation of that year or the next, sitting down with a sympathetic young woman and reading to her one of the latest

---

[30] Note to l. 428 of the 1793 edition (*WPW* i. 68: see Duncan Wu, *Wordsworth's Reading, 1770–1799* (Cambridge, 1993), 62). The controversy was about Virgil's use of the word 'castella'.

poems about sensibility in nature. If he then proceeded to compliment her by giving her the name of the young woman addressed in it that would be very much in keeping with the mode.

There is a little further evidence that this particular poem remained as a presence in Wordsworth's mind, moreover, since its second line resembles the opening to some lines that he set down in a notebook many years later as an adjunct to the lines that begin 'This is the spot . . .':

> Here let us rest,—here, where the gentle beams
> Of noontide stealing in between the boughs
> Illuminate their faded leaves . . .[31]

In spite of the fact that both passages probably owe something to the moonlight scene in *The Merchant of Venice* ('Here will we sit, and let the sounds of music | Creep in our ears . . .'[32]) the resemblance between them is close enough to suggest that the locution 'Here let us sit' had lodged itself in Wordsworth's mind, reappearing when he was writing lines that were associated both with Dorothy and with the train of ideas connected with the Lucy poems. It is even possible to spread the net wider.[33]

---

[31] *WPW* iv. 424, note: see also below at n. 57.

[32] v. i. 55.

[33] Years later Wordsworth wrote a famous sonnet about the abolition of the idea of death in a moment of vivid emotion that began with the words 'Surprised by joy . . .' and ended with lines recording the recognition 'That neither present time, nor years unborn | Could to my sight that heavenly face restore' (*WPW* iii. 16). These lines bear an interesting resemblance to the run of those in the *Gentleman's Magazine* poem about female lustre 'that, once set, | Nor months, nor years, nor ages can recall! . . .' The resemblance not only suggests that the lines might have continued to work in Wordsworth's subconscious mind (one may also compare the syntactical construction of the lines in the Immortality Ode: 'Nor Man nor Boy | Nor all that is at enmity with joy . . .') but raises in turn a further possibility. Wordsworth's Fenwick note on 'Surprised by joy . . .' reads 'This was in fact suggested by my daughter Catharine, long after her death' (*WPW* iii. 423). Catharine died on 4 June 1812 at the age of 3, to the great grief of her parents. The poem was published in 1815 and Mark Reed believes it to have been composed by mid-October 1814 at the latest: (*W Chronology MY* 520 and n.). There is no reason to doubt that the event was in some sense at the poem's source, but some readers have commented that there is something strangely unchildlike about the person being invoked. Could it be that behind the incident involving memory of Catharine the response of someone much longer dead might also have been brought momentarily to life?

From speculation based on possible verbal echoes in Wordsworth's later poetry we return to echoes of previous literature here. If we look at the first of the Lucy poems, 'My hope was one . . .' and ask what *poetic* writer stands behind its language and imagery, there is one obvious answer. The comparison of Lucy's lips to roses and her hair to woodbine harks back to poems such as Burns's 'Ye banks and braes o' bonnie Doon', where the jilted maiden goes out 'To see the rose and woodbine twine', and to his fondness for the line 'Her lips are roses wet wi' dew'. The violet, the star, and the broom are all images used several times by Burns, and even when Wordsworth produces a comparison with a river in these poems it turns out to be a Scottish one, the Carron.[34] When we come to the opening of the next poem, comparing Lucy to a rose in June, the reminiscence of Burns is even more unmistakable.[35]

In the late 1780s Wordsworth was already an admirer of Burns. *Poems, Chiefly in the Scottish Dialect* was published in 1786 and in the following year Dorothy recorded that when she had mentioned them to her brother he spoke of his own admiration and promised to get the book for her. In 1799, just after he had been writing the first Lucy poems, he wrote to Coleridge with further praise: 'The communications that proceed from Burns come to the mind with the life and charm of recognitions.'[36] If we suppose that he was recalling the love of an actual woman in the Lucy poems it is a natural further inference that as he recalled it and set it into verse he was attracted also to remember the writings of a poet who had meant a good deal to him at the time when he loved her, and who had probably continued to help shape his sense of her. The atmosphere of the Lucy poems supports this, suggesting as it does an early love. It may not be impossible to think of

[34] De Selincourt points out that if there is a literary source here the most likely candidate is 'Owen of Carron', a ballad by the Westmorland poet John Langhorne: *WPW* ii. 30. Langhorne was quoted in a rough draft of Wordsworth's associated with 'The Vale of Esthwaite' in 1788: Duncan Wu, *Wordsworth's Early Reading 1770–1799* (Cambridge, 1993), 84.

[35] 'O my Luve's like a red, red rose, | That's newly sprung in June', Burns, *Poems* (1794). The image of a woman's cheeks 'as fresh as rose in June' occurs also in 'Dulcina', a poem collected in Percy's *Reliques of Ancient English Poetry* (1765).

[36] Letter of 17 Feb. 1799, *WL* (1787–1805), 256.

Wordsworth writing in this way about a love that took place *after* he had fathered a child by Annette Vallon but it is certainly much harder.

In spite of their brevity the Lucy poems contain a surprising number of details from which to build up a picture of the young woman's life and its surroundings. If we assume that they all belong to one and the same girl she had a rose-like complexion with light hair; she lived near a stream, and perhaps close to springs that fed it; her cottage, set on a lonely heath and probably in a dell, was approached first across a broad lea and then by way of a rising path that passed through an orchard-plot. Having been unusually beautiful as a young girl she was attacked by a fatal malady which first deprived her of her liveliness and then destroyed her. From childhood she had been endowed with a playfulness and a sympathy that made her seem like a part of the nature she inhabited—even as if she embodied its very spirit. Assuming that the passages associated with 'Nutting' also refer to her, she had not only been trained in civilized ways but had received some education, yet she could behave occasionally in nature with a wildness and recklessness that seemed at odds with her customary gentleness, prompting her lover to recall her to the tenderness and sympathy he felt she should be cultivating, in correspondence with the essential spirit of nature. Although these details are scattered through the poems there is no disabling contradiction among them—as there might be, for example, if she were described with dark hair in one place and light in another.

In the later Lucy poems the question of her identity becomes more complex. When the second edition of *Lyrical Ballads* was published in 1800 Wordsworth included all the shorter poems so far quoted. 'Nutting' also appeared, though the original preamble in which 'Lucy' was addressed had already dropped out, never to be restored. By the following spring, when he was moving towards marriage with Mary Hutchinson, he had already discussed with her at least one of the poems already published (the poem that originally began 'My love was one from cities far . . .'), since on sending a further one in April he introduced it at the end of his letter with the words

We had a melancholy visit at Coleridge's—Adieu—love to Tom—I now transcribe a short poem to be read after She dwelt among

I travell'd among unknown men,
  In lands beyond the sea;
Nor, England did I know till then
  What love I bore to thee.

'Tis past—that melancholy dream!
  Nor will I quit thy shore
A second time; for still I seem
  To love thee more and more.

Among thy mountains did I feel
  The gladness of desire
And she I cherish'd turn'd her wheel
  Beside an English fire.

Thy mornings show'd, thy nights conceal'd,
  The bowers where Lucy play'd;
And thine is too the last green field
  Which Lucy's eyes survey'd.

God for ever bless thee, my dear Mary—Adieu.[37]

Had the evidence ceased at this point, the case for assuming that all the poetry quoted so far referred to an actual young woman whom Wordsworth had loved and who had died would have been virtually overwhelming. In the light of the group as a whole Coleridge's conjecture that 'A slumber . . .' had been occasioned by some gloomy moment in which he had imagined his sister to have died would have been regarded as a passing fancy, and the only other point that might have invited comment was the fact that in the original 'Nutting' opening Lucy had been addressed in the present tense rather than in the elegiac tones of the subsequent references; this could readily have been explained as a back-projection of Wordsworth's response to the time of the originating incident. If doubts about a straightforward factual interpretation had been entertained the alternative might have been to propose a totally symbolic reading, based on an assumption that Wordsworth brooded constantly on the death of loved women and was fond of embroidering such meditations with fanciful events that he made up to illustrate them.

A piece of evidence that stands solidly in the way of straightforwardly assuming Lucy to have been a real woman whom Wordsworth had formerly loved emerges, however, in the final

---

[37] Wordsworth to Mary Hutchinson 29 Apr. 1801: *WL* (1787–1805), 333.

poem of the group, composed in the following year, 1802, as he was riding home from seeing Mary, to whom he was not yet married. He sent copies both to her and to Coleridge:

> Among all lovely things my Love had been,
> Had noted well the stars, all flow'rs that grew
> About her home, but She had never seen
> A Glow-worm, never once—and this I knew.
>
> While I was riding on a stormy night,
> Not far from her abode, I chanced to spy
> A single Glowworm once; and at the sight
> Down from my Horse I leapt—great joy had I.
>
> I laid the Glowworm gently on a leaf,
> And bore it with me through the stormy night
> In my left hand—without dismay or grief
> Shining, albeit with a fainter light.
>
> When to the Dwelling of my Love I came,
> I went into the Orchard quietly,
> And left the Glowworm, blessing it by name,
> Laid safely by itself, beneath a tree.
>
> The whole next day I hop'd, and hop'd with fear;
> At night the Glowworm shone beneath the tree;
> I led my Emma to the place,—'Look here!'—
> O joy it was for her, and joy for me!

In this letter to Coleridge he added a note,

The incident of this Poem took place about seven years ago between Dorothy and me.[38]

'Emma' was the name which he normally used when referring in his poems to Dorothy. In the first of the 'Poems on the Naming of Places', composed and published in 1800, the characterization by which he identifies 'Emma's Dell' clearly refers to her, and in another poem of that year, ''Tis said that some have died for love . . .', it is reasonable to trace a reference to her in the 'Emma' who is being addressed. In the following year he wrote a sonnet, 'There is a little unpretending Rill', which was not published until nearly twenty years later. Having described its unnoticeableness, he recalled his first visit there with Dorothy ('my Love' in the manuscript) in 1794:

[38] Wordsworth to Coleridge, 16 Apr. 1802: ibid. 348.

But faithful Emma! thou with me canst say
That while ten thousand pleasures disappear,
And flies their memory fast almost as they
The immortal spirit of one happy day
Lingers beside that Rill, in vision clear.

In the 1802 collection the poem 'The Sparrow's Nest', dated in the previous year, includes a reference to 'my sister Emmeline and I', a phrase also used in 'To a Butterfly', composed on 14 March 1802.[39] The name Emma as an affectionate name for Dorothy continued to stand so in later collections.

In the case of the glow-worm poem the phrase 'seven years ago' would suggest that the incident took place while William and Dorothy were living at Racedown.[40] When the poem received its first publication, in the 1807 collection, on the other hand, the name 'Emma' was changed to 'Lucy', thus inviting the reader to group it with other poems in which she figured.[41] Why did this replacement take place? The most obvious explanation is that Wordsworth was embarrassed to use such affectionate terms ('Among all lovely things my love had been') in publishing a poem which other evidence pointed to as referring to his sister.[42] The decision to alter the name to Lucy is nevertheless striking in view of the normal association in his poems between Emma and Dorothy. If a private manuscript poem addressed to Emma is changed to 'Lucy' on its public appearance, and if

---

[39] *WPW* ii. 111–12, 33; iii. 4 and 419; i. 226–7.

[40] It might seem unlikely that while living so abstemiously Wordsworth would have had a horse to ride, but see the anecdote in Moorman, *Wordsworth*, i. 320 n.

[41] It appeared just before 'I travelled . . .', apart from which no 'Lucy' poem was repeated in the collection. The present one was never afterwards reprinted by him, a fact which de Selincourt thought might have had to do with the ridicule in the *Simpliciad* (1808) of poets who 'greet the glow-worm's flame, | Put it to bed, and bless it by its name': *WPW* ii. 532.

[42] The identification with Dorothy was not always made to others; in the notebook entitled 'Sara Hutchinson's Poets' the line reads 'I led my Mary to the spot' (DC MS 41, p. 13), which invites the reader to speculate about the other Marys in Wordsworth's early life; it is safest to assume, however, that this simply represents a gracious compliment to Mary Hutchinson, made by way of her sister. For Sara's benefit, it seems, he was using a tactful disguise which would not be appropriate when the poem was sent to Mary herself, since she was presumably familiar with the story already and knew that it had involved Dorothy. The disguise was then replicated in a different form for readers in general when the 1807 version was made to refer to 'Lucy'.

Wordsworth himself says in private that the incident took place between himself and Dorothy, it becomes a logical next step to recall Coleridge's conjecture about 'A slumber . . .' relating that poem also to her and then to ask whether all the early Lucy poems did not spring from fantasies, however unlikely, about his sister.

There is at least one further possible link between Dorothy and Lucy, moreover. The lines quoted earlier from the draft introduction to 'Nutting', where Lucy was addressed in a moment of uncharacteristic wildness, then modulated, as we saw, into a more tender invocation:

> Come rest on this light bed of purple heath,
> And let me see thee sink into a dream
> Of gentle thoughts, protracted till thine eye
> Be calm as water when the winds are gone
> And no one can tell whither—

These lines became favourites of Dorothy's. They form part of some lines entitled 'Travelling' that she would sometimes read repeatedly to her brother when he needed to be soothed. Eventually they were incorporated into a later poem, 'Lycoris', written as a tribute to her, which again brings together elements of radiance and trance that look back to the Lucy poems.[43]

Yet the fact remains that any attempts to identify Dorothy straightforwardly with Lucy sits strangely with what we know of her. By 1798 she had a reputation for wildness which disturbed her relatives. Her habit of 'rambling about the countryside on foot' was considered improper for a young lady.[44] There is indeed a note of anxiety in her brother's address to her in the 'Lines written . . . above Tintern Abbey', where he takes pleasure from the reflection of his own earlier enthusiasms in the 'shooting lights' of her 'wild eyes', yet fears lest 'solitude, or fear, or pain, or grief' may in time be her portion. The long description of her by De Quincey makes a similar point: sympa-

---

[43] In her journal for 4 May 1802 Dorothy Wordsworth wrote 'I repeated verses to William while he was in bed—he was soothed & I left him. 'This is the spot' over & over again'. *DWJ* (Woof) 96. For 'This is the spot' and its relation to the 'Lycoris' poems see also below at nn. 56 and 57.

[44] See her spirited letter of 21 Apr. 1794 to her aunt, Mrs Christopher Crackanthorpe, in reply to such criticisms: *WL* (1787–1805), 117.

thetic and sensitive she might be, but these characteristics were embedded in a different kind of personality:

> She was all fire, and an ardour which, like that of the first Lord Shaftesbury,
>
> > 'O'er-inform'd its tenement of clay;'

he writes, and

> . . . this ardour looked out in every gleam of her wild eyes, (those 'wild eyes', so finely noticed in the 'Tintern Abbey') as it spoke in every word of her self-baffled utterance, as it gave a trembling movement to her very person and demeanour.[45]

De Quincey speaks also of her ungainliness and lack of grace—which again he attributes to the immediacy and vehemence of her feelings: 'beyond any person I have known in this world Miss Wordsworth was the creature of impulse . . .'. Again, 'she was the very wildest (in the sense of the most natural) person I have ever known; and also the truest, most inevitable and at the same time the quickest and readiest in her sympathy . . .' Dorothy herself was to deny that as a girl she had been gentle. 'I was always the termagant, you know', she said in later years.[46]

While some pieces of evidence may seem to be pointing firmly towards the existence of a strong link between the Lucy of Wordsworth's poetry and Dorothy, then, any attempt at firm identification runs up against severe difficulties. If it were not for the glow-worm poem, indeed, it is unlikely that anyone would have been drawn to it, the Lucy of the earlier poems being so different in appearance and demeanour. Although the wildness that has just been noticed finds a counterpart in the original opening of the 'Nutting' passage, that is the only instance of such behaviour on Lucy's part, and it is there being remarked on as uncharacteristic. As for Dorothy's appearance, her complexion was dark (De Quincey says that 'her face was of Egyptian brown'[47]); her hair was not a 'woodbine wreath', nor was she tall, nor, according to De Quincey again, at all graceful. Until she took up residence with her brother her residence had been

[45] *DQ Recollections*, 188.
[46] William Knight, *Life of William Wordsworth*, 3 vols. (Edinburgh, 1889), iii. 492.
[47] *DQ Recollections*, 130–1.

mainly at the rectory at Forncett St Peter in Norfolk, where the
stream could hardly be described by the term 'springs', suggesting a more hilly region, and the village, though isolated, was
hardly a 'lonesome heath'. She did not live in a cottage during
this period, nor did she ever make a living by spinning.[48]

There is also a difference of tone between the addresses to
Lucy, which in the original 'Nutting' passage are indulgent
and even a touch patronizing, and those to Dorothy, who in
the contemporaneous 'Lines written . . . above Tintern Abbey'
and elsewhere is approached respectfully and even with some
stateliness.

Why, in any case, should there have been any need to
fictionalize Dorothy's life into a story of death? The actual
Dorothy, as we know from other accounts and from her own
writings, was immediate and intense in her responses to nature.
Why should this vivid living presence have been so firmly
killed off? F. W. Bateson attempted an answer: 'In the end,
Wordsworth *had* to kill the thing he loved, even though it was
only in poetry.'[49] But this is too facile, shunting him into a moral
attitude created by Oscar Wilde. Wordsworth's problem was
rather that of having to face the *potential* mortality of the thing
he loved. His responses to the untimely deaths of his mother,
father, his brother, two of his young children, and in his old age
of his daughter Dora all demonstrate the devastation such losses
caused him. There is no evidence that he felt a need to supplement this agonizing knowledge by killing off still more people
when he wrote his poetry. What the Lucy poems are about, it
has to be urged again, is the effect of *actual* loss.

The point is particularly apposite to the first two Lucy poems,
each of which raises it in a different form. In the first case, the
poem ends with the words

> But now she's in her grave, and Oh!
> The difference to me!

The enforced stress on the word 'difference' recalls other pas-

---

[48] According to Robert Woof one or two of the wheels preserved in the
Wordsworth Museum at Grasmere have been associated with the Wordsworths, but
these would have been used by Dorothy, if at all, only for the very simplest kinds of
spinning (private communication).

[49] Bateson, *Wordsworth*, 67.

sages in Wordsworth's writing where a word or phrase, spoken or otherwise, is intended to have a weight beyond any that is inherent in the simple poetic effect. One thinks of the woman who looks at a wagon delivering bread and in her poverty projects a human personality on it, saying, 'That waggon does not care for us';[50] or the discharged soldier who walks with the poet in the moonlight and refuses to seek accommodation, commenting, with 'ghastly mildness', 'My trust is in the God of Heaven, | And in the eye of him that passes me.'[51] In both cases the phrases are freighted beyond their normal content by the circumstances and the description leading up to them—the one by its bleak despair, the other by its trust in providence, both divine and human. To Sara Hutchinson, similarly, who claimed that the speech of his old leech-gather was tedious, he commented,

It is in the character of the old man to tell his story in a manner which an *impatient* reader must necessarily feel as tedious. But Good God! Such a figure, in such a place, a pious self-respecting, miserably infirm, and [ ] Old Man telling such a tale![52]

In the case of 'My love was one from cities far . . .', the word 'difference' is given similar weight by its crucial positioning in the last line, the effect of Lucy's death having been so much more overwhelming than anything the narrator could have expected. And in us, as readers, a faith that the poet himself actually underwent the experience ratifies this effect, much of which is lost if we learn that after all there was no actual death, the 'difference' having therefore existed only in Wordsworth's imagination. Similarly with 'Strange fits of passion . . .'. If there was no real death, the subsequent telling, Lucy's laughter, and the poet's tears, as recorded in the last stanza of the original version, simply provide a sentimental closure that has no business in the work of a maturing poet. If the telling and the laughing response *actually* took place, on the other hand, Wordsworth's reason for putting them into his first version becomes as understandable as his subsequent decision to omit them—presumably as looking over-sentimentalized: in terms of

[50] DC MS 13 p. 5 (cf. *WPW* i. 316).
[51] *W Prel* (1805), IV. 494–5.
[52] Letter to Sara Hutchinson of 14 June 1802, *WL* (1787–1805), 367.

the poem as a whole they were too cheaply acquired and their continuing presence could not compensate for the enhanced effect to be gained by cutting off the poem at the previous, exclamatory stanza.[53] At the time when the Lucy poems were composed, at least, Wordsworth was still willing to chance his arm in the interest of trying to convey the weight, beyond words, of a deeply felt emotion; but by then the risk was already worth taking only if the emotion was one that he himself had experienced, not one he might in certain circumstances have imagined himself feeling.

The supposition that in these poems he was recalling an actual Lucy whom he loved and who died gains credence from other circumstances surrounding the composition of the original poems about her. It has already been pointed out that the verses among which these lyrics were first included when they were transcribed and sent to Coleridge all consisted of memories from his own boyhood and youth. The evidence suggests that during the period in Germany immediately after Coleridge's departure for Göttingen he was reviving in himself such memories and musing on their possible significance. It is a reasonable supposition, therefore, that *all* the poems written at that juncture came out of endeavours to record resonant memories of unusual events.

Another point in one of these poems bears on the same question. When Wordsworth sent to Coleridge the manuscript of 'My hope was one, from cities far . . .', with its last stanza beginning 'Long time before her head lay low | Dead to the world was she . . .', he preceded it, as we have seen, with the observation, 'In the last stanza of this little poem you will consider the words "Long time" as put in merely to fill up the

---

[53] If Wordsworth did not weight his words so barely in his later writing this may have been because he came to feel that he was fighting a losing battle against unsympathetic readers, who simply converted such effects into bathos. Hartley Coleridge's parody of 'She dwelt among the untrodden ways', written about Wordsworth's lack of popularity as poet, ended with the comment on 'The White Doe of Rylstone',

> Unread his works—his 'Milk-white Doe'
> With dust is dark and dim;
> It's still in Longman's shop, and oh!
> The difference to him!

Quoted Bateson, *Wordsworth*, 2.

measure but as injurious to the sense.' As two scholars at least have pointed out,[54] it is hard to understand why he should have been at such pains to stress this unless the verses were referring to events that had actually happened. If the poetic narrator were simply imagining a young woman suffering from a slow illness and in the process becoming dead to the world the lines would make perfect sense; there is an 'injury' only if the writer is recalling that in real life she was not in fact 'dead to the world' for so long. The point adds force to the supposition that we are dealing with an actual young woman and with events that really occurred.

Yet as soon as the supposition has been made one returns to the stubbornness of the evidence that links the poems with Dorothy: the lines from the first extended drafts for 'Nutting' that were taken up into poetry later addressed to her; Coleridge's conjecture about 'A slumber . . .'; the explicit statement that the event behind the glow-worm poem took place in her company. How are such contrary indications to be reconciled?

The problem is a knotty one, yet further attention to the chronology of the relevant events points towards a possible solution. It has already been noted that the two poems suggesting most strongly that Wordsworth was dealing with a real death were also the first two to be sent to Coleridge; these, taken by themselves, contained little hint of overt symbolism, which might suggest that when they were written Wordsworth was responding to the impact of an actual event, either because it had recently happened or because it was being remembered from the past with unusual vividness. We may also acknowledge that they were composed at a time when the relationship between William and Dorothy was in a particularly sensitive state. A few months earlier Wordsworth had concluded the 'Lines composed . . . above Tintern Abbey', with lines of tenderness for Dorothy that were touched with apprehension for her possible fate in future years. Now, with the departure of Coleridge for another part of Germany at the end of September, they found themselves thrown together with unusual closeness

---

[54] See Moorman, *Wordsworth*, i. 425 n., citing also H. M. Margoliouth, *Wordsworth and Coleridge* (1953), 55.

while living in an unfamiliar culture. If Lucy was a real young woman they would surely have discussed the significance of her death and William's love for her. Dorothy, we know, particularly admired and was moved by the poems he wrote on the subject, while he could have held up to her the example of Lucy's deep attachment to nature as one from which she herself could profit. In these circumstances the way was open for her to become for him a kind of Lucy-surrogate. On this reading of the relationship, we may suppose that the events recorded in the early preamble to 'Nutting', recalling the original Lucy in a moment of uncharacteristically turbulent behaviour, would have seemed in their own way relevant to the untamed side of Dorothy's nature. (The words 'Thou, Lucy, art a maiden "inland bred" | And thou hast known "some nurture"'—the phrases in quotation marks being of course from Orlando's speech in As *You Like It*[55]—sound as if they were addressed to a young woman who had been brought up in wild country rather than, like Dorothy, in a country rectory. They were in any case added later, as we have seen.)

The lines inviting the young lady to calm which followed in the drafts were to have a quite different resonance for them, on the other hand, being woven and expanded into a later piece, given the title 'Travelling' by Wordsworth:

> This is the spot:—how mildly does the sun
> Shine in between the fading leaves! the air
> In the habitual silence of the wood
> Is more than silent; and this bed of heath
> Where shall we find so sweet a resting-place?
> Come let me see thee sink into a dream
> Of quiet thoughts, protracted till thine eye
> Be calm as water when the winds are gone
> And no one can tell whither. My sweet Friend,
> We two have had such happy hours together
> That my heart melts in me to think of it.[56]

Whereas the previous parts of the 'Nutting' drafts seem focused

---

[55] From Orlando's speech in the forest in Act II. vii. 96–7.

[56] The lines were printed by De Selincourt in *WPW* iv. 425 and dated by him in 1803–4 (mistakenly, if composition was in question: see Dorothy Wordsworth's 1802 journal entry quoted above in n. 43). See also below, next note.

elsewhere, these lines came to be associated with the relationship between William and Dorothy. As already mentioned
they were in fact used by brother and sister as a kind of poetic
charm in times of weariness or mental anguish. This again is
sufficiently explained if Wordsworth was encouraging his sister
to fashion herself into the image of the lost Lucy as a means of
calming her natural impetuosity. On such a reading the writing
of the 'Glow-worm' poem reflected the fact that by 1802 the
Lucy-persona had become sufficiently developed as part of his
relationship with her for him to be able to give the imagery and
connotations of a 'Lucy memory' to something that had actually
happened between himself and his sister and eventually to sub-
stitute for 'Emma' the other name, with its further connotations.
The more he could assimilate the dead Lucy to the living
Dorothy the more possible it became to reconcile himself to the
fact of her loss, feeling that Dorothy, at least, was cultivating
something of her inwardness with nature, and so, in her turn,
perpetuating the human benefit. The link between Nature and
Providence could thus be rescued.

In this connection we may turn again to the lines beginning
'Here let us rest . . .' (already associated above with a reading of
'Moon-light' in the *Gentleman's Magazine*) and look at them in
the context of a later notebook passage from which they were
adapted to form part of the 'Lycoris' poems:

> Here let us rest—here, where the gentle beams
> Of noontide stealing in between the boughs
> Illuminate their faded leaves;—the air
> In the habitual silence of this wood
> Is more than silent; and this tuft of heath
> Deck'd with the fulness of its ~~bloom~~ flowers presents
> As beautiful a couch as ere was framed.
> Come—let us venture to exchange the pomp
> Of widespread landscape for the internal wealth
> Of quiet thought—protracted till thine eyes
> Be calm as water when the winds are gone
> And no one can tell whither. Dearest Friend
> We two have had such blissful hours together
> That were power granted to replace them (fetched
> From out the pensive shadows where they lie)

> In the first warmth of their original sunshine
> Loth should I be to use it. Passing sweet
> Are the domains of tender memory[57]

The lines correspond to other aspects of the relationship with
Dorothy: the resort to 'This is the spot . . .' as a charm, the poem
addressed to Emma recalling 'The immortal spirit of one happy
day', and so on. But they fall in equally readily with lines from
the early drafts addressed to Lucy, as if the borders between
memories of her and memories of happy experiences with
Dorothy had by now become blurred.

Such assimilation might not be without its dangers—a point
to which another poem of the time, composed and published in
1800, bears witness:

> 'Tis said, that some have died for love:
> And here and there a church-yard grave is found
> In the cold North's unhallowed ground,
> Because the wretched man himself had slain,
> His love was such a grievous pain.
> And there is one whom I five years have known:
> He dwells alone
> Upon Helvellyn's side.
> He loved—The pretty Barbara died,
> And thus he makes his moan:
> Three years had Barbara in her grave been laid
> When thus his moan he made.
>
> Oh! move thou Cottage from behind that oak
> Or let the aged tree uprooted lie,
> That in some other way yon smoke
> May mount into the sky!
> The clouds pass on; they from the heavens depart:
> I look—the sky is empty space;
> I know not what I trace;
> But when I cease to look, my hand is on my heart.

---

[57] DC MS 86 (the MS is unfoliated; this is from the final inscribed recto, reading
forward). See also *WPW* iv. 96 and 424. My earlier discussion is at n. 31. The last
nine lines were later published in part in ll. 41–51 of the second of the 'Lycoris'
poems, entitled 'To the Same', addressed to Dorothy Wordsworth and written
as a tribute to her. The two poems bring together elements of radiance and trance
that again look back to the Lucy poems; dated probably, according to Ketcham, in
1817–18, they were first published in 1820. See *WPW* iv. 97 and note, pp. 423–4;
also *Shorter Poems 1807–1820*, ed. Carl H. Ketcham (Ithaca, NY, 1989), 253–5,
476–81.

'Oh! what a weight is in these shades! Ye leaves,
When will that dying murmur be suppress'd?
Your sound my heart of peace bereaves,
It robs my heart of rest.
Thou Thrush, that singest loud and loud and free,
Into yon row of willows flit,
Upon that alder sit;
Or sing another song, or chuse another tree!

Roll back, sweet rill! back to thy mountain bounds,
And there for ever be thy waters chain'd!
For thou dost haunt the air with sounds
That cannot be sustain'd;
If still beneath that pine-tree's ragged bough
Headlong yon waterfall must come,
Oh let it then be dumb!
Be anything, sweet rill, but that which thou art now.

Thou Eglantine, whose arch so proudly towers
Even like a rainbow spanning half the vale
Thou one fair shrub, oh! shed thy flowers,
And stir not in the gale.
For thus to see thee nodding in the air,
To see thy arch thus stretch and bend,
Thus rise and thus descend,
Disturbs me, till the sight is more than I can bear.

The Man who makes this feverish complaint
Is one of giant stature, who could dance
Equipp'd from head to foot in iron mail.—
Ah gentle Love! if ever thought was thine
To store up kindred hours for me, thy face
Turn from me, gentle Love, nor let me walk
Within the sound of Emma's voice, or know
Such happiness as I have known to-day.[58]

The extent of factual basis, if any, for this poem is hard to determine. The somewhat bombastic imagery at beginning and end is uncharacteristic of Wordsworth, leading one to suspect a connection with Coleridge's writing in the same year of 'The Voice from the Side of Etna; or the Mad Monk', a poem about a lovelorn solitary bewailing the loss of his loved woman (who

---

[58] Published in the 1800 edition of *Lyrical Ballads*. MS readings from DC MSS 15 and 16: cf. *WPW* ii. 33 and *Lyrical Ballads and Other Poems, 1797–1800*, ed. James Butler and Karen Green (Ithaca, NY, and London, 1992), 176–8.

in this case appears to have been murdered by him), which was characterized by similarly extravagant language and on first publication subtitled 'An Ode in Mrs Ratcliff's Manner'.[59] In Wordsworth's case the poem reads as if he were adopting a strategy for dealing with the grief he had felt over a bereavement and which he found it difficult to express directly. The narrator presents himself as haunted by the memory of a love followed by loss; he feels a subconscious agitation at every memory of that loss, transmitted through the caricature figure of the giant who could dance even though clad in iron mail. The conclusion, with its address to 'Emma', draws the relationship between William and Dorothy into the narrative as a whole. And if we then read the last line in conjunction with the poem already quoted that ends with the lines

> The immortal spirit of one happy day
> Lingers beside that Rill, in vision clear[60]

we may well ask if the same occasion is not being referred to in both cases: a day of quite unusual peace, affection, and happiness. It is as if on that occasion Dorothy had become inseparable from Lucy in his mind, both women being enfolded into a sense of their oneness with the spirit of nature; and as if thought of that trance-like enjoyment was liable to be succeeded, as in 'A slumber . . .', by an admonitory sense of the change involved in death—not a separation from nature, but rather a transformation in one's perception of nature. Just as Lucy had been lost, so might Dorothy be; and the thought of such a second bereavement is more than he can bear.[61]

If this was so, it was also a likely part of the process that memories of the actual Lucy in all her vividness as an individual living woman with a personality of her own should have begun to fade, giving place to a figure whose significance had been

---

[59] *CPW* (EHC) i. 347 n. The poem, published in the *Morning Post* on 13 Oct. 1800, was first collected in the 1880 edition of the *Poetical and Dramatic Works*.

[60] See above, p. 57.

[61] In an article entitled 'Brothers and Sisters', *Times Literary Supplement*, 13 Sept. 1974, Donald H. Reiman argues straightforwardly that Emma here was Dorothy; Derek Roper, in his edition of *Lyrical Ballads* (1968), 373, maintains equally straightforwardly that she is simply 'a name for the speaker's sweetheart'. According to Butler and Green, loc. cit., n. 58 above, 386, the name was added in a manuscript revision, probably between 8 and 13 August 1800.

created by the nature she at once loved and symbolized and whose characteristics could therefore be made part of his relationship with his sister. And this in turn prompts the question whether both relationships did not involve some element of betrayal of the woman involved—whether Lucy's existence as a whole woman was not jeopardized by Wordsworth's insistent alignment of her with the gentler powers of nature and Dorothy's by his pressure on her to calm her wilder instincts, to become less of the termagant in the interests of cultivating her relationship with that element in nature which was in his deepest belief its necessary peaceful centre.

Such questions are obscured by the fact that we do not know how or from what cause the original Lucy, supposing that she existed, died. The language of the poems would suggest one of the most familiar maladies of the time, a decline into consumption: the mortality rate from that illness was then high. But it is not impossible that she died, or that Wordsworth feared she had died, out of love for him—even, conceivably, that she had committed suicide. In that case his sense of responsibility would have come to the fore in a self-reproach that matched his physical love for Annette against his (presumably unconsummated) love for Lucy, leaving him feeling that he had been found wanting in both relationships. But here indeed we move into a realm of uncheckable speculation.

One virtue of the hypothesis advanced here concerning the relationship between Lucy and Dorothy Wordsworth is that it is not only the one that answers best to the various details of the poems, with their shifting points of emphasis, but that it helps explain the roles both of the original 'Lucy' and of Dorothy in a manner that respects both. To see Wordsworth first shocked by and grieving over the death of a woman he had loved, and then coming to terms with the experience by generalizing her significance and subsuming it into his affection for Nature and for his sister—an affection undershot nonetheless by tragic awareness of her potential mortality—may be a complex way of interpreting the process of the poems as a whole but it is the one that seems best to account for all the phenomena involved.

We are still left with difficult questions. Is there any way of discovering an original for 'Lucy'? One suggestion that has been put forward is that Wordsworth might have been recalling the death of Mary Hutchinson's sister Peggy, who died swiftly of consumption in March 1796. There is no positive evidence, however, for this identification;[62] to make it simply because there was a young woman known to Wordsworth who died young is to ignore the frequency of early deaths among women at this time: the parish registers record many such cases.

A further theory that has been advanced is that Lucy might have been modelled, partly at least, on Mary Hutchinson.[63] It is notable that when in the 1850 version of *The Prelude* Wordsworth came to pay tribute to his wife (in a passage that had been absent in 1805) he depicted her gift of inner radiance by invoking once again the star/glow-worm nexus of imagery that is found also in the Lucy poems:

> She came, no more a phantom to adorn
> A moment, but an inmate of the heart,
> And yet a spirit, there for me enshrined
> To penetrate the lofty and the low;
> Even as one essence of pervading light
> Shines, in the brightest of ten thousand stars,
> And the meek worm that feeds her lonely lamp
> Couched in the dewy grass.[64]

Yet while Mary Hutchinson's personality is closer than Dorothy's to that depicted as Lucy's—at least in Lucy's normal gentle moods—there are indications that her appearance was different. Although De Quincey described her complexion as 'fair' he also mentioned the description of her 'dark brown hair'

---

[62] It was proposed by H. M. Margoliouth, *Wordsworth and Coleridge* (1953), 52–6, prompted it seems simply by the discovery that a young woman in Wordsworth's circle of intimate friends had in fact died prematurely during the period in question. There seems to be nothing else to support such a link. She was not brought up in isolation among the mountains, having lived with her sister Mary at Sockburn for most of the period.

[63] See A. Beattie, *Representative Poems of William Wordsworth* (New York, 1937), esp. pp. 317–24 nn., cited Moorman, *Wordsworth*, i. 424 n. In his note for 'Three years she grew . . .' Beattie draws parallels between 'She was a phantom of delight . . .' and the *Prelude* descriptions of Mary Hutchinson; he also (p. 323 n.) cites Wordsworth's direction to her that 'I travelled . . .' was to be read after 'She dwelt . . .' (*WL* (1787–1805), 333) as offering clear evidence that Mary was to 'accept the poems in question as referring to her', which of course they do not.

[64] *W Prel* (1850), XIV. 268–75.

in the poem 'She was a phantom of delight . . .' written about her by her husband.[65]

There are important difficulties of another kind in proposing a closer association. In his comment on his own marriage Wordsworth described how he and Mary 'had known each other from childhood, and had practised reading and spelling under the same old dame at Penrith'.[66] As a result it has been generally assumed by scholars, especially those who comment on the early poetry, that from that time Wordsworth always regarded her as his sweetheart, so that when he finally proposed marriage he was fulfilling a long cherished plan. It is certainly true that in *The Prelude* he describes Mary in his early recollections (probably from 1787) as

> then to me
> By her exulting outside look of youth
> And placid under-countenance, first endear'd . . .

He also describes the time

> When in the blessed hours
> Of early love, alone or with the Maid
> To whom were breathed my first fond vows I roamed . . .[67]

While Wordsworth's deep affection for Mary when he was young is not in question, however, it is harder to believe that what used to be called an 'understanding' existed between them through the following years. Mary remained Dorothy's friend

---

[65] *WPW* ii. 213–14 (*DQ Recollections*, 130–1).

[66] 'Autobiographical Memoranda': *WPrW* iii. 375.

[67] *W Prel* (1805) VI. 234–6 and XI. 316–19 *variation*. The date of these remembered excursions is uncertain. Mary Moorman assumes that they took place in the summer vacations from Cambridge of 1788 and 1789 (Moorman, *Wordsworth*, i. 79) but this supposition seems to be based on the fact that the account of Mary in *The Prelude* comes just after the account of his time in Cambridge. She elsewhere points out that since Dorothy left Penrith in October 1788 there would have been little point in her brother's having spent a long time in Penrith after that time, and there is in fact virtually no evidence for a visit in 1788 itself. Moorman states that an entry in Ann Tyson's account for him of 1*s*. 6*d*. for 'Horsehire' is 'almost certainly to ride to Penrith', but it could as easily have been for a journey or journeys to Broughton and the south-west, particularly since from there Wordsworth would have been in a position to bring the horses back. In spite of its placing in *The Prelude* the reference to the walks with Dorothy and Mary seems more likely to refer to 1787, when we know that Wordsworth spent time at Penrith before going south to begin his time at Cambridge (*W Chronology EY* 74).

rather than his, and none of Dorothy's letters to her in the period contain contributions by or messages from her brother, or indeed any allusions that might suggest a special underlying relationship. If anything, Dorothy seems to keep determinedly silent about him. It was as her friend that Mary visited both in Dorset for a long period during the winter of 1796–7; even in that period our knowledge of the relationship remains meagre. It has recently been increased, it is true, by the discovery a few years ago of letters between William and Mary which contain at least one striking sentence. Writing to her in 1810 and affirming his lasting love for her, he speculates that if when she left Racedown in June 1797 Mary had taken the road for Bristol instead of going to London he would have accompanied her. In that case, he finds himself fancying, 'we should have seen so deeply into each others hearts, and been so fondly locked in each others arms, that we should have braved the worst and parted no more'. While this no doubt refers in some measure to the obstacles that lay in the way of marriage during those years of comparative poverty it also suggests that the question of marriage had not been deeply discussed, let alone settled between them at that time.[68]

Certainly if Wordsworth was thinking of Mary as his future wife from 1787 to 1797 he was one of the least assiduous lovers on record. In 1789 she moved to her great-uncle's farm at Sockburn in County Durham, yet there is no firm evidence of his having visited her there at any time before 1799, even if there may have been occasional meetings elsewhere. In the same years he was, by contrast, a frequent visitor both to Hawkshead, where he had been at school and where he returned each summer for a long period to lodge with Dame Tyson, and to the Furness coast in the south-west of Cumbria.

Another potent argument has already been mentioned: if the

---

[68] Wordsworth's letter is dated 11 Aug. 1810, *WL* viii (Suppl.), 29. Mary's brother Henry made no mention of any prior attachment between them in his autobiographical poem, when he described his 1797 journey with her into Dorset to see them: see *The Letters of Mary Hutchinson, 1800–1855*, ed. M. E. Burton (Oxford, 1958), pp. xxi–xxii. Wordsworth's brother John may well have had some hopes on his own account in 1800–1, before she and William became engaged: see the language of his last letter to her: Moorman, *Wordsworth*, i. 472–3. After John's death in 1805 Wordsworth recalled that in 1800 he himself had 'no thoughts of marrying': *WL* (1787–1805), 563.

Lucy poems were written partly about his relationship with Mary why should he have made any secret of the fact? All the indications are that once they were married he took advantage of any opportunity to express affection and praise for her; he would have taken particular delight in explaining to what extent poems such as these related to her.

If we turn from the young women with whom Wordsworth is known to have been acquainted in his youth and ask whether the poems themselves provide any geographical indications as to where a loved woman might have been located one clue to such a factual basis is found in the reference to 'the springs of Dove' in the first of the poems. This is of little help, however, particularly in view of the existence of various rivers with that name.[69] It is more likely that his usage is based not on memories of a particular stream but (as has also been suggested in relation to the name Lucy), on his liking for a poetic name that would run well in verse. It was not only a plausible name for an English river but euphonious and easy to rhyme.

In looking for geographical clues it may be more profitable, in fact, to return to De Quincey's account of Lucy, quoted earlier, and to consider that in its fuller context. There it appeared as part of a view that Wordsworth was 'no lover in a proper sense'—which prompted him to the counter-reflection, on the basis of verses such as those beginning 'When she I loved was strong and gay' and ''Tis said that some have died for love', that at some earlier period of his life he might have been. He continued,

---

[69] As happens elsewhere in this complex affair, such pointers as exist set up various possible trails. Wordsworth is known to have visited the best-known river Dove in England, which flows through Dovedale in Derbyshire and was the river where Izaak Walton practised his art of fishing, in June 1788, at the beginning of his summer vacation from Cambridge; but he seems to have stayed in the region for no more than two or three days. (*W Chronology EY* 84–5.) Two other rivers with the name are found in Yorkshire, one of them rising in the Cleveland Hills 20 miles from Sockburn where the Hutchinsons settled; but no connection has been traced with either. G. M. Harper noticed with pleasure that there is a Dovedale in Cumberland near Dove Crag, with an 'ancient manor house or superior farmhouse' called Hartsop Hall and believed this to have been the location of a love-affair in the summer of 1788, since he was sure that Wordsworth would have passed through it on his way from Hawkshead to Penrith (*William Wordsworth, his Life, Work and Influence* (1916; new edn., 1929, p. 43). However, the running water there is called Dovedale Beck, and there are scarcely any other habitations on the fells in that area, which in any case is hardly a 'heath'.

... yet if no lover, or (which some of us have sometimes thought) a lover disappointed at some earlier period by the death of her he loved, or by some other fatal event (for he always preserved a mysterious silence on the subject of that 'Lucy', repeatedly alluded to or apostrophized in his poems, and I have heard, from gossiping people about Hawkshead, some snatches of tragical story, which, after all, might be an idle semi-fable, improved out of slight materials)—let this matter have been as it might—at all events he made, what for him turns out, a happy marriage. Few people have lived on such terms of entire harmony and affection as he has lived with the woman of his ultimate choice.[70]

Since this is the only contemporary clue that survives as to a factual basis for the Lucy poems, it is worth examining in some detail. Its main importance is to locate in Hawkshead the main sources of gossip about the affair. From the evidence of the poems themselves one would not immediately think of Hawkshead itself as a setting for the events described; if they did indeed happen there it is surprising that no other tradition survived, given the relative compactness of its community. If they had taken place in the immediate neighbourhood it is likely that the gossip would have been specific enough for the story to have been retailed and handed down by others. Within his own lifetime Wordsworth was well known as an important figure, and when T. W. Thompson wrote *Wordsworth's Hawkshead* more than a century later a notable amount of reminiscence and record concerning the poet was still circulating among the local inhabitants. If the events occasioning the Lucy poems had occurred in their midst direct tradition would surely have kept them alive. On this basis, then, it seems likely that if there was such gossip in Hawkshead they had taken place at some distance from the town. The fact that Lucy is specifically said to have dwelt 'among the untrodden ways' is also an indication that she lived in an area less frequented than Hawkshead itself, already then quite a thriving community.

The existing evidence enables one to speculate a little further concerning the most likely time and place for such events. We know that after Wordsworth left Hawkshead School and went to Cambridge in 1787 he was in the habit of returning to the area each summer: there are indications that he visited it in each of the next two summer vacations. In 1790 and in 1792 he was

---

[70] *DQ Recollections*, 187–8.

in France. In 1791 and 1793 he may or may not have visited the Lakes; in 1794 he certainly returned there, and spent a summer at Broughton and Rampside in the south-west of the district which was to be viewed in retrospect as idyllic: the news then of Robespierre's death, brought across the Leven estuary on a day of unusual splendour, induced an ecstatic mood that would long be remembered and made the subject of a rhapsodic passage in *The Prelude*,[71] while the image of Peel Castle, reflected in a mirror-like sea day after day, was to become the wistful emblem of a state of mind he later felt to have been lost to him for ever, after the death of his brother John.[72] The nostalgic element in his recollection of that summer may have been further intensified by the fact that from the autumn of the following year, 1795, when he took up residence with Dorothy at Racedown in Dorset, there were no more long journeys to the north-west until his return from Germany in 1799, when he took Coleridge on a journey of rediscovery that also included a visit to the Hutchinson sisters at Sockburn in Durham.

A further source of evidence concerning the period and Lucy's possible identity remains to be more fully examined. The fact that there was another area that Wordsworth visited in the summers during his vacations from Cambridge and to which he continued to return afterwards has already been touched on. This was the Furness area in the south-west of the Lake District, including Broughton in Furness, a town close to the estuary of the River Duddon, about which he was later to compose his famous series of sonnets. When he published the latter he commented:

During my college vacation, and two or three years afterwards, before taking my Bachelor's degree, I was several times resident in the house of a near relative who lived in the small town of Broughton. I passed many delightful hours upon the banks of this river, which becomes an estuary about a mile from that place.[73]

The 'near relative' was his cousin Mary Wordsworth, who

---

[71] W *Prel* (1805), x. 539–66.

[72] In 1805: see his 'Elegiac Stanzas': *WPW* iv. 258–60.

[73] *WPW* iii. 504–5. Mary Moorman believes that the phrase 'before taking my degree' should read 'after taking my degree' (Moorman, *Wordsworth*, i. 122 n.): he took his degree in 1791 and it is likely that he stayed with the Smiths in July 1794, for example (*W Chronology EY* 157); Mary's father Richard Wordsworth had died in June of that year. Perhaps the best reading would be 'before and after'.

married John Smith, an innkeeper at Broughton. Six years older
than himself, she died in 1799, only a few months after the
first Lucy poems were composed. Broughton is about 15 to 20
miles from Hawkshead and it would not have been difficult
for him to visit a young woman who lived somewhere in the
area, particularly if he could have done so on horseback. An
innkeeper, moreover, would be likely to have horses that could
be used for the purpose. The possibility must be considered that
the original Lucy lived in the district—perhaps in the Duddon
Valley itself—and that this was a main reason for Wordsworth's
being attracted to return to the region each summer.

Wordsworth's love for the Duddon Valley is evident not only
from his sonnet sequence but from the account of it in his *Guide
through the District of the Lakes*. One has to look more closely
into the matter, however, before the long-standing nature of his
attachment becomes clear. It was in early boyhood that it first
began, having been originally sparked as a result of hearing its
praises sung by Hugh Tyson, the husband of Ann, his old nurse
at Hawkshead. Hugh claimed to have known it in his earlier
years, and in response to his enthusiasm Wordsworth set off to
visit its upper reaches when himself very young. On that occasion the immediate attraction was the prospect of fishing, a
sport which he had already practised in the Derwent but had
found disappointing round Hawkshead, where the stocks were
low:

I fell into the common delusion that the further from home the better
sport would be had. Accordingly, one day I attached myself to a person
living in the neighbourhood of Hawkshead, who was going to try his
fortune as an angler near the source of the Duddon. We fished a great
part of the day with very sorry success, the rain pouring torrents, and
long before we got home I was worn out with fatigue; and if the good
man had not carried me on his back, I must have lain down under the
best shelter I could find. Little did I think then that it would have been
my lot to celebrate, in a strain of love and admiration, the stream
which for many years I never thought of without recollections of
disappointment and distress.[74]

---

[74] *WPW* iii. 504. In his *Wordsworth's Hawkshead*, ed. Robert Woof (Oxford,
1970), 6–7, T. W. Thompson tells the story of the boyhood visit and its lugubrious
outcome, relating its provenance through several descendants, without apparently
recalling that Wordsworth had recorded it more directly in his own note.

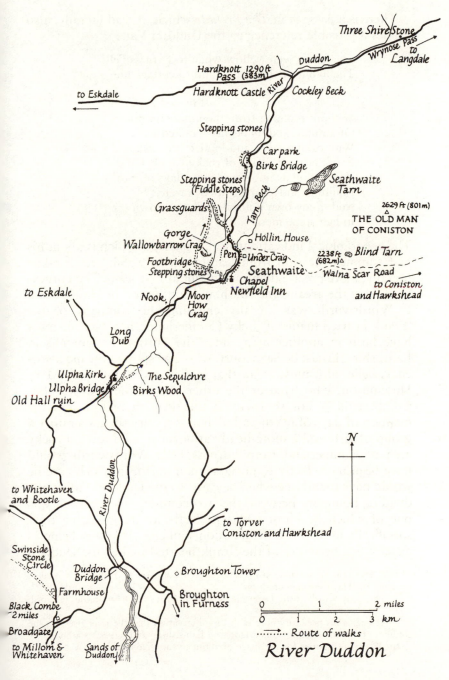

Three Shire Stone

Wrynose Pass to Langdale

Duddon

Hardknott 1290 ft Pass (383 m)

to Eskdale

Hardknott Castle River Cockley Beck

Stepping stones

Car park
Birks Bridge

Stepping stones (Fiddle Steps)

Grassguards

Gorge

Wallowbarrow Crag

Footbridge
Stepping stones

Pen

Tarn Beck

Seathwaite Tarn

2629 ft (801 m) △
THE OLD MAN OF CONISTON

Hollin House

2238 ft (682 m) △ Blind Tarn

Under Crag

Seathwaite Chapel
Newfield Inn

Walna Scar Road

to Coniston and Hawkshead

to Eskdale

Nook

Moor How Crag

Long Dub

Ulpha Kirk
Ulpha Bridge

Old Hall ruin

The Sepulchre
Birks Wood

N

River Duddon

to Whitehaven and Bootle

to Torver Coniston and Hawkshead

Swinside Stone Circle

Duddon Bridge

Farmhouse

Broughton Tower

Black Combe 2 miles

Broadgate

to Millom & Whitehaven

Sands of Duddon

Broughton in Furness

0        1        2 miles
0    1    2    3 km

........ Route of walks

River Duddon

There is a passage in *The Prelude* which, if read literally, also
carries a possible reference to the Duddon Valley:

> The leaves were yellow when to Furness Fells
> The haunt of shepherds, and to cottage life
> I bade adieu . . .
>                                 I turned my face
> Without repining from the mountain pomp
> Of autumn and its beauty (entered in
> With calmer lakes and louder streams); and you,
> Frank-hearted maids of rocky Cumberland
> You and your not unwelcome days of mirth
> I quitted, and your nights of revelry,
> And in my own unlovely cell sate down
> In lightsome mood . . .[75]

The geographical indications in this passage, which is about his
first summer vacation from Cambridge in 1788, are, if taken
literally, more precise than they might at first seem. The Furness
Fells lie in the area to the south and south-west of Hawkshead.
If Wordsworth was literally enjoying the company of the
'Frank-hearted maids of rocky Cumberland', however, he must
have been in another area, since the Furness region falls in
Lancashire. Ernest de Selincourt, who also spotted the inconsist-
ency, believed it must mean that he had spent time with Mary
Hutchinson, who lived at the other end of the county.[76] But
Cumberland is not so rocky in the Penrith region, and the
mention of days of mirth and nights of revelry suggests rather a
group of girls and a more heady atmosphere. To reach a rocky
area of Cumberland from Furness Fells Wordsworth would
have been more likely to go west than north, in which case he
would have found one when he came to the Duddon Valley, the
dividing boundary between the two counties. The division was
one of which he himself was perfectly aware, referring to it
specifically in a note to the Duddon sonnets;[77] if he was being as
exact when he wrote of the 'frank-hearted maids' the Duddon

---

[75] W Prel (1805), VI. 1–3, 9–17. The 1850 version reads 'Esthwaite's Banks',
stressing the Hawkshead connection.
[76] 'The Early Wordsworth' (1936) in *Wordworthian and Other Studies* (Oxford,
1947), 25 n.
[77] He begins his prefatory note with the observation that the river rises 'on the
confines of Westmoreland, Cumberland and Lancashire' and serves 'as a boundary
to the last two Counties for the space of about twenty-five miles': *WPW* iii. 244.

Valley could well have been in his mind. This would fall in with his statement that during his college vacation, and two or three years afterwards, he 'passed many delightful hours upon the banks of this river'.

After the summer of 1794 Wordsworth did not return to the area for some years.[78] When in October 1804 he revisited the valley accompanied by his sister, they stayed at an alehouse in Seathwaite, Dorothy describing the Duddon Valley to Lady Beaumont as

one of the most romantic of all our vales and one of the wildest. . . . In Duddon vale Rocks, hills, bushes and trees are striving together for mastery, green fields and patches of green are to be spied out wherever the eye turns with their snug cottages half-hidden by the rocks or so like them in colour, that you hardly know rock from cottage.[79]

A country, clearly, of 'rocks and stones and trees'. A few years later, when William and Mary Wordsworth had been spending a period in a cottage by the seaside on the west coast of Cumberland at Bootle they sent their two young children back with the maid by way of Coniston and walked up the Duddon Valley by themselves. On this occasion, Wordsworth recorded that they spent some time at Ulpha, a few miles below Seathwaite: 'Mary and I returned from Duddon Bridge, up the Duddon and through Seathwaite, the children with Fanny. We dined in the Porch of Ulpha Kirk and passed two Hours there and in the beautiful churchyard.' In a manuscript now known as the 'Unpublished Tour' he describes the churchyard further: 'The whole scene is inspirited by the sound and sight of the river rolling immediately below the steep ground upon the top of which the Chapel stands. The following pleasing Epitaph will be found upon a stone affixed to the Wall of the Chapel . . .' He goes on to quote the epitaph, which describes a woman 'worn out with pain and long disease' and concludes, 'So raise to heaven thy pensive heart, | Where dearest friends will never part.' He then points out that a tombstone in the wall was erected by a father to the memory of a daughter who 'died at the age of one & twenty' and continues, 'This . . . is the only

---

[78] Coleridge however spent a little time there during his 1802 walking tour. *CN* i. 1205–6, 1225.
[79] *WL* (1787–1805), 507–8.

record in the Church yard, except that a Person has availed himself of the naked surface of a corner stone of the Chapel rudely to engrave thereon a brief notice of One who is buried near it.' The Duddon Valley was closely associated in his mind with elegy.

Wordsworth later reverted to this 1811 visit with Mary when he dictated to Isabella Fenwick a note on the Duddon Sonnets:

I have many affecting remembrances connected with this stream. These I forbear to mention; especially things that occurred on its banks during the later part of that visit to the seaside of which the former part is detailed in my Epistle to Sir George Beaumont.[80]

One reason that the memories must have been 'affecting' was that the children who had been sent on ahead were within a short time both to be dead, but since they were not actually present on this occasion, the fact hardly accounts for the phrase concerning 'things that occurred on its banks'; indeed it is difficult to see why the memories should have been affecting unless further elegiac recollections there, beyond his experience on that particular occasion, were involved.

From 1807 onwards Wordsworth was composing the sonnets which eventually came together in his 1820 volume. Given his returning fascination, it is worth exploring further the possibility that on the occasions when he revisited the Duddon Valley he was recalling events that had been of unusual significance. It may also be noted that when the sonnets were published in his 1820 *Poems* they were set alongside the long poem 'Vaudracour and Julia', the disguised account of his love for Annette Vallon, which also appeared there for the first time. The possibility that in that volume not one but two relationships were being commemorated in disguised form, the one potentially scandalous, the other the very opposite of scandalous but still too intimate to be described openly, deserves serious consideration.

The overall structure of the sonnet sequence does not immediately betray such concealed intent. If there is a controlling theme it would seem to be rather Wordsworth's purpose to celebrate the Duddon while introducing symbolism by relating

---

[80] *WPW* iii. 505. The 'Epistle to Sir George Howland Beaumont, Bart. from the South-west Coast of Cumberland', was composed in August 1811: *WPW* iv. 142–50.

its flowing to the stream of time. Moral reflections were also included: without labouring the analogies it was possible to put in touches that treated the Duddon at the beginning as an infant spring ('Child of the clouds') and at the end as a mature estuary, reminiscent rather of a great commercial route such as the Thames. Wordsworth also explored the further symbolic possibilities raised by the historical connections of its setting, ranging from his reflections on the traces of primeval forests and primitive man in the second and eighth sonnets to the mentions of Roman remains at Hardknott in the seventeenth and of modern commerce and war in the thirty-second. Over and above this, there intervene occasional reflections suggesting how the sense of the stream as a whole relates the flux of time to intimations of eternity: these are present particularly in the sonnet on Ulpha Kirk, where the sound of the running water is dwelt on as giving resonance to the scene, and the final 'After-thought', with its comments on the relation between Form and Function and the voicing of an ultimate reassuring hope that 'as toward the silent tomb we go ... We feel that we are greater than we know.'

Intertwined with this play of possible significances, however, there are a number of points in the sequence where the run of the narrative suggests more local memories. Such signs also deserve attention, since whereas Wordsworth's sonnet-sequences are normally geared closely to their subject-matter, this series displays an unusual tendency to pursue digressive themes, linked only loosely to the point that has been reached in the sequence.

An example is the strange little pair of poems on 'Stepping-stones', in the second of which the teasing of a 'shepherd-lass' by her adolescent companion as she tries to cross the stream turns into a flirtation as dangerous for both as it is attractive:

> Chidden she chides again; the thrilling touch
> Both feel, when he renews the wished-for aid:
> Ah! if their fluttering hearts should stir too much,
> Should beat too strongly, both may be betrayed ...[81]

---

[81] *WPW* iii. 250. In *Through the Wordsworth Country* (1906), 263–4, William Knight quotes Mr Herbert Rix as locating this set of stones as at Black Hall and the 'Faery Chasm' of the next sonnet as 'the rocky gorge which is crowned by Birks Brig'.

A more specific touch of possible reminiscence is detectable as the sequence moves towards a more inhabited part of the valley at Donnerdale. The poet ends one sonnet by expressing a hope that if the weather becomes inclement he might be able to turn aside for shelter and

> While the warm hearth exalts the mantling ale,
> Laugh with the generous household heartily
> At all the merry pranks of Donnerdale![82]

The suggestion is that he has enjoyed similar pleasures in the past. Was it on such occasions that he shared the company of the 'frank-hearted maids of Cumberland', their 'days of mirth' and 'nights of revelry'? Lucy, remembered for her 'laughter light', would fit well into such a scene.

Whatever one makes of these possibilities there is one point at which remembrance of the actual breaks through quite unambiguously. The sonnet in question, the twenty-first, is crucial to the present enquiry:

> Whence that low voice?—A whisper from the heart,
> That told of days long past, when here I roved
> With friends and kindred tenderly beloved;
> Some who had early mandates to depart,
> Yet are allowed to steal my path athwart
> By Duddon's side; once more do we unite,
> Once more beneath the kind Earth's tranquil light;
> And smothered joys into new being start.
> From her unworthy seat, the cloudy stall
> Of Time, breaks forth triumphant Memory;
> Her glistening tresses bound, yet light and free
> As golden locks of birch, that rise and fall
> On gales that breathe too gently to recall
> Aught of the fading year's inclemency!

The 'kindred' of the third line must include his cousin Mary, who, as noted above, married John Smith of Broughton and died there in 1799. Wordsworth's note, it will be recalled, records how he stayed with them on various occasions and 'passed many delightful hours' upon the banks of the Duddon;

---

[82] *WPW* iii. 251. William Knight maintains (ibid. 266) that this sonnet, entitled 'Open Prospect', and the next must refer to 'The Pen' or 'Pen Crag', the only spot from which such a view might be gained.

when he speaks of 'some who had early mandates to depart' Mary's death must have been particularly in his mind. Since the word is 'some', however, he must be thinking of more than one person who had joined these expeditions and who had died young. This again prompts the thought that one of his companions there might have been the original young woman of the early Lucy poems, this being one of the 'affecting remembrances' which he 'forbore to mention' in his account of the river. If so, we have a strong clue to the identity of the person whose 'low voice' comes back to him as he walks by the Duddon, awakening memory of a figure whose 'glistening tresses' were 'bound, yet light and | free | As golden locks of birch'. If the voice is indeed that of the long lost Lucy the poem gains in emotional force—a force restrained by the use of stately locutions such as the word 'mandates' but nevertheless resurgent in the promise of renewal that subsists in the imagery of spring.

Given the existence of such a strong clue it is natural to pursue the enquiry further. It may be no accident that the very next sonnet relates the tradition of a 'love-lorn Maid' who met a tragic end. The sonnet, entitled 'Legend', describes how she died trying to pick a primrose that was blooming on a rock down a cliff just out of her reach whether she was straining downwards from above or upwards from below. It is as if after the memory of death in sonnet 21 the poet feels the need to expand the sense of loss by introducing a tragic event, even if the title gives it a fictional direction. The next sonnet moves to the sports that surround sheep-washing, where the effects of the clamorous play of the shepherds are compared to the results of the washing in the river, which are immediately swept away ('Frank are the sports, the stains are fugitive'). The next, beginning 'Mid noon is past . . .' brings the traveller temporarily to rest in a 'Nook— with woodbine hung and straggling weed'. The word 'Nook' may or may not have had a personal resonance for Wordsworth, as we shall see elsewhere,[83] and the appearance of the Burnsian word 'woodbine' might or might not involve accidental memory of the Lucy whose hair was a 'woodbine wreath'. It is even conceivable that the grotto-like place where he rests ('half grot,

---

[83] See the Appendix, pp. 322–3.

half arbour') reminds him of an occasion long before, recorded
in the lines cited earlier: 'While in the Cave we sate this Noon |
Oh what a countenance was thine.' The most remarkable thing,
however, is that at this point in the sequence he is suddenly
overcome by a sense of guilt at the absence of his wife ('The One
for whom my heart shall ever beat | With tenderest love') and
moved to introduce a further sonnet expressing his wish that by
some magical device she could be transported to join him: 'With
sweets that she partakes not some distaste | Mingles, and lurking
consciousness of wrong.' It is as if a sense of guilt, induced by the
fondness of the memories aroused at this juncture, is prompting
him to reaffirm his lasting love for Mary in this manner.

Certainly the theme of recollected affection continues, as he
thanks the Duddon in the twenty-eighth sonnet for

> hopes and recollections worn
> Close to the vital seat of human clay;
> Glad meetings, tender partings, that upstay
> The drooping mind of absence, by vows sworn
> In his pure presence near the trysting thorn . . .

Just what is being referred to here? And is there a further
reference to such meetings and partings in the next but one
sonnet? There he dwells on the fact that while one can leave the
river for a while and be sure one can rejoin it further along
without any change of relationship, it is not so with human
absences:

> Who swerves from innocence, who makes divorce
> Of that serene companion—a good name,
> Recovers not his loss; but walks with shame,
> With doubt, with fear, and haply with remorse:
> And oft-times he—who yielding to the force
> Of chance-temptation, ere his journey end,
> From chosen comrade turns, or faithful friend—
> In vain shall rue the broken intercourse . . .

This is an extraordinary weight of moral reflection to hang on
something so simple as a decision to walk across fields for a
while instead of continuing to follow the banks of a stream: it
again raises a question, this time whether in the past there had
been by the Duddon a 'tender parting' *not* to be followed by
so 'glad' a meeting—perhaps when Wordsworth returned from

his second visit to France in 1792, having yielded to 'chance-temptation' in the interval?

The next sonnet, on the Kirk of Ulpha, is relevant in a different respect to the questions raised here. As Wordsworth comes to it in his sonnet-sequence he greets it as a sight that 'to the pilgrim's eye | Is welcome as a star'. This involves an unexpected change of direction for the implied visitor. The church does indeed come into sight as one walks down the valley, but if it is to be seen as like a 'welcome . . . star' its positioning makes it difficult for the viewpoint of the traveller to be other than that of one going *up* the valley, where it will be seen standing on the skyline, rather than nestling in nearby fields. Yet the ordering of the sequence throughout has presupposed someone proceeding down and Wordsworth himself was in the habit of advising those planning a visit to follow the same direction if possible. On the occasions in the past when he visited the valley from Broughton, on the other hand, he would have come to the church at Ulpha on his way up; and if in some cases he had been on his way to see a young woman after an absence the familiar church might well have seemed at that point particularly welcoming.

It may finally be pointed out that if this part of the valley had been the scene of tender relationships in the past, that made it an appropriate place in which to meditate now on matters of life and death:

> How sweet were leisure! could it yield no more
> Than 'mid that wave-washed Church-yard to recline,
> From pastoral graves extracting thoughts divine,
> Or there to pace, and mark the summits hoar
> Of distant moon-lit mountains faintly shine,
> Soothed by the unseen River's gentle roar.

It is a good example of Wordsworth's need when facing the fact of human mortality to find a landscape fitting and fitted to his needs and emotions. The scene of distant illumination, coupled with the soothing sound of the nearby river, evokes elements frequent in Wordsworth's elicitings of consolation from nature. But one might also draw attention to an odd metaphor near the beginning of the sonnet, where the words 'welcome as a star' are followed by the lines

> that doth present
> Its shining forehead through the peaceful rent
> Of a black cloud diffus'd o'er half the sky . . .

The image of a star with a forehead, once attended to, is lugubrious; it is hard to think of a reason for its appearance here
except as answering to a desire on Wordsworth's part to give a
sense of personal presence, of a living head rising. This might
again answer to recollection of the mood of expectation in
which he he had sometimes formerly walked up the river. (It is
also possible to juxtapose it against the image of the moon
dropping into darkness behind Lucy's cottage in 'Strange fits of
passion . . .'.)

There is another issue to be considered. When in the early
drafts quoted above Wordsworth was admonishing 'Lucy' for
her voracious behaviour he pointed out, echoing the words of
Shakespeare's Orlando, that she was 'inland bred' and had
known 'some nurture'. If it is indeed the case that she was an
inhabitant of the upper Duddon Valley one might well ask what
kind of education or training she could possibly have enjoyed in
so remote an area. The prospect seems unpromising, given the
general lack of such opportunities in England at the time, but as
Wordsworth himself points out in the volume, they were here
unusually good, thanks largely to the efforts of one man. In a
note to his description of Seathwaite Chapel in the eighteenth
sonnet, he gives a long account lasting several pages, of its most
famous incumbent[84] Robert Walker, known as 'Wonderful
Walker' on account of his extraordinary piety and devotion,
the exemplary modesty and frugality of his life, and the range of
his good works. Among the qualities Wordsworth describes is
his enthusiasm for communicating to the pupils at his school his
own passionate admiration for nature:

He was skilled in fossils and plants; a constant observer of the plants
and winds: the atmosphere was his delight. He made many experiments on its nature and properties. In summer he used to gather a
multitude of flies and insects, and, by his entertaining description,
amuse and instruct his children. They shared all his daily employments,
and derived many sentiments of love and benevolence from his observations on the works and productions of nature. Whether they were

---

[84] *WPW* iii. 510–22.

following him in the field, or surrounding him in school, he took every opportunity of storing their minds with useful information.[85]

Children who had been born in that part of the valley during Wordsworth's early life and so formed part of Robert Walker's congregation would have found their feeling for nature enhanced both in and out of the schoolroom. With such a teacher at hand it would not be surprising if a young woman of innate sensitivity found herself encouraged to enter into an immediate intimacy with living things and a delight in nature, her upbringing in such a solitary place powerfully assisting the process.

A passage in the 1805 version of *The Prelude* also bears on the matter. Relating how at a certain stage in his youth, when his response to Nature was dominated by his immediate sensuous reactions, the 'inner faculties' were laid asleep, Wordsworth reflects that in the complex processes of growing up such 'thraldom of that sense' seems inevitable. 'And yet,' he continues,

> . . . I knew a Maid,
> Who, young as I was then, conversed with things
> In higher style. From appetites like these,
> She, gentle visitant, as well she might,
> Was wholly free. Far less did critic rules
> Or barren intermeddling subtleties
> Perplex her mind, but, wise as Women are
> When genial circumstance hath favor'd them,
> She welcom'd what was given, and craved no more.
> Whatever scene was present to her eyes,
> That was the best, to that she was attuned
> Through her humility and lowliness,
> And through a perfect happiness of soul
> Whose variegated feelings were in this
> Sisters, that they were each some new delight.
> For she was Nature's inmate: her the birds
> And every flower she met with, could they but
> Have known her, would have loved. Methought such charm
> Of sweetness did her presence breathe around
> That all the trees, and all the silent hills,
> And every thing she look'd on, should have had

[85] Ibid. 521.

> An intimation how she bore herself
> Towards them and to all creatures. God delights
> In such a being; for her common thoughts
> Are piety, her life is blessedness.[86]

When Ernest de Selincourt edited *The Prelude* he assumed that the description referred to Dorothy, and said so in his note. In her 1959 re-editing of his edition Helen Darbishire disagreed, saying that the description corresponded better with what was known of Mary Hutchinson's placid nature. In support of that identification, which has been followed by other editors,[87] she also drew attention to a version in one manuscript which ran,

> Who, though her years ran parallel with mine
> Did then converse with objects of the sense
> In loftier style . . .[88]

pointing out that Mary was born only four months after Wordsworth, whereas Dorothy was nearly two years younger.

'Parallel' need not be interpreted quite so precisely, however; and it should be noted that Wordsworth gives this description without any indication of the 'Maid''s identity. Other such allusions, when referring to Dorothy Wordsworth or Mary Hutchinson, are normally explicit. The idea that the person being described was Mary Hutchinson is, as noted earlier in connection with her sister Peggy, made even less likely by the description of her as living in a mountainous part of the country.

The possibility remains, then, that this description refers to another young woman whom Wordsworth knew in his youth—the one, perhaps, who, sitting in a cave, inspired him in his early draft by her 'love even for the unsubstantial clouds'. It may be, in other words, that we have here his longest description of the original Lucy. Everything that is said about this Maid fits well with the details about her in other poems.

If this is so, a further prospect opens, since the passage was first adumbrated as part of a long discussion about sensitivity to

---

[86] W *Prel* (1805), XI. 199–223.
[87] See William Wordsworth, *The Prelude* 1799, 1805, 1850, ed. Jonathan Wordsworth, M. H. Abrams, and Stephen Gill (New York, 1979) at this point.
[88] W *Prel* 612–13.

nature which was probably drafted about 1798. There the lines read as follows:

> But some there are, and such as I have known
> Far happier, chiefly one beloved maid
> For **she is** Nature's inmate, & **her** heart
> Is every where, even the unnoticed heath
> That o'er the mountains spreads its prodigal bells
> Lives in **her** love; friends also more than one
> Are **hers** who feed among the woods and hills
> A kindred joy. **And** blessed are your days
> That such delights are yours. For though we prize
> And by a          law the things
> Our hands have form'd & though as I believe
> The love of order is a sentiment
> Inherent in the mind yet does it seem
> That each access of strength this passion gains
> From human labours through a course direct
> Or sinuous, is productive evermore
> Of littleness & pride.

The language of the concluding assertion can be compared with that of some lines in the poem 'Lines left upon a seat in a Yew-tree', published in 1798 but perhaps already completed by 1797:

> If Thou be one whose heart the holy forms
> Of young imagination have kept pure,
> Stranger! henceforth be warned; and know that pride,
> Howe'er disguised in its own majesty,
> Is littleness; that he who feels contempt
> For any living thing, hath faculties
> Which he hath never used; that thought with him
> Is in its infancy.[89]

The correspondence in ideas is such as to make it likely that the two passages were written while the same complex of ideas was at work in Wordsworth's mind. But since in this early version the maid is spoken of throughout in the present tense,

---

[89] Lines 48–55: *WPW* i. 92–4. According to the editor, drafts appear in a notebook in use at Racedown in 1795–7, some lines being in the hand of Mary Hutchinson, who visited the Wordsworths there in the early months of 1797. Her name and address appear in one of these MSS near one of the drafts but not apparently associated with it. The reference to 'littleness and pride' may also be compared to Coleridge's 1797 account of the universe as being, for those unhabituated to 'the Vast', a 'mass of *little things*': *CL* i. 354; cf. 349.

Wordsworth when he wrote the lines must have believed her still
to be alive. This would mean that if the Lucy poems written at
the end of 1798 were indeed about the same young woman,
news of the death to which they represented a reaction must
have reached him only very recently.

The original manuscript (the relevant page of which is reproduced as an illustration to the present volume) reveals a point
of further interest: certain words, such as 'she', 'her', and
'hers' (printed here in bold type), appear in a blacker ink in
the manuscript, indicating that they must have been added
later.[90] Such additions are not notable elsewhere in the manuscript and it is hard to think of a reason for these unless the lines
originally contained a direct address to the young lady. This
would make sense of the use of the words 'your' and 'yours' in
the next sentence, which otherwise exhibits an odd shift of
pronoun.

If we imagine how the lines might originally have run, taking
into account a few signs of the original writing that have survived such as a dot over the 'hers' in line 5, we may attempt a
reconstruction of the text as follows:

> For **thou art** Natures inmate, & **thy** heart
> Is every where, even the unnoticed heath
> That o'er the mountains spreads its prodigal bells
> Lives in **thy** love; friends also more than one
> Are **thine** who feed among the woods and hills
> A kindred joy. **Then** blessed are your days
> That such delights are yours. For though we prize . . .

As with the alteration to 'Ah! what a crash was that', however, the possibility cannot be ruled out that one of the new
words, for example the 'And' in line 6, might have been written
over a name. If so, the run of the metre is such that it could
hardly have been of more than one syllable. Monosyllabic
names were not common in the late eighteenth century, the only
examples that spring readily to mind being 'Kate', 'Jane', 'Ruth',
and 'Anne'.

---

[90] DC MS 16 pp. 114–15. The erasures have been fairly thoroughly carried out.
See, however, below, Appendix, n. 16. It is just possible that a forensic expert,
equipped with the latest techniques, might be able to discover what was originally
there.

Investigation into Lucy's possible identity may also be accompanied by attempts at closer location of her dwelling-place. In geographic terms it has been noted that the region where Wordsworth's memories seem to come most vividly into play as he comes down the valley begins in the region known as Donnerdale. It is at the first broadening of the river plain into more habitable country that he places the sonnet referring to the delights in inclement weather of retiring into shelter with 'mantling ale' and laughter at 'all the merry pranks of Donnerdale'. The commemoration of Robert Walker at 'Seathwaite Chapel' is followed first by a sonnet entitled 'The Plain of Donnerdale' describing the future rougher course of the stream and then by the twenty-first, in which he is haunted by the 'low voice' from the past. If we suppose that he is calling on memories of real events this is the area of the river's course where they are most redolent.

Wordsworth's fondness for staying in this part, along with his frequent recommendations that the valley should be explored as a whole, was prominent in subsequent years. It is further evidenced by the fact that a drawing of Seathwaite chapel by a young friend, the Reverend Lionel Fraser of Peterhouse, Cambridge, became a valued possession, which he hoped to have reproduced as an engraving for a later edition of the Duddon Sonnets.[91] The tours in the valley described in his guides to the district were supplemented by further visits, which continued for the remainder of his life. In 1840 he lost his temper with his wife (an event rare enough for him to comment on it) over a misunderstanding of the route there.[92] In 1844 he spent a sleepless night near Seathwaite and told his companion afterwards that 'he had not slept well, that the recollection of former days and people had crowded upon him, and "most of all, my dear sister . . ."'. This had led on, he said, to the thought of others who had died and to the alteration of sonnets 'and that made the matter worse still'. Having said this, he turned to comment on the perfect beauty of a bunch of harebell and parsley fern.[93]

[91] *WL* (1829–34), 651; (1840–53), 447–8, 544–5.
[92] See his Fenwick note, *WPW* iii. 505.
[93] Lady Richardson, reported in *The Prose Works of William Wordsworth*, ed. A. B. Grosart (3 vols. 1876), iii. 447.

Although the final reaction looks at first like a classic displacement gesture at the onset of emotion, it may not in fact have
been so irrelevant to what he had been saying. Perhaps among
those 'others who had died' he was remembering with particular
force at that moment the loss of one of whom he had once
written,

> even the unnoticed heath
> That o'er the mountains spreads its prodigal bells
> Lives in her love.

Investigation of these matters of detail returns us to a question
touched on earlier. If we assume for the purposes of argument
that behind the Lucy poems there was a real woman who
Wordsworth knew and who actually died, how important is it?
Isn't it, after all, the poetry that matters, and that alone?

The argument that Wordsworth himself was deeply concerned with such matters of fact can be reinforced by considering his intellectual predicament during the period. This was a
time when, following the Terror in France and the subsequent
reaction against it, he was troubled by the increase of scepticism,
particularly among the young. His concern led him not only to
look for a grounded position from which to counter the current
tendency towards nihilism or despair but to contemplate the
making of a poem on a Miltonic scale which would address this,
the most urgent issue of the age.

As he did so the drafts began to shape themselves around
a single protagonist, a character who was in certain respects
autobiographical. Then, in a further development, much of the
autobiographical material already drafted was hived off to form
the separate poem which would become *The Prelude*. This
seems to have answered to a recognition that for the purposes
evolving in the larger poem, *The Recluse*, generalization from
the detailed memories of his own experience might not be of
service. The Wordsworth of his own history might have been
fortunate in his experiences in nature but he had also been on
his own admission a socially favoured creature, with the benefits
of upbringing in a well-to-do family supplemented by education
first in a good country grammar school and then in a major
English university. For his larger poem a different kind of
protagonist was needed. If the experiences, and the basis for

philosophy that he was adumbrating there were to be generalized, it was essential to make it credible that they could have
happened to, and been reflected on by, a man with no such
advantages, someone who had been cut off from such influences—living alone, perhaps, in the wildness of nature. While
the autobiographical purposes were increasingly realized in the
writing of *The Prelude*, therefore, the moral and social intent
for *The Recluse* devolved round the more restricted figure of
the pedlar, a man who could be regarded as having developed
in the same way as Wordsworth despite having been brought up
in a humbler environment. It was in consequence particularly
valuable to Wordsworth that he should have known one or two
figures in real life who corresponded to such a pattern—men
who, despite a lack of favouring circumstances, had learned a
considerable human wisdom.

His account of the formation of *The Excursion* in the note
dictated to Isabella Fenwick during the 1840s makes clear his
own attitude to the characterization that resulted:

had I been born in a class which would have deprived me of what is
called a liberal education, it is not unlikely that, being strong in body,
I should have taken to a way of life such as that in which my Pedlar
passed the greater part of his days. At all events, I am here called upon
freely to acknowledge that the character I have represented in his
person is chiefly an idea of what I fancied my own character might have
become in his circumstances. Nevertheless, much of what he says and
does had an external existence that fell under my own youthful
and subsequent observation. An individual named Patrick, by birth
and education a Scotchman, followed this humble occupation for
many years, and afterwards settled in the town of Kendal. He married
a kinswoman of my wife's, and her sister Sarah was brought up from
childhood under this good man's eye. My own imaginations I was
happy to find clothed in reality, and fresh ones suggested, by what
she reported of this man's tenderness of heart, his strong and pure
imagination, and his solid achievements in literature, chiefly religious
whether in prose or verse.[94]

In addition to this source from Sara Hutchinson's memories,
Wordsworth reports on his conversations in Hawkshead with a
Packman who in following the same trade had acquired 'an

---

[94] *WPW* v. 373–4.

intimate knowledge of human concerns, not merely among the humbler classes of society'.

This kind of reinforcement from an individual in the society about him enabled Wordsworth to feel that his generalizations were being forged from a larger stock of wisdom than that which had come to him simply by way of his own special educational advantages, so strengthening his authority in pronouncing at large on the relationship between human beings, society, and nature.

The problem recurred, however, and in a more acute form, at the very core of his philosophy. For in his musings on the state of human beings and society in the aftermath of the French Revolution and its subsequent decline into violence he had come to look at all evidence which suggested that the kind of grounding he had experienced in growing up close to nature's workings might be a resource for mankind generally. He was not so naive as to believe that her operations were always benevolent in their bearing on human affairs; a man who had been brought up in the bleak winters of a mountainous countryside such as that of Cumbria was unlikely to cherish such an illusion. Rather, he believed that in spite of all in nature that was indifferent to human welfare and apt to destroy it there were processes at her very heart that if rightly apprehended and appreciated would reveal themselves to be in touch with the most philanthropic propensities of human beings. This, a central insight of the 'Lines composed . . . above Tintern Abbey', was the potentiality that he was continuing to explore as he worked towards *The Prelude*. But in doing so was he simply manufacturing a delusion out of memories of his own sensibility? Just as it was important to him to be able to believe that his aspirations for humanity were not simply a result of his own favoured education but could be replicated by a thoughtful human being in any walk of life, so it would be a considerable gain for him to be able to recall any human beings in whom the alliance between the forces of nature and their own inward powers could be seen to operate fruitfully—if also unconsciously. To demonstrate the existence of even one such 'child of nature', who had grown to adult status without losing his or her inner bonding would be of immeasurable value, providing a solid resource to which he could turn in states of despondency or depression.

Such examples were rare, however. Even the young Hartley Coleridge, who had shown himself very much a child of nature in his earliest years, displayed an unreal quality that provoked forebodings about his future.[95] It was for this reason, I am suggesting, that the Lucy about whom the poems were written was so important to him; and, equally significantly, that she must have had an actual human existence. A straightforwardly simple girl who had shown an ability to respond to nature owing little to books or to a sophisticated cultivation of sensibility was exactly what was needed for his philosophy of nature at that time. Whether or not she might have proved a suitable permanent companion for Wordsworth, she acted as guarantor for the subsistence of a power at the heart of nature on which he could rely in the midst of much that suggested indifference or even malevolence. That there had existed someone who without advantages of income or education could appreciate the workings of nature in so direct a way furnished powerful evidence of a strong providential element, a potential resource of stability and of moral good which could be both a revelation and a foundation on which to build. The existence of even one Lucy in the world could transform one's sense of what was possible for humanity.

Such a transformation was needed, moreover. Robert Walker was a fine example of a man who had shown what it was to believe in providence under the old dispensation. In a letter quoted in the *Annual Register* for 1760 and picked up from there by Wordsworth himself,[96] he had excused himself from not having replied immediately to his correspondent on the grounds that 'the hand of Providence, then laying heavy upon an amiable pledge of conjugal endearment, hath since taken from me a promising girl . . .'. He went on to give an account of his financial position, explaining that he had never had an estate of his own; yet 'by a providential blessing upon my own diligent endeavors, the kindness of friends, and a cheap country to live in, we have always had the necessaries of life'.

Even Walker had to acknowledge that the hand of Providence might show itself not only in the distribution of blessings, but in

---

[95] See his poem 'To H. C. Six Years Old', ibid. i. 247.
[96] Ibid. iii. 512–13.

'laying heavy' on those one loved. For Wordsworth, to whom such events were rendered more disturbing by the doubts concerning Providence and Nature that had been increasingly stirred up by writers since Voltaire, making it a matter of urgency to find ways of linking the workings of Providence more closely and surely with those of Nature herself, the figure of the young woman on whom his Lucy was based provided, we may contend, the most ready means. Given his faith in her power to demonstrate such a link, on the other hand, the news of her death must correspondingly have been a blow of the same order as that experienced by Tennyson nearly fifty years later on the sudden death of Arthur Hallam. The fact that Nature could strike down one of her most innocent devotees with such casualness was cruel to any sense of an ultimate providential order. It was one thing to be able to look behind sudden death and still perceive the operations of a divine moral order, another to see those operations as in some way 'natural' when they showed a wanton ability to efface a young woman who had apparently embodied within herself simultaneously both 'law and impulse'.

In these circumstances, it is true, the *memory* of Lucy could still return as consolation, and even as a renovating power. But memory would be, by the same token, a treacherous resource. If one had rested one's faith in the existence of a bond between outermost nature and innermost humanity, tenuous to the outer eye yet overwhelmingly convincing in certain experiences, such as those of trance, and found a human being who at times seemed to embody that link, the memory of those moments of entrancement and their impressiveness could be a source of consolation. But what was one to say when memory went on to remind one that her bodily existence had been destroyed by that same nature, in an equally potent stroke of untimely death? Where then could be traced the existence of a supernatural mercy, divine or otherwise? The very word might turn into an exclamation:

> 'O mercy!' to myself I cried,
> 'If Lucy should be dead!'

For Wordsworth the alternation between the two kinds of possibility would never disappear. In moments of greatest loss they would return through life to haunt him as something more than a simple personal blow. In the face of such bleakness the only resource that could counterweigh was in fact that of 'Memory' herself in her cyclical mode, refusing to let him forget the young woman whose mediating image recalled the recurring mercy of spring in the natural world—a mercy of which her immediate personal presence had once been redolent,

> Her glistening tresses bound, yet light and free
> As golden locks of birch, that rise and fall
> On gales that breathe too gently to recall
> Aught of the fading year's inclemency!

This resurgent power of memory, at least, corresponding as it did to the seasonal round of the universe, could be seen as an enduring resource of the dependably providential.

## 3

# William Ellery Channing Visits
# the Lake Poets

THE name of William Ellery Channing is better known in the United States than in Britain, but it is doubtful whether even in present-day America he is known to many by much more than an occasional street-name. His earlier stature is best indicated, perhaps, by the ease with which T. S. Eliot could expect his allusions to be picked up when he wrote about his mother's dramatic poem *Savonarola* that her Savonarola spoke as if he had read Emerson, Channing, and the *Hibbert Journal*.[1]

By 1822 Channing was already well known in Boston as a liberal Christian thinker with progressive views on social matters: after the conclusion of the Napoleonic wars he had been one of the first to advocate a pacifist position, and had been prominent in establishing the Massachusetts Peace Society. He had also been active in opposition to the institution of slavery. His health had been poor, however, and his congregation had given him a long period of leave in the hope that it might improve. Accordingly he found himself crossing the Atlantic on his way to a long tour of Europe.

In recent years his religious views had made him a controversial figure: his early training had been for the Congregational Church, but he had increasingly urged on his contemporaries the advantages of a more liberal Christianity and in 1819, when he preached a sermon at the ordination of Jared Sparks and wrote two articles, 'Objections to Unitarian Christianity Considered' and 'The Moral Argument against Calvinism', it became clear that his orientation was changing. He objected to the name 'Unitarian', disliking it for its abstraction as much

[1] See his introduction to *Savonarola, A Dramatic Poem* by Charlotte Eliot (1926).

as the term 'Trinitarian', and believing that the differences between the churches were largely verbal. He objected still more to
Calvinism, with its doctrine of predestination: if that were true,
he thought, existence would be a curse.[2]

Channing's detestation of predestination went along with
a belief in the divine providence, an issue that had been brought
into prominence as much in America as in England by the
scientific investigations and observations of the time. It was
entirely consonant with that interest that one of his activities
on board ship should have been to make observations on the
elements around him. A representative sample from his entries
in the journal he kept as they journeyed,[3] shows him paying
particular attention to phenomena which might at first sight
seem to be of no significance yet could on reflection be seen to
show signs of a divine appointment and ordering:

> The light and heat of the sun on the ocean may seem unprofitable.
> Not so. The heat is absorbed in vapour, and when given out by
> condensation of vapour into rain, it is imparted to the atmosphere.
> Hence good done by raining, at sea as well on land. Air is softened . . .

> What a beautiful appointment, that the sun, which heats and dries
> the earth, should raise the cloud to shelter it, and the rain to moisten
> it; and that heat, which seems at first, at war with moisture, should
> conjoin with it in rearing the plant! . . .

> A beautiful appointment, that the sun gives impulse to the winds, by
> which his beams are mitigated on shore, by which the vapour of ocean
> is multiplied and transported, and of course, by which the earth is
> preserved from being parched . . .

The current spirit of the age, with its leanings towards psychological issues, showed itself most in Channing's contempla-
tion of the energies of nature and their possible providential
effects on the minds and souls of those who experienced them:

> Great powers in the universe, balancing one another by mighty
> energy, make creation more interesting. Would not less intensity of
> heat, creating and requiring less motion of winds, vapours, sea, be
> attended with less activity of animal and vegetable nature? These great
> powers in nature call forth great energy and skill in man, give impulse
> and life to the soul . . .

---

[2] Letter of 1812, quoted *Channing Memoir*, i. 357.
[3] *Channing Memoir*, ii. 208–10.

A feeling for nature was not uncommon among the New Englanders of the time, some of whom had followed with interest the activities of the early Romantic writers in the England to which he was going. As a young man Channing had heard of the plan that Coleridge and Southey had made to set up an ideal community in Philadelphia and had thought of emulating them.[4] When he tried in later years to express his own religious aspirations the imagery of freedom in nature came readily: 'I desire to escape the narrow walls of a particular church, and to live under the open sky, looking far and wide, seeing with my own eyes in the broad light, hearing with my own ears, and following truth . . .'.[5] Above all, he had been stirred by Wordsworth, whose poem *The Excursion*, published eight years before, had come as a revelation and now formed part of his favourite reading. Nor was this surprising, for Wordsworth had recently done more than anyone else to expound the beauties of nature when viewed against the sense of a divine providence. Channing later said that he read him more often than any poet apart from Shakespeare.[6] There is no evidence, however, that he went so far as to follow the young Wordsworth in tracing a relationship between providence and the inception of human love in natural surroundings, in the manner suggested in the last chapter. The Wordsworth he admired was older and more conventional in his views.

His discovery and admiration were reflected in his behaviour on arriving at Liverpool—the usual port of entry from North America. Most American visitors after the disappointment of arriving in a port that looked so like the New York that they had just left, travelled across the Mersey and to Chester, where they could hope to experience the medieval charm they were looking for.[7] The Channings, by contrast, though met with many offers of welcome in the city, made their way immediately into the Lakes and to Grasmere. The manuscript version of the journal, recently rediscovered in an American library, has made it pos-

    [4] *Channing Memoir*, i. 117.

    [5] Discourse at the Installation of the Revd M. I. Motte, 1828, in *Works* (1840), iii. 211.

    [6] *Channing Memoir*, ii. 95.

    [7] See Christopher Mulvey, *Anglo-American Landscapes* (Cambridge, 1983), 37–59.

sible to correct and supplement previously published accounts of his travels.[8]

The language used in his descriptions of the scenery shows how saturated in Wordsworth's writings he had become.[9] Most writers of the time would analyse what they saw in terms of the picturesque, but although Channing sometimes did so, he was even more interested in the effects of the scenery on his own imagination and psyche. He was particularly struck by the effect of the islands of Windermere:

The islands are numerous (some say 17), varying in size & to one who sails on the lake, their combination with one another & with the shore open an almost endless number of channels, & form mazes of beauty which attune the eye & stimulate the imaginatn by partially disclosed scenery, & a mysterious intricacy—

The influence of Wordsworth shows most fully in his account of Grasmere:

Next we visited Grassmere Water—a sacred spot, a seclusion from all that is turbulent and unholy in life. It was near sunset as we approached this water. We found ourselves descending a mount, called Loughrigg, into a valley, in which reposed this sweet lake, unruffled, smooth, hemmed in by sheltering mountains. The solemn heights towards the setting sun showed to us as we rode eastward of Grassmere, their dark sides, which were reflected with wonderful distinctness in the still bosom of the lake, within which they seemed to find even a more quiet abode than in the tranquil heavens into which they ascended—This repetition of the dark side of the mountain threw a solemnity over the part of the lake to which the reflectn was confined; whilst beyond this line, a mild light, answering to that of the heavens & other mountns gleamed from the water, giv$^g$ various though not unharmonious expressions &

[8] I am greatly indebted to Katherine H. Griffin of the Massachusetts Historical Society, who came across this when searching at my request for Channing's account of his visit to Coleridge (see n. 26 below) and very kindly made a xerox available to me. I am most grateful both to her and to the Society, which has allowed me to reproduce the extracts which appeared in the article on which this chapter is based, and the relevant parts of which are reproduced here by kind permission of the Oxford University Press. The accounts of the conversations with Wordsworth and Southey are given in full below.

[9] It should, however, be noted that Channing wrote up his descriptions of the Lakes after his visit to Wordsworth, so that he may also have been influenced directly by the language of the poems that Wordsworth read to him on that occasion, as related below.

investing it at one moment with the power of different forms of beauty—

The effect of this lake on the spirit was immediate, deep, penetrating the inmost soul, and giving us a feeling of something profound in our nature. . . . The character of this place is that of seclusion, but not a stern or sorrowful seclusion, congenial with the mind which injury or disappointment has made impatient or sick of the world. It invites the mild enthusiast, who amidst the deformities of life sees the lovely in human nature, and who at a distance from the tumults of society would resign himself to visions of moral beauty, perfect loveliness, and sublime virtue, unknown on earth—who is conscious of the capacities of human nature for what is good and great, and desires, under the kindliest influences of the universe, to call forth into new life these high principles in his own soul.

Channing enjoyed one advantage which was denied to many of his fellow-Americans visiting England. His brother-in-law was the painter Washington Allston, who had met Coleridge in Rome, and then renewed the acquaintance in London and Bristol.[10] Channing carried a letter of introduction, therefore, and could expect a welcome from Coleridge's friends as well. He called on Wordsworth as he passed through Rydal on his way to Grasmere and was invited to spend the next afternoon with him. In Grasmere, he recorded, 'a sick man, the clergyman of Ambleside, in the next room, was the only painful circumstance'. It was a reminder of his own condition; and indeed having spent the next morning walking in the lanes around the village he found some difficulty in reaching Rydal Mount that afternoon, the only vehicle available to a stranger being a cart belonging to the village. He accepted this, however, and once he had reconciled himself to a slow and rather uncomfortable progress was once again able to discern the workings of providence:

finding that it was intolerably jolty when the horse trotted, I made him walk the distance $2\frac{1}{2}$ miles. Happily the air was mild, and I began to think that Providence, in distributing lots, had not been as severe as

---

[10] For recent accounts of the friendship see E. S. Shaffer, ' "Infernal Dreams" and Romantic Art Criticism: Coleridge on the Campo Santo, Pisa', *The Wordsworth Circle*, 20 (1989), 9–19 and my 'Transatlantic and Scottish Connections' in R. Gravil and M. Lefebure (eds.), *The Coleridge Connection* (1990), 308–43—which also includes some references to Channing.

some wd think in limiting multitudes to a cart—for I enjoyed the fine prospects of Rydal & Grasmere, as I could not have done in a covered vehicle.

To be visited in these years by such a man as Channing must have been a strange experience for Wordsworth, whose devotion to nature had long been shadowed by the loss of his early idealism, following the violence of the French Revolution. Against such a conservatism Channing maintained undauntedly a belief in the possibility of human improvement. Wordsworth's basic pessimism concerning human nature was met by the idealism of a man who, while realistic about the ills which human beings suffered, found it extremely difficult to believe in evil. Twenty years later Wordsworth was still to recall one assertion that he had made during his visit—primarily, he said, on account of the manifest sincerity with which it was uttered—'that one great evidence of the Divine origin of Christianity was, that it contained nothing which rendered it unadapted to a progressive state of society, that it put no checks upon the activity of the human mind, and did not compel it to tread always blindly in a beaten path.'[11]

After leaving Grasmere Channing went on to Borrowdale by way of Derwentwater, which he found disappointing in terms of the picturesque. The mountains, however, had all the effect that he could desire:

My spirit rose with the mountains, which towered around me, & found something within itself corresponding to their might & sublimity—Exhilaration mixed with awe, at the sight of these monuments of the power which framed & actuates the universe—Their height, connecting them with a purer & more peaceful region & the visionary character given to the tops by distance, & by the softening atmosphere, formed a strange contrast with the weight & massiness of the foundations, so that they united many of the interesting thoughts which we associate with heaven & earth & gave them the power of both worlds over the mind.

He then went on to Keswick to visit Robert Southey, now Poet Laureate, whom he first saw riding in a cart with his family. The recently discovered journal mentioned earlier[12] contains a

---

[11] *Channing Memoir*, ii. 221.
[12] See above, n. 8.

hitherto unknown account of the conversation which followed. Southey, who received him courteously, spoke of his increasing preference for the literature of truth and fact, and went on to discuss the issues of the day in a manner likely to interest Channing greatly:

I saw Mr Southey Monday, Tuesday, Wednesday—His appearance expressive chiefly of an amiable character—He lives under Skiddaw, a mountain of inspiration to a poet—He talked however little of poetry or poets, told me that he should not now begin his American poem[13] (of which by the way Philip is not the hero, M$^r$ S having no love of savage life) but should prosecute it because begun, & that he had come to love truth & fact more than fiction—acknowledgments enough to show that he never possessed the highest gifts of a poet—Poetical power has been unfolded most in later life (Milton, Cowper) when realities of life incline us to look beyond & above them—he expressed his motives in writing on Methodism & Quakerism & spoke very candidly of their founders—spoke of his history of Brazil[14] as the work on which his reputation wd chiefly rest—of his works just completed or in preparation, as the 'peninsular war', the history of the 'Church in England' 'Dialogues on the progress & prospects of soc$^y$'.[15] He undertakes *too much*—We conversed on State of England, of whh he spoke discouragingly, as if Cobbet & demagogues had the ear of the common people—of the establishment, which, with few alterations, such as wd multiply clergy & bring them into contact with people, he thought admirable—of the want of religion, & of the frequency of infidelity in lowest classes & among the liberal party, even the leaders—of pauperism, as a subject on which no steady light had been thrown, & to which a partial application of M$^r$ Owen's plan[16] wd be useful—of Malthus, whom he esteems not more than myself[17]—of the danger, to spring from the present full agency of the reformists & the press—of Unitarianism, here as distinguished from

[13] i.e. 'Oliver Newman', a poem in the metre of *The Curse of Kehama* 'designed to have been an Anglo-American Iliad of King Philip's war', on which he worked from 1815 to 1829 without completing it.

[14] *The History of Brazil* (1810–19).

[15] i.e. his *History of the Peninsular War* (1823–32), *The Book of the Church* (1824)—followed by *Vindiciae Anglicanae* (1826)—and *Sir Thomas More: Or Colloquies on the Progress and Prospects of Society* (1829).

[16] For more on Southey's view of Robert Owen's ideas see his *Colloquies* (1829), 62 and 132–47. He also discussed them in e.g. letters of 1816 (*S Letters* (Warter), iii. 45 and *S Letters* (Curry), ii. 141) and of 1829: *S Letters* (Warter), iv. 146–7.

[17] Southey's lifelong hatred of the doctrines expressed in Malthus's *Essay on the Principle of Population* (2nd edn., 1803) was at its height in 1804, when he used particularly violent language: *S Letters* (Curry), 350f., 355, 357, 363.

that system among us[18]—of Buckminster's[19] & Benson's[20] sermons, which he seemed inclined to place at head of modern sermons—of preaching, & its general mediocrity &c—I found him not inclined to read answers to his books—averse to metaphysical discussion—fond of such books as Mather's magnalia[21] & Fuller's church history[22]—looking on religion as a subject for belief rather than reasoning—strongly attracted to existing institutions, though generous in his views of the possible progress of society thro the operation of these institutions— Gave me interesting account of Shelly's history[23] & of Wesley's letter as given by his wife[24]—Accorded with my views respecting the spirit which ought to unite England & America—I spoke to him with great freedom of the signs of the times, of the spirit & sacrifices demanded from the great &c—and was heard attentively—He offered me every aid in England, & gave me letters to Oxford & Cambridge[25]—His manners are simple—I first saw on the road from Lowdore, riding in a cart with his family.

[18] Southey thought of Channing's beliefs as being closer to Arianism, but later became persuaded that he was now 'an Unitarian of the lowest grade, that is as near Theophilanthropic as may be, and that in proportion as he has liberalised his own creed, he has contracted his charity for those who are travelling in the same direction': *S Letters* (Warter), iv. 160.

[19] The *Sermons* (Boston, 1814) of Joseph Stevens Buckminster (1784–1812), an American Unitarian minister. Writing to Longman's in Sept. 1824 Southey suggested that they issue an English edition: 'They are so striking and so good that they could not fail of success'.

[20] Christopher Benson (1789–1868) was at this time curate of St Giles's in London. The following December Southey urged his daughter Edith May to go and hear him: 'He is so far the best preacher I ever heard, as to admit of no comparison with any other.' The sermons which he put in Channing's hand (p. 119) may have been the *Seven Discourses upon the Duties and Doctrines of the Gospel* (Newcastle, 1821).

[21] i.e. Cotton Mather, *Magnalia Christi Americana: Or the Ecclesiastical History of New-England, from first planting in the year 1620 unto the year . . . 1698* (1702). For Southey's enthusiasm see e.g. *S Letters* (Warter), ii. 264 and *S Letters* (Curry), ii. 265.

[22] Thomas Fuller, *The Church-History of Britain* (1655 etc). See e.g. *S Letters* (Warter), iii. 429.

[23] Shelley visited the Lake District in 1811 with Harriet Westbrook and was cordially received by Southey: see *S Letters* (Curry), ii. 19, 20, 21. Later however, having long been repelled by Shelley's atheism and appalled by Harriet's fate, he rebuked him in a letter of 1820, later published in an appendix to *Correspondence of Robert Southey with Caroline Bowles* (1881), 363–6.

[24] According to Southey's letter of 1820, in *S Letters* (Curry), ii. 220, the letter in question, 'carried off' by Mrs Wesley 'when she finally separated from him', concerned the 'unwarrantable liberties' which he took with the person of one of his female disciples when he was 65.

[25] Two such letters have survived, one to Benson (see above, n. 20), and one, which was returned undelivered, to the Revd Peter Elmsley in Oxford. *S Letters* (CCSouthey), v. 119–20 and *S Letters* (Warter), iii. 321.

The Channings went on to visit Europe and to winter in Italy but the end of their trip was clouded with sadness, since at Florence they were informed of the deaths of a sister-in-law and of their youngest child. They hurried home by way of England, but there was still time for Channing to pay his last call on an English Romantic poet. According to his later account, he particularly admired Coleridge's *Biographia Literaria* and the 'spirituality of the philosophy' expressed in it.[26] Coleridge, meeting him, seems to have been struck by an outgoing spirit like that which he remembered in the Washington Allston who had provided his letter of introduction. After he had expressed his admiration for Allston, they spoke of the current state of literature. Coleridge, like Wordsworth, was evidently attracted by a man who recalled so much of his own idealism a quarter of a century earlier. But he was also disturbed to find him attracted towards unitarianism, the very doctrine that he himself had turned his back on after his youthful allegiance. He urged on Channing the importance of the doctrine of the Trinity, as expressing a relationship between wisdom, love, and spirit that was equally active in the Supreme Being and in the psyche of the true Christian; it was, he contended, 'the perfection of Reason, which can only be developed in us by our grasping the idea of the relation of the infinite Love and infinite Wisdom in one Spirit, communicated to those who are filial by a free obedience'.[27] Channing was particularly struck by the fact that Coleridge never used a word that was empty, or even careless.[28]

[26] Mentioned in the headnote to the entry on Channing in *CM* ii. 20 as from the 'memorandum book' in which Channing made his notes on the occasion. This memorandum book, from which other items are quoted in the *Marginalia* headnote and cited below, has not been found in spite of an extensive search, but Arthur W. Brown, who described the visit in *Always Young for Liberty: A Biography of William Ellery Channing* (Syracuse, NY, 1956), 149–50, has assured me that it exists. The locations of some Channing manuscripts have changed in recent years.

[27] Quoted from the transcript of the 'memorandum book' mentioned in n. 26 above. Peabody, *Reminiscences*, 70, quotes this in an almost identical form as supplied by Channing himself, adding 'I think he said that the formula Coleridge used for the Trinity was "the relation of Love and Truth in the Holy Spirit, in communion with which man finds his life—Love being the Father and Truth the Son".'

[28] Peabody, *Reminiscences*, 143.

Coleridge in his turn was evidently delighted to find that the spirit which had so pleased him in Allston's work as an artist was equally present in Channing. Writing to the former shortly afterwards, he expressed his pleasure at the meeting, using as he did so the very words that had formed an important element in his discourse on the Trinity:[29]

Highgate, 13th June, 1823.

MY FRIEND,—It was more than a gratification, it was a great comfort, to all of us, to see, sit, walk, and converse with two such dear and dearly respected friends of yours, as Mr. and Mrs. Channing.

Mr. Channing I could not be said not to have known in part before. It is enough to add that the reality differed from my previous conception of it, only by being more amiable, more discriminating, and more free from prejudices, than my experience had permitted me to anticipate. His affection for the good as the good, and his earnestness for the true as the true—with that harmonious subordination of the latter to the former, without encroachment on the absolute worth of either— present in him a character which in my heart's heart I believe to be the very rarest in earth. If you will excuse a play on words in speaking of such a man, I will say that Mr. Channing is a philosopher in both the possible renderings of the word. He has the love of wisdom and the wisdom of love.[30]

I was unfortunately absent the first evening. Had they been prevented from repeating their visit, I should have been vexed indeed, and yet not as much vexed as I now know I should have had reason to be. I feel convinced that the few differences in opinion between Mr. Channing and myself, not only are, but would by him be found, to be apparent, not real—the same truth seen in different relations. Perhaps I have been more absorbed in the depth of the mystery of the spiritual life, he more engrossed by the loveliness of its manifestations.

Channing was amused by the letter, and particularly by its implication 'that he had seldom met with a person so interesting in conversation'. 'My part was simply interrogative', he commented: 'I made not a single remark!'[31] His account of the

---

[29] Letter to Allston, *Channing Memoir*, ii. 221–2 (not in *CL*).

[30] Cf. his remarks on Schelling's pamphlet against Fichte, 'the spirit of which was to *my* feelings painfully incongruous with the principles, and which (with the usual allowance afforded to an antithesis) displayed the love of wisdom rather than the wisdom of love'. *CBL* i. 164.

[31] Peabody, *Reminiscences*, 75.

thoughts that Coleridge poured out in a flood on all subjects included also

his idea of the Church of England, which was wholly new to me, and not at all acceptable in England to any party, for he included in the National Church not merely the pulpits and curacies of the Establishment, but all the spiritual forces at work in the land,—the great schools and universities, and even the sectarian schools and pulpits![32]

Already Coleridge was revolving the ideas that would be developed in his short treatise *On the Constitution of the Church and State* in 1829. Channing was also to recall that Coleridge did not condemn Unitarians personally and 'had not suffered so much of a reaction as Southey, or even as Wordsworth'.[33] Like his brother-in-law, he came to regard Coleridge as one of the most important influences of his life, declaring that he owed more to him 'than to the mind of any philosophical thinker'.[34]

Coleridge for his part was evidently impressed by Channing but also found his views disturbing—partly, no doubt, because they echoed those which he himself had entertained in youth. After reading one of Channing's assertions he wrote a long vindication of the Trinity in a notebook entry of 1825–6.[35] When, in 1828, Channing sent him a pamphlet in further justification of his opinions, Coleridge, still disturbed that so fine a man should be mistaken in his religious beliefs, reiterated his objections to his use of certain terms. His marginal annotation[36] concluded, however, 'But I am vain enough to believe, that an hour's tete a tete with Dr Ch would leave little difference between him and me, on this point.'

[32] Memorandum book quoted in n. 26 above.
[33] Ibid.
[34] Peabody, *Reminiscences*, 75. After Coleridge's death he wrote to Wordsworth, paying his own tribute: 'Perhaps he has no where more enthusiastic friends & admirers than in this country, & among men of hostile sects. This is a proof that he is a teacher of Universal truths.' His admiration was evidently not unqualified: he went on to express a hope that Coleridge would find 'a biographer worthy of him, able to comprehend him, & just both to his excellencies & *defects*. So much is known of him, that no record of him, but a faithful one, will obtain confidence.' He was also impatient to see his great philosophical work. Letter of 19 Apr. 1835 among Wordsworth Library MSS, quoted *WL* (1835–9), 195.
[35] See his discussion of Channing's *Sermon Delivered at the Ordination of the Rev. Jared Sparks . . . in Baltimore, May 5, 1819* (Liverpool, 1824) in *CN* iv. 5291.
[36] *CM* ii. 22.

The point continued to nag at his mind and other Americans were treated to a word or two on the subject. When John Wheeler visited him in 1829, he recorded that Coleridge's first words to him were: 'Mr Wheeler, do you know D$^r$ Channing? I have seen him—we differ in theological opinions—D$^r$ C. is wrong—he contradicts himself.' And then, Wheeler continues, 'the floodgates were opened & he went on giving his opinions, not as his but as intuitive truth concerning the Trinity.'[37]

When an American journalist interviewed Coleridge in 1832 he wrote that he was 'not a little surprised at his remarks concerning Dr. Channing of Boston', which included the assertion 'that, as a theologian, Dr. Channing did not understand himself, and was not an unitarian.' After reporting his own somewhat ponderous response the correspondent observed that 'Mr. Coleridge seemed to wish better of Dr. Channing, and spoke of his talents with respect'.[38] Emerson, similarly, visiting him the following year, found that after some warm words concerning Allston he spoke 'upon Dr Channing & what an unspeakable misfortune it was that he should have turned out an Unitarian after all'. A 'declamation upon the folly & ignorance of Unitarianism' (in the course of which Emerson's polite interjection that he himself was a unitarian was swept briskly aside) was followed by a further judgement on Channing, not quite so favourable as the one in his letter to Allston:

Very sorry that Dr Channing a man to whom he looked up—no, to say he looked up to him would be to speak falsely,—but a man whom he looked *at* with so much interest should embrace such views. But when he saw Dr C he hinted to him that he was afraid he loved Christianity for what was lovely & excellent [—] he loved the good in it & not the true. And I tell you sir that I have known many persons who loved the good, for one person who loved the true. But it is a far greater virtue to love the true for itself alone than to love the good for itself alone. He knew all this about Unitarianism perfectly well because he had once been an Unitarian & knew what quackery it was. He . . . had been called the rising Star of Unitarianism. Then he

---

[37] Quoted (*variatim*) in *Coleridge the Talker*, ed. R. W. Armour and R. F. Howes (Ithaca, NY, 1943), 359–60. For the whole record see my 'Transatlantic and Scottish Connections' in R. Gravil and M. Lefebure (eds.), *The Coleridge Connection* (1990), 331–6.

[38] Ibid. 317–18.

expatiated on the Trinitarian doctrine of the Deity as being Realism &c
&c ...[39]

The two accounts are not necessarily in contradiction: both may
be seen as combining appreciation of Channing's character with
a sense that if only Channing would look more introspectively
into the elements that made it so good he would find them to
consist in an interworking of love and wisdom that would give
him a key to the nature of the Trinity. Channing for his part
found such an approach too subtle-minded, writing to Lucy
Aikin: 'Coleridge, I believe, loved truth, but, I fear, he loved
more that subtle, refined action of mind, by which he was
authorized in his own judgment to look down with contempt on
the common judgments of men.'[40]

What Channing saw as an unnatural over-refinement
Coleridge, by contrast, would have regarded as a discrimination
in the mind that must be made if one were to reach truth: indeed
he said as much in the notebook entry on Channing's pamphlet
referred to above:[41] 'A far steadier Intimacy with Ideas, a larger
grace of that spiritual discernment, which, the profound Apostle
assures us, can penetrate into the deep things (or depths) of God
himself, is required to the right apprehension of God manifest in
the flesh.' Channing in turn helped to confirm Coleridge's judgement on him that he loved Christianity mainly for what was
lovely and excellent in it when he told Elizabeth Peabody[42] that
Coleridge's true insight into the divine was to be found in
Alvar's speech in *Remorse*—meaning, presumably, the address
to Nature that concluded it:

> With other ministrations thou, O Nature!
> Healest thy wandering and distempered child:
> Thou pourest on him thy soft influences,
> Thy melodies of woods, and winds, and waters!
> Till he relent, and can no more endure
> To be a jarring and a dissonant thing
> Amid this general dance and minstrelsy;

[39] *The Journals and Miscellaneous Notebooks of Ralph Waldo Emerson*, ed.
W. H. Gilman et al. (Cambridge, Mass., 1960–   ), iv. 408–11.
[40] Letter of Feb. 1837: *Correspondence of Dr Channing and Lucy Aikin, 1826 to
1842*, ed. A. L. Le Breton (London and Edinburgh, 1874), 329–30.
[41] See n. 35.
[42] Peabody, *Reminiscences*, 72.

> But, bursting into tears, wins back his way,
> His angry spirit healed and harmonized
> By the benignant touch of love and beauty.[43]

In this speech he no doubt traced the link he was looking for between the view of the divine as a harmonizing and healing power and the view of nature that had so impressed him in Wordsworth's poetry. 'I find in the poetry of Coleridge and Wordsworth,' he wrote, 'a theology more spiritual than in the controversial writings of either Unitarians or Trinitarians.'[44]

Despite the greater congeniality of some of Coleridge's views, nevertheless, the meeting that proved most memorable when Channing looked back on his English visits was probably the one in Grasmere. The record of his conversation with Wordsworth on that occasion (also in the recently discovered journal[45]) is all the more interesting since it not only comes from a period when records of Wordsworth's talk are sparse but shows him opening his mind freely to his visitor.

Perhaps Channing himself raised the question of the pacifism with which his record opens, but if so he must have found the ensuing discourse at one and the same time congenial and disturbing, for while Wordsworth expressed his horror of war in tones that were convincingly sincere, his main theme was that of the necessary role of war within the providential order of things—an assertion which Channing had explicitly rejected in a sermon on War in 1816.[46]

Mr W's conversation was free, various, animated. He spoke of the importance of a national spirit to the development of imagination—& considered war as appointed by providence to give men a generous interest in the country. Poetry, he thought, must be national at least in its origin, & quoted Greece—Scott's popularity he considered as a proof of general interest in national topics—He considered too general benevolence as consistent with nationality—& read me an account of

---

[43] *CPW* (EHC) ii. 871–2.

[44] Peabody, *Reminiscences*, 72.

[45] See above, n. 8.

[46] 'The common argument, that war is necessary to awaken the boldness, energy, and noblest qualities of human nature, will, I hope receive a practical refutation in the friends of philanthropy and peace.' In addition, he had devoted a whole appendix to the demolition of other such arguments in favour of it. 'War: A Discourse before the Congregational Ministers of Massachusetts', *Works* (1840), iii. 53, 55–8.

Ld Falkland—On my opposing these views, he repeated two of his sonnets[47] accordant with my views, & delighted me by his tones of feeling—He *recited*, if the *recitative* be the origin of the word—He conversed on the effects of the different methods of disposing of property in England & America, & whilst deploring the love of gain in England, observed that large profits cherished the arts & ornaments of life, & rescued the whole country from being given up to vulgar utilities.

In view of Wordsworth's insistence upon his horror of war, as expressed later in this conversation, the account of Lord Falkland which he read to Channing is likely to have been from Clarendon's panegyric, which mentions how he, 'sitting among his Friends, often after a deep silence, and frequent sighs, would with a shrill and sad accent, ingeminate the word *Peace, Peace*, and would passionately profess "that the very agony of the War, and the view of the calamities and desolation the Kingdom did, and must endure, took his sleep from him, and would shortly break his heart". This made some think, or pretend to think "that he was so much enamoured on Peace, that he would have been glad the King should have bought it at any price ..."' Clarendon dismisses such a view as 'a most unreasonable Calumny', going on to record Falkland's courage and even cheerfulness in battle.[48] Wordsworth would have found such a mixture of deep feeling and principled fortitude more congenial to his own position than Channing's thoroughgoing pacifism.

Having explained his more conservative position Wordsworth proceeded to a disarmingly frank account of his own poetry and that of his contemporaries:

He spoke freely of his own want of general popularity, & yet of his influence on the literature of the age—of other poets—Scott, whom he considered as faulty, in keeping the spirits in constant exhilaration by rapid movement & who confirmed my opinion of the advantages of universal over local poetry—Scott's poetry being now seldom read—of

---

[47] These are difficult to identify in view of the obscurity of the discussion but the sonnet that begins 'Not Love, nor War, nor the tumultuous swell | Of civil conflict ... | Not these *alone* inspire the tuneful shell ...' *WPW* iii. 24 is a possible candidate, particularly since it was first published in 1823.

[48] Edward Hyde, Lord Clarendon, *History of the Rebellion and Civil Wars in England* (Oxford, 1705–6), ii. 358–9. Although the volume was missing from the copies of this edition that were sold from the library at Rydal Mount after Wordsworth's death it may be presumed that he had earlier had a full set.

Ld Byron, whom he thinks destitute of all true love of nature, & owing his success in delineating it, which is very rare, to his mocking-bird or imitative propensities—observing that his pictures were almost always *false*, such as showed he had not looked on nature with his own eyes, & painted it from a constraining love. He thought however that he had a perception of female beauty—Of Pope he spoke as having added much to English literature, & as excelling in giving the spirit & manners of society, but not as a master of the soul & its depths—'His translation of Homer discovers an insensibility to the spirit of the original, which argues almost impotence'—'Gray shows little of himself, his own feeling & character, in his writings—& frequently is chargeable with logical errours.'[49] He considered the present race of poets as too imitative, as mannerists. His own manner had been copied rather than his spirit imbibed. When I spoke of the third canto of Child Harold, he complained of it as wanting that organization, that organick life, which shows the product of a creative mind—It is disjointed . . .

The last comment, with its Coleridgean insistence on the importance of the organic by comparison with the mechanical in art, shows Wordsworth indulging in a piece of Romantic criticism which may have gained some of its urgency from a desire to convince Channing that his own poetry was not merely on the side of life but showed itself to be so in the very way that it was written.

After continuing his series of literary judgements Wordsworth returned to the question of war and its role in the scheme of things:

He seemed to enjoy Cowper much. He considered M^r Allston as the first of living historical painters. He spoke of Coleridge freely, & whilst giving him superiority of genius to Southey, spoke of his habits as inconsistent with productive labour, & as contrasted with those of the latter, who is singularly exemplary. He considered war as an evil, but as a counteracting one, needed by the frivolousness, sensuality &c of men, whilst he shrunk from its horrours. He considered religion as the key to poetry, without which even the finest parts of the Greek tragedians (who were the profoundest of ancient poets) could not be understood—Poetry carries us up to the *infinite*, which is undefined, i e, *mystical*.—He supposed nationality to be often as extravagant as *love*; but the last, tho a species of idolatry, confining all that is lovely &c, to one object is still a mode of purifying the soul. He was in early

---

[49] Wordsworth may here be echoing the strictures of Johnson in his Life of Gray.

life struck with the extravagancies of *love*, & perhaps never felt its power deeply,[50] but now he viewed it as a process of raising mind— Such were principal topicks.

Channing also commented on Wordsworth's readiness to bring poetry into his discussions:

In course of conversation, he introduced short passages of his own poetry, or of others, & recited them as if they were his inmost joy—We talked so eagerly as often to interrupt one another. He was simple, unaffected, earnest—his eyelid sometimes half-closed, as if he were looking inward, or abstracting himself from outward things, his mouth seeming to argue an Irish origin—On my return, we walked together until I was wearied, then took our places in the cart, & talked till we reached our distant inn—As I descended into Grasmere near sunset with the placid lake before, & Wordsworth by my side in a village cart talking of poetry with a poet's spirit, I felt the combination of circumstances to be such as my hopes could never have anticipated—His son, a youth of 16 or 17 eager to catch our conversation, walked by the side of the cart & at last took his seat behind us, proving the interest which his father's pursuits had awakened. M[r] W staid with us till 10—& we parted, perhaps to meet no more—His guide to the lakes[51] is a present which I shall retain as a monument of our interview. He lives in a favoured spot, on a mountain's side, whence he looks down on Rydal Water, & upward to the mountain top, & has a glimpse of Windermere thro the valley which opens southward—

The memory of the visit remained fresh in the minds of everyone concerned. In 1828, when he sent a message of greet-

---

[50] Cf. Coleridge's remark in a letter to Crabb Robinson of 12 Mar. 1811: 'Wordsworth is by nature incapable of being in Love, tho' no man more tenderly attached . . .', *CL* iii. 305, an assertion apparently echoed (though this time with no specific mention of Wordsworth) in his *Table Talk* of 27 Sept. 1830. Sara Coleridge made the same point in her MS essay for Aubrey de Vere 'Reasons for Not Placing "Laodamia" in the First Rank of Wordsworth's Poetry': 'Mr. Wordsworth was never in *love*, properly speaking. I have heard him boast of it, in [the] presence of his wife, who smiled angelically, delighted that her husband should be so superior to common men.' Printed in the appendix to Bradford K. Mudge, *Sara Coleridge, A Victorian Daughter* (Princeton, 1989), 247. I am grateful to Rachel Trickett for this reference. Wordsworth's assertions make interesting reading in view of the discussions in the chapter above. Had his memory of the power of former loves diminished over the years? Or was he simply recalling the fact that he had been unwilling to himself surrender so totally to any of the young women whom he loved in his youth?

[51] A new edition of Wordsworth's guide, previously published as part of other volumes, appeared in 1822 with the title *A Description of the Scenery of the Lakes in the North of England*.

ing, Dorothy Wordsworth recorded that she distinctly remembered him, and the bad health from which he had been suffering. 'My Brother was very much interested by him, and thinks highly of [his] Talents . . .'[52] For his part Channing remained devoted to Wordsworth's poetry: in 1835 he expressed his gratitude for 'the quickening influence of your writings on my mind and heart'[53]—a tribute to be expanded in 1841 in an address entitled *The Present Age*, where the long account of him as 'the poet of humanity' pleased Wordsworth so much that he suggested to his daughter and son-in-law that they might lay out two pence on a copy.[54]

At the same time the fact that their discussion survived in Channing's mind as well is indicated by the 1835 note, which also mentioned a recently published sermon on the evils of war. Recalling their interview, he went on to say, 'Among other things we talked of War. All my impressions on that subject have gained strength with time, & some of them I have embodied in this discourse of which I ask your acceptance.'[55] In his sermon (which Wordsworth had still not received a year later[56]) he allowed for the possibility of a just war in certain circumstances; he also conceded that 'in almost all wars, there is some infusion of enthusiasm; and in all enthusiasm, there is a generous element'; apart from that, however, his views were what they had been in 1816: he made no attempt whatever to fit war into a providential scheme.

In his covering letter Channing stated that his sermon had been 'called forth by the present State of this country', but that state was still comparatively peaceful, just as belief in divine providence was still relatively uncontroversial. The outbreak of the American Civil War and the publication of the *Origin of Species* would in the course of time raise such questions with a new kind of immediacy; in 1835, however, they were still a quarter of a century away.

---

[52] *WL* (1821–8), 606–7.
[53] Ibid. 606 n.
[54] *WL* (1840–53), 241 and n.
[55] Letter of 19 Apr. 1835. Reproduced by kind permission of the Trustees of Dove Cottage.
[56] *WL* (1835–9), 195.

## 4

# Myers's Secret Message

THE questionings concerning divine providence that began to agitate minds in the eighteenth century and were at work in Channing's mind as he crossed the Atlantic were slow to gain ground in the English provinces. Ways of interpreting human experience did not change quickly, even in the great centres of English culture, and the difficulty was even more marked as one moved away. Yet those who had sufficient leisure to read and think in an area such as the Lake District could not ignore the issues that were being raised: the very fact that Wordsworth himself was still a living presence in their midst was a stimulus to such reflections.

One such figure was Frederic Myers, first Vicar of the newly designated St John's church in Keswick. While Wordsworth and Southey were spending their last years in the district the local inhabitants had been coming to terms with the effects of growing tourism in the region and an influx of people wishing to settle there. In Keswick it was felt that the town had outgrown the capacities of Crosthwaite church (where Southey was buried in 1843) and the building of a new church on a site with a fine view overlooking Derwentwater was accordingly put in hand. Prominent in the enterprise were the Marshall family, who, having made a considerable amount of money in Leeds from their flax-spinning business[1] had been buying various properties in the Lake District. As it happened, they also had a strong link with the Wordsworths: John Marshall, the man primarily responsible for their fortune, had married Jane Pollard, one of Dorothy's oldest friends and correspondents, and moved with her to Hallsteads, a house by Lake Ullswater where William and Dorothy visited them on several occasions.

---

[1] See W. G. Rimmer, *Marshalls of Leeds: Flax-Spinners 1788–1886* (Cambridge, 1960).

Frederic Myers, who was recommended to the Marshall family as a suitable first incumbent for the new parish, and who was a widower at the time, proceeded to seal his relationship to them by marrying as his second wife Susan, one of their daughters. A man of learning and notable tolerance,[2] he also pioneered adult education in Keswick, overseeing the setting up of an evening school there for which he secured the support of Wordsworth.[3] In 1850, the year of Wordsworth's death, his health failed and he died soon afterwards. By then he had fathered three sons, the eldest, Frederic William Henry Myers, being 7 years old.[4]

This eldest son, subject of the present chapter, was later to become known to readers of poetry through his study of Wordsworth and to a wider audience through his interest in psychical research. Strong Wordsworthian links had already been established in his mind: it is quite possible that as a child he met the poet himself, either in the company of his father, or while visiting his cousins at Hallsteads. He was certainly aware of the way in which Wordsworth had set his stamp on the area. 'To those who were young children while his last years went by,' he wrote later, 'he seemed a kind of mystical embodiment of the lakes and mountains round him—a presence without which they

[2] He wrote a number of books on religious topics. The novelist Elizabeth Lynn Linton, daughter of the Vicar of Crosthwaite, who lost his wife just after she was born but refused to try and increase his income, telling the bishop that he would commit his children to the care of providence, discussed her religious doubts with Myers, but found that his own eclecticism, rejecting the doctrine of eternal punishment and the personality of the devil while accepting equally difficult dogmas without cavil, only increased her perplexity, until he charged her with wilful and intentional perversity: see G. S. Layard, *Mrs Lynn Linton: Her Life, Letters, and Opinions* (1901), 4, 39. From time to time Myers corresponded with his friend and neighbour at Mirehouse James Spedding (a friend of Tennyson's who in his time had been elected to the Cambridge Apostles) on topics of mutual interest, including the implications of the new developments in science. When Robert Chambers's *Vestiges of the Natural History of Creation* was published in 1844, for instance, they exchanged views about its implications in letters that still survive: TCL MS Myers 16[150, 157(2)].

[3] When this was opened, Wordsworth was invited to attend and, to the excitement of Myers and his associates, accepted. By this time he was very deaf, however, and when asked to say a few words showed some reluctance. On being further pressed he rose and said, 'My friend Mr Myers has requested me to say whether I agree with him in what he has spoken to you, I have no hesitation in saying that I agree with every word of it.' When this proved to be all that he had to say there was considerable disappointment. See TCL MS Myers 17[69].

[4] After his father's death the family moved to Badminton and then to Cheltenham, where he showed his unusual abilities at the newly founded College.

would not have been what they were.'[5] The effect on him resembled that on Channing. It was as if Wordsworth had so powerfully appropriated the local scenery that to anyone familiar with his writings they could hardly be seen in any other way—as if he had not just produced poems about it, but in an important sense had composed the Lake District itself.

Mentioning the sources of his factual information at the outset of his study Myers remarked, 'It has, however, been my fortune, through hereditary friendships, to have access to many manuscript letters and much oral tradition bearing upon the poet's private life; and some details and some passages of letters hitherto unpublished, will appear in these pages.' He was referring partly to the letters from Dorothy Wordsworth to Jane Pollard that had survived in the family and were to be quoted from in his book; but his claims suggest that when visiting the family he had heard further reminiscences and gossip about the Wordsworths.

Myers, who might well have entered the Church but in the event decided against doing so,[6] found in Wordsworth's thought a response to the moral questions of the age that promised to solve his intellectual problems. Upbringing and temperament alike made him responsive to the teaching that Wordsworth had himself wished to imprint on later generations:

To compare small things with great—or rather to compare great things with things vastly greater—the essential spirit of the *Lines near Tintern Abbey* was for practical purposes as new to mankind as the essential spirit of the *Sermon on the Mount*.[7]

This was Victorian Wordsworthianism at its most intense; an unusually sympathetic reader of any literary text that had to do with nobility and honour, he responded warmly to the official persona that Wordsworth had constructed for himself in his later years and regarded the self-probings of the posthumous *Prelude*, published during his childhood, simply as a pendant to works in which those qualities were promulgated more straightforwardly. The divisions in Wordsworth's mind that a

[5] Myers, *Wordsworth*, 181.
[6] A letter of 14 Feb. 1868 from Myers's mother to James Spedding among the Spedding papers in the Wordsworth Library at Grasmere mentions that he has given up the idea of taking orders.
[7] Myers, *Wordsworth*, 131.

twentieth-century reader traces were not directly apparent to him: he read much of the writing at its face value—even if he glimpsed that it might sometimes be approached profitably at more than one level.

Despite his veneration he was by no means uncritical, being one of the first to acknowledge a falling off in the later years. Wordsworth's musical gift had declined, he declared, until, by about 1818, 'We feel that he is hardening into self-repetition, into rhetoric, into sermonizing common-place, and is rigid where he was once profound. The *Thanksgiving Ode* (1816) strikes death to the heart. . . . the accent is like that of a ghost who calls to us in hollow mimicry of a voice that once we loved.'[8]

Myers's connection with the Marshalls also made him alive to the controversial nature of Wordsworth's later political opinions: 'One of the houses where Mr Wordsworth was most intimate and most welcome was that of a reforming member of parliament, who was also a manufacturer, thus belonging to the two classes for which the poet had the greatest abhorrence.'[9] Nevertheless, he goes on, Wordsworth felt so sure of the affection with which he was regarded there that when visiting he 'expounded the ruinous tendency of Reform and manufactures with even unusual copiousness':

> The tone in which he spoke was never such as could give pain or excite antagonism; and . . . the only rejoinder which these diatribes provoked was that the poet on his arrival was sometimes decoyed into uttering them to the younger members of the family, whose time was of less value, so as to set his mind free to return to those topics of more permanent interest where his conversation kept to the last all that tenderness, nobility, wisdom, which in that family, as in many others familiar with the celebrated persons of that day, won for him a regard and a reverence such as was accorded to no other man.[10]

Myers's own unusual abilities again became evident from 1860 onwards, when he proceeded to Trinity College, Cambridge, and won most of the prizes for classical learning and ability to compose verses in Latin and Greek. Among the ancient writers there was one, however, who in his eyes reigned supreme. In his autobiographical writings he tells how when he

---

[8] Ibid. 121.    [9] i.e. Hallsteads. Ibid. 162.    [10] Ibid. 163.

was 6 his father began to teach him Latin and gave him a copy of Virgil, and how even at that tender age the power of his writing made a deep impression.[11] His father's death shortly afterwards may well have imprinted this admiration still more firmly. He is probably the only person who ever claimed to have learned the whole of Virgil's works by heart while still at school; for the rest of his life they were to provide a continuing touchstone for his own ideals and the standard by which he judged other writers. Even in the case of Wordsworth, poems of his later career such as the Virgilian 'Laodamia' escaped his misgivings.

At first sight this may look like an exemplary opening to a career in classical studies, yet there were other facets to his personality. One incident in particular during his undergraduate career, which caused a small Cambridge scandal at the time and even set up a ripple in the outside world, points in a different direction. In 1863, having competed successfully in previous years for various prizes, Myers decided to enter again for the Camden medal for classical verse, which he had already won. Following the end of the Indian Mutiny, the subject proposed was 'India pacificata'. Once again he was successful, but shortly after the award had been announced another candidate, who had won the medal two years before and had also been competing again, wrote to the Vice-Chancellor pointing out that a large number of lines in Myers's entry had previously appeared in a collection of Oxford Prize Poems. He also stated that in the event of there being a further competition he wished his own entry to be withdrawn. During the summer, controversy about the matter erupted into the columns of the *Cambridge Chronicle*. A correspondent calling himself 'Crispinus' gave examples of the passages that had been lifted; another (or perhaps the same one returning to the attack under another name) gave more. A reply by a correspondent calling himself 'Codrus' tried to defend Myers, only to be countered by an even more angry letter from 'Crispinus'. It was a point of particular concern that in the copy available for scrutiny the only instance in which Myers had acknowledged a debt had been his inclusion of a line from his contemporary R. W. Raper, who might have been

---

[11] Myers, *FIL* 6.

expected to notice it. (Myers was later to offer an explanation of this anomaly.) By September the matter had reached the national press: a report in the *Athenaeum* concluded,

Much speculation is going on in the University as to what action the authorities will take in this matter. So flagrant a case of plagiarism cannot be overlooked; and the general opinion is, that the examiners will have to review their decision, and call upon Mr Myers for an explanation of his conduct.[12]

The matter rumbled on during the autumn. The entries in Myers's own journal (always laconic in form, a space of one line being left for each day of the year) read on 2 December 'New Camden Row' and on the 3rd 'Resigned Camden'.[13] H. W. Cookson, who had recently become Vice-Chancellor for the second time, had evidently decided that the matter must be taken further: in the Register of Prizes for the University the announcement of the award to Myers is followed by a further note in his hand: 'It appeared subsequently that M^r Myers had borrowed largely from an Oxford Prize poem. As I was not satisfied with his explanation I requested him to return the medal, though I accepted his disavowal of dishonourable motives.'[14]

Cookson himself seems not to have gone into the matter very far, since the borrowings took the form not, as his note suggests, of extracts from a single poem but of numerous phrases and lines from various verses in the collection. In reply to letters from various MAs he relayed a comment from the Electors that if they had not given the medal to Myers they would not have awarded it at all; he also reported that Myers had returned the medal. One of the chief agitators in the affair, Richard Shilleto, a considerable Greek scholar of the time who had never been made a fellow of his and Myers's college, Trinity,[15] remained unsatisfied. He wrote satirical verses about the affair which he sent to Samuel Romilly, Registrary of the University—who duly recorded their receipt and kept them.[16] Romilly himself did not

[12] *Athenaeum*, no. 1873 (19 Sept. 1863), 369.
[13] TCL MS Myers 14^{1-2}. Hitherto unpublished.
[14] Register of Prizes (Cambridge University Library Add. MS Archives Char. 1 1). Hitherto unpublished.
[15] He was later elected to a fellowship in Peterhouse.
[16] They remain in the University archives along with Romilly's *Diary* (see next note).

take the matter so seriously. When as a result of the affair there was in the following April an attempt to persuade members of the university to vote against Myers's degree he wrote in his diary.

Yesterday there was an attempt to prevent Myers (the Plagiary) from taking his degree: I am happy to say that the Persecution failed egregiously: only 25 to 3 were the n$^{OS}$ for & against his degree:—his degree was from the Classical Tripos.[17]

The following week Shilleto wrote to the *Cambridge Chronicle*, where the proceedings had been reported, explaining that his proposal had been made primarily as a protest from one who was 'jealous for the fair fame of my University', after which the matter rested, re-emerging only once or twice, in volumes of reminiscences. Years later G. G. Coulton recalled how it had on one occasion been the subject of a paper by Henry Jackson, who offered it to a group in Trinity College as a case of 'literary kleptomania', remarking also that Myers had had his 'queer side' and reminding the company of his enthusiasm for psychical research. He also related that when he discussed the affair with Lee-Warner, the candidate whose complaint had begun the whole altercation, 'he spoke without undue bitterness, but added, "he was always a queer fellow. Once, when I came into my room, I found him reading my letters." '[18]

The final comment shows Myers acting in a way that was according to the conventions of the time 'ungentlemanly', yet which he evidently did not regard as an important breach of the code. He adumbrated a similar distinction in his own account of the affair, which he left among his autobiographical writings:

'Jugend ist Trunkenheit ohne Wein,' [Youth is drunkenness without wine]—and few have known either the delight or the folly of that intoxication more fully than I. On the sensual side of my nature I shall not dwell. Of the presumption of those early years I take as an example one braggart act. Having won a Latin prize poem, I was fond of

---

[17] Romilly, *Diary* (CUL Add. MS 6842) entry for 2 Apr. 1864. Hitherto unpublished.

[18] G. G. Coulton, *Fourscore Years: An Autobiography* (1944), 106–8. In 1903 J. E. McTaggart set down a brief record of the affair, having heard it from Jackson, in which he mentioned that the affair had come to be known in the first place because Myers told his friends what he had done: TCL Add. MS c. 183$^{105}$, dated 2 Aug.

alluding to myself as a kind of Virgil among my young companions. Writing again a similar poem, I saw in my bookshelves a collection of Oxford prize poems, which I had picked up somewhere in order to gloat over their inferiority to my own. I laid this out on my table, and forced into my own new poem such Oxford lines as I deemed worthy of preservation. When my friends came in, I would point to this book and say, 'Aurum colligo e stercore Ennii'—'I am collecting gold from Ennius' dung heap,'—a remark which Virgil used to make with more valid pretensions. My acquaintances laughed; but when my poem was adjudged the best, a disappointed competitor ferreted out these insertions; and the Master of Trinity, although he roundly asserted that I had done nothing illegitimate, advised me to resign the prize. Many another act of swaggering folly mars for me the recollection of years which might have brought pure advance in congenial toil.[19]

The context of Myers's course of action helps to explain why he was drawn to act as he did. The scholar John Conington had just published the second volume of his major edition of Virgil's writings, containing the first half of the *Aeneid*. In his introduction he discussed Virgil's reputation for taking ideas and lines from his predecessors, recalling how he had written of Homer, whom he was clearly wanting to imitate in the *Aeneid*, that grappling with him was like trying to rob Hercules of his club, whereas when it came to his appropriations from the historical poet Ennius they were as 'the gold which a man rakes from a dunghill'.[20] Myers's allusion suggests that he had read Conington's new volume and that in composing his prize poem he had had the idea of scoring off the sister-university by taking as many lines from their prize poems as could be incorporated into his own while producing a piece of work that would stand on its own merits and—in his own view at least—surpass the Oxford productions. It was a witty way of emulating his own hero—though of course if offered as an explanation of what he had done it would sound impossibly arrogant.

Myers's method of composition would raise fewer eyebrows now, when it might be regarded as an interesting example of postmodern composition; even now, however, a prize entry of this kind might well prove controversial. Further evidence about

[19] TCL MS Myers 72[144]: Myers, *FIL* 9.
[20] *P. Vergilius Maronis Opera: The Works of Virgil with a commentary by John Conington* (1858–71), ii (1863), 23, citing Donatus XVIII. 71.

the affair, showing that Myers had himself developed a theory for what he did, has recently become available in an exchange of letters about it with William Whewell, master of his college. Whewell also had married into the Marshall family, so that Myers's mother was his sister-in-law; in September he mentioned to her that he would like to have some explanation from Frederic of his behaviour and received a long letter, the draft of which still survives. Frederic explained that his action was partly to be understood in terms of his own theory of poetic composition:

Brandon House
Cheltenham
Saturday Sept. 26/63

My dear Uncle

My Mother tells me that you say you would be glad that I should write to you about the affair of my Camden.

I am very glad to do so, as I had wished to do so before, but did not know whether it would be fitting. It seems to me that there are two questions which anyone might naturally ask, firstly, How could you steal the lines without feeling that you were doing wrong? Secondly: How could you fail to see that others would think that you were doing wrong? I will try to answer these.

Firstly. I had not intended to write for the Camden this year, & till a late period had not done so, when a method of treating the subject occurred to me which I thought would make a good poem. I became interested in the subject & wrote, rather from enjoyment of the act of composition than from any special craving for the prize.

I had thought a good deal on the theory of poetry, & had come to the conclusion, of course very probably erroneous, but at any rate sincerely held, that the essence and value of a poem consists entirely in the impression which it makes as a whole, and that the special parts have no separate function, as it were, but are only valuable as building up & subserving the symmetry of the whole. For example any criticism which was content to compare two poems by comparing the beauties of their special portions, as for example Mr. Gladstone's criticism on Homer & Virgil, appeared to me unsatisfactory. I looked wholly to the indefinable nobility of the general style & manner of thought, and most of all to the rhythm, which appeared to me the highest manner of implying poetic thought, and the true test of the poet. Thus no one poet could be materially assisted by plagiarising from another: if he did not possess that breadth of thought and power over rhythm to which I refer no theft could enable him to assume it: if he did possess those powers I considered that the works of others might fairly be useful to him where thro' some casual fitness they were capable of amalgamation with his own peculiar and essential style. [Thus, tho' of course the cases are not precisely parallel, a philosopher may be great not by inventing new views only, but by assimilating the views of others and perhaps giving them a depth and significance which they did not before possess.] I fancied that I discerned traces of a similar view in several of the poets whom I most admired: most of all in Virgil of whom after Mr Conington's edition it is surely hardly too much to say that almost every line in his works is a translation an adaptation or an actual theft. At any rate the number of such thefts in him is enormous, but it seemed to me that this did not in the least detract from the merit or real originality of the work, which I considered to be in the masterly rhythmical and poetical judgment which enabled him to select and arrange his booty. I will go no further into this theory: I only wish to say enough to show in what manner I conceived of plagiarism. While writing my poem, & with such theories in my head, I chanced to notice an old book of Oxford Prize Poems, which I possessed by chance & had hardly ever opened, as I am not in the habit of reading such compositions. It is natural to me to be desirous of immediately reducing to practice any theory which I may have formed & I seized on the opportunity of doing so then. So to act and from such a motive may have been foolish, reckless, & headstrong, and I am painfully aware of my danger of acting on crude and sometimes presumptuous opinions without considering or regarding what others will think. Of some such fault as this I feel now that I must have been guilty, but I am quite sure that I acted with no dishonourable motives. I mean that I certainly did not steal lines, knowing such theft to be dishonourable, but wishing even dishonourably to obtain the prize. I do not remember its once occurring to me that I might be charged with such conduct, or if it did so occur, the idea was indignantly rejected. I do not think that such petty cheating is one of the faults to which I am by nature prone, or over which I am wont to stumble.

As to the second question: How was it that I did not see that others would think my conduct wrong? I answer that I made no secret of the plagiarisms, that I mentioned them to any acquaintance who was interested in the subject, and that not one word of warning or remonstrance was addressed to me: with the single exception of one gentleman's advising me to leave out the quotation from Raper. When I showed this man the poem it contained the lines from Raper with *no notes*: at his advice I omitted the lines from Raper in the copy I sent in: in which copy there were no notes. Therefore the argument: you acknowledge one theft: then why not all? does not apply to the copy on which the decision was pronounced. In that copy there were no thefts acknowledged. I afterwards re-inserted the lines and added the note, partly to please Raper, partly for the sake of introducing some curious words and spelling in the note: certainly not ὧς τ'αλλ' ἀφανιῶν κλέμματα [as disguising the other thefts], as Mr. Shilleto says: a purpose which would probably have been better answered by leaving the poem as it was when the prize was adjudged to it: with a line of my own instead of the quotation from Raper & with no notes of acknowledgment whatever.

But to return. This piece of advice, essentially partial, & accompanied as far as I recollect with approval of the rest of the thefts, or at any rate with no recommendation either to refrain from sending in the poem or to acknowledge the thefts: this I say I mention as absolutely the only piece of anything that could be construed into warning of what people would think of my proceedings. A copy of the poem is I believe now in the possession of a graduate in honours, bracketed by my own hand, before the poem was sent in so as to mark the plagiarisms. I made no secret of the matter: if anything I was obtrusively anxious to discuss my theory. I sent a copy to Mr Conington, and, tho' usually he comments freely on such compositions as I send him, he made no remark. He has since been kind enough to say that he regrets not having warned me. I regret it also, as one word from him would have been sufficient to make me withdraw the poem from competition, even had it been already sent in.

I hope I have shown that I had some excuse for being, as I certainly was, perfectly unprepared for the strong view that has since been taken of my conduct. Indeed I cannot understand how anyone can think that I knew that if the lines were identified I should be thus spoken of, and that I yet underwent the risk for such additional chance of the prize as the lines gave me. My name has been held up to scorn and reproach in a great number of newspapers, [for example Athenaeum, (as I am told), Guardian, Clerical Journal, Leeds Mercury, Glasgow Advertiser] many of my acquaintance have had their opinion of me greatly shaken & my Mother has been and is seriously distressed. Had I for one moment conceived that discovery w^d subject me to the least chance of one tenth of these evils I would not have run the risk for all the prize-poems in the world. I blame myself for folly in not foreseeing all this, for rashness in acting without enough consideration, but I do not blame myself for fraudulently risking everything to gain the prize. I have endeavoured to be perfectly candid in the expression of my motives that you may have every means of judging of what I have done. I should be very much obliged if you would be kind enough to send me a short note to tell me something of what your judgement is. If you wish it I will write other lines in the place of the stolen ones. The poem, as it is, is about 13 lines longer than my poem of last year.

What I am most afraid of is that the Adjudicators thinking that some notice ought to be taken of my thefts may unintentionally inflict a far severer punishment than they wish.

The attention of every one who has ever heard my name must have been, and I know in many instances has been awakened by the newspaper letters &c w^h have already appeared. Should any adverse decision be pronounced against me, or should I be deprived of the poem, altho' such a decision might be qualified by some such modifying expression as 'You have rather been foolish than fraudulent': I fear, I say, that such modifying expression would be lost sight of, and that the adverse decision appearing in the papers would lead every one who had read the previous letters to think: 'Here is the official confirmation of the charge of dishonourable conduct which we noticed before.'

I need hardly say that I could hardly be punished more severely for any fault whatever than by all my acquaintances thinking that I had committed a fraudulent action. Such a punishment I think would be severer than any one would wish knowingly to inflict on me who was not himself thoroughly convinced of my want of honour.

I must apologise for giving you this long defence to read: but felt sure that you would kindly wish me to write fully on the matter, as it is one of great importance to my future prospects. I would have written a day or two sooner, but have [*the draft breaks off at this point*][21]

Two letters from William Whewell himself, which also survive, show that he received Myers's account sympathetically. The first was written directly in reply:

> Trinity Lodge
> Cambridge
> Sept. 30. 1863

My dear Fred

I was glad to receive your letter for I wished to know what view you took of your way of composing your Latin poem. I always supposed that you had no purpose of obtaining the prize by any means which you could not avow, but I did not exactly guess your theory of literary annexation—I may call it. Even now I am surprized that you should have carried it so far; especially in a prize poem. However

---

[21] TCL MS Myers 12^{222(1)}. Hitherto unpublished. So far as I have been able to check the other journals that Myers mentions they seem to have been taking their accounts from the *Athenaeum*.

much other compositions may be judged of by the general effect, prize poems are always, I think judged of by special passages—at least in a great measure. It is quite true that the plan of your poem is quite original—so much so indeed that it startled some of the judges. There is nothing in the lines which you have borrowed which could in any way suggest the general design of your poem. But all prize poems are necessarily imitations of classical works, and it is understood I think, that such imitations are not to be appropriated without some modification. Imitate as Virgil has, and you are welcome to your materials.

I am very much grieved that so much has been said about this matter and that your mother has been troubled about it. I do not think that anything will or can be done by the judges to alter or modify the judgement of the prize. I think it likely that the Vicechancellor will call the Judges together, but I do not think that they can do anything. And the talk on the subject—such as has been in the newspapers—very silly most of it, must be allowed to die away, as it will. You have ability and originality enough not to be permanently affected by this accident. Wait till the business of the term begins, and then you will see whether any good is likely to be done by writing your own poem as you conceived it, with lines all your own. I doubt whether such a task is worth the trouble.

With my best wishes that this vexation may be speedily and well ended I am, my dear Fred

Affectionately yours<br>
W Whewell[22]

This letter was written before Myers decided to return the medal. In December of that year Whewell wrote again, this time in the course of a letter to Myers's mother:

I trust that Fred's misadventure will be quite forgotten. I do not think that it has made any one who attends to the circumstances think at all the worse of him. I mean morally; for of course most persons will see in what he did a good deal of self-opinion . . .

He continued,

I do not exactly know how the matter ended. I told him I thought that he might make as widely known among his friends as he liked the V.C's letter in which he declared that he did not believe there was anything dishonourable in his intentions. I thought that if his letter was diffused among his friends it would get into the newspapers in the way in which everything gets into the newspapers. I do not know if he

---

[22] TCL MS Myers 4[141]. Hitherto unpublished.

followed this advice,[23] or if any notice on that subject appeared in the newspapers.

Whewell, knowledgeable in many fields, had less experience, unfortunately, of the media and of the difficulty involved in getting a fair account published once a distorted one is in circulation. No further report is known to have appeared in the press, and the point he made in the next sentences of his letter, re-emphasizing what he had said to his nephew, remained unknown:

I do not think that a fair criticism of Fred's verses ever appeared. It would have been reasonable to show how entirely independent the *plan* of his poem was, and how ingeniously the lines which were borrowed were offered in a way quite different from their original purpose.[24]

Myers's composition was certainly not plagiarism in the ordinary sense, where whole chunks of another person's work are incorporated into one's own in a manner designed to gain credit from the other's conceptions; he was, however, sailing near the wind, given that some of the passages used ran to several lines and that a quarter of the poem was made up in this way. It is a pity that no copy of the poem is known to have survived intact, since this would have made possible a fuller appraisal of the matter; as it is, the published instances of lines and sequences that were actually borrowed[25] give no hint of the whole design. Nevertheless Whewell's decision to exculpate him of dishonesty was telling. As his uncle he might be expected to be well disposed; in Victorian Cambridge, on the other hand, it was unlikely that a man of his stature would have allowed family feelings to sway his sense of justice in a matter as serious as plagiarism; indeed, he might well have felt it necessary to be all the more scrupulous.

It is also significant that in spite of the move to stop Myers from gaining his degree he was subsequently elected to a fellowship in his own college—a strong indication that the fellows of

[23] There is no manuscript record of this particular 'advice', which was probably given to him privately—perhaps when he returned to Cambridge for the new term.

[24] Letter dated 30 Dec. 1863: TCL MS Myers 17[28]. Hitherto unpublished. Whewell died from an accident just over two years later.

[25] These were given in the *Athenaeum* account, the fullest I have seen.

Trinity, at least, regarded the Camden affair as not involving culpable guilt. Their view may well have corresponded with that hinted at by Whewell—that Myers's course of action told less about his moral state than about his youthful arrogance. Trinity College has never been averse to electing clever young people to its teaching staff, however high their self-opinion.[26]

Although Myers's behaviour may be regarded as injudiciously clever the affair suggests a somewhat unreal state of mind. The influence on him of Wordsworth has been mentioned, but there are aspects that are more reminiscent of Coleridge. Like Coleridge Myers was a clergyman's son, precocious in ability and intellectually ambitious. Like him also he could behave in a controversial manner. Even the charge of plagiarism corresponds to incidents in Coleridge's life which, being neither unambiguously culpable nor unquestionably honest, are not readily explained. In Myers's case, the affair is also worth attending to for the manner in which it prefigures other incidents. There was a lack of fit between his evident desire to preserve an honourable reputation and his willingness to press on the boundaries of conventional behaviour. Another episode that might seem fool-hardy, though in a totally different context, was his lone swimming of the falls below Niagara one night (a feat which he believed himself the first Englishman to have accomplished).[27] And Jackson was probably not alone in his willingness to make a connection between Myers's behaviour over the Camden medal and his later interest in psychical research, given the deep suspicion with which that subject was regarded by many in Victorian England; yet that too can be seen as having taken further the willingness to follow the enquiring spirit wherever it might lead that Coleridge had exhibited.

Even in terms of his academic career Myers's behaviour did not follow the simple course that might have been predicted for a man in his position, working as a classical scholar and teaching the young to live by the best standards of the ancient world.

---

[26] It was Whewell's successor W. H. Thompson who, when a very clever young fellow had been holding forth at a college meeting, remarked, 'We are none of us infallible, Mr X, not even the youngest of us.' Henry Jackson later insisted that the remark was not at the time regarded as the 'brutality' it might have seemed: see R. St John Parry, *Henry Jackson, O. M.* (Cambridge, 1926), 166.
[27] The incident is described both in TCL MS Myers 11[218] and in Myers, *FIL* 12.

The times were changing, as the controversy provoked by Darwin's *Origin of Species* caused young men of Myers's generation to question the foundations of their intellectual position. A previous generation had been ready enough to read Greek and Latin writers alongside the Bible and find in the classical virtues a proper complement to those invoked in Christian teaching: just before Myers's time, Thomas Arnold had reformed Rugby School on that very basis. But now there was a new challenge, with Darwin's and Wallace's picture of a human existence that evolved out of the animal creation and still retained some of its principal features such as the struggle to survive, supervening as it did on other criticisms of the idea that the human race had been a special creation by God, undermined the Christian element in that concordat. The universe now looked a starker place, particularly as the writings of those physicists who were currently formulating the laws of thermodynamics came to be known. Increasingly, it seemed, it should be regarded as a vast machine, not only producing all living creatures, including man, according to fixed laws, but gradually and inevitably running down towards a final exhaustion of its energy. Myers, who had passed through a brief intensification of his Christian beliefs in the late 1860s,[28] was overwhelmed a year or two later by apprehension of the new intellectual forces and their significance. He gave up overt religious allegiance and in a letter of 1871 to his friend Henry Sidgwick described Darwin as 'a TIDAL progenitor'.[29]

It was also possible, on the other hand, to take a more optimistic view of contemporary scientific work. One might contend that physical evolution had its counterpart in the realm of the spirit, by way of a movement in human affairs that was gradually raising men and women further and further above the animal creation in which they were rooted. In that case, and so far as they were taught to perceive the existence of such a pattern and co-operate with it, they might then learn the benefits of acting disinterestedly rather than out of a simple urge to survive. If the workings of divine providence were to be looked for in such a dispensation it would be found not in the universe

[28] See below, at n. 54.
[29] Letter to Sidgwick 11 Mar. 1871: TCL MS Myers 12[100].

at large but in the consciousnesses of those human beings who took a loftier view of their destiny.

For this reason the publication of Benjamin Jowett's new translation of Plato's writings in 1871 proved timely, offering to a new generation the thought of a philosopher who had not been bound by the observations of empirical science and who among other things offered metaphysical backing for the ideal of Love. In these years, also, John Ruskin's voice became increasingly portentous, recalling young people who might find themselves disturbed by the new intellectual developments to the ideal of 'nobility'. If a noble view of humanity could be elicited and cultivated it might yet be found to be attuned to the universe at its deepest level, just as Wordsworth had believed.

In 1869 Myers's chief friend and mentor at Trinity, Henry Sidgwick, deeply concerned by the implications of current intellectual movements, took the momentous step of resigning his Tutorship and Fellowship, being no longer able to subscribe conscientiously to the Thirty-nine Articles of Faith in the Church of England, as Fellows were then required to do. The respect in which he was held by his colleagues was shown when they immediately appointed him to a lectureship in Moral Sciences, thus enabling him to continue teaching in the university. Myers, also, resigned his teaching post at Trinity in 1869, partly out of sympathy with Sidgwick's ideals, including his desire to promote the cause of women's education,[30] but also because he believed himself to be more adapted to a career in research and writing than to university teaching (he was later to describe himself as 'minor poet and amateur *savant*' and to earn his living, like Matthew Arnold, by joining the recently formed Inspectorate of Schools).[31]

His life in London during the following years brought him into touch with various notable intellectuals, including George Eliot, whom he and Sidgwick, as they read the successive instal-

---

[30] His interest was aroused particularly by the fact that Josephine Butler, whom he greatly admired (see below at n. 54, and Chapter 6, n. 3) was president of the North of England Council, founded in 1867 with Miss A. J. Clough as secretary: *Sidgwick Memoir*, 174–5.

[31] Myers, *FPP* 2 (TCL MS Myers 26[63(7)]). He followed that occupation for the remainder of his life, becoming in time an inspector of schools in Cambridgeshire.

ments of *Middlemarch*, came increasingly to admire. When the final segment appeared late in 1872 he was moved to draft an enthusiastic letter:

> Brandon House
> Cheltenham
> Dec 7/72

Dear Mrs Lewes,
 I have often wanted to write to you while Middlemarch was coming out, but have restrained myself ⟨hitherto⟩, partly because you must be bored with many letters of the kind from slight acquaintances, like myself, or even strangers, and partly because I felt hindered by the idea that you might think that I expected an answer, ~~in spite of any disclaimer I might make~~. But after reading the last volume my impulse to write is so strong that I shall yield to it. I do *not* expect an answer, and I write to give myself the pleasure and relief of thanking you for an enjoyment which has brightened the whole year. Each ~~of your~~ reader ⟨of complex books like yours⟩ will care most for some particular strain ~~in the very complex web of your books~~ which appeals most ⟨directly⟩ to his personal tastes and experience. Tho' I thoroughly enjoy the whole ~~of Middlemarch~~ I care far the most for the scenes between Ladislaw & Dorothea. Noble lovemaking,—the surprised and pure contact of lofty souls—is hardly ever described ~~naturally~~ truly. When it is described ~~naturally~~ truly to read the description is better than to live thro' any scenes but such as those. Life has come to such a pass—now that there is no longer any God or any hereafter or anything in particular to aim at—that it is only by coming into contact with some other person that one can be oneself. There is no longer anything to keep an isolated fire burning within one, all one can do is to feel the sparks fly from one for a moment when one strikes a kindred soul. Such contact in real life can make one feel for the moment immortal; but the necessary circumstances are so unusual! mere love, delicate or passionate, will not do: to have its best savour love must be set among great possibilities and great selfsacrifices, and must demand the full strain of all the forces within one. Unless things can so happen the first moment of love is apt to be the best. And therefore it is that to read of Dorothea's night of struggle and visit to Rosamond is better, tho' it is only on paper & in a book, than an ordinary passion; for this is what one wants, tho' it be ~~only~~ but a shadow; this is the best conception of life that in this stage of the world we can form. Scenes like those go straight into the only imperishable world; the world ~~of~~ which is peopled by the lovely conceptions which have ~~detached~~ disengaged themselves in successive generations from the brains of men. The

interest of such conceptions is more than artistic; they are landmarks in the history of the race, showing the height to which, at successive periods, ~~the life of man has risen~~ man's ideal of his own life has risen. And you ~~appear to me~~ ⟨seem now⟩ to be the only person who can ~~now~~ make life appear potentially noble and interesting without starting from any assumptions. And others who have ~~had something~~ shown more or less of the same power of rising into clear air—M^me de Stael in Corinne, M^rs Craven in Fleurange, George Sand in Consuelo—have all needed some fixed point to lean against before they could spread wings to soar. (De Stendhal ~~I think, alone has~~, perhaps, while himself detached from all illusions, has painted life in the same grand style. But he remains too much outside his characters, and tho in his books nobleness seems possible it seems possible only as an aberration). But one feels that you know the worst, and one thanks you ~~for not having~~ in that you have not despaired of the republic.[32]

Subsequently, as friendship developed, he invited her and G. H. Lewes to visit Cambridge with him in the spring of 1873— almost certainly the occasion of a walk with her there[33] in which she pronounced her views on human destiny, perhaps in direct response to the assertion in his letter that 'there was no longer any God or any hereafter or anything in particular to aim at'. His subsequent account has become well known:

I remember how, at Cambridge, I walked with her once in the Fellow's Garden of Trinity, on an evening of rainy May; and she, stirred somewhat beyond her wont, and taking as her text the three words which have been used so often as the inspiring trumpet-calls of men,—

[32] Draft letter of 7 Dec. 1872, TCL MS Myers 11^118. The finished letter was completed next day and is now in the George Eliot and George Henry Lewes Collection in the Beinecke Library at Yale. See below, Ch. 5, n. 18. The mention of the republic at the end may carry an allusion to Swinburne, whose *Songs before Sunrise* celebrating the republic (including 'Love the Beloved Republic' in 'Hertha') had appeared in 1871.

[33] Myers's journal for 20 May includes the entry 'Mrs Lewes in roundabout'. Professor E. J. Kenney tells me that this term is a traditional one for the Fellows' Garden of Trinity; it was also used by Caroline Jebb in a letter of 1879: see Bobbitt, *Dearest Love*, 152. It should be noted, nevertheless, that George Eliot visited Cambridge again a few years later, in 1877, at the invitation of Mr and Mrs Sidgwick and that Myers's entry in his journal for 3 June then read 'Mrs Lewes in Roundabout. Stuart. Bowling Green at night.' This suggests a meeting with her in the earlier part of the day, however, while Myers's 1881 account speaks specifically of 'an evening in rainy May' and uses the word 'once', suggesting a date earlier in their relationship; the 1873 dating carries more weight, therefore. When George Eliot accepted an advance invitation to breakfast with Sidgwick for the earlier visit she remarked that the weather was bad. See below, Ch. 5, at n. 20.

the words *God, Immortality, Duty*,—pronounced, with terrible earnestness, how inconceivable was the *first*, how unbelievable the *second*,
and yet how peremptory and absolute the *third*. Never, perhaps,
have sterner accents affirmed the sovereignty of impersonal and
unrecompensing Law. I listened, and night fell; her grave, majestic
countenance turned toward me like a Sibyl's in the gloom; it was as
though she withdrew from my grasp, one by one, the two scrolls of
promise, and left me the third scroll only, awful with inevitable fates.
And when we stood at length and parted, amid that columnar circuit
of the forest-trees, beneath the last twilight of starless skies, I seemed to
be gazing, like Titus at Jerusalem, on vacant seats and empty halls,—
on a sanctuary with no Presence to hallow it, and heaven left lonely of
a God.[34]

While George Eliot's citation of 'the inspiring trumpet-calls
of men,—the words *God, Immortality, Duty*' and her demolition of the first two to make way for the 'peremptory and
absolute' claims of the third was Kantian in its terms, the final
insistence suggested also a responsiveness to the later philosophy of Wordsworth, invoking by implication his equally em-
phatic stress on the need to cultivate the human affections.

The Wordsworthian strain was familiar enough to Myers,
who would have been equally conscious how these same values
were the stuff from which George Eliot's novels were made. But
the point that must have struck home to him with particularly
deadening force was her refinement of his point about a 'hereafter'. If human immortality were so unbelievable (and in spite
of the Wordsworth who had made much of the intimations of
immortality that he traced in his own experience, particularly in
childhood), then the fate of the human race must ultimately be
devoid of real hope.

Yet as mentioned above, revulsion at the harsher implications
of Darwinsim and the attempt to rescue human spirituality were
generating the search for a counter-force. Another field for
investigation lay in the possible existence of laws other than
those that had so far been discovered in the natural sciences. The

---

[34] 'George Eliot', *Century Magazine*, 23 (Nov. 1881), 62–3. Rosemary Ashton
(*George Eliot: A Life* (1996), 334) finds this account overdrawn. There is no doubt
a touch of conscious exaggeration, but the description corresponds convincingly
with other contemporary accounts of her at her most intensely serious. In response
to Professor Ashton's sarcastic question 'What does a Sibyl's face look like?' (ibid.)
one may respectfully refer her to Michelangelo and the Sistine Chapel.

result (whether consciously or otherwise) was a rise of interest in
psychical phenomena of all kinds, a curiosity which Myers
shared. Recognizing the potential importance of such matters
for a world that seemed more and more dominated by the
straightforward evidence of the senses and quantitative meas-
urement, he found himself asking whether the time had not
come for a group of trustworthy intellectuals to set themselves
the task of sifting thoroughly all the evidence for paranormal
mental activity, examining it from both sides in a disinterested
and uncommitted fashion. It might then be possible either to
establish indisputable evidence for the existence of life beyond
death, or, failing that, to conclude once and for all that the
phenomena being investigated were illusory.

The story of this quest (to be considered in further detail
elsewhere) began with a 'star-light walk which I shall not forget'
with Henry Sidgwick in which Myers asked him

almost with trembling, whether he thought that when Tradition, Intui-
tion, Metaphysic, had failed to solve the riddle of the Universe, there
was still a chance that from any actual observable phenomena,—
ghosts, spirits, whatsoever there might be,—some valid knowledge
might be drawn as to a World Unseen.[35]

Although the exact date of this walk is uncertain[36] it took place
no later than 1871. Sidgwick gave his support, writing to him in
1872,

I sometimes feel with somewhat of a profound hope and enthusiasm
that the function of the English mind with its uncompromising matter-
of-factness, will be to put the final question to the Universe, with a
solid passionate determination to be answered which must come to
something.[37]

Following his guarded approval there were initial investigations.
The two men were joined by Edmund Gurney, a young fellow of
Trinity already known for brilliance of conversation and general

---

[35] Obituary of Sidgwick: *Proceedings of the Society for Psychical Research*, 15 (1901), 454.
[36] Alan Gauld points out (*Founders*, 103) that it is here given as 3 Dec. 1869, but in *Fragments of Inner Life* the interest is dated from 13 Nov. 1871. In Myers's Journal the entry for the first date is marked 'On Ghosts?', that for the second 'H.S. on ghosts'.
[37] Letter to Myers, Apr. 1872: *Sidgwick Memoir*, 259.

intelligence. (Jane Harrison described him as 'perhaps the most lovable and beautiful human being I ever met' and George Eliot was equally enthusiastic, as noted in the next chapter.[38]) In May 1874 Myers and Gurney visited Gurney's aunt Lady Mount-Temple at Broadlands, where they met the Reverend William Stainton Moses, a clergyman who, having become interested in spiritualism and formed a 'home circle' with two friends, had had experiences that startled him. Myers was deeply impressed by what he felt to be his manifest probity, and as a result of this meeting began to shape an informal association of people (largely associated with Trinity) who had already displayed interest in the phenomena concerned. Although the results were by no means conclusive enough remained unexplained for curiosity to be aroused further and in January 1882, at a meeting under the chairmanship of Professor W. F. Barrett, the Society for Psychical Research was formally set up, with Sidgwick as president. The full story of all these events, including the appointment of Gurney as secretary and his tragic death in 1889, must, again, be left for discussion elsewhere; all that needs to be related here is the energetic part played by Myers, who eventually began putting together the materials for a study of what was for him the central issue, to be entitled *Human Personality and its Survival of Bodily Death*—his own attempt, one might say, to produce in modern times a counterpart to the Virgilian epic. When twenty-five years later, Myers, suffering from heart trouble after an attack of influenza, was told by a medium that he had not long to live he turned to the production of his book with increased urgency, but the medium's prophecy of the period left to him proved over-optimistic, and he died on 17 January 1901. The book remained incomplete at his death but his widow was nevertheless able to put together a full version of what had already been produced and publish it in 1903.

In view of the need for extreme stringency when dealing with the evidences presented, one of the better-attested cases investigated made a particularly strong impression on Myers. It concerned a young man who had hidden a piece of brick and a sealed envelope containing a message in a secret place, telling his relatives that after his death he would try if he could to let them

---

[38] *Reminiscences of a Student's Life* (1925), 55, cited Gauld, *Founders*, 175 n.

know where they were. In the event the exact location of the brick and the contents of the message were revealed to them by means of alphabet tappings which proved accurate. Myers proposed this as an excellent model for an experiment which anyone might undertake:

I think it very desirable that as many persons as possible should provide a decisive test of their own identity, in case they should find themselves able to communicate through any sensitive after their bodily death. The simplest plan is to write down some sentence embodying an idea or name which you feel it probable that you will remember, if you remember anything, and then to seal this sentence up in an envelope, without communicating it to any person whatever. . . . If, then, the writer (it may be many years afterwards) finds himself capable of sending a message from the other world, let him mention this test sentence, and try to reproduce it. The sealed envelope can then be opened; and if the spirit's message should be found to coincide with the words therein written, there will be as good a proof as we can get that that message has at any rate not emanated from any living mind . . .[39]

'Small as may be the chances of success,' he also wrote, 'a few score of distinct successes would establish a presumption of man's survival which the common sense of mankind would refuse to explain away.'[40] In accordance with his own precept Myers himself left a sealed message in the manner described, which he deposited with Oliver Lodge in January 1891 and which after his death in 1901 remained for some time unopened.

An important part was now played by a Cambridge researcher, Margaret Verrall,[41] who had become interested in the investigations of the Society and taken up crystal-gazing, for which she had shown some aptitude. Having been deeply impressed by Myers's growing certainty concerning a future life, she had after his death begun to concern herself with automatic writing, a form of psychic experimentation that could, it appeared, be carried on in independence from the activity of the conscious mind—and which indeed seemed to work better under such conditions. The individual practising it might engage in some other activity at the same time; in any case there would not

---

[39] Myers, *HP* ii. 499.        [40] Ibid. 182.
[41] Her Husband, A. W. Verrall, was to become the first King Edward VII Professor of English Literature. Both husband and wife had received a classical education.

be conscious awareness of what had been written until it was read back. After a period during which Mrs Verrall had little success, she found herself transmitting phrases and sentences that seemed significant, some of them including various Latin phrases to do with evergreens, dew, and fragrant flowers. A year or two later, on July 1904, she was particularly intrigued to find that she had written down the sentences, 'I have long told you of the contents of the envelope. Myers' sealed envelope left with Lodge. You have not understood. It has in it the words from the Symposium—about Love bridging the chasm.'

For the pioneers of the Society for Psychical Research this was understandably exciting, a golden opportunity to carry out the kind of test that Myers had hoped for. The words mentioned as being in the *Symposium* could easily be found, moreover: they were from a passage in Socrates' dialogue with Diotima concerning the nature of love:

'What then is love?' I asked; 'Is he mortal?' 'No.' 'What then?' 'As in the former instance, he is neither mortal nor immortal, but in a mean between them.' 'What is he then, Diotima?' 'He is a great spirit (*daimon*), and like all that is spiritual he is intermediate between the divine and the mortal.' 'And what is the nature of this spiritual Power?' I said. 'This is the power,' she said, 'which interprets and conveys to the gods the prayers and sacrifices of men, and to men the commands and rewards of the gods; *and this power spans the chasm which divides them*, and in this all is bound together, and through this the arts of the prophet and the priest, their sacrifices and mysteries and charms, and all prophecy and incantation, find their way. For God mingles not with man; and through this power all the intercourse and speech of God with man, whether awake or asleep, is carried on. The wisdom which understands this is spiritual; all other wisdom, such as that of arts or handicrafts, is mean and vulgar. Now these spirits or intermediate powers are many and divine, and one of them is love.'[42]

If Myers's sealed envelope, once opened, were found to contain some part of the extract just quoted there would evidently be a strong case for believing in his survival. On 13 December, accordingly, Oliver Lodge summoned a group of his close associates in the Society to gather together in a formal session, at which the envelope was opened and the sentence it contained

---

[42] Plato, *Symposium*, 202–3 (Jowett trans. (1871) i. 518–19. My italics).

read out. It ran 'If I can revisit any earthly scene, I should choose the *Valley* in the grounds of Hallsteads, Cumberland.' A note was prepared for insertion in the next number of the Society's journal (withholding exact details of the message in case there should be any later development) which concluded: 'It has, then, to be reported that this one experiment has completely failed, and it cannot be denied that the failure is disappointing.'[43]

The notice duly appeared and was circulated to members of the Society; it then reached the popular press and for many years all that was known to the general public was that there had been an experiment which had failed. Mrs Verrall, meanwhile, claimed that although she was a classical scholar she had not read the *Symposium* when she began her automatic writing, and that it was not until after the occasion in May 1901 when she found the name of Diotima occurring in her scripts that she read the whole dialogue (early in 1903). In Myers's posthumous work *Human Personality and its Survival of Bodily Death*, after insisting on the link between telepathy and other bonds between individuals, asserting as he did so that 'Love is the energy that makes a Cosmos of the Sum of Things,' he had made explicit mention of Diotima, through whose mouth, he said, 'Plato insists that it is an unfailing sign of true love that its desires are *for ever*; nay that love may be even defined as the desire of the *everlasting* possession of the good.'[44] The book appeared in 1903, and Mrs Verrall had already read it when she wrote down the communication that led to the opening of the posthumous message.[45] Since she knew Myers well she would in any case have been bound to know of his passion for Plato's views of love, examples of which appear constantly in his published writings. Some of her subliminal writing represented constructive dramatization on her part.

This was not, however, the end of the story. Soon after the account of the opening was sent for publication some of Myers's associates realized that the experiment had not been quite as

[43] *Journal of the Society for Psychical Research*, 12 (Jan. 1905), 11–13.

[44] Myers, *HP* 113–15.

[45] Myers's widow, always anxious to play down the significance of that episode, claimed that proof sheets had earlier been lying round her house and that Mrs Verrall could have seen them there before writing down the name of Diotima in her earlier writing, a point which Mrs Verrall acknowledged in a footnote to her account. Some of the correspondence is preserved in TCL MS Myers 2$^{1-8}$.

decisive a failure as had at first been assumed. Although those who assembled in London for the opening and reading of the message acknowledged that in the terms in which Myers had set it up it had failed, one or two people present recognized the existence of a connection between the message transmitted by Mrs Verrall and the message Myers had actually left. This was particularly evident to those who had had the opportunity to read some pieces of intimate autobiography entitled *Fragments of Inner Life* that Myers had written before he died, privately printed and circulated to selected friends and relations in sealed packets, with instructions that they were not to be opened until after his death. To those who had then read it, mention of the Valley at Hallsteads had a special significance. Mrs Verrall, on the other hand, was not in a position to appreciate the relevance of the platonic love mentioned in her writing to this valley: although she knew by then that there had been an episode of love in Myers's earlier history she had no reason to associate it with any particular location. It was not until 21 December 1904, when Eleanor Sidgwick showed her passages from the full version of the autobiography,[46] that she became aware of the connection.

Myers's widow, meanwhile, who had not been invited to attend the opening of the message, was appalled when news of its contents reached her, since she grasped immediately the reference to this episode, which was mentioned in the autobiography and had been already known to her; she hoped its last vestiges had died with her husband. Although she did not believe the events in question to have been to his discredit, she was convinced that their disclosure could do untold and lasting harm to relations of his and to other surviving members of their family and had already tried to reclaim existing copies or to extract promises that the contents would not be revealed to anyone.[47]

---

[46] W. H. Salter, 'F. W. H. Myers's Posthumous Message', *Proceedings of the Society for Psychical Research*, 52 (1958), 32.

[47] The only person to demur was Oliver Lodge, who thought it would be a breach of trust to Myers if the story were covered up completely; Mrs Myers, made desperate by his attitude, wrote to William James, begging him to intercede: letter of Mar. 1902, TCL MS Myers 29[65]. In the event, it seems, Lodge did return his copy, but only after having typewritten copies made of all the most confidential passages. His record is preserved in TCL MS Myers 13[50].

One of those who had read *Fragments of Inner Life* was Eleanor Sidgwick, Henry's widow, who found her copy in circumstances which themselves touched on the paranormal.[48] The effect of her reading was to bring home to her the significance of the place that had figured in the posthumous message. As mentioned earlier, Hallsteads had been built by Dorothy Wordsworth's friends Jane and John Marshall about 1816 and visited on several occasions by the Wordsworths themselves. In this house Myers's mother, like other members of the Marshall family, had been brought up; he himself had stayed there on many occasions. For Myers, however, it had also provided the central scene of a crucially important love relationship. While he did not give precise details in *Fragments of Inner Life*, his widow knew the whole story, which he had told her before their marriage.[49] Eventually she dealt with the problem by publishing most of the text in 1904 along with a selection of Myers's poems under the title *Fragments of Prose and Poetry*; at the same time she took care to cut out everything that referred to the story concerned. The original version survived, nevertheless, both in Oliver Lodge's typescript and in other printed copies, and sixty years later details of it were published for the first time by W. H. Salter in the Society's Journal,[50] using the

---

[48] When Henry Sidgwick was sent his packet, he had given it to his wife to look after with some other papers and she had placed it in her room in Newnham College. Since Sidgwick died before Myers Myers's widow asked Mrs Sidgwick whether there was a sealed packet among his papers. Mrs Sidgwick, who had completely forgotten the incident, replied that there was not. In the following month Mrs Verrall's scripts began to contain a description of a room, and of a box in that room which had come from Florence. On reading it one of her friends remarked that the room sounded like Mrs Sidgwick's in Newnham. It was not until more than two years afterwards, however, that Mrs Sidgwick happened to look in a box in her room which corresponded to the description and found in it the sealed packet containing *Fragments of Inner Life*. This was in December 1903, a few months before Mrs Verrall transmitted the crucial sentences. After the opening of the sealed envelope she read the autobiography and discovered evidence in it for the existence of a connection between the sentences that Mrs Verrall had written down and the one in the envelope.

[49] 'I have told her about Annie:—at once she felt all I would have her feel, and only longed that the likeness which I see should grow more complete . . .' Letter of 1 Jan. 1879: TCL MS Myers 12[151].

[50] W. H. Salter, 'F. W. H. Myers's Posthumous Message', *Proceedings of the Society for Psychical Research*, 52 (1958), 1–32. In 1946 Salter, the husband of Mrs Verrall's daughter Helen (who had also practised automatic writing with some success) and a member of the Society for Psychical Research wrote to Myers's

version that had been left to Sidgwick. In 1961 it was published in full by the Society.

Although Salter's article, drawing on the Society's archives and on other accounts over the years, was reasonably accurate, he did not have full access to the family archives,[51] which make it possible not only to piece together the story more fully but to see better how it relates to some of the intellectual developments already described.

For some years Myers had been interested in young women in a phase which he later described as belonging to the 'sensual side' of his nature.[52] It has further been suggested that he passed through a homosexual phase, though the evidence for this is thin;[53] in 1866–7, having come under the influence of Josephine Butler, he tried to persuade Henry Sidgwick's brother Arthur to

surviving son and daughter asking whether they might now be willing for the full version of the autobiographical fragments to be published. They refused, his daughter writing that the omitted passages referred almost wholly to 'one supremely painful episode in my father's life . . .' 'Nor,' she continued, 'can I imagine any thing more repugnant to my father than delving into details in connection with that tragedy.' A few years later, nevertheless, Salter decided (probably because the surviving children had died in the interval) that the time had come to give a full account of the affair in his article.

[51] It was not until 1970, when they were deposited in Trinity College Library, that they were made generally available to scholars and it became possible to fill in the full details of the story from previously unpublished letters and journals. Some scholars such as Alan Gauld (see my Preface above) and Frank M. Turner were able to use them earlier.

Myers's papers were carefully weeded by his widow; his correspondence with Annie Marshall, for instance, was almost completely destroyed. References to their relationship were by no means excluded, on the other hand: indeed it appears that Mrs Myers was anxious that most of them should remain, to support her contention that in his dealings with Annie her husband had always played a thoroughly honourable part. In a note expressing her wish that *Fragments of Inner Life* should not be reprinted in its entirety, for instance, she insisted 'Remember there is nothing but what is beautiful Pure and Holy . . .': TCL MS Myers 13[42].

[52] Myers, *FIL* 9: see above, p. 122. In 1864, in one of his more abandoned-seeming letters, he wrote to Arthur Sidgwick, Henry's younger brother and his friend, 'I advance daily in amorousness feebleness folly & sin': letter of 16 Sept. 1864: TCL MS Myers 12[193]. It is hard to know at what level of seriousness to take this.

[53] In *John Addington Symonds, A Biography* (1964) Phyllis Grosskurth quotes (pp. 114–15) some comments by Symonds that suggest he traced homosexual tendencies in Myers. It is true in addition that Myers introduced him to the writings of Walt Whitman (p. 119) but the passage she quotes from him on the experience of finding the foundations of one's moral position shaken during a dark night of the soul (*Essays Classical* (1883), 220) might as easily refer to the conflict between heterosexual love and conventional morality that he experienced in the 1870s. See also Gauld, *Founders*, 90n.–91n.

join him in adopting a more serious frame of mind and embrace Christianity wholeheartedly.[54] By 1869, as mentioned earlier, he had come to appreciate more fully the implications of Darwinism[55] and changed his standpoint again.

After a further period of emotional turbulence[56] an already existing acquaintance developed into the most crucial relationship of his life. The members of the Marshall family whom Myers sometimes met at Hallsteads included a cousin, Walter, who in February 1866 had married a young woman named Annie Hill, a clergyman's daughter from Thornton Dale in Yorkshire whom Myers had met by the summer of 1867.[57] She herself remains an elusive figure, being usually seen in the surviving records only through his eyes. Such other references to her as survive invariably emphasize her sweetness and grace. Almost all her correspondence was later destroyed but there is a letter in the Myers archive which appears to be signed by her (though the handwriting differs markedly from another of hers in the collection, written in 1871). It is a playful fragment, preserved perhaps for that very reason;[58] if by her it probably dates from the first year of her marriage, and was sent from some place where she was staying with a number of relatives

---

[54] TCL MS Myers 12[194]. For a colourful account of Josephine Butler at this time see Gauld, *Founders*, 95–6.

[55] See above, n. 29.

[56] August 1870 was marked by trouble of some kind, probably to be associated with entries in his journal that record a stay at Hallsteads and Lakeland walks with various young women. See his MS 'Account of friendship with H[enry] S[idgwick]': TCL MS Myers 13[22(2)]. It may well be that he was in love but found his love unrequited: the entry for 15 Aug., for example, reads, 'Patterdale with her. O temps, suspens ton vol.' In the following May he proposed marriage to 'Miss E.' and was presumably rejected; this he later said 'marked the last wave of the subsiding agitation' (ibid.).

[57] In his MS Journal, TCL MS Myers 14[1], the entry for 22 June records a lunch party at Patterdale. An annotation (by whom it is hard to say) states that it was their first meeting. Beneath, there appears a quotation: 'Benedetto sia'l giorno e'l mese e'l'anno' ['Blessed be the day and the month and the year'], a quotation from the opening of one of Petrarch's sonnets to Laura (*Canzoniere* LXI), in which he recalls their meeting.

[58] It is possible that Annie's writing changed sharply during the succeeding years, or that she used a more formal script when writing to her aunt. The dates given in the letter suggest that it was written in June or July, since those are the months when strawberries are most plentiful, and in 1866, since it is hard to find another year during the period when the days of the week and dates correspond. In that case it belonged to the summer immediately following her marriage. If it is not by her, it gives a vivid picture of the female ambience in which Myers moved.

(possibly on Derwent Island, where members of the Marshall family sometimes stayed). The mood that emerges is one of humorous boredom touched by seriousness:

& every now and then  (portrait of a midge of the country which just perched on my finger) a moral sentiment epigram or poem, as (I. busi- ness) 'evening bags or trowsers. Good Lord have I any?'— 'The devil invented talking to show his diabiolical power in enabling any body to torture his neighbours without giving him- self the least enjoyment.'—'My conscience is a surly brute to whom I throw a sop now and then just to keep him quiet.' I hope you care to hear these as much as I did. My diary of the time I have spent here consists in (besides the usual amount of morality, totaly unconnected with this place;)
'Wed. 4 Walked in aft.
Thur 5. Walked in aft.
Frid 6 Walked in aft.
Sat 7 Walked in aft.
Sund 8. Walked in aft.' (the latter followed by long and accurate notes of the sermon.) Did you not say that Aunt Dofo asked which of the two (Mary & Aileen) you thought the bestlooking? I sh$^d$ hardly have doubted

I sh$^d$ put A 5th below M. Frederica (=Mousie) Theo and Catkin. I don't know y$^r$. opinions about them all, do tell me. **do write** (another midge). We (two J's, M. & I) have german lessons every day w$^h$. are the great opportunity for laughter & mirth. The weather has been warm. Thermometer at 102–5 in the shade (you may publish the last sentence of my letter.) I have the indegestion, consequent upon taking no exercise, bathing, drinking nothing but milk at breakfast & eating only cheese at lunch & dinner & unlimited strawberries all day long. There is an *awful* amount of music here, All the time except that so occupied Theodosia employs in drawing Mary w$^h$. Mary likes very much as she must be idle and T makes her very good looking though utterly unlike herself. The great employment of the evenings besides music is criticising the exactitude & beauty of the above portraits, an occupation w$^h$. M seems very fond of.

There is before most of the windows a lawn C. on the opposite side of a gulph D going down to somewhere naughty

one has to step over a vast sofa A to the window B & jump across this 3$^{yds}$. or so about once every 5 minutes w$^h$ is trying for my mussles but infinitely worse for my nerves. E. represents 10 or 12 elegant female cousins scoffing at me B about to jump.

> I remain   Yr v—y
> Æ Marshall[59]

The central impression is of a writer who combined humour, liveliness, and sensitivity with an underlying seriousness. Such qualities would have endeared her immediately to Myers, who came from a similar background. Annie's feeling for nature, not expressed directly in this letter, linked him with his Wordsworthian roots, helping him to discern a spiritual affinity.

In the early years of her marriage Annie bore five children in quick succession. She and her husband, neither of them in good health, spent the winter of 1870–1 at Vevey in Switzerland, and Myers, who had reached their neighbourhood in the course of a long European tour, wrote to his mother that he might either go straight on or stop for a day or two to visit them and walk with Walter.[60] In the event he opted for Vevey, a decision which proved momentous for him. His journal mentions walks with both Walter and Annie; some years later, when he sent a poem entitled 'Vevey' to Sidgwick he noted that seeing Annie there in February 1871 had been 'the beginning of all things'.[61] In a manuscript note a little later he wrote, 'On Feb 21, 22, 23, 24, 25 on the shores of Lake Geneva I learnt certain lessons which made me stronger ever after. . . . I learnt that suffering is not shame, and that isolation is not overthrow, and that discouragement is not despair. I learnt how divine a thing human courage can be, and that "there is nothing a spirit of such magnitude cannot overcome or undergo".'[62]

It is clear that Annie laboured under various burdens. In the

---

[59] TCL MS Myers 3$^{115}$. Hitherto unpublished.

[60] Letter to his mother, 8 Feb. 1871: TCL MS Myers 12$^8$. Myers said that he would enquire from Annie about the question of smallpox in relation to one of the children, and evidently satisfied himself about this before visiting them. There had already been visiting between members of the family: in 1870 Annie and Walter visited the Myerses at Leckhampton near Cheltenham, where Frederic walked with them from time to time; he and his mother also visited them nearby at Malvern.

[61] TCL MS Myers 12$^{144}$.     [62] TCL MS Myers 13$^{22(2)}$. Hitherto unpublished.

following September, when she wrote to Myers's mother from Switzerland giving an account of their activities and improvement in health, she added, 'Walter seems to like this place too. He has had more good days than usual lately.' Her next sentences indicated that troubles previously discussed with her aunt were continuing:

Oh Aunt Susan, I would give anything to have a few talks with you—and still—if I had the opportunity—I don't think I would use it—for I could say nothing but what would pain you—. I often think of what you would advise—knowing you has been one of the greatest blessings of my life—you can never know what that last week at Cheltenham has been to me ever since,—but it grieves me to think what pain it must have been to you, who should I think be surrounded by unvarying peace & calm.[63]

At the end she signed her letter 'Your loving child', assuming the persona that others, including Myers, found attractive. What the 'troubles' were she did not specify, but later records help to fill out the picture, showing that all was not well in the marriage. Walter, we learn, had had a nervous illness in 1859 from which he had later recovered. On seeking medical advice as to the prudence of marrying he was advised that it would probably be good for him. At the same time he proved subject to long fits of depression, interspersed with periods of excitability. (Later he thought this might have been due to his having been prescribed a drug, chloral, which another doctor afterwards told him was the worst thing he could have taken.[64]) According to an account prepared by Annie at a later stage, he was in his normal condition 'gentle, courteous, moderate in all ways, of sound & deliberate judgement & most truly generous & kind' but in his depressive states either 'interested in little or nothing, & despondent as to all personal matters, & inclined to no exertion or act', or, in his states of excitement, 'impulsive, talkative, prone to excessive exercise, exaggerated in speech & intention & extravagant in expenditure & easily roused to anger'. The death of his father in 1872, leaving him with more money, unsettled him further.[65]

Towards the end of her letter to her Aunt Myers Annie wrote, 'I hope Fred will contrive to take us in his way if he should come

---

[63] Letter of 30 Sept. 1871 from Bex, Canton de Vaux, Switzerland: TCL MS Myers 17[22(1)]. Hitherto unpublished.     [64] *Committee Report* minute 9327, p. 426.
[65] Submission by Annie Marshall among records at Ticehurst.

abroad this winter.—Had he anything to do with the Educational Commission, as I think he had reason to expect . . .'[66] Compared with her husband, depressive and over-energetic by turns and essentially self-regarding, Myers, with his wide interests, his poetic aspirations, and his conscientious desire to work in the new fields opened up by the 1870 Education Act, must have been an exhilarating companion. Although he was evidently coming to admire Annie deeply, however, that at the time seems to have been all. He did not go abroad that winter, and was not to see anything of the Marshalls until the following year, 1872, when after a stay with Henry Sidgwick at Southend in June he encountered Annie again, this time in London:

June 23 was in many ways a memorable day to me. Coming up to town full charged, as it were, with friendship, I met at Onslow Gardens,—in a carriage in front of the door, to speak more accurately,—a lady whom I had not seen since Feb. 25, 1871,—no very long time, perhaps, but time enough for many things to happen in, if they crowd up—We talked on the leads of 17 O. G. on subjects w^h (as the Pope says) 'it would be out of place to define more particularly'. Suffice it to say that when I left the house that night & thought of the day gone by, ~~the world~~ Earth seemed to me as if it were so full of wisdom, beauty, love, that it was 'becoming already the fabled heaven'.[67]

Meanwhile, like many of his generation, he was enjoying Tennyson's praise of chivalric honour in the *Idylls of the King*. At the end of October he read 'Gareth and Lynette', with its picture of the knights of the Round Table at their noblest:

> the listening eyes
> Of those tall knights, that ranged about the throne,
> Clear honour shining like the dewy star
> Of dawn, and faith in their great King, with pure
> Affection, and the light of victory,
> And glory gained, and evermore to gain.[68]

The following month the final part of *Middlemarch* arrived, prompting him to draft the letter to George Eliot quoted above,

---

[66] TCL MS Myers 17^22. Hitherto unpublished.

[67] TCL MS Myers 13^22(3). Hitherto unpublished.

[68] Lines 320–5. In December 1869 he had written to his mother, 'I think much of Tennyson's new vol. very poor—especially the Coming of Arthur: but some of the Grail seems to me better—more ethereal & impalpable—than anything else of his': TCL MS Myers 8^117.

where he expressed particular appreciation of scenes between Ladislaw and Dorothea on the grounds that 'Noble lovemaking,—the surprised and pure contact of lofty souls—is hardly ever described truly'. Some of his other statements there—that in the absence of a God or a hereafter it was only by coming into contact with some other 'kindred soul' that one could be oneself, that to have its best savour love must be set among great possibilities and great self-sacrifices—were to prove portentous.

Despite the enthusiasm of his letter to George Eliot Myers was himself suffering from bouts of depression at this time, which were broken in January 1873 when he went to visit an old friend at Scarborough, where Walter and Annie were staying. As usual his journal entries were laconic:

21 Called on Annie
22 Dined with W. & A.
23 Ride on sands with Annie
26 Walk on Spa with Annie
27 To London

When one's eye travels to the foot of the page, however, it is caught by a line of verse which is picked up at the foot of each of the following three pages so as to form a complete couplet:

> Love is enough;
> while ye deemed he was sleeping
> There were signs of his coming
> and sounds of his feet.

The stanza is from William Morris's 'Love is Enough', the leading poem in his collection of that name, which appeared in that year[69] and which Henry Sidgwick mentioned to him in a letter.[70] It is followed by a further line on the next page, this time a quotation from the Bible:

> They should hunger no more, neither thirst any more.[71]

[69] From William Morris, *Love is Enough* (1873).

[70] In March 1873 Sidgwick wrote to him, 'I saw Morris the other day, and taxed him with putting nineteenth-century sentiment on the provincial stage of a medieval Arcadia. He said Middle Ages were subtle to any extent in amatory matters. I said they might be subtle, but they weren't sceptical of their own emotions, did not "tremble for the death of desire". He grinned good-humouredly and admitted.' Myers noted that this was a reference to 'Love is Enough': *Sidgwick Memoir*, 278 and n.

[71] Rev. 7: 16.

Other entries record a visit by Annie to Cheltenham in late
March and April and a visit to the racecourse with her followed
by a ride, a walk through the woods, and a visit to Worcester
with her and Walter. A quotation inserted from Virgil's
*Georgics* reads: 'Ver magnus agebat' ('The great spring was at
work'). Then in May came the visit to Cambridge with George
Eliot and G. H. Lewes, including, almost certainly, the walk
with her in the Fellows' Garden of Trinity already described,
during which she insisted on the supreme necessity of Duty.[72]
On 13 June he was on his way to the Lake District.

At Hallsteads, where he was to stay for several weeks, he again
saw a good deal of Annie. If his visit to Scarborough in January
had been made under the sign of *Middlemarch* and its portrayal
of noble love-making, this visit must have taken place with
George Eliot's words about duty still ringing in his mind. The
day following his arrival his journal records a drive to Patterdale,
with a further note the next day, 'Dove-coloured dress for first
time'; an entry on the 18th speaks of a visit via Keswick to the
falls at Lodore and Derwent Water, with a note in German, 'Wie
sollen beide'. On the same day is dated a four-line verse:

> When that wild storm o'er Skiddaw swept
>   And melted in red-purple air,
> And Love within us lit and leapt
>   And sank, and still was fair.[73]

On the 21st appears a further note, 'The longest day, and
possibly the best', with a later addition: 'Was *that* the land-
mark?' and a deleted opening: 'There is nothing which a spirit of
such'.[74] The entry for the next day has a line in German, 'Und
dennoch uns nicht gerauft und geschlagen', the next but one
'Stormy row Wo mag wohl jetzo weilen' and the day after that
'Wenn ich in deine Augen seh'; since this last is the first line of
a song from Schumann's *Dichterliebe* it is likely that German
*lieder* were forming a part of their entertainment. On 13 July the
entry runs 'O rock and torrent, lake and hill', the first words of
a poem of his about Hallsteads evidently composed at that time:

> O rock and torrent, lake and hill,
> Halls of a home austerely still,
>   Remote and solemn view!

---

[72] See above, pp. 134–5.     [73] TCL MS Myers 29[15].
[74] See above, p. 146.

O valley, where the wanderer sees
Beyond the towering arch of trees
    Helvellyn and the blue!

Great Nature! on our love was shed
From thine abiding goodlihead
    Majestic fostering;
We wondered, half-afraid to own
In hardly-conscious hearts upgrown
    So infinite a thing.

Within, without, whate'er hath been,
In cosmic deep the immortal scene
    Is mirrored, and shall last;—
Live the long looks, the woodland ways,
That twilight of enchanted days,—
    The imperishable Past.[75]

In the manuscript version there appears after the second stanza
another—later cancelled though not, apparently, by Myers
himself:

There came a day; thy calm we knew
Which can the beating heart subdue
    The impassioned heart controls;
No lover's oath our lips would frame,
But the eyes' interchange became
    A sacrament of souls.[76]

From these pieces of evidence a coherent story emerges.
Myers, still under the sway of George Eliot's portrayal of noble
love-making followed by her insistence on the absoluteness of
Duty, had come to recognize the existence of a love which could
combine passionate attraction with stringently moral behaviour,
enabling the lovers to feel for each other with the strenuousness
that he had described in his letter as the only kind worth having.
If the fact of Annie's marriage made it impossible for their love
to be realized in a physical relationship he could still feel himself
invited to a high calling. Its existence did not at all inhibit him
from undertaking a tour to Madeira with Walter in August—
presumably, in the hope of improving the latter's health. Their
love might never be consummated in anything more than an

---

[75] Myers, *FIL* 23–4, from TCL MS Myers 29[15], p. 37, the conclusion revised 4
May 1891.
[76] TCL MS 29[15]. This seems to be in another hand.

interchange of eyes and a touch of hands, yet that would be enough.

Annie Marshall's combination of the childlike with a womanly dignity was accompanied by a tremor of piercing vulnerability. The blend was commemorated in a poem entitled 'Love and Death':

> O painter, match an English bloom,
>   And give the head an English air,
> Then with great grey-blue stars illume
>   That face pathetically fair.
>
> As though some sweet child, dowered at will
>   With all the wisdom years could send,
> Looked up and, like a baby still,
>   Became thine equal and thy friend;
>
> And kept the childly curves, and grew
>   To woman's shape in wondrous wise,
> And with soft passion filled anew
>   The sea-like sapphire of her eyes.
>
> Look on her, painter; is there aught
>   Of well-beloved that is not here?
> Could chance or art be guessed or taught
>   To make the lovely child more dear?
>
> And yet herself he sees not;—no,
>   To me alone the clue she gave;
> My bird, so wounded, soaring so,
>   At once so tender and so brave.
>
> He knows not through how stormy skies
>   My dove maintains her waveless way;—
> To woe and wrong my child replies
>   With woman-glances, gently gay.
>
> Ay, first the unconquerable heart
>   Electing through those eyes to shine,
> Found in my soul the soul thou art
>   And, more than beauty, made me thine.
>
> All human passion merged in one;—
>   The whole soul in one act set free;—
> Mother for daughter, sire for son,
>   Feel faintlier what I feel for thee.
>
> Here, take me; this is all; for us
>   Earth has no love unknown to know

> God, if a God have wrought it thus,
>   Surely shall always keep it so.[77]

In his autobiographical account Myers concealed Annie's identity under the name Phyllis, quoting a line from Virgil's *Eclogues* which translated reads 'When my Phyllis comes every wood shall be green'; mention of Hallsteads there is accompanied simply by the comment that she had been brought up in a place of that kind. His anxiety to convey the quality of their love was matched by a desire not to reveal its full details—mainly out of concern for the other people involved; these included his future wife, who was later told the story but may not have appreciated the full intensity of his feelings, at least during his lifetime. Although Annie's husband must have known something of what was involved he too may not have grasped it fully: Myers left specific instructions that his manuscript account should not be published during Walter's lifetime.[78]

Annie and Frederic saw a good deal of each other from time to time in the next few years, both in London and the Lake District, and Myers was occasionally to recall their experiences in further poetry. The opening of one lyric in particular catches vividly his delight at seeing her at a new meeting, the moment of impulsive joy being caught with exactitude in the rhythms of the lines:

> Oh, when thro' all the crowd she came,
>   My child, my darling, glad and fair,
> How seemed she like a flying flame
>   That parts at eve the dusk of air!
> How leapt my heart, regarding there
>   Her ways in coming, softly fleet,
> Her starry aspect, shining hair,
>   The light grace of her eager feet!
>
> But when from those blue deeps divine
>   The tender glory quivering shone,
> And her eyes' ardour met in mine
>   The love she loved to look upon;—
> Then rainy mist or crowded floor
>   Became as heaven for her and me,

---

[77] Myers, *FIL* 18–19 from TCL MS Myers 29^15, pp. 34–5, dated 1873.
[78] TCL MS Myers 26^63(5).

> The London whirlwind, London roar,
>      As sighing of an enchanted sea . . .[79]

On other occasions such meetings in London gave rise to a
mystical feeling that he and Annie were living the true reality in
an unreal world. His journals record a number of visits to Hyde
Park and the Serpentine, which are evidently referred to in some
lines from 'The Renewal of Youth', published in the collection
of that title in 1882. The Argument asserts that the poem is
about the problem of the unseen world, and the author's sense
of having found a solution to it, even if he disclaims the power
of being able to do more than lead others to the same point. He
describes how minds like his 'draw a particular delight from
the interpenetration of the common scenes of life by their far-
reaching memories, meditations, and hopes', his illustrations
including an experience of transcendence in London's Hyde
Park:

> To them the aspects of the heavens recall
> Those strange and hurrying hours that were their all;
> For to one heart her bliss came unaware
> Under white cloudlets in a morning air;
> Another mid the thundering tempest knew
> Peace, and a wind that where it listed blew;
> And oped the heaven of heavens one soul before
> In life's mid crash and London's whirling roar:—
> Ay, and transfigured in the dream divine
> The thronged precinct of Park and Serpentine,
> Till horse and rider were as shades that rode
> From an unknown to an unknown abode,
> And that grey mere, in mist that clung and curled,
> Lay like a water of the spirit-world.[80]

He also accompanied Annie to other cultural events in London:
exhibitions at the Royal Academy, opera at Covent Garden.
One of the latter expeditions included a moment of particular
poignancy, recorded in the *Fragments*. The original manuscript
reads as follows:

I noticed often the effect which the sight of her produced on strangers,
most strongly perhaps on girls growing to womanhood, whom the

---

[79] TCL MS Myers 29[15]. Myers *CP* 343.      [80] Ibid., 292–3, 302.

combination of her innocent look, her loveliness, & the tremor of a hidden tragedy which hung over her eyes, seemed sometimes to fascinate with a sudden insight into the pathos & bewilderment of human fates. I remember (for instance) that I was once descending the stairs of Covent Garden opera-house with a party of whom Phyllis was one, and that at the foot of the stairs we were to part; and that she stopped me in an embrasure to ask my counsel on a sad and urgent matter. I remember that ~~as I looked up in perplexity from her softness of aspect and & face of troubled appeal~~ looking up I saw close to us a high-bred beautiful girl, unknown to me, moving calmly downwards among her kin. I saw her manage to stand and wait where she could look at Phyllis still; I saw her grow forgetful of the outward scene in sympathy with that unknown sorrow. The girl never once looked at me, nor Phyllis at her; but when, a minute later, all was over, & I ~~was walking thro the moonlit streets~~ walked away alone, I felt how swift, how secret, how subtle are the ties betwixt soul & soul . . .[81]

Apart from an occasional prose cameo of this kind Myers preferred to retail the main events of his narrative in a series of poems. As one would expect, given his literary gifts, these are extremely accomplished, owing much in form and movement to his admired Tennyson. The power they exercise over the reader, however, comes partly from a sensed intensity of feeling which increases as one pieces together the full story behind his recollections.

Several of the poems have already been quoted from; another, 'Honour', dwells on the stresses set up in the relationship through its platonic nature;

And the darkness of death is upon her, the light of his eyes is dim,
But Honour has spoken, Honour, enough for her and for him.

Lines such as these remind one that Myers is a near-contemporary of Sir Henry Newbolt: a similar rousing beat drives them on in their unquestioning devotion to honour, regarded as a paramount virtue. At the same time there is in these poems a growing note of sadness. This is not explained in the autobiographical account, where they simply suggest, without relating, the remainder of the story.

[81] TCL MS Myers 26^{63(76)}. This may have taken place on 24 July 1873, when Myers recalls that Sidgwick accompanied him and others to the Italian Opera: TCL MS Myers 13^{22(3)}. His Journal for that day records a visit to Covent Garden, with a note 'H.S. meets Annie'.

As the events reached their culmination they came increasingly to involve her husband. About the relationship between his wife and his cousin Walter always preserved silence, but he could not have failed to notice their growing intimacy—particularly since their visits and meetings in London were supplemented by a constant exchange of letters. He seems to have acquiesced, accepting the relationship as fully honourable; not himself drawn to cultural events or Platonism he presumably found the situation not unacceptable. While pursuing the more active life of sport and politics he preferred, he continued to suffer from bouts of depression, which in 1874 resulted in his travelling abroad again. Annie, meanwhile, passed through periods of unspecified illness. She spent some time confined to an invalid chair, and when he journeyed abroad was too ill to join him.

During the next eighteen months much less is known about the progress of the love between Frederic and Annie, which presumably continued to be cultivated when both were in London; in 1876, however, events took a new turn, the details of which can be traced by putting together various records, including testimony from Walter himself. It was an extraordinary imbroglio, verging sometimes on the melodramatic, sometimes on the absurd. According to Walter's later account[82] his taste for activity meant that during his more manic phases he was always in danger of over-exertion. Annie's version went further, recording that following a period of better health he had recently been announcing himself to be inspired and to be doing God's work—this, however, resulting only in 'boastful talk', accompanied by 'aimless and foolish expenditure'. Describing himself as possessed of such extraordinary talent that in a few years' time he would be 'among the first ten men in England and possibly Prime Minister', he had taken in addition to reckless riding about the parks and streets, as well as secreting a knife and announcing an intention of taking his own life.[83]

During the spring of 1876 he spent a good deal of time campaigning for the Liberal party during the election of a member for Cumberland. In the midst of the excitement he also found time for other activities: he bought a horse from someone

---

[82] *Committee Report* minutes 9306–22, pp. 425–6.
[83] Report on his previous condition by Annie Marshall, 27 May 1876, among patient's notes at Ticehurst.

he had recently come to know and agreed without proper security to lend him £4,000 towards the purchase of property in Park Lane that was expected to yield a good profit. The cheque went through his solicitor, who presumably contacted Annie to express concern at the apparent rashness of his current actions and to question his state of mind. She certainly heard of the transaction in some way and became desperately anxious. Things came to a head on the evening of 2 May, when, spending the evening in the company of friends, including both herself and Frederic Myers, he indulged in extravagant behaviour and began using violent language. (Perhaps she raised the question of his recent transactions and was told briskly to mind her own business.) At her request Myers sent telegrams next day to her father and to Walter's brother George, asking them to come at once. Meanwhile she went out during the same night to find their local doctor (who lived close by) and ask whether something could be done to restrain her husband's actions. Since the cheques had already been drawn there was in fact only one means of stopping them at this stage.

What followed for Walter Marshall next morning was a scene not unworthy of Kafka. As he was eating breakfast in his room he glanced out of the window, saw a man coming to the front door, and went down to let him in. This turned out to be their doctor, Dr Seton, who came into the breakfast room, asked about the health of his wife and children, and then told him that he had been behaving in a very excited manner and that he required medical care. Walter demurred and after further conversation and breakfast left the room to go to his study, only to find Seton following him and in his study another man sitting whom he had never seen before. This man, introduced as Seton's friend Dr James, began talking to him in turn; after a while, as he began to suspect what was going on, he heard the voices of two further men downstairs. He suggested that he should send a note to a friend of his whom he would like to bring into the discussion and Seton agreed but asked him to put on his boots so that they could go together. Complying with the request, Walter told him that he trusted him on his honour that that was what was going to happen. When they reached the front of the house, a hansom cab and a four-wheeler were standing outside and Walter made for the front one. Immediately, however, he was seized by the two other men, who turned out to be keepers from a local asylum, and while Seton went off in the hansom he was bundled into the second cab and driven to Munster House in Fulham, where he was kept in a public room until the afternoon, when the supervisor, Dr Blandford, explained that he was being detained there because he had been certified by the two doctors. Walter did not know on what evidence he had been committed or who had asked for the order. In trying to affirm his sanity he found himself in a situation that was again reminiscent of Kafka: the more violently he protested, the more his behaviour was seen to confirm the symptoms of excitability. Since his wife had consented to the certification and signed the document, moreover, the matter was now out of her hands; Walter was left to make what appeals he could on his own. On the 13th he was transferred for the time being to Ticehurst Hospital in Sussex,[84] a fee-paying institution, which at least enabled him to maintain himself in greater comfort, being allowed a carriage and horses for excursions into the country and running up modest bills with the tailor, the hosier, the stationer, the tobacconist, and the perfumer. He also purchased cricketing pads.[85] He still continued to protest, nevertheless, that he was not insane and should not be there at all.

The records kept at Ticehurst survive, including the original certification and the doctor's case notes. From these, and from his own later account to the Commissioners for Lunacy, it emerges that Walter Marshall corresponded with them and that two of them visited him but recommended against him. On 31 May he was offered an interview with Sir William Gull, who reported, 'I cannot doubt the necessity of medical supervision and care in this case';[86] he then asked his wife to request that he should be examined by two doctors independently. When this eventually happened, on 28 July, they wrote differently:

That Mr. Marshall during a long conversation said nothing that was incoherent, or, so far as we were informed, inconsistent with fact. That

---

[84] I am indebted for initial knowledge of this part of the story to Charlotte Mackenzie's *Psychiatry for the Rich* (1992), where her account of Ticehurst includes the case of Walter Marshall in outline. It was also from her book that I learned of Marshall's evidence before the Select Committee.

[85] See the Patients' Bill Books for 1876, p. 301.

[86] *Committee Report*, 421.

he was excitable in manner, and rapid in his mode of reply to questions; but the excitability of manner, and rapidity of talking, were not such as to appear morbid.[87]

'From what we saw of Mr Marshall,' they reported further, 'we should have felt it to be impossible for us to certify that he was of unsound mind.' They commented in addition, however, 'that serious disease of the brain was imminent, and that it was probable that "general paralysis" would be developed hereafter': they were therefore 'of the opinion that Mr Marshall need not be any longer detained in an asylum; but also that it would be unsafe for him to be placed entirely at liberty at the same time'. Their concluding recommendation was that he should have leave of absence for a period, during which time he should have an attendant and be under the supervision of a medical man. Since it was not then clear who should act on this report, nothing was done for a time.

When Walter was eventually discharged he remained, not unnaturally, resentful of the way in which the affair had been handled and was given an opportunity to testify before a parliamentary select committee on lunacy laws.[88] In appearing before it he was apparently allowed access to his certification and so was able to comment on its evidence point by point, seeking throughout to establish a clear distinction between his excitability (fully admitted by him but regarded simply as a nervous affliction) and insanity proper. While the extravagance of his behaviour and the unaccustomed violence of his language no doubt brought him into a zone where his sanity might be questioned, his contention that he was not clinically insane seems justified.

In registering his protest he was presumably not given access to his own case notes, which record that after settling in reasonably well at first he began to behave disruptively, being extremely active and talkative and awaking early each morning. He was also said to be abusive to the attendants but well-

---

[87] Ibid. 422

[88] His testimony was subsequently published in *Committee Report*. The surviving sources of information concerning the episode are of different kinds, therefore, consisting of the medical records left by the doctors who certified his insanity (including the certificate itself), Annie Marshall's report on his recent condition, the hospital's case notes, and Walter's formal testimony before the select committee.

mannered to those in a position of authority. Since the latter were kept fully informed of his behaviour towards everyone else who was treating him, however, they were not likely to be favourably impressed by such selective deference.

Although such behaviour evidently induced some hostility, it is nevertheless hard at first sight to see why the report by the two doctors was not acted on immediately, and indeed why they seemed to be facing in two directions, saying in one and the same document that there was no need for him to be detained and that it was not advisable for him to be released. The key to this curious equivocality is to be found by reading between the lines of the case notes, which record that on 24 May he confessed to having suffered a severe attack of syphilis at the age of 21. Although the notes contain no direct comment, this information evidently convinced the doctors that his current behaviour was a result of the earlier episode and that his condition was moving steadily towards that of General Paralysis of the Insane. This view was presumably communicated to others who saw him. From now on behaviour that would support such a diagnosis was faithfully recorded: it was noted for instance that his paintings were 'mostly of a gaudy, sensational and jerky character' and that some, where much colour was grouped into purposeless masses, presented the 'typical G.P. appearance'.

While the later doctors were no doubt moved partly by a desire to save the face of their colleagues the duality of their report was consistent with a belief that though Walter was not at present insane he soon would be. After Gull examined him, Myers had reported on the situation to Sidgwick: 'Gull has seen W. & expresses a very unfavourable opinion. Newington tells me he thinks he will never leave Ticehurst. W. is now angry and complaining of plots etc. w^h. much distresses A.'[89] It is not clear whether Annie was ever apprised of the reasons for the further working diagnosis, but in either case its effects could not but be unwelcome. To know that her husband was not considered insane after all, yet that on medical advice he was being kept in confinement must have been bewildering. Nor can it have been a comfortable reflection that the most pressing motive for her

[89] Letter of 3 June: TCL MS 12[132].

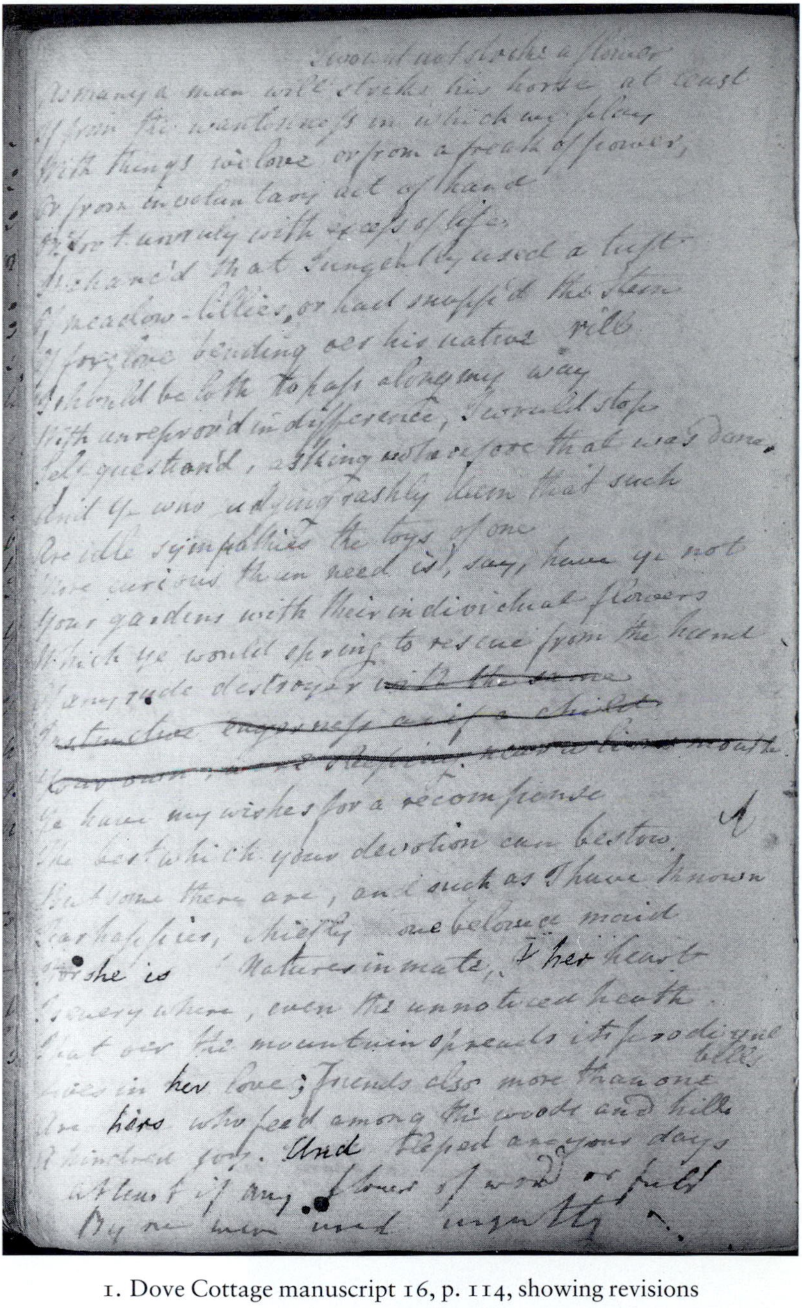

I would not strike a flower
As many a man will strike his horse at least
If from the wantonness in which we play
With things we love or from a freak of power,
Or from involuntary act of hand
Or foot unruly with excess of life
It chanc'd that I ungently used a tuft
Of meadow-lillies, or had snapp'd the stem
Of foxglove bending o'er his native rill
I should be loth to pass along my way
With unreprov'd indifference, I would stop
Self-question'd, asking wherefore that was done.
And ye who judging rashly deem that such
Are idle sympathies the toys of one
More curious than need is, say, have ye not
Your gardens with their individual flowers
Which ye would spring to rescue from the hand
Of any rude destroyer ~~[illegible]~~
~~[illegible]~~
~~[illegible]~~
Ye have my wishes for a recompense
The best which your devotion can bestow.
But some there are, and such as I have known
Far happier, chiefly one beloved maid
For she is Natures inmate, & her heart
Is every where, even the unnoticed heath
That o'er the mountain spreads its prodigal bells
Lives in her love; Friends also more than one
Are hers who feed among the woods and hills
A kindred joy. And blessed are your days
At least if any flower of wood or field
By one ever used ungently

1. Dove Cottage manuscript 16, p. 114, showing revisions

2. F. W. H. Meyer in Scarborough at the age of 30

3. F. W. H. Meyer in later life, painting by William Wontner

4. Hallsteads as it is today

5. Broadlands in the late nineteenth century

6. Ruskin: portrait of Rose La Touche
in water colour

7. Ruskin: portrait of Rose La Touche
in water colour

8. Ruskin: portrait of Rose La Touche
in water colour

9. Ruskin: pencil drawing, *Portrait of a
Girl's Head on a pillow*

original night expedition to seek medical help had been to stop the payments just authorized—even if certification was the only means by which this could have been accomplished. As she reflected on her recent conduct she must have felt that it had fallen below the highest moral standards. Walter himself was to report that during the six days in May between his first confinement and the visit by the Commissioners 'there was a greater strain on my powers than ever I wish to go through again'; his own previous behaviour might have been insensitive but the action she took had brought him acute suffering.

The fact that Walter was 'complaining of plots' was a further source of anxiety. While apparently accepting that the relationship between Annie and his cousin was honourable he might well have felt jealousy, accompanied perhaps by a suspicion that they would find it not inconvenient to have him out of the way. There is said to be a tradition in the family that at this time Annie and Myers decided not to see one another while Walter was still confined.[90] In view of his condition Annie may have insisted on a more permanent separation: an entry in Myers's diary on 2 July reads simply 'Miss Froude and A. on balcony. Farewell.' (The last word may have been written in later.) Myers was making preparations for a tour of Norway with his brother Arthur, while it had been decided that she should go off to Yorkshire to stay with her father. In early August he departed, his boat being by chance on the Humber during a moonlit night by the shore of the county where she had gone.[91] He referred to the subsequent separation later in his memoir, when he was looking back on the spiritual ecstasy their love had brought:

I felt all this through saddest separation; while on Norwegian fjords above the long gulf of liquid darkness 'the immeasurable heavens Brake open to their highest,' and the precipice barred with blackness the desolate influx of the sea. 'I shall see her some time,' I would say to myself,—'ἔσσεται ἤ ἤως ['there will be the dawn']—morn or noon or evening shall it be when my eyes shall meet hers once more, and I shall

---

[90] Gauld, *Founders*, 121.

[91] The incident is recorded in a poem 'Iamque Vale': Myers, *FIL* 20–1. It is likely that Annie's father took her at this time to The Hall in Thornton Dale where she had been brought up and which was still his home: Gauld, *Founders*, 121. Myers visited him there in September of the following year: TCL MS Myers 12[133].

speak and hear my fill.' But that was not to be by morn or noon or evening of any earthly day.[92]

The last sentence hints at the tragic conclusion to the affair. Annie was now trapped in a situation where her love for her children kept her locked into her role as mother, while the husband to whom she felt equally bound was in confinement for the foreseeable future. Meanwhile the man she loved most was separated from her, perhaps for good.

The decision that her father should look after her for a time seems in these circumstances to have been particularly unfortunate, since it restored Annie to the environment she had left at her marriage: that of a clergyman's daughter, with its implicit moral demands. For someone brought up in accordance with a strict conventional code the nobility of Myers's love for her could not obscure the fact that she had involved herself in betrayal of her marriage vows. The move away from orthodox Christianity that she had been following in Myers's company must have become a matter for regret also, her sense of guilt being further barbed by recollection of the financial motive for seeking her husband's certification. Matters were compounded by Walter's current condition and his talk of plots.

The fiction of the time is again relevant: Sue Bridehead's reversion to her former religious allegiance in *Jude the Obscure*, published twenty years later, provides a parallel instance of the religious dilemmas a young woman could face from alternating allegiance to the demands of love and of conventional morality and the consequent effects on her mental and physical health. Myers, like other members of the family, was evidently concerned about her current plight, as may be judged from his comment on a similar case in the following year.[93]

When she returned from her stay in Yorkshire Annie, finding

---

[92] Myers, *FIL* 40. The quotation is from Tennyson's 'Specimen of a Translation of the Iliad in Blank Verse', lines 14–15, where the reference is to the appearance of the stars in all their profusion: *The Poems of Tennyson*, ed. C. Ricks (1969), 1157.

[93] 'Mrs Stuart is in a most distressing state; very severe & heartbreaking sorrows have reduced her to a state of exhaustion & nervousness much resembling Annie's. I fear that it is by no means impossible that she may become insane. She is one of the best & noblest people whom I have ever known, and it is most terrible to me to see her sliding down the dark path way w[h] may have such a tragedy at its foot.' TCL MS Myers 12[143]. Hitherto unpublished. Once again 'noble' has become the key word to describe the tragedy of a person in such a state.

her responsibility too much 'in the face of perpetual reproaches' asked, together with her father, for a family conference at the Marshalls' house on Derwent Island to discuss the current problems. She offered to take charge of Walter; such a course of action was immediately ruled out, given her present state of health; instead it was decided that Walter should leave Ticehurst and be put under a doctor in Brighton. Five people should be in charge of his affairs and Annie's father would deal with any communications, all responsibility being taken out of her hands.[94] Her aunt, Myers's mother, returned with her to Old Church, the house by Hallsteads on the shore of Ullswater where she and Walter stayed when visiting there, and then left her on being reassured that she did not need any one to stay with her, hoping that her state of mind would improve now that she was back with her children and a governess who was 'helpful & cheerful'.

Instead, however, an event followed that was to shock the neighbourhood. The subsequent report in one local newspaper began, 'It is our painful duty to record a very melancholy event'; that in another, 'Probably a sadder and more determined case of self-destruction is not to be found in local annals than that which we record today.'[95] Susan Myers, who heard what had happened while travelling alone in Edinburgh, hastened to write to Scandinavia so that her son should learn what had happened and not hear the news from elsewhere:

Dearest Fred   it is very terrible to me to have to write bad news to you—but it may reach you by newspapers—Our poor darling Annie is gone from us—the strain on mind and body was too great. Indeed indeed we must try and think that she has found the rest and peace which have been so sorely wanting to her lot. I *know* you will feel this after a time—and that her life had little prospect save of continued pressure & suffering. But the manner ⟨of her death⟩ has been a terrible shock. I sup. you will see that—but it may be that your attention will not be drawn to it. If you *can* keep it from Arthur during the rest of your time—I shd. be thankful—I fear it will destroy much of the good of his travelling.

---

[94] Letter to Myers from his mother of 22 Aug. 1876, TCL MS Myers 15[131].
[95] *Penrith Observer* for 5 Sept. 1876, p. 6; *Penrith Herald*, 2 Sept. 1876, where the account appeared under the headline 'Painful Suicide of a Lady in Lake Ullswater'.

I had been very anxious—we all had—at the fixed stony look in her face—She grew silent towards me, after havg been *quite* frank & loving—& I could not with all my entreaties get her to speak of what was in her mind, after she had once said that she saw she had been quite wrong in every thing—in this last step for W. (the certif.) & altogether @ religion—in rejecting Xtianity—hoped she w^d pass thro' this crisis—& get a fuller happier faith—she was continually praying & getting me to read T. a. Kempis to her—We came together on Mon^y—& she brightened up during the drive & talked more like herself—I left her at O. ch. at 7 P.M. thinking the children w^d. cheer her. Next morng. she was missing—a shawl lay by the lake—& in deep water she was found—It has been a terrible time—but I have not broken down—& all have tried to do their best.—I think of little else—but indeed I grow calm in thinking of her as at peace.

Along the top of the letter she wrote

A letter from you came too late & is burnt. ~~the~~ Mr and Mrs Hill came—& will write—the funeral at Thornton. Don't hurry home—There is nothing to be done. E. will be with me.—

and then, in addition,

I know how much M^r Gurney will feel this—My kindest remem^ces to him—I open my note & put in—[96]

The reference to Thomas à Kempis's *Imitation of Christ* suggests that in her extremity Annie may have felt kinship with Maggie Tulliver, who had turned to the same devotional writer in her distress.[97]

The suicide took place on 29 August. Full reports of the inquest, which was held at Old Church on the 31st, appeared immediately afterwards, with particularly detailed accounts in newspapers at Penrith and Carlisle, the nearest large towns. They confirm and amplify Mrs Myers's account, adding details which she either did not know or withheld to spare her son. Annie's maid, Ada Watson, reported how the morning after her mistress had returned from Derwentwater she had entered her room to find her absent, with her dress lying on a chair; she had also noticed blood in her footbath and the apparent remains of blood in the basin, with a pair of blood-stained scissors nearby.

---

[96] TCL MS Myers 15^150. Quoted in part Gauld, *Founders*, 122.
[97] See *The Mill on the Floss*, Book IV, ch. iii.

When the lake was searched her body was found in it at a depth of 12 feet, dressed in a nightgown, a pair of red stockings and a petticoat. A wound had been inflicted on either side of the jugular vein.

Her father, also called as a witness, 'gave his evidence amidst painful emotion, and several of the jurors were also moved to tears'. He reported that she had been in 'intense trouble'[98] in May and that he had stayed with her on that account. At Derwentwater she had made a proposal to him concerning her husband (presumably that she should now look after him) which had been regarded as quite impossible in her state of health, and when he left on the Tuesday she told him she had had no sleep during the night. He had noticed 'a particular stony look in her face' that he did not like; this was intensified when he bade her goodbye after breakfast. Both he and her maid attested her devotion to her children.[99]

Myers's mother wrote again to him and spoke of her increasing sense of irreparable loss, remembering 'her sweet affectionate patience, her angelic grace'.[100] He was naturally devastated, expressing his reactions in a succession of poems in the original version of *Fragments of Inner Life*. The tragic end, coming just over three years after they had first fallen in love, may not have been totally unexpected, since one of the poems speaks of illness, and even madness, but his grief was no less intense. The next chapter of his memoir contains an account of his state of mourning after his return to England; in Wordsworthian fashion, he sought consolation by contemplating the beauties of nature at their finest:

Some of the serenest hours of those mourning years were spent in that valley in the grounds of Hallsteads, on Ullswater, which has been

---

[98] It has been suggested, notably by Alan Jarman (see n. 146 below), that the 'trouble' (a word used also by Miss E. M. Froude in a letter to Myers at that time (TCL MS Myers 2[61])) was partly due to a new pregnancy on Annie's part. If so, it is to be assumed that Walter, not Frederic Myers, was the father. This would certainly help account for the intensity of her depression, but there is no hint of such a development in the surviving documents and certainly no hard evidence. The current situation with Walter was 'trouble' enough to account for use of the word.

[99] See reports mentioned above and that in the *Carlisle Journal* for 1 Sept. 1876, p. 5. Further reports which appeared in the *Carlisle Express* and the *Yorkshire Post and Leeds Intelligencer* for 2 Sept. (pp. 13, 3) add little or nothing of significance.

[100] Letter of 12 Sept. 1876: TCL MS Myers 15[132].

the setting of much of my inward life. Outside it lie the wilder beauties of Cumberland; within are a grandeur and solitude which foster without overwhelming the heart. There are tower and spire of cedar and cypress, high walls of flowering laurel, and rhododendrons massed amid the shade. There for many a twilight hour I have paced alone, and shaken from the thick syringas their load of scent and rain. The childhood of Phyllis also had been spent in a scene resembling this; she had been nurtured amid antique simplicity, and in an ancestral moorland home.

After quoting from William Morris he continues,

When I think of that valley I understand the hauntings of the earthward-hovering soul. For I haunt it now; even now, when I would think steadfastly of myself, my image comes to me as pacing that glade of silence, between the ramparts of impenetrable green. I feel a twilight that deepens into darkness, a calm where winds are laid, and in my own heart a grave intentness, as of one who strives to lift into an immortal security the yearning passion of his love.[101]

The description of the scene at Hallsteads here connects closely with another poem of Myers's, not published till long after his death, which is called 'In Twilight':

> When in late twilight slowly thou hast strayed
> Thro' wet syringas and a black-green shade,
> With one communing so, that each with each
> Knew not the interludes of ebbing speech,
> Marked not the gaze which thro' the dimness fell
> On beauty in the daylight loved so well:—
> Since in that hour the still souls held as nought
> The body's beauty or brain's responsive thought,
> Content to feel that life in life had grown
> Separate no longer, but one life alone;

---

[101] Myers, *FIL* 28, quoting lines from William Morris's *Sigurd the Volsung* in which Brynhild recalls her upbringing to Sigurd, concluding,

> There morn by morn aforetime I woke on the golden bed;
> There eve by eve I tarried mid the speech and the lays of kings;
> There noon by noon I wandered and plucked the blossoming things.

Morris's poem was published in 1876, the year of Annie's death, and the story of the lovers who lay with a sword between them preserving their chastity must have seemed poignantly relevant. The Valley at Hallsteads is in a part of the grounds that a visitor would pass through on the way to Old Church, the house on the banks of Ullswater a little way away where Annie and Walter usually stayed with their children when visiting.

Ay, and they guessed thereby what life shall be
When Love world-wide has shown his mystery.[102]

Such passages leave no doubt why Myers framed his posthumous message in the way that he did. The grounds of Hallsteads were henceforward associated for him with the central inner experience of his life, interpreted in Platonic terms.

As for the situation Annie had left behind her, the records are fragmentary. After her death Walter's brother took over responsibility as arranged, organizing his discharge from Ticehurst and his supervision by a doctor in Brighton. The case notes on 20 August record that his mind was as much disordered as on admission, and on 3 September that the news of his wife's death a week before had been communicated cautiously by his brother. ('He was excited . . . then . . . subdued—but he did not seem to be grieved to the extent that might have been expected.') The final note reads 'Discharged—Unimproved'. Two months later, when Walter sent some money to Ticehurst to be divided among his attendants, he enclosed a note in which he reported, 'I have been very well since I left and very busy'.[103] Whatever bravado there may have been in this his self-estimate was supported when he returned, taking up his former life and public duties. He remained deeply disturbed about the course of the whole affair, nevertheless, and on hearing that a Select Committee on Lunacy Law was sitting decided to appear before it. Whether in connection with this, or for his own satisfaction he enquired further into the circumstances of his certification, and in January 1877 received a letter of clarification from Myers, drafted as follows:

Dear Walter,
  Ernest has shown me your letter of the 25th, & his reply, to which I have little to add. Dr Jones seems not ⟨quite⟩ accurately to recollect the conversation at 20 Wilton Place. I, like Ernest, knew nothing of Mr Hall except what your Wife had told us of your account to her of transactions with him—We ~~gave~~ could therefore give no evidence on this point. As the Certificate will show you, my evidence was limited to two statements.

---

[102] This poem (the uncharacteristically wayward syntax of which might point to the existence of an omission) was commented on by W. H. Salter in 'F. W. H. Myers's Posthumous Message', loc. cit. n. 50 above, p. 9.
[103] Note among patient's papers at Ticehurst.

(1) That your normal manner showed the well-bred ⟨composure⟩ of an English gentleman.

(2) That your manner on the evening of May 2 was of an opposite character. My only other action in the matter was to despatch two telegrams, at your Wife's desire & in her name, on the morning of May 3, to her Father & to your brother George, requesting their immediate presence in town, & one to Julian, of similar purport. There can, I think, be no doubt that under any view of the circumstances it was right to despatch those telegrams:—which would doubtless have been sent whether I had consented to despatch them or not—I have no reason to believe that the steps which were taken were in any way suggested or modified by any opinion of mine.

~~I can most heartily unite with you in an expression of the profoundest regret that those steps were taken; not that I wish in any way to impugn the judgement or conscientiousness of any person concerned, but simply because I cannot conceive that any course of action or inaction could have resulted in greater misery~~.

I am very glad to receive your assurance that you have no unfriendly feeling towards Ernest or me. It would, I think, be a needless aggravation of calamities already sufficiently heavy if there were any division of feeling between you & those who ~~revere the memory of your noble Wife, and who ⟨earnestly⟩ desire that your and her children should be reared up to be all which she could have wished them to be~~ have deeply felt the sorrows of the past year, & earnestly desire your & your children's wellbeing.

I am always, ⟨dear Walter⟩

> Yours sincerely,
> FWH Myers

Walter duly appeared before the Select Committee and gave a long account, preserved in the minutes. Throughout his testimony he insisted that he did not wish to criticize the actions of any of his relatives, and that his purpose was simply to raise questions about the ease with which a person could be certified and taken away without their consent or proper evidence of insanity. Only once in the course of his evidence was the veil of his discretion lifted for a moment. When a member of the Select Committee sought to confirm that he was not attributing any malicious or interested motives to any person Walter replied 'Certainly not'. 'Throughout the whole transaction?' asked the member, to which Walter replied, 'No, certainly not malicious; I do not know about interested.'[104]

---

[104] Letter to Walter Marshall of 27 Jan. 1877: TCL MS Myers 11[185] *Committee Report*, minutes 9335–6, p. 426.

The pessimistic prognoses at Ticehurst proved in the event to be mistaken. He did not pass into General Paralysis of the Insane and once he returned to his former life there were apparently no signs of his condition recurring or deteriorating. Instead, he settled to a normal life—chastened no doubt by his experiences. He inherited Patterdale Hall from his brother and in due course became Deputy Lieutenant of the county. He married again in 1898, only a year before his death, after which his remains were buried in Patterdale churchyard, where a monument erected over them still stands.

Myers, meanwhile, who shared Shelley's view that human loves were not mutually exclusive, did not feel inhibited from finding happiness elsewhere if it were to offer itself, since the relationship with Annie seemed in any case to have belonged to another dimension of his life, and after two years began to look about him. When he wrote to his mother in February 1879, reassuring her about his feelings for the future, he again invoked Wordsworth:

Do not be anxious about earthly happiness for me:—I have nothing to complain of: my grief is of a kind w^h is common to the whole race, (& I would not change my memories for any other ~~life~~ hope)

Moreover I have really little fear but that most of my remaining years will be tranquil & fully occupied, & that some close affection will be raised up for me to make even this earth a home—

> 'The kindly nurse does all she can
> To make her foster-child, her inmate Man' &c[105]

The Wordsworthian quotation appealed to a code of reassurance shared between mother and son. Some years later when he had fathered children of his own, she was able to write to him 'May they also become "beings breathing thoughtful breath— As travellers betwixt Life & death." '[106]

At the same time his tendency to be drawn to attractive young women did not go unnoticed in Cambridge circles. Caroline Jebb, American wife of his friend Richard Jebb (now Professor of Classics in Glasgow) was in the habit of commenting drily on

---

[105] TCL MS Myers 12^12, citing the 'Ode: Intimations of Immortality', ll. 82–3 *variatim*: *WPW* iv. 283.

[106] Letter of 4 Feb. 1893 (TCL MS Myers 15^57) quoting *variatim* from 'She was a phantom of delight . . .': *WPW* ii. 213–14.

the local scene each summer when she and her husband returned
to stay. In June 1878 a letter to her sister about her pleasant
times with the Butcher sisters (daughters of the late Bishop of
Meath) included the observation:

> Fred Myers is a goose, and we can't help all looking upon his affair
> as a sort of comedy. He is very companionable and with an insidious
> nature. Fanny says her mother is so afraid of him that she believes if
> there were no other way of keeping Eleanor, another sister, from his
> influence, she would leave London altogether. English people believe in
> prevention. Thus far he has had small chance of seeing Eleanor alone,
> and can have hardly made much impression on her affections.[107]

Myers knew the Butcher family well, and it is possible that the
mother, widow of the Bishop, had been put on her guard by
picking up some suggestion of the recent tragedy.[108] Meanwhile,
when Caroline heard in the following year that Myers was
visiting her native America her tongue was sharpened again:

> Henry James' story in the *Cornhill*, 'The International Episode', struck
> his imagination as presenting a very attractive picture of American
> young ladies, and I am sure he has gone over with many ideas of
> amusing himself. *He* does not see that his girth is wide, his hair thin, his
> thirty-five years fully printed on face and figure, and that the only kind
> of person fitted to *attract* him, would scorn him.[109]

This time, however, her forecasts proved wide of the mark:
shortly after his return Myers was introduced in London to a
young woman, Eveleen Tennant, whose portrait by Millais he
and Annie had admired a few years earlier when they saw it at
the Royal Academy.[110] He proposed and (after some hesitation
on her mother's part) was accepted. (Apart from commenting
on her once as a 'barmaid beauty'[111] Caroline Jebb ignored her
thereafter.) Myers was self-admonitory: 'May I so learn these
lessons in my felicity that it may never seem needful to Provi-

---

[107] Bobbitt, *Dearest Love*, 141.
[108] The accounts of the tragedy involving Annie Marshall appear to have been
confined to newspapers published in the North of England; it is unlikely that anyone
in his own circle who did not already know of his attachment to her heard of it, or
would have connected it with him if they had.
[109] Ibid. 153.
[110] See his letter of 1 Jan. 1881: TCL MS Myers 12[146]?
[111] Bobbitt, *Dearest Love*, 159.

dence to send me desolating sorrow again!'[112] In the following year his delight was still being darkened by forebodings of further tragedy,[113] but these remained unfulfilled and the marriage was duly celebrated in the Henry VII chapel of Westminster Abbey. By his own account all turned out happily; among their three children was Leopold Henry Myers, later to achieve success as the author of novels that included the trilogy *The Root and the Flower*.[114] Towards the end of his autobiographical fragment Myers describes the pleasures of his married life, with his children outside bounding 'like leverets' on the lawn, and insists that his reason for not dwelling on their happiness there is simply that in the present context that is not his concern. During his lifetime Eveleena herself became an accomplished amateur photographer.[115]

The tragic episode of a few years before remained meanwhile a powerful, even overwhelming memory, Myers being firm in his conviction that the love he had known with Annie Marshall differed from and transcended other kinds. Although he could not write about it openly its effects haunted his writings for the rest of his life. In an essay on Virgil, for instance, he dwelt on the splendour of Dido and her love for Aeneas, yet maintained that Virgil's description did not contain the essence of his beliefs concerning love, which he found, surprisingly enough, in his references to the young female warrior Camilla. Her brightness and grace, he thought, pointed to the kind of femininity that was coming to be valued in Virgil's time, and looked forward to the view of woman that would develop in the Middle Ages, culminating in Dante's Beatrice. At the height of his first feelings of love for Annie, in June 1873, he had written in his journal 'TIBI ENIM · VIRGO QUAS DICERE GRATES' [For to thee O maiden,

---

[112] Letter to his mother of 12 Mar. 1880: TCL MS Myers 12[16]. Hitherto unpublished.

[113] '. . . such deep & continuous drafts of [happiness] . . . And one fears lest it be taken from me.' Letter of 1 Jan. 1881, TCL MS Myers 12[17].

[114] No doubt things did not always run smoothly. Alan Gauld quotes Leo Myers's description of his father as 'Theodore Pontifex the Second' (Gauld, *Founders*, 331 n., from Granville Bantock, *L. H. Myers: A Critical Study* (1956), 137) and mentions a report of an unpublished poem by J. K. Stephen satirizing Myers's tempestuous relations with his wife (Ibid. 329 n.). Whatever the truth of the matter her entries in his Journal after his death bear witness to her utter dereliction.

[115] Examples of her work were shown in an exhibition 'Three Women Photographers' at the National Portrait Gallery in 1994.

what thanks shall I utter?]—a phrase which in the *Aeneid* is addressed to Camilla.[116]

In his *Modern Essays*, a few modern figures held up as deserving of admiration for their loftiness of intent include Mazzini, as a statesman who combined the qualities of lover, patriot, and saint and whose love for Italy resembled 'that love which the world has agreed to take as the loftiest type of individual passion, the love of Dante for Beatrice', loves 'wholly free from self-assertion and jealousy', both of them 'intensified and exalted by sorrow'.[117] A similar adherence to high principle is found in other contemporary figures: in France George Sand, Ernest Renan, and Victor Hugo, in England Archbishop Trench, Arthur Stanley, and George Eliot. All are characterized for him by a high seriousness, a striving to reach a truth which they can honour. The last essay, 'Rossetti and the Religion of Beauty' strikes an even more distinctive note. While by no means uncritical of the new aestheticism and religion of beauty that was growing up about him, he argued, throughout, that it was an irresistible current in an age when artists had been set free both from the spirit of self-mortification and from the enslavement of jealous orthodoxy, and the increasing material riches available for the purchase of works of art and the resulting security for artists had given them an increasingly powerful place in society. It was all the more important to ensure a due purification and refinement of this new culture.

Rossetti, who was not only named after Dante but had translated his *Vita Nuova*, was quoted repeatedly—especially his verses on the phenomena of love and its elevating power:

...as the lover moves amid these mysteries it appears to him that Love is the key which may unlock them all. For the need is not so much of an intellectual insight as of an elevation of the whole being—a rarefaction as it were of man's spirit which Love's pure fire effects, and which enables it to penetrate more deeply into the ideal world...

[116] Virgil, *Aeneid*, XI. 508. The chief description of her as warrior-maiden is in book VII. 803–17. Brief quotations from Virgil, usually in capitals, are notably frequent in the Journal. Myers may have been seeking apposite tags for particular occasions, or he may possibly have had recourse to the 'sortes Virgilianae', the practice of opening Virgil at random and lighting on the first phrase that met one's eye, noting it down if it seemed appropriate.

[117] Myers, *EM* 54.

Myers goes on to clarify how in this rarefied air the lover has, in the words of Plato, set sail upon the ocean of Beauty:[118]

The inexplicable suddenness with which Love will sometimes possess himself of two several hearts—finding a secret kinship which, like a common aroma, permeates the whole being of each—has often suggested the thought that such companionship is not in reality now first begun; that it is founded in a pre-natal affection, and is the unconscious prolongation of the emotions of an ideal world.[119]

The whole of this long discussion is freighted with memories of his own, together with a significant distinction: 'Rossetti could never have summoned us to the clear heights of Wordsworth's *Laodamia*. Yet who can read *The House of Life* and not feel that the poet has known Love as Love can be—not an enjoyment only or a triumph, but a worship and a regeneration . . . Love, as Plato said, is . . . "the interpreter and mediator" between things human and things divine'.[120]

This is the point to which Victorian Wordsworthianism had arrived, and although Wordsworth himself would not have endorsed such a development it was consistent with Myers's ideals. The story of his love for Annie Marshall and their attempt to maintain it on the highest level can be read as a sublimer version of the values of affection and duty that Wordsworth had bequeathed to his successors. However absolute the demands of a human love might seem they are still submitted to the stern code of honour. Read against knowledge of the sacrifice which he believed that he and Annie had made in response to those demands the discussion of Wordsworth's *Laodamia* in his 1880 study resonates beyond the poem into an affirmation of high principle. For reasons which will by now be

---

[118] Ibid. 323–4.

[119] Ibid. 322.

[120] Ibid., 333–4. Without knowing much of Rossetti's life he claims that he must have known deep bereavement, and goes on to speak of lovers in whom, after such loss 'the change which comes over the passion of love is not decay but transfiguration, in a manner that recalls Plato's belief that admiration could extend itself "from one fair form to all fair forms" and from fair forms to noble and beautiful ideas and actions, and all that is likest God'. Later he emphasizes the point: 'When Love had been made known to him by life itself and death—then he had at least gained power to show how the vaguer worship may become a concentrated expectancy: how one vanished hand may seem to offer the endless welcome, one name to symbolize all heaven, and to be in itself the single hope.' Ibid. 328–31.

sufficiently evident, he deplored the final versions that concluded with the reflection that Laodamia's fate was that of one
'not without crime', preferring the first, used also by Matthew
Arnold in his 'admirable volume of selections':

> Ah judge her gently who so deeply loved!
> Her, who, in reason's spite, yet without crime,
> Was in a trance of passion thus removed;
> Delivered from the galling yoke of time
> And these frail elements—to gather flowers
> Of blissful quiet 'mid unfading bowers.

The avowed origin of Wordsworth's poem brought Myers
back once again to the admiration for Virgil he had sustained
throughout life. At the same time his account of Wordsworth's
achievement reflects the dignity and pathos of his own situation:

Under the powerful stimulus of the sixth *Aeneid*—allusions to which
pervade *Laodamia* throughout—with unusual labour, and by a strenuous effort of the imagination, Wordsworth was enabled to depict his
own love *in excelsis*, to imagine what aspect it might have worn, if it
had been its destiny to deny itself at some heroic call, and to confront
with nobleness an extreme emergency, and to be victor (as Plato has it)
in an Olympian contest of the soul. For indeed, the 'fervent, not
ungovernable, love,' which is the ideal that Protesilaus is sent to teach,
is on a great scale the same affection which we have been considering
in domesticity and peace; it is love considered not as a revolution but
as a consummation; as a self-abandonment not to a laxer but to a
sterner law; no longer as an invasive passion, but as the deliberate habit
of the soul. It is that conception of love which springs into being in the
last canto of Dante's *Purgatory*, which finds in English chivalry a noble
voice,—

> I could not love thee, dear, so much,
> Loved I not honour more.

For, indeed, (even as Plato says that Beauty is the splendour of Truth,)
so such a Love as this is the splendour of Virtue; it is the unexpected
spark that flashes from self-forgetful soul to soul, it is man's standing
evidence that he 'must lose himself to find himself,' and that only when
the veil of his personality has lifted from around him can he recognize
that he is already in heaven.[121]

---

[121] Myers, *Wordsworth*, 114–15.

There are other moments in his book—his accounts of the 'Lucy' poems, for instance—when the experience of his own love helped to shape his sense of what Wordsworth had been about as a poet. I have argued above, against some common asssumptions, that the first two, at least, of the poems normally grouped under that heading must have been based directly on an actual experience of love and bereavement on Wordsworth's part and that all are related to it in some way. Myers, at least, would have needed no convincing at all, since his own experience had brought him to a similar conclusion:

And here it was that the memory of some emotion prompted the lines on *Lucy*. Of the history of that emotion he has told us nothing; I forbear, therefore, to inquire concerning it, or even to speculate. That it was to the poet's honour I do not doubt; but who ever learned such secrets rightly? or who should wish to learn? It is best to leave the sanctuary of all hearts inviolate, and to respect the reserve not only of the living but of the dead. Of these poems, almost alone, Wordsworth in his autobiographical notes has said nothing whatever. One of them he suppressed for years, and printed only in a later volume. One can, indeed, well imagine that there may be poems which a man may be willing to give to the world only in the hope that their pathos will be, as it were, protected by its own intensity, and that those who are worthiest to comprehend will be least disposed to discuss them.[122]

This passage can be set against the reference in the autobiographical fragments to his love for Annie Marshall:

There are reasons—reasons which discredit neither her nor me—why I cannot give this tale in full. Nor are its actual names and facts of any permanent importance. Its inner meaning I shall give, and should any reader attempt to discover what is here held in reserve, let him know that it is not for him that I have written; and that I scorn him as a prying intruder upon joys and sorrows such as he can never share.[123]

Later he writes that (in contrast to Wordsworth's Peter Bell)

Lucy's whole being is moulded by Nature's self; she is responsive to sun and shadow, to silence and to sound, and melts almost into an impersonation of a Cumberland valley's peace.[124]

[122] Myers, *Wordsworth*, 34.　　[123] Myers, *FIL* 17.
[124] Myers, *Wordsworth*, 139.

Did Myers know more about Wordsworth's Lucy than he was prepared to reveal? The possibility is at least worth considering. If as he believed the poems recorded actual events the person most likely to have known about them was Dorothy; and if Dorothy in turn had ever revealed them it would as surely have been to her closest friend Jane Marshall. It is just possible, therefore, that the story continued to circulate in confidence among members of the Marshall family, reaching Myers himself, and that his 'fortune, through hereditary friendships' to have had access to 'many manuscript letters and much oral tradition bearing upon the poet's private life'[125] included some knowledge about this episode.

However that may be, further tragic elements in the decline of Annie Marshall are reflected in Myers's account of Wordsworth. Just after one of his comments on the 'Lucy' poems he makes reference to another poem often associated with that group: 'The poem which begins " 'Tis said that some have died for love" depicts the enduring poignancy of bereavement with an "iron pathos" that is almost too strong for art.'[126] The lament in Wordsworth's poem, attributed to the man who lives 'Upon Helvellyn's side' and who has lost his Barbara, runs at one point

> 'Roll back, sweet Rill! back to thy mountain bounds,
> And there for ever be thy waters chained!
> For thou dost haunt the air with sounds
> That cannot be sustained . . .'[127]

It is notable that the poem Myers wrote reflecting on the fact (which he evidently found it hard to credit) that Annie had died without his being aware in the same instant, included the same image:

> No sound or sight, no voice or vision came
>     When that fulfilled itself which was to be,—
> The crash that whelmed mine inner world in flame
>     And rolled its rivers backwards from the sea.[128]

An unexpected Wordsworthian relevance emerges at another point in his study, also, when he refers to 'one home of pre-

---

[125] See above, p. 118 (Myers, *Wordsworth*, 2).
[126] Myers, *Wordsworth*, 114.
[127] *WPW* ii. 33.     [128] 'Feror ingenti circumdata nocte', *FIL* 21.

eminent beauty' as one of those which 'owed to Wordsworth no small part of their ordered charm':

In this way, too, the poet is with us still; his presence has a strange reality as we look on some majestic prospect of interwinding lake and mountain which his design has made more beautiful to the children's children of those he loved; as we stand perhaps in some shadowed garden-ground where his will has had its way,—has framed Helvellyn's far-off summit in an arch of tossing green, and embayed in towering forest-trees the long lawns of a silent Valley,—fit haunt for lofty aspiration and for brooding calm.[129]

As a grandson of Jane Marshall Myers was himself one of the 'children's children' of persons whom the poet had loved. We know that in 1816, when John Marshall bought some land by Buttermere and Crummock and consulted him, Wordsworth gave advice concerning the landscaping of the property,[130] but it has not hitherto been recognized that he had a hand in the landscaping of Hallsteads itself. By a strange twist to the story, in other words, Wordsworth himself helped to design the beauty of the scenes among which the sub-Wordsworthian romance between Frederic and Annie reached its intensest moments and where he spent many later hours mourning her loss.

The influence of Wordsworth on Myers emerges unobtrusively at other points in his career. He opposed the extension of the railways in Lakeland, for instance;[131] and as a young man, at least, he shared the view of capital punishment expressed in the later sonnets.[132] There was one respect, however, in which he did

---

[129] Myers, *Wordsworth*, 68.

[130] Moorman, *Wordsworth*, ii. 163, citing *The Letters of Sara Hutchinson*, ed. Kathleen Coburn (Toronto, 1954), 93.

[131] Just as Wordsworth had inveighed against the construction of a railway line between Kendal and Windermere, arguing that ordinary people needed to be educated in the wilder beauties of nature before they could profit from day excursions to see them (*Kendal and Windermere Railway: Two Letters Reprinted from the Morning Post* (1845): WPrW iii. 331–66). Myers, writing in 1883 against the proposal to drive a railway from Braithwaite to Buttermere (thus affecting Borrowdale) cited social reasons that differed only by invoking the doctrine of a higher evolution: 'What the children of poor artisans want is green grass, shady trees & blue sky:—such space for recreation as a park or Arboretum affords. The enjoyment of such scenery as Borrowdale comes at a higher stage in the social scale;—just as it came at a later date in our historical development.' (TCL MS Myers 11[212]. Hitherto unpublished.)

[132] See Una Taylor, *Guests and Memories* (Oxford, 1934), 258–60, cited Gauld, *Founders*, 100n. In 1868, when Henry Taylor was hard at work writing on the

not share his predecessor's habitual caution. Whatever his earlier attachments may have been, Wordsworth would not have been prepared to commit his central affections to a young woman simply because she radiated a sense of illumination. Such a phenomenon might in itself be amoral, shedding a delusive light that could lead the lover astray. His own attitude is expressed with precision in the verses about his wife that begin with the words 'She was a phantom of delight . . .',[133] where his appreciation of her early attractions includes the lines

> A dancing Shape, an Image gay
> To haunt, to startle, and way-lay . . .

Against this attractive but potentially dangerous effect he sets his growing appreciation of her human qualities, coming finally to

> The very pulse of the machine;
> A being breathing thoughtful breath,
> A traveller between life and death . . .

question of criminal reform, he wrote to him with his current views: 'I cannot agree in your wish to assimilate (the criminal's) condition to the condition of a lunatic in a well managed asylum. On the contrary, I think that of all classes whose treatment the nation is in any way called to determine, the lunatic ought to receive the best treatment and the confirmed criminal the worst.'
Myers went so far as to assert that once it had been established that a criminal was irretrievably set in his ways it would be better for everyone if he were put to death. It was a young man's conclusion, typical of his tendency to pursue a train of ideas to its logical conclusion; we have no means of knowing whether he later sustained that view—or indeed how it might or might not have been modified by his later views on immortality. The exact nature of Myers's political views is not easy to discover. He certainly liked the company of titled people and had a romantic enjoyment of the glamour involved. Through his friend R. H. Collins he came to know Prince Leopold, whom Collins had tutored (see below, p. 290) and even thought of asking him to be best man at his wedding as his closest friend, but was afraid the gesture might seem presumptuous. In this context it is worth noting that although Annie Marshall was brought up in stately surroundings, her family were not particularly aristocratic. In a letter to Myers after spending time with her mother and sisters while Annie and Walter were in Germany, his mother wrote, 'It is astonishing that Annie sh^d be what she is when one sees her family! Mrs H. is good-natured—but common-place & 2nd class in every way . . .': letter of August 1872 from Patterdale Hall: TCL MS Myers 15[95]. Hitherto unpublished. Myers was constantly brought into touch with people of all social classes through his work as a school inspector and his researches for the Society for Psychical Research, and his social views were probably, like those of many Victorians, mobile. The ambiguity of the word 'noble' could (as with Ruskin) move it up and down the actual social scale.

[133] *WPW* ii. 213: see also above, n. 106.

His wife has, in other words, spanned for him the gulf opened at the centre of 'A slumber . . .' by establishing a link between the revelatory quality that was so disturbingly undermined there and the depressing yet reassuring dependability exhibited by the rolling round of rocks and stones and trees.

Myers was more willing to commit himself to the spiritual when revealed in a physical illumination; in that respect, once again, his career and impulses corresponded less with those of Wordsworth than of Coleridge. We have already suggested a parallel between Myers's youthful tendency to push his behaviour to an extreme that might be condemned by the cautious and some incidents in Coleridge's early career. In his mature years, similarly, his love for Annie Marshall mirrored the course of Coleridge's for Wordsworth's sister-in-law Sara Hutchinson, which rested likewise on a belief that true love was revelatory. Coleridge wrote disparagingly of Wordsworth's idea of love, which he characterized as 'a compound of Lust with Esteem and Friendship'. Love, in his own view, was 'no more a compound, than Oxygen, tho' like Oxygen, it has an almost universal affinity, and a long & finely graduated Scale of elective Attractions.' His favourite comparison was with the moment of sunrise, when, however long and closely one had been watching for it the sun 'always *started* up, out of the horizon—!' The relation of love to other emotions was for him like that between the sun and a cloud, which, once called up by its presence, became equivalent to 'the Veil of Divinity'.[134] His thought found expression in a notebook poem, evidently about his love for Sara Hutchinson, which was first published (in a slightly different version) in the year of his death:

> All Look or Likeness caught from Earth,
> All accident of Kin or Birth,
> Had pass'd Away: there seem'd no trace
> Of Aught upon her brighten'd Face,
> Uprais'd beneath the rifted Stone,
> Save of one Spirit, all her own/
> She, she herself, and only she,
> Shone in her body visibly.[135]

---

[134] Letter of 12 Mar. 1811, *CL* iii. 304–5.

[135] *Poems*, ed. J. Beer (1993), 383. The poem, given the title 'Phantom', appears in one of Coleridge's 1805 notebooks (*CN* ii. 2441) but had evidently been written

Myers wrote similarly of such an experience:

> She wears her body like a veil
>     And very life is shining through;
> Her voice comes ringing on a gale
>     Of spirit-passion wild & new;
> O soul without a mate or name,
>     Divine & mortal, maid & boy,
> Shine out, & with a cry proclaim
>     The unguessed infinity of joy![136]

At the time when Myers wrote his studies of Wordsworth and of George Eliot the psychical research on which he had embarked was proving baffling and inconclusive. His goal of throwing light on the question of immortality seemed far away. His optimism was revived, however, when he heard of the work of a medium in America, Leonora Piper, who became one of the most successful psychic practitioners of her time. While other mediums were detected in fraud, or suspected of it, she submitted to every test proposed to her and was never detected in doubtful dealings. Some of the most hard-headed psychic investigators, including William James and Richard Hodgson, came to believe in the genuineness of her powers. In September 1893 Myers visited James at his house in the United States and was deeply impressed by what he heard from her—all the more so since he found her personally unappealing. Writing to James afterwards he thanked his wife for the warmth of her hospitality:

I shall not forget her gracious welcome . . . when in the midst of all her fatigue and her settling down after long absence she accepted as guests not only RH & myself but also that insipid Prophetess, that tiresome channel of communication between the human & the divine . . .[137]

---

by early 1804 (cf. 2055). Either it or the experience that inspired it might have been known to Wordsworth when he wrote the lines beginning 'She was a phantom of delight' (*WPW* ii. 213) about his wife.

[136] TCL MS Myers 29[15], p. 53, dated 1876. Myers, *CP* 353.

[137] Letter of 3 Feb. 1897, TCL MS Myers 11[155], p. 3. Others found her equally unattractive. Thinking about her own death, William James's sister Alice wrote that she 'hoped to Heaven that the dreadful Mrs Piper won't be let loose on my defenceless soul': *The Diary of Alice James*, ed. L. Edel (New York, 1964), 231. Alan Gauld examines the case against her as a medium critically in Gauld, *Founders*, 361–3, finding it heavily biased.

What she succeeded in conveying to him marked a 'great epoch'.[138] At some point in the same period Hodgson reported to Myers that Mrs Piper had begun receiving messages from a figure whom she called 'the bright lady', and who appeared to be Annie Marshall. When Myers expressed some scepticism— not surprisingly in view of the fact that after some early apparent messages so much time had elapsed without communication and that the message was now coming from so far away—he was told by Hodgson that Annie had asked Mrs Piper to put as a test of her identity the words 'syringa blossom'. Myers was deeply impressed—understandably in view of the descriptions of Hallsteads quoted earlier, in both of which the mention of syringa is associated with the memory of their love and twilight walks there.[139] The calmness with which he henceforward approached the question of human survival owed much to a renewed conviction that Annie Marshall had lived on in some form and that he would be reunited with her. In 1899, after sessions with another medium, Mrs Thompson, he wrote to Oliver Lodge that the year had brought him '*certainty*'.[140]

In a further series of essays, published under the title *Science and a Future Life* as he was gaining these new assurances, he presented the questions of survival less tentatively. Contending in an essay on 'Tennyson as Prophet' that the later poetry included some of his best—a view which was strengthened by Tennyson's late enthusiasm for Virgil—he also claimed him as having suggested the existence of a power of communication between human minds without sensory agency and as having been 'the prophet of a Spiritual Universe'; after Tennyson's death he referred back to that discussion in a footnote to a further essay, on 'Modern Poets and Cosmic Law': 'I have reason to believe that the line taken there, based partly on his own conversation, was not unacceptable to Lord Tennyson.'[141] In this culminating essay he affirms once again that the process

[138] TCL MS Myers 11[155], p. 2.

[139] See above, p. 166. It should be noted, however, that as W. H. Salter points out ('F. W. H. Myers's Posthumous Message', loc. cit. n. 50 above, p. 9) the poem was included in Myers, *FPP* 148, but not in the earlier collections or in Myers, *FIL*. This one could have been written *after* Mrs Piper's mention of 'syringas', therefore.

[140] Letter to Oliver Lodge, quoted Frank M. Turner, *Between Science and Religion* (New Haven, 1974), 114.

[141] Myers, *SFL* 160 ff, 168 n.

of evolution, whose message is 'Lay hold on Life', is to be fulfilled in the perception that there is in the end no limit to life, and that true lovers will discover this. Once again Plato on love as the realization of hidden yearnings is cited; he then continues,

Shall they not recognise that no terrene Matter or Energy, but Love itself is the imperishable of that higher world: so that earth's brief encounter with some spirit, quickly dear, may be the precursory omen of a far-off espousal, or the unconscious recognition of fond long-severed souls? Shall they not find that the lifelong loyalty to the touch of a vanished hand has been no vain or one-sided offering of the heart; but that the affection has been stablished by an unseen companionship, and that the Beloved has answered all?[142]

The mention of a 'vanished Hand' suggests something more than a simple quotation from Tennyson's 'Break, break, break . . .'. Myers remained haunted by the touch of a particular hand.

Twentieth-century attitudes have swung so far against belief in the kind of synthesis that Myers was looking for that it is now difficult to find a steady mode by which to contemplate his relationship with Annie Marshall. In its time it was simply an unusually intense, puritanical version of a situation that would have been familiar to readers if only from contemporary novels—particularly French ones. Several examples may be mentioned: Myers might, for example, have seen strange parallels in the adventures of his namesake Frederic in Flaubert's *Education Sentimentale* or in the behaviour of Eduard in Goethe's *Elective Affinities*. He himself, writing to George Eliot, had mentioned 'M$^{me}$ de Stael in Corinne, M$^{rs}$ Craven in Fleurange, George Sand in Consuelo' as writers who had achieved nobility, remembering, no doubt, that *Corinne* had been mentioned in *The Mill on the Floss*[143] and mindful, perhaps, that Maggie Tulliver could be compared with Consuelo—as indeed she had been by George Eliot's friend Sara Hennell.[144] A novel nearer in space and time, and more relevant to his own condition, was J. A. Froude's *The Nemesis of Faith*, first published by George Eliot's friend John

---

[142] Myers, *SFL* 207.        [143] Book v, ch. iv.
[144] Letter to George Eliot of 28 June 1860, MS at Yale, quoted Haight, *Eliot*, 335. Haight also mentions her reading of *Consuelo* (ibid. 59).

Chapman in 1849, about a young man who having lost his Christian faith formed an intense but platonic relationship with a married woman encountered on the shores of Lake Como while travelling on the continent. As in Goethe's novella the story ends tragically with the loss of the young woman's child, followed by her remorse and death. For those who find it difficult to believe that a relationship such as that between Myers and Annie Marshall would not have culminated in physical love-making, this novel provides an important contemporary corrective: not only is there no hint of adultery, but the narratorial tone is condemnatory in spite of that. It is assumed that notwithstanding his restrained behaviour Markham Sutherland was wrong to breach the conventional moral code by allowing himself to become involved with Mrs Leonard at all; the reader is even permitted to think that the culminating event, the death of the heroine's young child because the lovers were too preoccupied to notice when she became wet and cold in their boat on a summer evening, was a kind of divine judgement. Yet the fact that the novel was presented within the terms of conventional morality did not prevent its author from being condemned in contemporary Oxford for having published it, or the book from being publicly burnt in the hall at Exeter College, Oxford. Myers presumably knew Froude and his work;[145] to read *The Nemesis of Faith* as a characteristic novel of the time is to appreciate how far he was cutting across contemporary assumptions in acting on a belief that a platonic love affair with a young married woman could be sustained with perfect honour. It was a bold mediating stroke, an attempt to show how human beings might rise above the demeaning implications of living in a purely Darwinian universe by cultivating their affection while maintaining a strenuous devotion to principle. At that moment of intellectual history the ideals of Romantic love and the intellectual demands of a post-Darwinian world could between them channel thinking into the compacted apotheosis of a twin concept. Against conventional beliefs and the distillations of practical experience it was being held that true nobility could

---

[145] It is not clear whether the E. M. Froude who was also a friend of Annie Marshall's was a relation of J. A. Froude, who had a town house near them, at 5 Onslow Gardens.

transcend all the objections that a transgressive love would normally arouse.

From one point of view, clearly, Myers's conduct represented a kind of derangement, an extreme example of the tendency to overreach that was noted earlier in his behaviour. So far as he was concerned, one might reflect, it was all very well to undertake such a strenuous platonic love; he, after all, had no other commitments. But what did it mean for a woman who was married to a man no better or worse than most of his fellows and who had the responsibility for children whom she loved? How could such contradictory demands be sustained? His pressure on Annie to accept the tension involved, however much it might be attuned to the higher ideals of the period, seems in such a light an act of cruelty, however unconscious. Under this view what was for Myers a matter of principle and heroism turns him at the very best into a subject of pathos.

To treat Annie Marshall purely as victim is, however, to slight her own status as a mature woman, capable of making her own judgements. Any verdict on Myers's behaviour meanwhile involves appraisal of his personality as a whole, which is not altogether easy. There has been at least one attempt to brand him as a villain, pure and simple.[146] The few accounts of him that have survived from contemporaries present him in a variety of lights but not that one. Even Caroline Jebb thought of him simply as a 'goose'. Jane Harrison, describing him and his associates, wrote briefly, 'Frederic Myers rang, perhaps, the most sonorously of all, but to me he always rang a little false.'[147]

---

[146] After the publication of *Fragments of Inner Life* Myers's character was attacked by Alan Jarman, who believed that the relationship between the two lovers had become a physical one and that the reason for Annie's desperation was that she had been made pregnant by him. He found Myers's version unconvincing, citing his account of the Camden affair as an example of the mealy-mouthed way in which, he believed, he always shrugged off past crimes and misdemeanours: see 'Failure of a Quest', *Tomorrow* 12 (Winter 1964), 17–29 and *Dr Gauld and Mr Myers* (privately pub. 1964). His attacks were ably answered by Alan Gauld, who through his access to the Myers archive was able to demonstrate the falsity of some of Jarman's assumptions and give a fuller, better informed account. See Gauld, *Founders*, 122 n. and refs.

[147] *Reminiscences of a Student's Life* (1925), 55. First as an undergraduate (1874–9) and then as a lecturer (from 1898) at Newnham College, Jane Harrison had various opportunities of meeting Myers—notably through the Sidgwicks; it is a pity she said no more.

Her hint of an over-grandiloquence may be set against A. C. Benson's account:

I thought of him rather as something medieval and lordly—a Venetian merchant-prince, perhaps, with an outlook on life and letters, and with none of the limitations in life, nothing of the timidity of dealing with its fulness, that my own more puritanical bringing-up had imposed on me.[148]

This from the son of an Archbishop of Canterbury and a man whose private income enabled him to be elected a fellow of his college without needing to be paid may seem strange; it is even more unexpected to find Benson commenting, 'The perfect smoothness of his brow and cheek, the absence of all lines or dints of stress or experience, his leisurely carriage, gave a feeling of self-contained prosperity and stability. It still remains to me a thing to be wondered at that so little of the eagerness or rapture of life should have been visible, and no touch of dissatisfaction or unrest.'[149] This contrasts with an account by an earlier writer that referred to a smouldering effect in him, a hint of underlying vehemence,[150] with his own repeated insistences in *Fragments of Inner Life* on the passionateness of his nature, and with his daughter's mention of the supreme painfulness of the episode involving Annie Marshall.[151] It is clear that there was a marked disparity between the impression of himself that he gave to others through his demeanour, particularly in later years, and the workings of his inner nature, not unlike the duality that some of Wordsworth's contemporaries detected in him, even in old age.[152]

---

[148] *The Leaves of the Tree* (1911), 178, quoted Gauld, *Founders*, 145. Benson was related to the Sidgwicks and could have met Myers both through his family and during his undergraduate career at King's College, Cambridge (1881–4).

[149] Ibid. 180, quoted Gauld, *Founders*, 328.

[150] 'Fred Myers was exceedingly agreeable, but there is a fiery vehemence half apparent in him which made one feel that he might not be so to all men and in all moods.' Henry Taylor, quoted in Una Taylor, *Guests and Memories* (Oxford, 1934), 249.

[151] See n. 50 above.

[152] Isabella Fenwick commented that if his intellect had been less powerful he would have been destroyed long before by the strength of his feelings and affections: Letter to Henry Taylor of 4 Jan. 1839, quoted E. Batho, *The Later Wordsworth* (Cambridge, 1933), 37 n. See also my *Wordsworth and the Human Heart* (1978), 241.

The stress in Myers's psyche was not perhaps of equivalent intensity, since his faith in human immortality gave him an increasingly strong overriding sense of assurance. It resulted rather from his grand conception of the resulting beliefs. This was reflected in his own literary style, which modern readers may sometimes find jarringly florid. Although he could write on occasion with the rhythm of his own natural feeling and achieved his best effects when he was content to give himself up to the workings of his own intelligence, he suffered from the effects of an intellectual situation in which the tendency to write naturally and informally was in conflict with, and over-taking, older, classically inspired models. The language of aspiration is not always easily distinguished from that of false grandeur; indeed, Myers recognized something of this when he wrote in a comment on the manuscript of *Fragments of Inner Life*, 'I am perfectly aware of the literary detects of the style in which these chapters are written . . . But I cannot feel that I am entirely candid unless I write in this emotional, over-decorated style, wh. corresponds in some subtle way to the idiosyncrasy of the soul within.'[153] He was alive to the paradox set up by the twin demands of his vocation, remaining true both to his classical, Christian upbringing and to his youthful absorp-tion of sceptical modes while still working ardently for an end that he believed to provide a key to the problems of the age and a means of restoring the spirit, if not the letter of religion. The resulting blend would always be in danger of sounding a note of falsity.

His growing belief in human survival simply intensified the paradox of his situation: the more he became convinced that communication from beyond the grave was a reality, the more he had to recognize that his desire to solve the problem for mankind generally remained unsatisfied, since the kind of uni-versally acceptable evidence that he and other members of the Society felt it essential to discover was precisely what eluded them.

The episode of the posthumous message perpetuated the di-lemma for his successors. From one point of view its effect was

---

[153] Marginal note on MS of *FIL*, TCL MS Myers 26[63(7)], quoted Gauld, *Founders*, 330.

simply to emphasize the cryptic gap that lay between his memories of love and the beliefs that had continued to sustain him in his loss. If the automatic writing *really* came from him there was a neatly self-reinforcing effect: the gap to which it referred could be said truly to have been bridged—bridged by platonic love in precisely the manner it was itself claiming. If not, on the other hand, a chaotic gulf of uncertainty remained, to be dealt with by noble but logically-minded Darwinians in the manner that Sidgwick had envisaged: bravely but 'with an agnosticism growing yearly more hopeless'. The love between Frederic and Annie could then be contemplated only as a matter of pain and pathos.

To contemplate these alternatives and their ramifications could be dizzying, making it easier to set the question aside altogether; yet one's sense of this particular moment in Victorian intellectual history is not complete without the episode and all that surrounded it. The principals were participating, unawares, in a human tragedy; but for the truly disinterested reader it remains impossible to know whether or not it also irradiated, as Myers came to believe, the lineaments of divine comedy.

In the end, Myers's career may be said to have revolved round two conversations in gardens with two very different women, which between them brought to a fine point the most characteristic issues of the time. George Eliot's asseverations spelt out in starkest terms the implications of the Darwinism that he had recently found 'tidal'. In one sense there was a finality about her prophetic figure, standing permanently in his memory, sibylline in the gloom, as she withdrew from him two of the three scrolls of promise and left only the alternative of a stern adherence to duty, to be supplemented, in her terms, by a strenuously Wordsworthian cultivation of affection. For Myers that desperate sense of the modern predicament could be alleviated only if one could discover, through equally strenuous efforts, some assured evidence of personal immortality, underpinning human affections by restoring the awareness of a divine providence. Without such an assurance his position could be sustained only by falling back on the tentative platonic solution he had already formulated when he wrote in his letter to George Eliot that since there was no longer anything to keep an isolated fire burning within, 'All one can do is to feel the sparks fly from one for a moment when one strikes a kindred soul.'

Once that affirmation has been translated into the terms of Victorian innocence and cultivation of aesthetic sensibility the power, and the enigmatic effect, of the statuesque grouping that is the other focal point of the narrative is reinforced, giving that also a kind of permanence. One is left with the mediating image of Frederic Myers and Annie Marshall, still standing in the Valley at Hallsteads in the season when the syringa was giving off its subtle scent, as if they might stand there for ever— discovering as they looked, talked, and touched 'a secret kinship which, like a common aroma, permeates the whole being of each'. By the late nineteenth century it was the best version of providence a scientifically aware puritan Platonist could hope for.

# George Eliot and the Cambridge Ethos

GEORGE ELIOT came late to the older universities. Like Wordsworth and Southey, she found much to recommend itself in English provincial culture, with its grasp on practical realities and its high valuation of ordinary life; like Coleridge, she found it necessary to spend the most important part of her career in London, where her editorial role with the *Westminster Review* set her at the heart of current intellectual developments. In the first respect her discovery of Wordsworth had been, as is well known, an important turning point in her career. Coming to him from her Evangelical Christian background she announced in her enthusiasm, 'I never met with so many of my own feelings, expressed just as I could like them.'[1]

As she modified and retreated from her Christian orthodoxy Wordsworth offered a point of stability. The insistence in his later works that the twin values by which humanity must now guide itself were those of duty and affection seemed to her indisputable, providing a point of stability in the midst of change. It also helped her find a basic polarity in her own personality. It had long been a basic insistence in Evangelical Christianity that the sense of mercy with which one was urged to look on the shortcomings of others should be matched only by the severity with which one regarded one's own—a requisition that penetrated even the conclusion of Lewis's *Monk*;[2] Wordsworth's doctrines pointed to a way in which one could extrapolate this teaching from religion and convert it into one for humanity at large. Kant's philosophy, through its emphasis on the centrality of the human Will, gave powerful support to Wordsworth's insistence on duty; the Wordsworthian stress on

[1] The remark was made on her 20th birthday: Haight, *Eliot*, 29.
[2] Matthew Lewis, *The Monk* (3 vols., 1796), iii. 315.

affection, meanwhile, was matched by her own ideal of sympathy, giving scope for the cultivation of wit and humour—again in a fully humane setting.

While these values provided, as it were, twin pillars to her general position she could explore the full range of intellectual discovery that was exciting and appalling her contemporaries, a project in which she was greatly assisted by her partnership with George Henry Lewes from 1854. Their meeting of minds not only gave her strong support in her career as a novelist, but kept her fully *au fait* with the latest scientific developments—particularly those flowing from Germany.

It was Lewes who first brought her into contact with Oxford, through his being invited to the 1868 meeting there of the British Medical Association.[3] When she visited the university in 1870 she saw some of the customary sights of the colleges and visited Mark Pattison and his wife, who drove her by Littlemore, where the conventual dwellings set up by Newman were still to be seen. She also spent a good deal of time learning about the current state of science—watching Dr Rolleston dissect a brain, for instance, or hearing about the latest methods of mensuration from Sir Benjamin Brodie in his laboratories.[4]

At the same time she was completing and publishing *Middlemarch*, the novel in which she first showed fully what the play of her gifts and values could achieve. Yet although its publication enhanced her reputation in Oxford, there are no signs that she formed a deep attachment to the place. In 1873 Benjamin Jowett invited her to spend a day or two as his guest, and she found herself lionized; she returned speaking of the continuous excitement she had enjoyed and thereafter visited Jowett in most years at about the same time. Yet an element in her seems to have preferred the severer intellectual and moral atmosphere she experienced in some circles at Cambridge. When asked by Oscar Browning to characterize the two societies she told him that 'at Cambridge they all spoke well of each other, but at Oxford they all criticized each other'.[5] But at another level, she might well have endorsed the sentiment behind her friend Emily Davies's rather different summing up: 'I

---

[3] Rosemary Ashton, *G. H. Lewes: A Life* (Oxford, 1991), 248.
[4] Haight, *Eliot*, 428.
[5] Oscar Browning, *Memories of Sixty Years at Eton Cambridge and Elsewhere* (1910), 194.

am well used to the cool Cambridge manner. It is not half so pleasant as the way kind gushing Oxford men have, but it comes to more.'[6] That was the kind of setting in which her current concerns could be discussed more readily. On her first visit in February 1868, when she and Lewes were invited to Trinity College by William George Clark (an old friend of Lewes's who was then Public Orator) and Oscar Browning, Browning noted the seriousness of her mood at dinner:

We dined in the evening, a small party, in Mr Clark's rooms. I sat next to her, and she talked to me solemnly about the duties of life, about the shallow immorality of believing that all things would turn out for the best, and the danger of fixing our attention too much on the life to come, as likely to distract us from doing our duty in this world.[7]

Something about Cambridge—and particularly this college, perhaps—brought out the serious side of her personality. Trinity College had had an especial association with Wordsworth, where his brother Christopher had been master; during the same period Julius Hare, as Tutor, had championed the ideas of Coleridge. That had been in the 1820s, however, and although the university had later entertained Wordsworth and given him an honorary degree the effects of his teaching had by now dwindled; inasmuch as they lived on, it was by way of the moral and intellectual stringency displayed by individual members at their best—in the work of Henry Sidgwick, for example, whom she met for the first time on this visit.

The sense of growing intellectual crisis in England had found a point of particular focus in Cambridge. Four years earlier Leslie Stephen had departed, having decided that he could no longer subscribe to the Thirty-nine Articles of the Church of England and resigned the college fellowship which required him to; in the following year Clark himself was to resign his orders, followed soon by Sidgwick's resignation of his fellowship on the same grounds as Stephen's. Such sacrifices appealed to the moral strenuousness which was strong in her.

Sidgwick has already been mentioned as one of the most striking figures in the Cambridge of his time. His status as a leading philosopher whose studies included central work in the field of ethics was augmented by wide intellectual and literary

[6] Quoted by Q. D. Leavis, 'Henry Sidgwick's Cambridge': *Scrutiny*, 15 (1947–8).
[7] Oscar Browning, *Life of George Eliot* (1890), 99.

interests. He was also a pioneer in the cause of women's education, playing a major part in the founding of Newnham College.[8] Although, along with his friend Myers, he apparently met George Eliot for the first time during the 1868 visit, he already valued her novels for their realism.[9] When he called on her and Lewes in London he was relieved to discover that on such an occasion her solemn side was less dominant: 'Mrs Lewes said one or two things like the subtle humour of her books, which I should not have detected in her at Cambridge.'[10]

In the next few years George Eliot became depressed by the fact that she and G. H. Lewes were both in bad health and must be drawing towards the end of their lives. She was also deeply disturbed by events on the continent of Europe, as the Franco-Prussian War took its grim course and the realities of mechanized warfare began to be revealed. Sympathetic at first with Germany's cause, she was revolted by reports of Prussian ruthlessness at the battle of Sedan and realized that the kindly, scientific Teutonic nation she knew had now shown an ugly face, partly as an effect of the brutalization brought about by all warfare.[11] In 1871 she wrote of 'the myriad sorrows produced by the regression of Barbarism from that historical tomb where we thought it so picturesquely buried—if indeed one ought not to beg pardon of Barbarism, which had no weapons for making eight wounds at once in one body, and rather call the present warfare that of the Devil and all his legions.'[12]

---

[8] His role in the development of the Society for Psychical Research was mentioned earlier. In 1876 he married Eleanor Balfour, who between 1880 and 1910 became Vice-Principal and then Principal of Newnham and who shared his many interest in psychical research, serving as the Society's honorary secretary for many years before being elected to its presidency in 1908. For an account of Sidgwick's wide range of interests and his impact on the Cambridge of his time, particularly on the cause of feminine education there, see Q. D. Leavis, 'Henry Sidgwick's Cambridge': *Scrutiny*, 15 (1947–8), 2–11.

[9] See his letter of 1863, quoted *Sidgwick Memoir*, 91. Henry Jackson recorded that when several people who were in his rooms in 1865 drew up lists of their five favourite novels, he named the five of hers that had then been published: R. St John Parry, *Henry Jackson, O.M.* (Cambridge, 1926), 170.

[10] *Sidgwick Memoir*, 185. He did not like *The Spanish Gypsy* as poetry (ibid., 185–6) but remained devoted to her fiction. Later he remarked that (in contrast to Mrs Oliphant) 'her conversation is full of eager sympathy, but there is comparatively little humour in it' (ibid., 270).

[11] Letter of 2 Jan. 1871: *GEL* v. 131–2.

[12] Letter of 27 Jan. 1871: *GEL* ix. 9.

The War was for her a triumph of the amoral, mocking the ideas of human progress that had raised such hopes during her lifetime. It also threw into relief the virtues of England and the uncompromising integrity and strength of mind that impressed her in figures such as Sidgwick. Soon she was writing to Mrs William Cross,

Mr Henry Sidgwick is a chief favourite of mine—one of whom his friends at Cambridge say that they always expect him to act according to a higher standard than they think of attributing to any other chief man or of imposing on themselves. 'Though we kept our own fellow-ships without believing more than he did,' one of them said to me, 'we should have felt that Henry Sidgwick had fallen short if he had not renounced his.'[13]

In a manuscript account of his friendship with Sidgwick written in 1873 Myers recorded how it was Sidgwick's example that had led him to adopt a policy of complete candour—an ideal which he himself put into practice as he described his progression from an initial dislike of Sidgwick's apparent coldness on coming across him as an undergraduate (a dislike shared by a number of his contemporaries) to his present soaring opinion: 'He and M[rs] Lewes alone of people whom I know have given me the feeling that on their wisdom one may depend; that where their counsel or their example stops one has reached the present limit of man as a moral being.'[14]

Sidgwick's own regard for George Eliot did not preclude criticism. Having read *Middlemarch* as the successive instalments appeared, he wrote to Myers in December 1871,

I feel as if I could have planned the story much better; I don't see why the Dryasdust hero need have been more than, say, thirty-five, and he might have had an illusory halo of vague spiritual aspiration; the end of the story could have been made just as tragic. The *style* is the finest intellectual cookery.[15]

When he wrote to George Eliot with a request on Myers's behalf soon afterwards he included with his critical candour a reference to her novel that was nevertheless tactfully economical:

[13] Letter of 11 Oct. 1873: *GEL* v. 445.
[14] 'Account of my friendship with Henry Sidgwick', TCL MS Myers 13[221] fo. 5 (dated 10–24 Oct. 1873).
[15] Letter to Myers, 20 Dec. 1871, TCL Add. MS c. 100[222], quoted *Sidgwick Memoir*, 256.

I am going to make a request which, I trust, you will not consider too presumptuous.

I want your leave to bring with me when I next come to see you—that is on the next Sabbath holiday that I am able to allow myself—my friend Frederic Myers. I should not venture to ask this merely because he is a man who I think would interest you: but, in fact, you met him here once, and were kind enough to invite him to call on you. Unfortunately so long a time elapsed before he could avail himself of your invitation that when the opportunity came he was too shy to take it, and would not now venture to recall himself unceremoniously to your recollection. I therefore offered to ask your leave to bring him with me.

I have just read the second part of *Middlemarch* twice through with equal pleasure and profit. It seems to me to surpass all previous books for exquisite expression of delicate psychological observation.[16]

George Eliot replied:

> The Priory
> 21 North Bank
> Regents Park
> Feb. 5. 1872
>
> Dear M^r Sidgwick
> I shall be happy to see M^r Myers with you any Sunday—the earlier the better. Indeed I felt a little injured that he seemed not to have remembered us.
> Your judgment about what I do will always be a matter of interest to me. It is with much fear & trembling that one undertakes to represent the action of those small but potent social conditions which have hitherto been most neglected by art.
>
> Always yours truly,
> M. E. Lewes[17]

The invitation was taken up, and initiated frequent visits by Myers, who was at this time living in London, to her Sunday afternoon receptions. When the final instalment of *Middlemarch* appeared late in 1872 he was moved to draft the enthusiastic letter quoted in the previous chapter, which was sent in its final version on 7 December.[18] George Eliot, who was clearly pleased

---

[16] *Sidgwick Memoir*, 257–8.
[17] TCL Add. MS c. 93^111. Hitherto unpublished.
[18] The final version is in the George Eliot and George Henry Lewes Collection in the Beinecke Library at Yale; part of it was reproduced by Gordon Haight in *George*

to have certain of the purposes of her novel so fully appreciated, replied at once, renewing a friendship that was to last for the rest of her life.

As a result of *Middlemarch* and its reception George Eliot was at this time attracting reverent attention from her many visitors. After seeing her on Palm Sunday in 1873—presumably at one of her afternoon receptions—Louise Creighton, wife of Mandell Creighton, wrote to Myers of her feelings:

. . . we were most kindly received. There were so many people there that I could not get much talk with M$^{rs}$ Lewes but still I had enough to feel the wonderful charm of her presence. It is very curious and I don't know how it is but when one sees her one somehow feels at once that one is in the presence of someone quite noble, at whose feet one would like to sit and learn. I don't [think] anyone has ever impressed me so much. She spoke affectionately of you, which I am sure you will be glad to hear. I like their way of receiving their guests and making everyone feel at home, there was no stiffness of constraint, but everyone seemed happy and at ease—.[19]

Shortly after reading this mention of her affection for him Myers invited the Leweses to visit Cambridge with him as his guest. Having agreed, George Eliot wrote to Sidgwick, accepting an invitation from him also:

21 North Bank
Regents Park
May 16. 7[3?]

Dear M$^r$ Sidgwick
    We ask nothing better than to breakfast with you on Tuesday morning, since our guardian M$^r$ Myers permits it.
    Let us hope that the weather will have changed its mood by Sunday. M$^r$ Lewes sends his best regards, & I am always

Yours very truly
M. E. Lewes[20]

*Eliot: A Biography* (Oxford, 1968), 451. The reference to Stendhal is omitted and there are one or two unimportant stylistic alterations; it concludes 'I remain, dear M$^{rs}$ Lewes, | Yours very truly | Frederic W H Myers.' Permission to reproduce extracts from this and other items of the Beinecke collection in the present article is gratefully acknowledged. I am also indebted to Pegram Harrison for obtaining copies of them at my request.

[19] Letter of 1 May 1873, TCL MS Myers 2$^{28}$. Hitherto unpublished.
[20] TCL Add. MS c. 93$^{114}$. Hitherto unpublished.

G. H. Lewes noted in his diary the events of the visit, which took place from the 19th to the 21st of May:

Monday 19 May 1873

Went to Cambridge on a visit to Myers. At lunch there was Mrs. Huth and her daughter, H. Sidgwick, Gurney, Jebb, etc. Trinity Library and music in the chapel. Tea. Then to the *boat race*. Brilliant day but very cold. Dr Phelps and his wife. At supper several of the fellows. Home at 12 knocked up.

Tuesday 20 May 1873

Breakfasted with Sidgwick. Capital talk. Took a walk with Polly behind King's till lunch. After lunch went to a choral festival in King's Chapel. Anthems etc. Tea. Boat race. Supper. Hallam Tennyson, and the two Balfours. Good talk till $\frac{1}{2}$ past 11.[21]

Wednesday 21 May 1873

Breakfasted with Myers: Sidgwick, Mrs. Huth, Jebb, Gurney. We went over the University Library. Started at 1.30. Home to find quantity of letters.

George Eliot's own journal account includes some different details:

Monday May 19. We paid a visit to Cambridge at the invitation of Mr Frederick Myers, and I enjoyed greatly talking with him and some others of the 'Trinity Men'. In the evenings we went to see the Boat race and then returned to supper and talk—the first evening with Mr. Henry Sidgwick, Mr. Jebb, Mr Edmund Gurney; the second, with young Balfour, young Lyttleton, Mr Jackson, and Edmund Gurney again. Mrs and Miss Huth were also our companions during the visit. On the Tuesday morning we breakfasted at Mr. Sidgwick's with Mr. Jebb, Mr G. W. Clark, Mr. Myers, and Mrs. and Miss Huth.

Myers's journal (always laconic[22]) describes the arrival of the Huths on the 18th and then reads:

19 Leweses come up. Boatraces & supper
   20 Breakfast H. Sidgwick. do. Mrs Lewes in roundabout.
   21 Mrs Lewes goes . . .

As has already been explained, it is virtually certain that the evening of the 20th was the occasion of the notable walk in Trinity Fellows' Garden during which George Eliot avowed the

---

[21] *GEL* v. 409–10.
[22] TCL MS Myers 14[1]. See above, Ch. 5 at n. 13.

inconceivability of God and the unbelievability of Immortality, leaving humanity with the single, but absolute necessity of Duty.[23] The same sombreness of mood seems to have infected her as she watched the excitement of the May Races on the river, since it was on that evening or the previous one that she responded to some undergraduates who wanted to know what she thought of it all with the bare statement, 'All human joys are transient'. The questioners, we are told, were less impressed than Myers by such earnestness; she fell in their estimation.[24]

The Cambridge visit proved a memorable occasion for her growing company of admirers, including Reginald Brett, who had recently come to know both Edmund Gurney (later to become, as we have seen, the chief associate of Myers and Sidgwick in their psychical researches) and Henry Jackson. Brett wrote,

Last week George Eliot and her husband, Lewes, came to stay with Myers. They brought with them a Miss Huth, a young girl, very clever and interesting, who took Gurney's heart by storm. George Eliot was more than an interesting visitor. Her presence has hallowed the place. Her sweet low voice thanked me for giving her tickets for the Choral Festival at King's, to which she, interested in every or any religious service, took her husband, who had not entered a church for years.

He told us how she had been into some Roman Catholic church abroad and sat there watching the women and children praying round her.

Her face reminds me of Savonarola's bust and pictures at San Marco, Florence . . .[25]

Richard Jebb had been alerted to the forthcoming visit by receiving from Myers some mock Pindaric verses containing the lines

[23] See above, pp. 134–5.

[24] The incident is related in *The Works of Arthur Clement Hilton . . . together with his Life and Letters* [by Robert P. Edgcumbe] (Cambridge, 1904), 81. Edgcumbe mistakenly recollects it as having happened during the May Races of 1872, when he shared the excitement as Lady Margaret, the boat club of St John's, pursued Trinity College for the headship of the river and finally caught them on the last evening. In 1873, when it must have taken place, Trinity were in their turn pursuing Lady Margaret, but did not catch them until the Wednesday evening, after the Leweses had returned to London. I am grateful to Graham Chainey for this reference.

[25] *Journals and Letters of Reginald, Viscount Esher*, ed. M. V. Brett, 4 vols. (London, 1934–8), i. 8–9.

Shortly another message shall fly to thee on the herald's wand
For men say that there is a woman now,
Man-named, anonymous, known of all, George Eliot, wiser than the
    wise,
Her too, methinks, my subtle net shall bear within the academic
    wall . . .[26]

When Jebb wrote a letter a few days after the visit he was still
full of it:

I had known Mrs Lewes before; but acquaintanceship sprang into
friendship by one of those impulses which cannot be explained except
by some hidden law asserting itself in a moment. . . . one of the things
which brought our minds closest together was a talk about criticism:
I was saying (*à propos* of Pater's essays on the Renaissance) that the
'precious' school seemed to be destroying everything—their finesses
and small affectations blinding people's eyes to the great lineaments of
the great creative works,—blinding them to the mind which speaks
from these faces:—the creators, if they could revive, would never know
their own thoughts under this veil of finikin yet thoroughly opaque
ingenuities. Her face lit up in a moment, and she said, 'It is such a
comfort and a strength to hear you say that'—and then she said why,
so eloquently. I asked her how Sophocles had influenced her:—(we had
been talking about him, and she had said that she first came to know
him through a small book of mine):—and her answer certainly startled
me. Probably all people,—or most people who have any inner life
at all—sometimes write down things meant for no eye but their own.
Long ago I was putting down in this way some things that had been
passing through my mind about Sophocles, and this among the rest,—
that George Eliot was the modern dramatist (in the large sense) most
like him, and that he had told upon her work probably *in the outlining
of the first emotions*. Her answer to my question was—'in the delineation of the great primitive emotions.' *Verbally* this was an accident;
but hardly in substance. Of course I did not tell her. But was it not
curious? . . . Her husband is very delightful:—he is accomplished, and
he has a good heart. What I admire in him is his faithfulness in laying
everything—knowledge, social power, reputation, all, at his illustrious
wife's feet. . . . We went together to the Choral Festival at King's, and
as I was walking with her, I heard some people whisper—'Mr Lewes is
here; but is *she* here?' He was close behind, but I doubted whether he
had heard it. When we came out, he quoted it to her . . .[27]

[26] Lady Caroline Jebb, *The Life and Letters of Sir Richard Claverhouse Jebb*,
(Cambridge, 1907), 154.
[27] Ibid. 155–6.

Henry Jackson, having dined in the company of the Leweses on both the 19th and the 20th, was less enthusiastic:

The assembled multitude worshipped in a very amusing way, but I confess to being rather bored by the stiff way in which she wraps up platitudes in stilted language delivered in a peculiar formal manner in a low voice.[28]

Whatever the effect of her manner on others George Eliot's journal shows that she herself found the occasion as stimulating as similar ones in Oxford, which she visited again a month later[29]). Shortly afterwards she wrote apologetically to Myers to say that a brooch which she thought she had mislaid in Cambridge had been in a drawer at home all the time, the result of her 'false imagination, which you perceive has a fatal facility in representing things as they are not'. She went on to thank him for 'two full days of enjoyment'.[30] Her writing also profited from the experience, one oblique result being the poem 'A College Breakfast Party';[31] the most important pleasure was that of talking to 'a hopeful group of Trinity young men',[32] which contributed to her planning of *Daniel Deronda* and particularly to the delineation of its hero. Leslie Stephen expressed a belief—without evidence, he admitted—that Daniel himself was modelled on Edmund Gurney, whom he described as 'a man of remarkable charm of character, and as good-

---

[28] R. St John Parry, *Henry Jackson O. M. . . . A Memoir* (Cambridge, 1926), 28. Anne Thackeray Ritchie, taken to call on George Eliot on 18 Jan. 1872 and 18 Feb. 1873, was also critical, finding the atmosphere rather ' "Too precious" at the "shrine" and the cult of the "divinity" too oppressive'. See her Journal, quoted Winifred Gerin, *Anne Thackeray Ritchie: A Biography* (1981), 162. George Eliot was appreciative of her work.

[29] See *GEL* ix. 100 and n. In Oxford, also, her presence was impressive: in a letter of 31 May 1876 J. A. Symonds recalls among a list of his most memorable experiences, 'There is a wall, for instance, in Magdalen with Mrs Lewis [*sic*] talking upon the fundamental truths of ethics and the way of adjusting the scientific interest to sentiments sacred': *The Letters of John Adddington Symonds*, ed. H. M. Schueller and R. L. Peters, 3 vols. (Detroit, 1967–9), ii. 417.

[30] Letter of 22 May, *GEL* ix. 95–6.

[31] Originally published in *Macmillan's Magazine*, 38 (July 1878), 161–79, and included in the 1878 edition of *The Legend of Jubal and other Poems, Old and New*; repr. in *Collected Poems*, ed. L. Jenkins (1989), 160–84. The MS is dated April 1874: see *GEL* vi. 388 and n., 414, 421. There is nothing to indicate that the Cambridge occasion influenced more than the setting of the poem.

[32] Letter to Mrs Richard Congreve, 25 May 1873: *GEL* v. 412.

looking as Deronda'.[33] Oscar Browning, whom she had met with Myers, wrote that in speaking of a young man who might have been the prototype of Deronda she said that he was so handsome that for some time she thought of nothing else, but afterwards she discovered that his mind was as beautiful as his face; this too seems a reference to Gurney.[34] She may also, however, have found elements for Daniel's character in other members of the group. Although Leslie Stephen thought that in the Cambridge of Deronda's day there had been 'a certain element of rough common sense which might have knocked some of her hero's nonsense out of him' the ardent idealism voiced in the letter from Myers quoted earlier shows that her portrayal was not without basis in contemporary fact.

In September of the same year Sidgwick wrote to her, mentioning that she had been kind enough to invite him to Black-brook, where they were living, and that he would be in London and able to visit them on 4 or 5 October.[35] An additional request from Myers that Edmund Gurney should accompany them is indicated in her reply, in which she said that since Lewes had not been well recently and they regarded themselves as 'en retraite' they would prefer not to have Gurney, continuing 'You and Mr Sidgwick are just the sort of exceptions that we choose, but please don't tell.'[36] Given the comment reported earlier, her reluctance may have been due to a fear of the disturbing effects of Gurney's ebullience and charm rather than to any undesirable quality. At all events when the lunch party duly took place on the 4th Myers had evidently told Gurney about her response, to judge from the reference to him in an account which he sent to Annie Marshall:

Then yesterday I went with Henry Sidgwick to the Leweses at Chiselhurst. I wrote to Mrs. Lewes & asked to bring Gurney, but she

[33] *George Eliot* (English Men of Letters Series, 1906), 191 (cited *GEL* vi. 140 n.).

[34] Oscar Browning, *Life of George Eliot* (1890), 116. A comment recorded by Alan Gauld from the manuscript diary of Lady Battersea, wife of one of Myers's friends, shows Gurney unwittingly returning the compliment: 'Mr Gurney is a fine, good creature. We talked of George Eliot and of Daniel Deronda. Mr G. thinks it the most remarkable of her works, as it contains a grand idea: How one fine nature can become the salvation of a narrow egotistical one, how it can open the gates of heaven to a poor earth bound soul.' Entry for 3 June 1879: BM Add. MS 47934, quoted Gauld, *Founders*, 175 n.–176 n.

[35] *Sidgwick Memoir*, 283–4.        [36] *GEL* ix. 103.

refused, in the enclosed note. I wrote also to Mrs. H. Huth and asked to bring Gurney hither for the Sunday, w^h she gladly accepted. I enclose Mrs Lewes' note & Gurney's comment thereon,—you can keep Mrs L's for an autograph & burn G's. We found Mrs. Lewes very nice, & had a great discussion as to the advisability of her putting in so many snobs & low people into her novels. She said that she thought that in order to give a just representation of the noblest people it was necessary to bring out, much more than was usually done, the milieu in which their existence was necessarily in great measure passed,—to show what kind of people they are whose opinion is 'public opinion', & weigh sometimes so painfully upon nobler natures. Still, I begged her to write one book in w^h all the people should be refined, & where the tragedy should be unmixed with vulgar elements, and depend wholly on the collision of high natures, and on such sorrows as are felt most keenly in the purest air—then we talked about the apparent bitterness of her books, & I remarked that whereas in her actual presence she seemed to bring out the best side of every one, in ~~her books~~ Middlemarch she said things about human nature w^h depress one and bring out all one's own and other people's faults. She defended herself by saying that she had so great a love for human beings that she never got to hate or despise them whatever their faults might be, and that therefore she could present their faults to herself in the plainest manner, without ~~hating them for it~~ feeling that she was putting them outside the pale of sympathy. Altogether she was very nice, & I wished you were there, for I think she has sufficient greatness not to be jealous of the advantages which in certain directions you have over her, tho' she would perceive them with great distinctness.[37]

During the same visit she commented on a matter that has concerned many readers of *Middlemarch*, as Myers was later to recall in his essay on her:

Mr Lewes and she were one day good-humouredly recounting the mistaken effusiveness of a too-sympathising friend, who insisted on assuming that Mr. Casaubon was a portrait of Mr. Lewes, and on condoling with the sad experience which had taught the gifted author-ess of *Middlemarch* to depict that gloomy man. And there was indeed something ludicrous in the contrast between the dreary pedant of the novel and the gay self-content of the living *savant* who stood acting his

---

[37] TCL MS Myers 3[18]. Hitherto unpublished, apart from some lines in Gauld, *Founders*, 331. It seems likely that this letter from Myers to Annie Marshall was preserved, unlike others, on account of the reference to George Eliot. The word 'snob' is used in its earlier sense of a person belonging to the lower classes of society.

vivid anecdotes before our eyes. 'But from whom, then,' said a friend, turning to Mrs Lewes, 'did you draw Casaubon?' With a humorous solemnity, which was quite in earnest, nevertheless, she pointed to her own heart.[38]

A marginal note to the letter just quoted establishes this as the occasion.[39]

In November George Eliot wrote to Sidgwick,

> 21 North Bank
> Regents Park
> Nov. 24. 73
>
> Dear M^r Sidgwick,
>     I want to remind you that we are in town now & shall feel a jealousy of indefinite friends who attract you more than we do.
>     Shall you not be coming to town soon, & will you not send us word that you will come & lunch with us some Sunday or other day?
>     I could not tell you enough, when we were walking along the railway platform, of the fellow-feeling with which I entered into what you said about your work. I should like to know that it is making progress.
>                                          Yours always sincerely,
>                                                   M. E. Lewes[40]

The work to which she referred was *The Methods of Ethics*, the task of writing which he had described to her in his September letter as like that of 'weaving a sieve to hold the water of life in'. 'However tight one tries to draw the meshes,' he had continued, 'everything of the nature of Wisdom seems to have run through when one examines the result'.[41] Meanwhile it is likely to have been accounts by Myers of their growing interest in psychical research that prompted the Leweses in the following January to pay what may well have been their only visit to a séance, held at the house of Erasmus Darwin. George Eliot's diary mentions among those present 'The Charles Darwin family, Myers, Mrs Bowen, Galton etc.'; she goes on to record,

---

[38] Myers, 'George Eliot', *Century Magazine*, 23 (Nov. 1881). 60. The 'friend' who posed the question was presumably Sidgwick, since no one else was present; the 'too-sympathizing friend' she quoted might have been Edith Simcox, who first came to know George Eliot in December 1872, shortly after the publication of *Middlemarch*.

[39] 'We asked her from whom she had drawn Mr. Casaubon. She pointed to her own heart.'

[40] TCL Add. MS c. 93^112. Hitherto unpublished.

[41] *Sidgwick Memoir*, 283–4.

however, that 'as complete darkness was insisted on we left in disgust'.[42] In her memoirs Henrietta Litchfield, daughter of the Darwins, gives a full and spirited account of the occasion:

Spiritualism was making a great stir at this time. During a visit of my father and mother to Erasmus Darwin in January, 1874, a *séance* was arranged with Mr Williams, a paid medium, to conduct it. We were a largish party, sitting round a dining-table, including Mr and Mrs G. H. Lewes (George Eliot). Mr Lewes, I remember, was troublesome and inclined to make jokes and not play the game fairly and sit in the dark in silence. The usual manifestations occurred, sparks, wind-blowing, and some rappings and movings of furniture. Spiritualism made but little effect on my mother's mind, and she maintained an attitude of neither belief nor unbelief.[43]

A longer account, based on all the available documents, records that Charles Darwin, like the Leweses, retreated from the scene, but on different grounds from theirs: he claimed to find the stuffy room 'hot and tiring'.[44]

Incidents such as this serve as a reminder that at this time George Eliot had embarked on the writing of her last novel. Still in the afterglow of her achievement in *Middlemarch*, she had been uncertain about her next step. As far as English provincial life was concerned she had now made her strongest statement, yet some intellectual problems took her well beyond, as she now demonstrated in *Daniel Deronda*, a novel which has been the subject of both admiration and unease ever since its first publication in 1876. In general most critics have taken their starting point from comments such as those of Henry James and, many years later, of F. R. Leavis, who both drew attention to a mixture of qualities in the novel. Leavis, in particular,

---

[42] *GEL* vi 6 n.

[43] H. E. Litchfield, *Emma Darwin: A Century of Family Letters, 1792–1896* (1915), 216–17.

[44] Adrian Desmond and James Moore, *Darwin* (1991), 607–8. When Huxley and George Darwin arranged another séance, as a result of which they concluded that Williams was a cheat, Charles Darwin was relieved, having earlier commented 'The Lord have mercy on us all, if we have to believe such rubbish.' When his niece Snow Wedgwood reported his view that it was a great weakness if one allowed wish to influence belief his wife (who remained neutral on the question of psychical phenomena) commented, 'Yes, but he does not act up to his principles' (ibid. 608). Darwin's cousin Hensleigh Wedgwood, by contrast, was so impressed by the séance that he continued his investigations, corresponding with Myers (see for example his letters in TCL MS Myers 4[135-7]), and became a spiritualist (*DNB*).

was struck by the liveliness and novelistic intelligence that surrounded everything to do with the presentation of Gwendolen Harleth, as opposed to what he saw as the unreality of the relationship between Deronda and Mordecai, including the 'wastes of biblicality and fervid idealism' devoted to the latter. He even went so far as to propose the extrication from the whole of a shorter (though still sufficiently long) novel to be entitled *Gwendolen Harleth*, and its presentation for separate publication—though when a publisher encouraged him to undertake his plan he had to report that a rereading had reinforced his 'already growing sense that the surgery of disjunction would be a less simple and satisfactory affair' than he had thought; in a still later assessment he maintained that it would be impossible to purge such a reconstructed piece completely of 'the voluminous clouds of Zionizing altruism and Victorian nobility that Deronda trails and emits—and for the most part is'.[45] We do not need to question the force of Leavis's critical judgements on the novel—within his own terms, at least—to see that his insistence on George Eliot's 'maturity' in creating Gwendolen, the favour shown to Deronda continuing the 'immaturity' he had diagnosed in *Middlemarch*, disregards the kind of maturity that had been shown by her in treating the intellectual issues raised by Deronda's story. In many respects her impulse in setting up the Zionist element in the novel corresponded to that of Wordsworth many years earlier as he worked with Coleridge on the idea of a great philosophic poem. Just as they wished to offer some grounds of hope for young men who had become disillusioned by the course of the French Revolution[46] so she was hoping to show in the midst of Victorian uncertainties what commitment to a course of positive action might look like.

The importance of making such a distinction is that it clarifies George Eliot's purpose in writing her last novel, which was not

---

[45] See his introduction to the Torchbook edition of *Daniel Deronda*, p. xiv, and his posthumously published essay in *The Critic as Anti-Philosopher*, ed. G. Singh (Cambridge, 1982), 73. His reference to 'this date' at the beginning of the former suggests that his sentiments may have been somewhat modified in the light of current events in Palestine, which had shown George Eliot a more accurate prophet of future events than had been readily appreciated by English critics.

[46] See Coleridge's letter to Wordsworth, Sept. 1798, *CL* i. 527; and cf. Wordsworth's *Excursion*, Bk iv ('Despondency Corrected') and his note, *WPW* v. 375.

simply to achieve greatness as a commentator at the human level (in which case some of Leavis's criticisms might be justified) but to resolve the intellectual complexities of her own society—to be a teacher in precisely the manner than Wordsworth had set out to be. For this reason study of the *process* of writing *Daniel Deronda* has a fascination that transcends that of the product— and indeed helps to explain its effects. The achievement of an organic whole in *Middlemarch* in the terms described by Vargish[47] left her still in need of a view that would extend to her larger European experience and to her desire to mediate be-tween the demands of the everyday and the needs of the spirit. As she compassed the scientific concerns of her contemporaries she was led, in a far more radical way than contemporaries such as Dickens, to question the providential, which was being further undermined by the implications of Darwinism.

Her work on the novel began in real earnest in the early months of 1874. The story of its origins has been investigated by others, including in particular her friendship with Emanuel Deutsch, the effects of which were sharpened by his death in June 1873, and her sorrow at the sight of Miss Leigh, Byron's grandniece, at the gaming table in Homburg in 1872;[48] but her contacts with the young men from Cambridge—notably Gurney, Myers, and Sidgwick—also had a part to play. It is interesting that the last two should have pressed her to write a novel dealing only with the more refined classes in society, since this is virtually what she now sets out to do. Even in the one instance where she deals at length with people of a different class, the Cohen family who look after Myra Lapidoth, it is noticeable that she actually emphasizes their vulgarity—indeed almost goes out of her way at times to do so: 'few, it is to be hoped, will be offended to learn that among the guests at Deronda's little wedding-feast was the entire Cohen family . . .' The easy acceptance of provincial comedy that characterized her earlier works has diminished.

The influence of her immediate intellectual surroundings ran much more deeply than this, however. Henry James, as is well known, reviewed this novel in the mode of a 'conversation'

[47] See above, Ch. 1 at n. 45.
[48] See Haight, *Eliot*, and *GEL*, v. 314–16, ix. 353.

which allowed a number of characters to express their respective enthusiasms and misgivings about it. Doing so enabled him not only to express his sense of the variety available to the novelist but to show how intelligent people could disagree about her achievement. Despite his reiterated achievement for her qualities as a novelist, however, it is not clear whether he appreciated the extent to which they depended on her particular view of life. At one point Constantius, the character who seems closest to a central view, remarks on the fact that there seem to be two distinct elements in George Eliot: 'a spontaneous one and an artificial one. There is what she is by inspiration and what she is because it is expected of her'. There is certainly some truth in this, but no one in the 'Conversation' seems to ask about another possible project, that of showing how a novel of manners might also be an intellectual and moral construction. Constantius sees clearly enough that what is going on in the case of Gwendolen is a discovery all human beings must make:

We think we are the main hoop to the barrel, and we turn out to be but a very incidental splinter in one of the staves. The universe forcing itself with a slow, inexorable pressure into a narrow, complacent, and yet after all extremely sensitive mind, and making it ache with the pain of the process—that is Gwendolen's story.[49]

None of those taking part in the conversation seems to recognize the corollary to this discovery: the entailed sense of duty. This is the point George Eliot had made in other terms to Myers in Trinity College Garden; and on it depend many of the elements found suspect by later readers, including Deronda's 'priggishness'. Behind this Wordsworthian articulation, moreover, lies the question that he had asked and which she was posing in her turn, reaching a similar solution. The twin duty and affection he had found the need to cultivate were values she shared and to which she continued to cling.

The perceptiveness she assuredly shows in the delineation of Gwendolen is partly a result of the concentration on physiological study that resulted from her discussions as she worked with G. H. Lewes on his *Problems of Life and Mind*, partly of the larger questions raised in that pursuit. The legacy of Victorian

[49] '*Daniel Deronda*: A Conversation' (from *Atlantic Monthly*, 38 (Dec. 1876)), in Henry James, *Selected Literary Criticism*, ed. M. Shapira (1968), 75.

public thinking is evident in her portrayal of the Reverend Mr
Gascoigne, whose advice to Gwendolen on the question of
marriage with Grandcourt is, 'If Providence offers you power
and position—especially when unclogged by any conditions that
are repugnant to you—your course is one of responsibility, into
which caprice must not enter.' He is startled by the bareness
with which she accepts his arguments, his response being even
more Wordsworthian: 'he wished her not to be cynical, to be, on
the contrary religiously dutiful, and have warm domestic affections.'[50] Even in the earliest chapters of the novel there is a
concern for the teaching of nobility which may reflect her contact with the younger men at Cambridge. Her Wordsworthian
concern for the correctness of her facts was in line with Cambridge scientific thinking, while her attendance at the séance
may well have had to do with a desire that the introduction of
spiritualism into her novel should have an accuracy according
with the methods advocated by researchers such as Myers and
Sidgwick. During the summer of 1873 she and Lewes toured
English places that might serve as scenes for some of the events;
it was not enough to get just the topographical settings right,
however: during the following year, she sought the advice
of academic friends concerning an incident she wished to
insert into the novel to illustrate Daniel's character during his
university career at Cambridge:

> The Priory
> 21 North Bank
> Regents Park
> Ap. 5. 75

Dear M<sup>r</sup> Sidgwick
   Here is a quotation of all I want to say on the subject we spoke of.
It will perhaps enable you to imagine the exact amount of fact that will
suffice me.

> Yours gratefully,
> M. E. Lewes

'However, the needy man missed the prize, & the man who could do
without it won. When the result was made known & *A* saw that *B*,
being bracketed with a winner, would come in for a vacancy, he at
once made up his mind to resign his scholarship & allege his intention
of quitting the university. The prospect which had long floated before

---

[50] Ch. xiii.

him as something possible & perhaps desirable, had suddenly condensed itself into a resolve under the pressure of his disappointment on behalf on B.'[51]

The reply from Sidgwick was evidently critical of the factual basis of the device, since three weeks later she wrote back,

> The Priory
> 21 North Bank
> Regents Park
> Ap. 26. 75

Dear M^r Sidgwick

Grateful thanks. I must give up the scholarship affair. That is a grievance to me because the thing one would often like to do in life— go back & alter—is what I most shrink from in writing.

I had in the first instance devised the commission by B of an offence causing rustication, which offence A took on himself, enduring the penalty instead of B & making light of the sacrifice because he had been beforehand meaning to quit the university. But an Oxford Fellow who happened to be at hand washed away all probability from my ingenious construction by making me understand the Dons of the period to be too wise & moderate for anything worse than 'gating' to be inflicted in a case of light devilry such as would be credible of an honourable man. It is so much easier to fancy myself ingenious than to be true! My Oxford acquaintance, however, is one for whom all practical affairs seem to have a washy, Indian ink sort of appearance. He admitted that a man might be 'sent down' for annoying & insulting a Don if the latter happened to be very cantankerous. My green device was of offensive caricatures attached to a door. He said, that the Proctor's Scout would take them down & nothing would be said about them.

M^r Lewes suggested a watering can sending a shower over a Don from his window—but really played by B. I had become sceptical.

Finding myself altogether astray in my ingenuity, I chose the barest incident I could think of & told it in five lines—the felicity of my imagination apparently being to pass from the diffuse Improbable to the condensed Impossible.

Pity me that I must go backward. These are the evils of not having lived when Shakspeare did, when there were sea-ports in Bohemia & Aristotle was quoted at the siege of Troy—at least & for all his audience cared. External improbabilities are ~~my~~ momentous in art only because they hinder the aesthetic effect.

---

[51] TCL Add. MS c. 93[113]. Hitherto unpublished.

I am confident that you are too goodnatured to mind the trouble I have given you.

Always

Yours truly & gratefully

M E Lewes[52]

The question had also been discussed with Leslie Stephen.[53] In the event, as readers *Daniel Deronda* will recall, she adopted a less pointed device by which Daniel slackened his efforts sufficiently to allow Hans Meybrick to win the scholarship for which both of them were candidates.[54] This may have been suggested by Sidgwick, since at the end of the following month she wrote again:

The Priory

21 North Bank

Regents Park

May 27. 75

Dear M^r Sidgwick

I think that the conditions your goodness has found for me will suffice for my needs—small so far as they are measured by any effect to be produced in my work, but not small in relation to my comfort. You would hardly believe how much I suffer when I have not a complete vision of the circumstances amongst which my characters move—no matter whether I have to describe the circumstances or simply to conceive them as part of my inward picture. The imperfection of my experience, & of my knowledge generally, has been the hairshirt that I have always worn in writing. Some things in life 'I know that I know'—how would one have courage to begin to write without that little lantern area?—but I am only the more miserable in my ignorance.

Have you ever felt what it is to have something quite specific to say in an interesting conversation that is going on in a foreign language?— you caring very much about your ideas & being all the while uncertain whether you are using the right phrases? A vivid imagination of what a language might be & is not will not serve one to impress the natives.

---

[52] TCL Add. MS c. 93[115]. Hitherto unpublished. The Shakespearian references are to *The Winter's Tale*, III. iii. 1–2 and *Troilus and Cressida*, II. ii. 166.

[53] Stephen consulted Sidgwick and reported back to her that the incident would not do as it stood, and that the nearest parallel he could find in his own college's recent history would not be satisfactory for the purpose she was seeking. Letter of 6 May 1875: *GEL* vi. 140–1.

[54] Ch. xvi.

We had fixed our flight from town for the 3ᵈ but there is a vexatious hitch about the house we had thought ourselves sure of. I have been so much of an invalid lately that I am yearning for the unbroken peace of the country. But a compensation for remaining here an extra week would have been found in seeing the friends whom June will bring to town.

With much gratitude

Yours always & sincerely

M E Lewes

Henry Sidgwick Esq[55]

When *Daniel Deronda* was published in 1876, there were those who thought it contained a profound providentialism. Reviewing it in 1876, R. H. Hutton wrote of its 'distinctly religious,' tone, its 'faith in the power which overrules men's destinies for purposes infinitely raised above the motives which actually animate them', continuing, 'it would be as idle to say that there is no conception of Providence or of supernatural guidance involved in the story, as to say the same of the Oedipean trilogy of Sophocles.'[56] Vargish takes a different line at this point, contending that in this novel George Eliot, finally free of previous considerations, is able to construct a fiction in which the characters, not believing in a providence, can interpret the world without it. At the same time, he points out, she introduces some of the machinery of the providential novel, notably the occurrence of coincidental events, for which the characters will need to find an alternative interpretation. It is certainly true that Gwendolen and Grandcourt are at least as self-centred as the equivalent characters in her previous fictions and that neither assumes coincidental events to be providential. Gwendolen, described as a 'spoiled child', takes it for granted that they work in her favour, but she does not believe in a benevolent overseeing power. This is one reason for the terror that subsists at times in her thinking. When, in the same way, Daniel turns up by apparent coincidence in Genoa, Grandcourt has no sense of any controlling power at work, but reads it

---

[55] TCL Add. MS c. 93[116]. Hitherto unpublished. The house they had been 'sure of' was probably at Tonbridge (or Tunbridge Wells): see her Diary for 14 May, *GEL* vi. 142n.

[56] Quoted, *George Eliot: The Critical Heritage*, ed. David Carroll (1971), 366 (Vargish, *Providential Aesthetic*, 229.)

simply as an instance of his sinister behaviour. It is harder to follow Vargish's line when dealing with the Jewish element in the novel, if only because Mordecai's view of things so completely assumes the existence of a benevolent order that it becomes extremely hard to read the part of the novel to which he belongs as anti-providential. The most that can be said is that readers are left to make up their own minds, and that their interpretations of the novel will differ considerably according to the degree to which they sympathize, or do not sympathize, with Mordecai and his aspirations.

The issue haunted real life as much as it hovered behind her fiction. In her own terms there could be no reassurance of providential workings in tragic events, except insofar as they evoked human sympathy. At the end of 1876 Myers wrote to her with some terrible news that had just been broken in the circle of their common friends:

Brighton
Sunday Jan 2/76

Dear Mrs Lewes,
You will have heard what has happened to the Gurneys. Three sisters who had taken an invalid brother to Egypt have been drowned in the Nile. The remaining family, 4 brothers & 1 sister, are here at Brighton, at 8 Marlboro' Place, the house of one of the brothers. It is hard for them to realise that with no warning, no sight or sound, the arrival of a single telegram has changed their life. They are a most united family, all gentle and noble-natured, with not one thought or one look to wish otherwise in the past. The number of the survivors does not lessen the loss. The central home is gone,—the background of unquestioning unwavering love w^h gave unity to scattered lives & comfort under every fortune. Each has his special loss. Edmund Gurney loses in the youngest the very darling of his heart,—and in both of the younger ones the only unfailing and instinctive sympathy ~~which he~~ in music which he knew; the inborn identity of appreciativeness which was present to him thro all his passionate apprehension of musical joy and efforts after adequate musical expression,—the invisible audience in whose imagined ears the notes seemed to be sounding complete and strong. But deepest of all are the old child-memories of brother & sisterhood,—that relation which when I hear him speak of it seems to me to have the grace of love without its passion and to carry thro' adult years the trust & gladness of the child. This feeling—as what deep feeling does not?—recalls words of yours, & we have ~~talked~~

thought much of you this Sunday. You will not be surprised at his wishing me to write to you. Living so habitually inter apices vitae [among the high points of life] & encountering there ~~those~~ from time to time those whom a great passion or sorrow has lifted into that larger air, you must be accustomed to the written expression of affections more intimate & sacred than there is wish or need to show in ordinary intercourse. We at least feel moved to say to you that it is in a grief like this, a grief profound & pervading, but without one regret, or shame, or sting, that one feels most stayed by the knowledge that one ~~does~~ has not suffered alone, that the *power*, at least, of perfect sympathy exists in high & tender souls. And if we have known one of these in the flesh, if we can imagine the voice, & remember the regard, & feel sure that that great heart will understand & identify itself with our sorrow, then human friendship is doing for us almost all it can, & hardly even presence or message are needed to make the consolation complete.

This is what he feels; & I write to you instead of him in order that you may not feel it necessary to write in reply,—*of course not to me*, & not to him either unless you really prefer to do so, for he will know without a sign from you that you have felt with him.

Further particulars will probably not be received for a week. Letters are expected tomorrow,—letters *from the sisters*.

Please let Mr Lewes see this; ⟨it is addressed to him as well as to you⟩. We count on his sympathy as undoubtingly as on yours.

I am always

Yours most truly
FWH Myers[57]

The letter which he suggested she should write to Gurney is (though not there identified as such) one that he quotes from in his essay on her,[58] where he follows his account of her severity in the Fellows' Garden at Trinity by illustrating how different could be her attitude when seeking to console. 'Writing to a friend who was feeling the first anguish of bereavement,' he comments, 'she approaches with tender delicacy the themes with which she would sustain his spirit':

[57] TCL MS Myers 11[119].

[58] Myers *EM* 269–70. This letter was not collected in *GEL*. That Gurney was its recipient is established by the existence of an unpublished letter from him to George Eliot herself after the death of G. H. Lewes, in which, after expressing his hesitation in writing to her at all, he continues, 'But remembering the words you once wrote to me, how the clinging fellowship in the mysteries of human experience is a privilege which gives to life such value as it has, I cannot wholly refrain . . .' MS letter of 17 Dec. [1878] in the George Eliot and George Henry Lewes Collection in the Beinecke Library at Yale.

'For the first sharp pangs,' she says, 'there is no comfort;—whatever goodness may surround us, darkness and silence still hang about our pain. But slowly the clinging companionship with the dead is linked with our living affections and duties, and we begin to feel our sorrow as a solemn initiation preparing us for that sense of loving, pitying fellowship with the fullest human lot which, I must think, no one who has tasted it will deny to be the chief blessedness of our life. And especially to know what the last parting is seems needful to give the utmost sanctity of tenderness to our relations with each other. It is that above all which gives us new sensibilities to "the web of human things, Birth and the grave, that are not as they were." '

Providential questions were raised again in the following year, when Myers revealed to her the tragic story of his love for Annie Marshall and sent her some of the poems he had written concerning the episode.[59] In her reply she thanked him for taking her into his confidence, continuing,

Indefinable impressions had convinced me that since we began to know something of each other a blight had passed over your energies and it was painful to me to feel in the dark about one of whom I had from the first thought with that hopeful interest which the elder mind, dissatisfied with itself, delights to entertain with regard to the younger, whose years and powers hold a larger measure of unspoiled life.

What you have disclosed to me affects me too deeply for me to say more about it just now than that my sympathy nullifies to my mind that difference which we were trying to explain on Sunday. When you write—'My own mournful present and solemn past seem sometimes to show me as it were, for a moment, by direct revelation the whole world's love and woe, and I seem to have drawn closer to other lives in that I have lost my own'—you express that spiritual result which seems to me the fount of real betterness for poor mankind.[60]

Her knowledge of the situation from which he wrote to her at that time also explains the precise wording of the note with which she expressed her pleasure when he told her, just over two years later, about his forthcoming marriage to Eveleen Tennant (whom he may have met in her company[61]): 'with this steady light of a thoroughly sanctioned affection you will do better and

[59] Some of these are printed in *FIL*.

[60] Letter of 16 Nov. 1877: *GEL* ix. 201.

[61] Myers's journal carries an entry for 13 May 1877 which reads 'Mrs Hollond. Mr S. Howard Tennants & Mrs Lewes'. A further marking (not necessarily by Myers) indicates the presence of Eveleen's sister Dolly, but does not make it clear whether Eveleen herself was there. Lewes's diary for 8 July 1875 had recorded his

better things of the same sort as those you have already done so well.'[62]

During these years Myers's journal shows that he continued to attend the Leweses' Sunday afternoon gatherings from time to time. His own growing conviction that psychical research was beginning to establish a firm basis for belief in personal immortality made him feel at times, however, that he was living in a different intellectual world:

At George Eliot's Sunday receptions I now would sit in strange confusion of mind. I heard the eager talk, the race of intellectual novelties which so recently had seemed to myself also to range over all the field which fate allowed to men. But now I felt a knowledge almost greater than I could bear; a knowledge beside which the last experiment of the biologist, the last speculation of the philosopher, seemed trifling as the sport of a child; and yet a knowledge which none would receive from me, an answer to which none cared to listen, although the riddle was at the heart of all.[63]

It was a subject he felt bound to argue about with her. His autobiographical reflections include the recollection of one telling discussion:

'Do you understand,' said George Eliot to me one day, 'that the triumph of what you believe would mean the worthlessness of all that my life has been spent in teaching?' ~~Of course I do not admit this.~~ This, indeed, is an exaggerated view. All valid appeals to moral sentiments must remain valid, however widely our knowledge of the laws of the Universe may extend. But from the point of view of the agnostic moralists themselves there was much truth in the saying. It was on their opposition to 'supernatural ethics' that this group mainly dwelt. They had led the race, they thought, out of its ancient bondage; & here were men striving to form chains for it again—[64]

On this occasion, or an equivalent one, he was prompted to

introduction to Mrs Tennant, 'who introduced me to her pretty daughters' (GEL vi. 155).

[62] Letter of 9 Jan. 1880: *GEL* ix. 286.

[63] Myers, *FPP* 15, *FIL* 16.

[64] TCL MS Myers 26[63(75)]. Hitherto unpublished. Myers goes on to describe a conversation with John Morley on these lines and also mentions a conversation with Ernest Renan, who, 'as late as 1887', still believed hypnotism to be a fraud. In the record of a séance after Myers's death (TCL MS Myers 20[36(7)]), reference is made to the 'Eliot seat' in Cambridge where he and George Eliot were said to have discussed the question of a future life.

write her a long letter (including a quotation from Tennyson) which was reproduced after his death among his autobiographical fragments:

My dear Mrs. Lewes,

—Our conversation of last Sunday has left me anxious to say a few words as to the belief in immortality; for I feel that I must have seemed to give an uncomprehending assent to what you said, and then to relapse into my former opinion.

The fact is that I so deeply admire all, and agree with most, of what you say on the matter that I cannot quickly find words which combine the expression of reverence for your teaching with the statement of a different view, to which my own experience of life has led me.

I entirely agree that the impulse to virtue should not depend on any hope of reward, and that since we find human life actually existing, and have no practical expectation of its being stopped by a general suicide, we are bound, however poor a thing life may be, to do all we can to improve it for our successors.

I think that to do this without any enthusiastic confidence in the result of happiness, even to those for whom we toil, is an act of heroic courage; and I am deeply grateful for the opportunity which you have given me of trying to catch from you something of this spirit. But when I come to apply these principles I find an unexpected difficulty—I find that life may be rendered painful not only by faults and vices from which we may hope that our successors will be free, but also by the very elements which may be expected to gather strength, namely love and religious aspiration. I find that love in its highest—in its most spiritual—form is a passion so grossly out of proportion to the dimensions of life that it can only be defined, as Plato says, as 'a desire for the eternal possession' of the beloved object,—for his or her ever-growing perfection and bliss; while removal by death, if no reunion be looked for, at once reduces this life to an act of endurance alone; and I find also that religious aspiration, reverence, worship (towards however unknown a God), tend to become the very aliment of what is truly life. Now if we can believe that any object for these feelings indeed exists, they are painful only from their intensity (*y muero porque no muero* [and I die because I do not die]), and have in them also an intermingling of the profoundest joy.

But if death be the end of all, I must consider these deep-seated instincts as a sad delusion—my sense of justice, my sense of mercy, will not permit me to reverence a Being, or to admire a system of forces, which brought into existence a world in which so many pure and sensitive creatures receive nothing but unmerited torture.

No happiness of my own, or of the mass of mankind, can excuse in

my eyes the impotence or cruelty which looked on while these inno-
cents perished.

If such be the scheme of things, I may try to be brave enough to do
what I can to improve it, I may reverence those who have so tried
before me, but I must sweep away my instinct to *worship* as a dream,
and again, it will be well if my moral nature does not narrow into
endurance alone. I can hardly have the heart to wish that future men
should be born with natures higher and more susceptible to love and
reverence than my own, that they may endure in consequence a fruitless pain greater than I can know.

And yet I cannot wish for any creature that he should lack what I am
forced to regard as the higher elements in myself.

The supposition that death ends all thus leaves me in a dilemma from
which I see no escape.

All is made plain if you once allow to love and virtue their own
continuance,—no reward consisting of anything except themselves,—
no rest except in higher energies,—only 'the glory of going on, and still
to be.'

I have come, on many grounds, to believe that this will be so. And
if this *is* to be so, it is surely well that men should think often of it,—
that life, so discrowned of glory, so poor and pitiable a thing at best,
if it end in the grave,—should be often set forth, not indeed as the
probation which earns beatitude, but as the watershed of illimitable
destinies, the first step in an endless progress,—a progress to higher
duties which will become joys in proportion as duty here has become
our joy.

This is the message which I feel moved to deliver, and I earnestly
desire so to conceive and present it as that it may not be out of moral
harmony with those fuller tones in which you speak of a courage and
a nobleness which I shall always gaze on from so far below,—tho' I
may believe that there is to their attainment a yet more excellent way;
and I am confident the day shall come when you, splendidly deceived,
shall stand in no shadow, but in the very presence among the 'choir
invisible,'—Yours always with grateful reverence,

Frederic W. H. Myers[65]

Despite her regard for Myers, George Eliot stopped short of

---

[65] From the abridged 'Fragments of Inner Life' in Myers, *FPP* 34–7. This letter is
reproduced neither in Mrs Myers's reprint of the essay in *Collected Poems: With
Autobiographical and Critical Fragments* (1921) nor in *FIL*. The 'quoted' letter from
George Eliot which follows in the 1904 edition and which was never reprinted in this
form consists of sentences selected and in one or two cases altered from the letter
George Eliot sent to Myers after learning from him of the loss of Annie Marshall: see
n. 60 above. The quoted line is from Tennyson's 'Wages'.

endorsing such sentiments; her own position was presumably closer to Henry Sidgwick's, scepticism offering a more acceptable *modus vivendi* between the demands of ethics and those of scientific research. Like him she looked to the extension of University education—especially for women—as offering the best grounds of hope for the future. In these years the Sidgwicks sometimes met her and Lewes at Six Mile Bottom near Newmarket, where, although they did not often return to Cambridge itself, they occasionally visited their friend W. H. Hall.[66] Meanwhile the work of establishing women's education further in Cambridge was going ahead through the foundation of Newnham College. Mrs Sidgwick may have had this in mind when in 1877 she wrote inviting the Leweses to pay another visit. George Eliot replied:

The Priory
21 North Bank
Regents Park
April 10. 77

Dear M^rs Sidgwick

Your kind letter is irresistible—if only my health, which continues to be troublesome, will allow me to carry out the kind proposal that I should see my friends in Cambridge towards the end of May. I dare not yet think of the journey very confidently, but I am not unhopeful, & there is time enough for me to get stronger before we are on the verge of summer. M^r Lewes and I should both value the opportunity of being with you more quietly and continuously than we could do under other conditions than those you kindly offer us. And as soon as I feel that I can count on the pleasure of visiting Cambridge, I will write to consult you as to the day & hour.

It seems to me a long while since I saw you & M^r Sidgwick at Six Mile, when our talk was too interrupted & our stay together too soon at an end. I do hope I shall be able to get the pleasant amours of being with you two or three days in May.

Sincerely yours,
M. E. Lewes[67]

---

[66] In an annotation on the back flyleaf of a copy of Oscar Browning's *Life of George Eliot* (1890) now in Cambridge University Library, someone, presumably its former owner A. C. Benson, has written, referring to a visit described on p. 128, 'On this occasion, Mr Hall who had an old & very conventional butler, said to him at the door as the Lewes's drove away "There are two of the greatest writers in England", "Yes sir," said the butler, "I thought they were something of the kind."'

[67] TCL Add. MS c. 103^32. Hitherto unpublished.

At about the same time Edmund Gurney also wrote proposing a joint visit to Cambridge. Lewes replied:

> The Priory
> 21 North Bank
> Regents Park
> Tuesday

Dear M$^r$ Gurney,

  Your seductive invitation comes at a time when I have only just recovered from an attack of gout and M$^{rs}$ Lewes still suffering from her old & painful malady—These infirmities warn us of the uncertainty which must hover round all such pleasant prospects as that you hold out; but should health permit we shall be only too glad to renew our Cambridge experiences at the end of May—say about the 30$^{th}$. We shall, I hope, see you many times before that & can arrange with you when the visit shall take place.

> Yours Ever,
> G. H. Lewes

G. Gurney Esq.

I was at the rehearsal yesterday of the Brahms & Joachim pieces which alas! I cannot hear at Cambridge.[68]

The visit duly took place from 31 May to 4 June 1877, in the company of Edmund Gurney and Kate Sibley, his betrothed, whom he was to marry on the 5th. George Eliot had long taken an interest in the foundation of Girton College, which she had discussed with the foundress, Emily Davies, both personally and in correspondence.[69] She had also given money to the College while it was still at Hitchin, asking that the gift be described as from 'the author of *Romola*' (the novel which she perhaps thought of as best establishing her 'respectability'); both she and Lewes had donated books. Since her previous visit, Girton College had opened its new building in Huntingdon Road in October 1873, but Emily Davies, who as mistress had overseen the crucial move of the College from Hitchin to its Cambridge

---

  [68] TCL Add. MS c. 101$^{122}$. Hitherto unpublished. The Leweses attended a number of concerts in London during this time, but the 'rehearsal' in question has not been identified.

  [69] The relevant correspondence is to be found in *GEL*: see vols. iv. 467–8, viii. 408–11, 427–9, 434–5, and 465–6 and the general index in vol. ix. An account of a conversation between the two is given in D. Bennett, *Emily Davies* (1990), 252–4.

venue, had left in 1875, having decided the time had come for her to stand down from a headship which she accepted in part because of the previous incumbent's illness. Now, having been invited to visit the College by Frances Henrietta Muller, a student rather older than most and afterwards to become an active feminist,[70] George Eliot learned to her dismay that the proposal had caused friction between the new Mistress (Marianne Bernard) and the students. She considered omitting any visit, but in the event found it possible to make a private call there,[71] in addition to her reception at 'Newnham Hall' (as the latter was known at that point). She also saw Myers,[72] and the Leweses revisited Six Mile Bottom, where Reginald Brett met her again and recorded his delight at spending four hours in her company:

She talks like the best part of her books, the parts where she analyses without dissecting, the parts out of which the compilers get her 'wise, witty and tender' sayings. She is wonderfully thoughtful, even in trifles. She shut up George Lewes when he tried to talk about her. She does not seem vain. She adores Charles Darwin because of his humility.[73]

The visit to Cambridge, which was recorded in George Eliot's diary as one of 'uninterrupted excitement', was, as in 1873, followed by anxiety about what might have been left behind— more articles being missed on this occasion. By now the Leweses had taken possession of their new house in the country at Witley:

[70] Gordon Haight cites an obituary notice in *The Times*, 17 Jan. 1906, for the information that she had been born in Chile and while at Girton became interested in feminist issues, including the efforts to establish women's trade unions. She later travelled extensively alone in Europe, America, and Asia, including China, and lived as a native in India, studying the position of women: *GEL* vi. 374 n.

[71] I am told by the Girton archivist, Dr Kate Perry, who has kindly assisted me with a number of my enquiries, that in the College no manuscript record relating directly to the affair has survived. This suggests either that any correspondence was later suppressed or that the matter was dealt with personally between the mistress and Miss Muller. The main surviving evidence comes in a letter from George Eliot to Barbara Bodichon of 19 May 1877 (*GEL* vi. 374–5 and nn.) which provides only a partial record. According to a traditional account (which may have been handed down orally) her private visit to the College involved entry through the back drive: see Bradbrook, *Infidel Place*, 51.

[72] For the possibility that this visit could have been the occasion of the famous conversation in Trinity College Garden, and for the arguments against, see n. 34 of the previous chapter.

[73] *Journals and Letters of Reginald, Viscount Esher*, op. cit. i. 40.

The Priory
21 North Bank
Regents Park
May [June[74]] 8. 77

My dear M[rs]. Sidgwick

I am one of those undesirable visitors who are apt to leave trifles behind them & give trouble in consequence. But pray let this note give you no further trouble than that of asking the good servant who waited on me whether such droppages from my travelling-bag & writing-case as a silver pencil-case, two penholders, one mother-of-pearl, one bone, both with pens turned inward & a small pair of nail-scissors may be found lurking in the rooms we occupied. If the answer turns out to be negative, take no notice of this letter, & leave me to infer that I made a mistake in fancying these small goods present in my bag & case & tumbled out in some hurried movement. They are none of them valuable in themselves, but the penholders & pencil case have for me the convenience of use & want & some charm of memories.

We are getting quickly settled in our country home, & have had some delightful walks in which we have talked of Cambridge & all the kindness shown us there by such people as one loves to feel indebted to.

We had the advantage of seeing more of M[r] Stuart as a fellow-passenger on the way to London.[75]

I suppose you as well as we have had to shiver with cold again, since the two sunny days that crowned our stay with you. But at this moment I am warm in the morning sunshine which is lighting up a broad woody valley & showing me a hazy line of distant hills.

I hope you have been resting well, & that the hay-fever has somehow been exorcised.

The thought of you and M[r] Sidgwick is very helpful to me. Think kindly of me, too, & believe me

Always yours most truly
M. E. Lewes[76]

She continued to follow the development of Newnham College with interest. When the possibility of having a man and woman in charge at Girton had been raised by Emily Davies in 1867 she had opposed it, saying that people who recommended such a course could not have much knowledge of life.[77] She saw

---

[74] Corrected in another hand to 'June'.
[75] See below, n. 85.
[76] TC Add. MS c. 103[33].
[77] MS letter of 20 Mar. 1867 at Girton College, quoted by Bradbrook, *Infidel Place*, 50.

no such impediment in 1880, however, when it was decided that the Sidgwicks should live together at Newnham College, writing on the contrary to Barbara Bodichon, 'they have had and have the admirable public spirit to let their house and arrange to live for a year[78] in the new Nuneham House in order to facilitate matters for the double institution'.[79]

During the same years Myers continued to visit the Leweses at their receptions in London. The death of G. H. Lewes in 1878 induced him to write a letter of sympathy in which he again referred to his belief in immortality:

Dear Mrs Lewes,

I venture to send you one word to say how profoundly I sympathise with your overwhelming bereavement.

I believe that such separations are not for long.

With deep respect

Yours sincerely
Frederic W H Myers[80]

Henry Sidgwick had written at greater length:

Hill Side,
Chesterton Road,
Cambridge.
Dec 5th

My dear M[rs] Lewes

I have hardly ventured to intrude by telling you of the shock and pain that Monday's news gave us. It can be no consolation to you to know how much poorer the world seems to so many by this loss. But it may be something to feel how undying a memory we shall retain of the nature and life so full and rich in genial development. If I had not known him, I should not really have imagined how possible it was to combine the driest light of philosophic sincerity and impartiality and devotion to truth, with so keen and deep a sensitiveness to all sources of human joy. The example is difficult to follow; but it will remain 'part of our life's unalterable good'.

My wife wants me to tell you her sympathy. You will believe in its sincerity and in mine.

---

[78] In the event they stayed for two years, during Mrs Sidgwick's term of office as Vice-Principal under Jemima Clough.

[79] *GEL* vii. 322.

[80] George Eliot and George Henry Lewes Collection in the Beinecke Library at Yale. Hitherto unpublished.

Ever yours
Henry Sidgwick.
Please do not trouble to answer this.[81]

Since Sidgwick had put his finger on the qualities that George
Eliot would herself have valued most in Lewes she no doubt
found his letter closer to her way of thinking than that from
Myers—all the more so since her husband had shown so little
interest in the movements for psychical research. Lewes had
always kept her down to earth; although ready to praise her
intellectual abilities to an extent she could find embarrassing,
he could also cut across the air of reverence that some set up
around her, as Oscar Browning vividly recalled.[82] While he did
not necessarily share the extreme commitment to the demands
of duty and affection she had developed in the course of her
career, his own commitment to dispassionate scientific research,
along with his liveliness of spirits, had provided for her an
intellectual touchstone, to be found valid even when other
values (along with any surviving faith in the providential) were
being tested to the uttermost. It was not surprising, then, that
when, early in 1879, she mastered the effects of her grief so far
as to think of establishing an award in his memory her immediate impulse was to further the study of physiology. The plan was
discussed first at the end of January with Sir James Paget, who
was giving her advice concerning her health; he suggested a
scheme for lectures at the College of Surgeons.[83] On 20 February
she wrote to Thomas Clifford Allbutt of her desire to found in
Lewes's memory 'some Lectureship or other efficient instrument
of teaching Biology (including Psychology)'[84] and on the same
day to Sidgwick, whose part in the plan has not hitherto been
fully documented:

[81] George Eliot and George Henry Lewes Collection in the Beinecke Library at
Yale. Hitherto unpublished.
[82] During the Cambridge visit of May 1877, 'A rather large party had been asked
to meet them, and as most of the guests had never met George Lewes and his wife
before, there was some excitement to hear the words which might fall from their lips.
The silence was broken by Lewes saying to her, "Why my dear, you surely don't like
that heavy black Bavarian beer, do you?" an unexpected beginning of memorable
table-talk.' Oscar Browning, *Life of George Eliot* (1890), 119–20.
[83] *GEL* vii. 100n.
[84] Ibid. 104.

The Priory
21 North Bank
Regents Park
Feb. 20. 79

Dear M^r Sidgwick

I am feeling very ill just now & have not yet been able to see any of my kind friends. But this only makes me the more anxious to take some steps towards carrying out a purpose in which I trust that you will give me a little sympathy.

I desire to institute some sort of educational instrumentality which will be a help to poor students of the subjects in which my husband was most interested—lectureships, for example, *to be called by his name*. I know some of the difficulties in the way of making any endowment permanently useful, & I am anxious to get advice on the subject from the judges whom I think the most competent both as to practical experience & as to their care for the public education. My mind has turned to you & Professor Stuart[85] as among the first of those who would be likely to help me, but I write to you as the longer known friend & will trust to your goodness to communicate my wishes to Professor Stuart.

I have just been reading in the 'Times' the report of the meeting on University Teaching at the Mansion House, & it has seemed to me that if I had a clearer view of the mechanism set going by the London Society for the Extension of University Teaching some practicable notion of what might be done in fulfilment of my desire would possibly get framed in my mind—to be corrected or amplified by wiser persons.

I would devote four or five thousand pounds to the purpose. Will you discuss the matter with M^r Stuart?—& with any other Cambridge man whom you think likely to aid with ideas, D^r Michael Foster, for example.

The letter you wrote me is kept by me among the precious records of respect for what I most care should have respect. Please offer my

---

[85] James Stuart, a Fellow of Trinity mentioned earlier, was Professor of Mechanism and Applied Mechanics from 1875–89, after which he spent more time in business and politics. He founded the University Extension Lectures in 1873 and was active in the development of Newnham College: see also *Sidgwick Memoir*, 175, 182, 272. In his *Reminiscences* (1912) he described (p. 123) how he met George Eliot at Mr Hall's and how she seemed thoroughly to enjoy humorous stories but during the whole four days never told one herself: 'Her conversation was very interesting but perhaps rather stately, and she laid down the law somewhat.' Like Reginald Brett (see above, p. 197) he commented on her resemblance to Savonarola; he thought she must have a Jewish ancestry.

best love to M^rs Sidgwick. I hope you are both well & in all things happy.

Yours always truly
M E Lewes

I wish to carry out the purpose I have written of at once & during my life, not as a matter of bequests.[86]

The idea of a lectureship as the most suitable means of commemoration soon gave place to other schemes, as shown in a further letter a fortnight later:

The Priory
21 North Bank
Regents Park
Mar. 3. 79

My dear M^r Sidgwick

Your letter is a precious light to me. It seems to make practicable the sort of scheme which lay in my mind, but which, in the lack of experienced opinion, I could only entertain vaguely & doubtfully.

The condition of the Laboratory I see to be all-important, & on this ground I concur in excluding the consideration of the London Society. Indeed, one vision of the impossible which had flitted through my mind had been the founding of a Biological Institute, which would require a fortune.

But it seems to me now that the right path—one in agreement with my husband's views of usefulness—has been struck out, & it remains for me to ask you & my other good friends who are competent in such matters to help me with their further advice.

I am not yet seeing even intimate friends, but I would thankfully see those who will be kind enough to aid me in this object which I have at heart, & I would go through any business connected with it.

The gravest question is, what university or college offers the best machinery for the purpose. Another—what conditions should be fixed as checks on the idle abuse of the studentship. If you, Prof. Stuart, D^r Foster or M^r. Frank Balfour will kindly give me some of your time when you come to town, I shall be most grateful. After four o'clock I am disengaged, or I would be so at any hour on any day with notice on a postcard.

I do not thank you in words for your help, because you know that I thank you in feeling that words will not suffice for.

---

[86]  TCL Add. MS c. 93^177. Hitherto unpublished. Many more letters relating to the scheme are gathered together in *GEL*: see the index to vol. ix under 'Lewes'.

> Always yours most sincerely,
> M E Lewes[87]

Sidgwick went to see her on 9 March and four days later she was visited by Michael Foster,[88] who suggested suitable trustees, including Sidgwick himself. Sidgwick revisited her on 6 April[89] and the plans progressed so well that she became impatient to see the whole scheme in operation:

> The Priory
> 21 North Bank
> Regents Park
> May 7. 79

Dear M^r. Sidgwick

A little while ago I received a letter from D^r Foster in which he said that he had recovered from his illness & that the Draft of conditions for the Studentship would not be much longer delayed. Can you tell me what is the cause of the further delay? I should be thankful to have the draft before I go into the country because I want to show it to Sir James Paget, who has suggested as a fruit of his observation on somewhat similar cases, that the appointment should be made to require confirmation *each* year; & not simply at the end of three years.

I am also anxious to know whether all the proposed Trustees have accepted the trust. Altogether I have got into a state of nightmare in which I want something to be done & can neither stir nor cry.

Forgive my troubling you. Whatever delay is clearly stated as necessary I shall resign myself to quietly. But it is not in my nature to begin a thing & put off the completion without good reason.

> Always yours most truly
> M E Lewes[90]

This was followed within a few days by another:

> The Priory
> 21 North Bank
> Regents Park
> May 12. 79

Dear M^r. Sidgwick,

Certain anxieties of mine as to the conditions of the Studentship

---

[87] TCL Add. MS c. 93[118]. Hitherto unpublished.

[88] Praelector of physiology at Trinity College and shortly to become professor of that subject in the University.

[89] *GEL* vii. 127.

[90] TCL Add. MS c. 93[119]. Hitherto unpublished.

have been clinched by a discussion of the subject with D$^r$ Andrew Clarke, who has promised that he will at once communicate his criticisms & suggestions to M$^r$. Huxley, while I of course turn to you as my original helper & the one in whose impartiality & comprehension I have the most complete reliance.

D$^r$ Clarke, without any leading from me, gave a voice to my own dread lest the Studentship instead of being a continual *public* memorial of my Husband's life should sink into a mere hole & corner affair, known only to a narrow circle in a particular institution, who would come within the chances of being benefited by it.

I had said no more than that it had been proposed to give the nomination of the Student to the Professor, when D$^r$. Clarke exclaimed 'Then it will come to be a mere provision of an assistant for the Professor!' and he then remarked that as there was no medical school at Cambridge, the physiological students there would not only be comparatively few, but would be for the most part of the more dilettante sort. He insisted strongly on the importance of a wider range of choices, so as to extend the chances of getting the fittest man, & in his opinion the fittest would be more likely to be found in Edinburgh or London than at Cambridge, not because he undervalues the teaching at Cambridge but for the reason already intimated. I sent you notes of his suggestions which you can show to anyone you like. And he is quite willing that his name should be mentioned in the matter. You will discern the ground of each suggestion.

But pray let his letter be private.

Always yours sincerely

M E Lewes

D$^r$ Clarke justly observed that a student such as I have in view—one fitted to carry on effective research—should not be simply following the lead of the Professor & merely helping him to carry out his ideas, but should have an independent line of work.

There is no question about the present localization at Cambridge: only about widening the range of choice from among promising men.[91]

The G. H. Lewes Studentship was in due course established, the first recipient being Charles Stuart Roy, a leading young physiologist who had studied at Edinburgh and then in Germany and who in 1884 was to become Professor of pathology at

---

[91] TCL Add. MS c. 93[120]. Hitherto unpublished. Much further relevant correspondence is preserved in the George Eliot and George Henry Lewes Collection at Yale University.

Cambridge. Further Students were elected in turn, two of whom went on to win the Nobel prize.

The establishment of the Studentship was a tribute to Lewes's feeling for science and for intellectual honesty. It was also a gesture in the direction of the small group of men whose exhibition of the integrity and idealism that were to be found among the members of an all-male college in Victorian England had called out her respect and prompted some important elements in her last novel. What she could not fully express in material terms was her interest in the all-female institution, based on secular ideals like her own, which Henry Sidgwick, reinforced by his marriage with Eleanor Balfour, was now helping to bring into being. While, as in her friendship with Myers, she could give serious attention to those who showed interest in psychical research, it remained for her of uncertain validity and dubious moral value. It was the work on behalf of feminine education which—though equally controversial among her contemporaries—corresponded, like the advancement of physiology, to her sense of the way things should be developing. Could she have continued to believe in providence, this might have been the manner in which she envisaged its operation, for such Cambridge initiatives pointed a way to the future of a kind that she could readily understand and support.[92]

The gap in her life created by the loss of Lewes continued to lie behind all—the more grievously in view of the closeness of their relationship. The creative stimulus set up by a liaison

---

[92] The connection with Cambridge continued after her death. In addition to the furtherance of scientific research through the G. H. Lewes Studentship women's education was supported: John Cross made gifts to Newnham College, presenting the College with £200 for the purchase of books for the Library and £50 towards setting up the Balfour laboratory. Acknowledging the gift, Eleanor Sidgwick mentioned that the College wanted to show its appreciation in a practical manner:

Dear Mr Cross,

Thank you very much—on behalf of Newnham College—for your new donation. I hope when you come back—and come to stay with us as you promise to do that we shall be able to show you how it & the others have been spent. We do not propose to keep your books separate from the others, as it is more convenient to classify by subjects—but we are having as you know a separate label for them.

The annual meeting of the College was held yesterday and you were elected a member of the council in place of Mr Albert Dicey who retires,—by rotation. I suppose you will in due course receive an official communication on the subject from

between two of the outstanding intelligences of the age had been stifled, it seemed. Even the respect in which she was held by the public had come to seem hollow. After the triumph of *Middlemarch* it had no doubt been gratifying for a time to enjoy greater respect in society, including homage from a succession of admirers, but now the spectacle—which as we have seen some of her visitors viewed with a scepticism her novelist's eye might have appreciated[93]—began to pall. Georgiana Burne-Jones recalled a remark of hers from April 1880: 'I am so tired of being put on a pedestal and expected to vent wisdom.'[94]

She had studied duty long enough and affection was now what she needed most. Indeed, while Lewes had been able to offer intellectual companionship of the highest order, praising and supporting her while sometimes teasing her, it is not clear that even he had always given her as much as she needed. A letter to John Cross the previous October had shown an extraordinary tenderness and indulgence, to the point of flirtatiousness:

the secretary. I hope you will consent to serve. The council generally meets about once a term.

I suppose you are enjoying bright sun & clear skies at Grasse. Winter has just begun here.

Believe me

Yours sincerely
Eleanor Mildred Sidgwick.

Cross accepted the offer, and served on the Newnham Council from 1883 to 1886. (I am indebted to Dr Carola Hicks, archivist of Newnham College, for this information, for showing me Mrs Sidgwick's letter and for other kind assistance.) Henry Sidgwick refers to a visit by him for a meeting in May 1886, when Cross mentioned that he was writing on Dante: *Sidgwick Memoir*, 448.) The fact that his gift was made to Newnham rather than (as in the earlier case) Girton, may indicate that some transference of allegiance on his and George Eliot's part had taken place, reflecting the contrast between Miss Bernard's chilly attitude at the time of her 1877 visit (by comparison with what she might previously have expected from Emily Davies) and the warmth of her reception at Newnham. It would be unwise to read too much into this particular gesture, since Cross himself had been a friend of the Sidgwicks before his marriage to George Eliot, whereas he had had no previous connection with Girton. Yet it is clear that once George Eliot came to know the Sidgwicks and their circle she recognized in them ideals which were near to her own and which therefore stirred a closer sympathy with the institution that was springing up under their tutelage than with the one that had emerged from her earlier discussions with Emily Davies.

[93] Additional satirical accounts, by Charles Eliot Norton and George Meredith, are recorded by Rosemary Ashton, *G. H. Lewes: A Life* (Oxford, 1991), 252–3.

[94] Georgiana, Lady Burne-Jones, *Memorials of Edward Burne-Jones*, 2 vols. (1904), ii. 103–4, quoted Haight, *Eliot*, 537.

Through everything else, dear tender one, there is the blessing of trusting in thy goodness. Thou dost not know anything of verbs in Hiphil or Hophal or the history of metaphysics or the position of Kepler in science, but thou knowest best things of another sort, such as belong to the manly heart—secrets of lovingness and rectitude. O I am flattering . . .'[95]

After reading this it is less surprising to learn that in the spring of 1880 she should have made known her decision to marry him. Given contemporary attitudes to marriage (including re-marriage after one's spouse's death) her decision to accept his proposal must have been taken with apprehension; and it was correspondingly gratifying to receive a message of support from Jowett: 'You know that you are a very celebrated person and therefore the world will talk a little about you, but they will not talk long and what they say does not much signify. It would be foolish to give up actual affection for the sake of what people say.' He also urged her not to let her new marriage stand in the way of more writing.[96] When, similarly, the Sidgwicks were told the news by Cross himself they wrote immediately and separately to give their good wishes,[97] receiving a reply from her by return of post:

The Priory
21 North Bank
Regents Park
April 30. 80

My dear M<sup>r</sup> Sidgwick

Your sympathy satisfies a need which without such satisfaction I should have felt very keenly, and my heart was much cheered yesterday when M<sup>r</sup>. Cross read me a letter he had received from M<sup>rs</sup> Sidgwick. You are both among those whose favourable judgment is felt by me as a sanction. But I should have thoroughly justified you if you had found incomprehensible what I myself had once thought impossible. Good wishes such as yours are a sort of progress which have an assured efficacy. I feel that I gather strength from them.

M<sup>r</sup>. Cross thought that you were not looking your very best. I hope the next holidays will set you up.

[95] *GEL* vii. 212.
[96] Ibid. 289.
[97] Their letters are in the George Eliot and George Henry Lewes Collection in the Beinecke Library at Yale. A note of 20 May from Myers is also in the collection.

Please thank M<sup>rs</sup>. Sidgwick for me & believe me
Always yours sincerely<br>M E Lewes[98]

That the path of the marriage did not initially run altogether smoothly is suggested by the strange incident in June during their honeymoon stay in Venice when John Cross jumped out of their hotel window and into the Grand Canal. However one may choose to interpret this incident, it meant that at a crucial moment George Eliot was deprived of the very kind of support she had been most looking for.[99]

Such adverse comments on the marriage as have survived from the outer circle of her acquaintance were feline rather than straightforwardly condemnatory. Lionel Tennyson's wife commented that she had been seen shopping for her trousseau at all the fashionable milliners and dressmakers in London, choosing whatever money and taste could do to make her look not too unsuitable a bride for a man of 40, while when Caroline Jebb met her with the Sidgwicks during a visit to Six Mile Bottom in August she remarked that such a marriage was 'against nature' but tempered her customary tartness with touches of pathos:

George Eliot, old as she is, and ugly, really looked very sweet and winning in spite of both . . . In the evening she made me feel sad for her. There was not a person in the drawing-room, Mr Cross included, whose mother she might not have been, and I thought she herself felt depressed at the knowledge that nothing could make her young again; to her we were young of a later generation. She adores her husband, and it seemed to me it hurt her a little to have him talk so much to me. It made her, in her pain, slightly irritable and snappish, which I did not mind, feeling that what troubled her was beyond remedy.[100]

---

[98] TCL Add. MS c. 93[121]. Hitherto unpublished.

[99] In *George Eliot: A Biography* (1995), 629–33, Frederick Karl speculates freely as to the possible background of the incident. He discusses the possibility that Cross had been stunned by her sexual rapacity. Against this should be set Charles Lewes's approval of the marriage on the grounds that his father would only have wished her happy and that 'she was of such a delicate fastidious nature that she couldn't be satisfied with anything but an ideal tete-a-tete': *Letters of Anne Thackeray Ritchie*, ed. Hester Ritchie (1924), 181. Both husband and wife afterwards explained the episode as one of illness. The nearest we have to further evidence is a MS note from Lord Acton (Haight, *Eliot*, 544 n.) that George Eliot feared Cross to be mad and was just explaining this to a doctor when she heard about the jump. Episode of madness or not, Cross went on to live a long and useful life.

[100] Bobbitt, *Dearest Love*, 163–4.

The sharpness of this insight, with its bleak overtones, might in certain moods have been appreciated by George Eliot herself, yet it was not necessarily as penetrating as Lady Jebb thought, springing as it did from an observation of Cambridge society that was less humane and open in its inquiry than the Sidgwicks'. 'What troubled' George Eliot was more directly physical than Lady Jebb seems to have realized: her health was not good and she did not survive to the end of the year. It also stretched far beyond interpersonal dynamics at an evening party. Lewes's death had left her facing more starkly the implications of living without providence. When she listened to the music in Trinity chapel on the day she walked in the Fellows' Garden with Myers she can hardly have failed to see in the antechapel there the statue of Newton, described by her admired Wordsworth as 'The marble index of a mind for ever | Voyaging through strange seas of Thought, alone.'[101] Her attention must in any case have been drawn to it by Lewes, an enthusiastic admirer of Newton's life and thought.[102] During her visit to the Library there the same day she may well have talked about, and reflected upon the degree to which Newton's discoveries left him with a sense not only of physical gain but of metaphysical loss, since in the light of his discoveries Heaven had become no more than a metaphor; hence, we may conclude, the enormous—and at first sight incomprehensible—efforts he devoted for the remainder of his life to discussions (still preserved there in manuscript) concerning the prophecies of Daniel and other such matters.

Newton's statue was flanked by those of other great Trinity men, including not only Francis Bacon and Isaac Barrow but (more recently) William Whewell. George Eliot might well have envisaged that in the course of time her friend Tennyson, who in writing *In Memoriam* had faced, more profoundly than most, the implications of a Nature from which Providence seemed absent would also take his place among them.

[101] *The Prelude* (1850), iii. 62–3. See also the reference to his 'ethereal self': ibid. iii. 267.

[102] A short piece by him on 'The boyhood of Newton' had appeared in the *Leader* for 16 June 1855, p. 578; eighteen months before the Cambridge visit he had enthusiastically recommended the *Life* of Newton by Jean Baptiste Biot: *GEL* ix. 30. Together they had admired a portrait by Kneller at Kensington in May 1867.

What she could not foresee was that just over half a century later the negative complement to all this grandeur, correlative to Newton's apparent sense of a metaphysical lack requiring remedy, would find physical embodiment in the same building. As one passed from the commemorations of individual greatness in the antechapel to the chapel proper, traditional imagery of Christian art would hold its own in the large stained-glass windows, and a single painting behind the altar. It was only after dark, in time to come, that the bleaker implications of the new intellectual order would be reasserted for visitors, as the panels at the end of the chapel came into prominence to either side of the altar, displaying in gilded paint the lists of those hundreds of members of the college who fought and were sacrificed during the World War of 1914–18 in the name of duty and love. The horror which had momentarily opened out behind her glimpse of Byron's great-niece wagering and losing at the gaming-table at Homburg and which she then shadowed out in the similarly feckless behaviour of Gwendolen Harleth, would meanwhile have found physical realization for a later generation in a resumption of that war between France and Germany which had so shocked her in 1870 by its demonstration of the latest technological developments in armed warfare. In the new world conflict, unabashed by their awareness of such potentialities, the generals on either side, now joined by those of other countries, including her own, would have continued to play for higher and higher stakes, making appeals always to the traditional demands of honour—which would have sounded more and more hollow as, in the inexorable course of improvident history, they lost the tens of thousands of troops they gambled, over and over again.

# 6

# Ruskin's Differences

F. W. H. MYERS'S first impression of Ruskin, caught one day when he was in the Lake District, proved unforgettable:

I met him first in my own earliest home, beneath the spurs of Skiddaw,—its long slopes 'bronzed with deepest radiance,' as the boy Wordsworth had seen them long since in even such an evening's glow. Since early morning Ruskin had lain and wandered in the folds and hollows of the hill: and he came back grave as from a solemn service from day-long gazing on the heather and the blue.[1]

Given his own early upbringing in that same countryside at a time when Wordsworth was still alive it was natural that Myers should immediately cast Ruskin in the role of a devout worshipper at Nature's shrine—even if he instinctively (and appropriately) turned back to Wordsworth's description of his earliest days to find the most authentic image for his sense of that worship.

The incident may have happened in Myers's own boyhood, in which case it could have coincided with Ruskin's own approval of Frederic Myers senior during a stay at Keswick in 1848: describing his happiness there, he remarked, 'We have a good clergyman, Mr Myers.'[2] It is much more likely, however, that it took place in the summer of 1867, when Myers stayed at his boyhood home for a fortnight and met him at least twice.[3] This

---

[1] F. W. H. Myers, 'Obituary Notice VI: John Ruskin': Myers, *FPP* 89–90. The quotation from Wordsworth is from *W Prel* (1850) i. 296.

[2] Letter to Mary Russell Mitford, 21 Apr. 1848: *R Works* xxxvi. 87.

[3] If the meeting referred to took place then, its exact date is hard to determine; nor is it clear from Myers's account whether it took place in the open air or indoors. According to his Journal (TCL MS Myers 14[1]) he met Ruskin on 22 July and at dinner on 30 July, and himself climbed Skiddaw ('with Stephen') on 3 August. Ruskin records in his diary that on 22 July he 'called on the Butlers on the island' and that on 30 July he climbed Saddleback (which is in the same range as Skiddaw) and then dined with the Butlers: *R. Diaries* ii. 625, 626. In a letter to his mother he recorded how he had gone straight up the steep front of Saddleback by the central

was halfway through the three-year period when Ruskin was waiting for Rose La Touche's answer to his proposal of marriage: in a letter to Joan Agnew he described how he knelt on Skiddaw and recalled the supplication of the Litany for pity 'upon all prisoners and captives', followed by a feeling of 'boundless liberty' as he saw below 'leagues of moorland tossed one after another like sea waves'.[4] This was probably a little later than the meeting with Myers; his mood on the occasion was certainly more complicated than the simple adoration of nature suggested in that account. But if the concluding experience there was prompting a faith in nature's power to liberate him from his current love-bondage his optimism was not, unfortunately, to prove justified.

In one respect, Myers was right to associate a Wordsworthian devotion to nature with Ruskin, who had only recently been exploring the possibility that one might be able to gain direct revelation of truth through contemplating natural scenery. On 19 July, later to be described as 'that wonderful day' and to prompt regret when he found that he had recorded so little about it in his diary,[5] he wrote to Joan Severn, asking, 'Is it actually possible ... that God should speak to any single *one* of his creatures, ... through His cloud and blue heaven?'[6] The sense of a revelatory quality in the natural world that hovered in that question had put him on terms with Wordsworth's writings from a much earlier age. On a tour to the Lake District in 1830

ridge to the summit and come down in good time to dress and go out to dinner with 'Acland's friends the Butlers'—chiefly to meet a young Scotchman whom he would tell her about in Joanna's letter: *R. Works* xix, p. xxxi. In spite of the editors' conjectures the young Scotsman was almost certainly James Stuart: see above, p. 223 and n. 206 below. The Butlers were Josephine Butler and her family: E. Moberly Bell, *Josephine Butler* (1962), 69, quotes a person who met them at the Marshalls' house on Derwent Island and reported the happy atmosphere around them; Ruskin visited them also in Liverpool: ibid. 70. This is the most likely occasion, therefore, for the meeting with Myers, who was both a member of the Marshall family and devoted at this time to Josephine Butler (to whom he dedicated his poem 'St Paul').

[4] Letter of 15 Aug. 1867 (ALS L.33 Bembridge), quoted Burd, *Christmas Story*, 75. He had recorded in his diary for 3 Aug. (ii. 627) that he would reach 'half of my time' (in his waiting for Rose's answer) that night at 12, but there is no explicit mention of climbing Skiddaw on that day or the next; indeed, the first mention of the mountain by name is on 15 Aug., when he came back to Keswick for a short stay. The kneeling may have taken place just before the letter was written, therefore.

[5] *R Diaries* ii. 625 and n.

[6] Letter to Joan Severn of 19 July 1867 (Bembridge MSS), quoted Burd, *Christmas Story*, 72.

he and his parents had attended Rydal Chapel with the express intention of seeing the Laureate—whose appearance in the event disappointed the 11-year-old, 'especially as he seemed to be asleep the greater part of the time'.[7] As he grew up he could not escape the influence, however—and in a letter of 1843 to his college tutor, who had been comparing Coleridge and Wordsworth to the latter's disadvantage, he entered a spirited defence. In the last analysis, he wrote, Coleridge was an 'intellectual opium-eater'; as a human being, Wordsworth was infinitely greater:

Wordsworth has a grand, consistent, perfectly disciplined, all grasping, intellect—for which nothing is too small, nothing too great, arranging everything in due relations, divinely pure in its conceptions of pleasure, majestic in the equanimity of its benevolence—intense as white fire with chastised feeling.[8]

If one were asked which was 'the most beautiful statement of God's providence', *The Ancient Mariner* or 'Hartleap Well', he went on, one would be bound to choose the latter: 'This is absolute, perfect truth; it is the law of God's daily providence, no diseased dream of a heated imagination.' He also dwelt on the poems that had impressed him most: the 'noble notion of parental love' in 'Michael', the 'pure pathos' of 'The Brothers'—

And then read the 'Affliction of Margaret,' and the 'Female Vagrant,' and 'Lucie Gray,' and 'She dwelt among the untrodden ways,'—and then with the magnificent comprehension—faultless majesty of the 'Excursion,' to crown all ... how could you say what you did?[9]

The figure he was holding up for admiration was Wordsworth as he had presented himself in his later years—the Laureate of Victorian admiration, his main theme the potential nobility of human nature. It was entirely appropriate that when Ruskin won the Newdigate Prize for poetry a few years later with a poem much influenced by him and was called upon to recite it in the Sheldonian Theatre at Oxford the occasion coincided there with the award of an honorary degree to the poet, who presented him with the prize.[10] The first volume of *Modern Painters*

---

[7] *R Works* ii. 286–97.
[8] Letter to the Revd W. L. Brown, 20 Dec. 1843: Ibid. iv. 392.
[9] Ibid. 393.      [10] Hilton, *R Early Years*, 53.

in 1843 (along with each subsequent one) bore on its title-page a motto from *The Excursion* in which Wordsworth affirmed his devotion to 'Truth and Nature'; in its pages, likewise, he was quoted as exemplary, not only for his power of rendering precise natural detail but for the insight shown in the attitudes he fostered, such as the need to see the sky not as a level plane or passing-place for clouds but

> rather an *abyss*
> In which the everlasting stars abide . . .[11]

His gift of conveying the sense of a 'trembling transparency' made him in Ruskin's view fit for comparison with Turner.[12] It was the same with the description of the skyscape and water-scape in book nine, concluding with the little floating clouds,

> . . . giving back, and shedding each on each,
> With prodigal communion, the bright hues
> Which from the unapparent fount of glory
> They had imbibed, and ceased not to receive.
> That which the heavens displayed the liquid deep
> Repeated, but with unity sublime.[13]

'There is but one master whose works we can think of while we read this,' commented Ruskin.[14]

Wordsworth himself, having received the second volume of *Modern Painters* as a gift from Ruskin, praised him to the bringer for having 'given abundant proof how closely he has observed and how deeply he has reflected'.[15] Afterwards he was to commend it to visitors at Rydal Mount as the work of 'a brilliant writer'.[16] Ruskin, in turn, was to write of Wordsworth as 'one whose authority is almost without appeal in all questions relating to the influence of external things upon the pure human soul' and to speak of his 'intense penetrative depth',[17] while also praising individual passages such as the lines of the Immortality

---

[11] Wordsworth, *The Excursion*, III. 97–8.
[12] *Modern Painters* III. III. i. 8: R *Works* iii. 347.
[13] *The Excursion*, IX. 603–8.
[14] *Modern Painters*, II. III. ii. 9–10. R *Works* iii. 363.
[15] See Wordsworth's letter to William Boxall of 21 May 1846: WL (1840–53), 780–1.
[16] William Knight, *Life of William Wordsworth* (1889), ii. 334, iii. 243, cited Hilton, R. *Early Years*, 73.
[17] R *Works* v. 330.

Ode that began 'Heaven lies about us in our infancy'.[18] Yet despite such praise his attitude became more critical in the course of time, so that when he produced the third volume of *Modern Painters* he was able to write of Scott's superiority as an observer of nature, commenting that Wordsworth

cannot altogether rid himself of the sense that he is a philosopher, and ought always to be saying something wise. He has also a vague notion that Nature would not be able to get on well without Wordsworth: and finds a considerable part of his pleasure in looking at himself as well as at her.[19]

In the same volume, similarly, he bracketed Wordsworth with Goethe as men whose conversations gave an impression of their own self-estimation which did not compare well with those of writers such as Scott and Turner: 'The *slightest* manifestation of jealousy or self-complacency is enough to mark a second-rate character of the intellect.'[20] Even the 'Lines written . . . above Tintern Abbey', much admired for expressing a passionate youthful devotion to Nature, did not remain wholly sacrosanct. The lines beginning 'Nature never did betray the heart that loved her' were quoted in a talismanic manner in the first volume of *Modern Painters*,[21] but in 1873 he could after fourteen days of incessant wind and rain declare to Charles Eliot Norton that Nature herself had been 'traitress' to him— 'whatever Wordsworth may say'.[22]

It is possible that the modifying of his veneration had been set off initially by what was apparently his first visit to the poet, in 1847.[23] The appearance shortly afterwards of *The Prelude*, with its strong autobiographical element, may also have contributed to an impression that the poet was more self-absorbed than he had at first grasped. Certainly many of his later references are laced with criticism. Revising *Modern Painters* for the edition of 1883, for instance, he substituted for the passage from the Immortality Ode mentioned above the one about 'obstinate

[18] *R Works* iv. 78.
[19] *Modern Painters*, III. XVI. 38. *R Works* v. 343. This volume appeared six years after Wordsworth's death.
[20] Ibid., III. XVI. 25: *R Works* v. 332.
[21] Ibid., II. VI. 3, note to sect. 23: *R Works* iii. 628n.
[22] Letter of 13 Jan. 1873: *R Works* xxxvii. 57.
[23] Rydal Mount Visitors' Book, cited *WL* (1840–53), 780n.

questionings', adding in a note that while Wordsworth was indeed 'almost without appeal' (in the favourable sense) as to the impressions of natural things on the human mind, he was by no means so 'as to the logical conclusions to be surely drawn from them'.[24] One of Wordsworth's chief interests being in the relationship between nature and the human mind he did not always adopt the humility before Nature that Ruskin found proper: hence the appearance of various statements that he was likely to find puzzling or disturbing. Despite his admiration for the Immortality Ode, for example, he wrote, 'I think that what Wordsworth speaks of as a glory in the child, because it has come fresh from God's hands, is in reality nothing more than the freshness of all things to his newly opened sight.'[25] He did not question the feeling itself, affirming that it was one that he himself had experienced.[26] It may be doubted, however, whether he ever appreciated Wordsworth to the full, since in spite of the latter's insistence on accuracy in the representation of nature, he had not given that the same predominance over other qualities. By 1885, indeed, when Ruskin produced 'On the Old Road', he was sufficiently provoked by Matthew Arnold's recent praise of Wordsworth at Byron's expense to write,

Wordsworth is simply a Westmoreland peasant, with considerably less shrewdness than most border Englishmen or Scotsmen inherit; and no sense of humour, but gifted (in this singularly) with vivid sense of natural beauty, and a pretty turn for reflections, not always acute, but, as far as they reach, medicinal to the fever of the restless and corrupted life around him.[27]

He was also satirical at the expense of Wordsworth's 'complimentary addresses to the Deity upon his endurance for adora-

---

[24] *R Works* iv. 78 n. This view is further explained in Letter 92 of *Fors Clavigera* (*R Works* xxix. 457), where he affirms the relevance of the line to the innocence of childhood and declares that it is untrue only in the implied limitation to that period of human life, since he is sure that the sense of heaven's nearness deepens with advancing years.

[25] *R Works* v. 369 (cf. 363–4).

[26] He describes his own experience of it in *Modern Painters*, IV. XVII. 18: *R Works* v. 368 (referring also to iv, p. xxvi and v, p. xix). See also *Praeterita* I, ch. xii: 'On the journey of 1837, when I was eighteen, I felt, for the last time, the pure childish love of nature which Wordsworth so idly takes for an intimation of immortality.' *R Works* xxxv. 218.

[27] *R Works* xxxiv. 318.

tion'[28]—though in spite of such patronizing comments he insisted later in the same volume that he had used Wordsworth as a daily textbook from youth to age and had lived 'in all essential points according to the tenor of his teaching'.[29]

If he was unwilling to follow even the speculations that Wordsworth undertook concerning the relationship between the childhood imagination and immortality of the soul, this was because he had from an early age devoted himself even more assiduously to exact observation of nature, being for his own part rather sceptical of any evidences concerning immortality. Keeping one's eye on the object was for him a discipline more testing even than that envisaged by Wordsworth (who had spoken rather of endeavouring at all times to look steadily at his *subject*[30]). For Ruskin the prime duty was to be faithful to Nature exactly as she revealed herself. Wordsworth, by contrast, with his equal concern to understand the role of the human mind in relation to nature, could all too readily adopt a stance that would seem to Ruskin unacceptably egotistical.

Yet Wordsworth's egotism at least allowed for an active relationship between the human mind and the nature it observed and for the achievement in *The Excursion* of a vision that made that partnership seem providential. As the intellectual developments in the middle of the century proceeded, the kind of structure that Wordsworth had attempted to set up seemed less sure in its foundations. Commenting on the disappearance of faith around him Ruskin named the chief infidels in his society, remarking shrewdly as he did so that Wordsworth was 'anchored but anxious in faith'[31]—a formulation that might have been applied interestingly to himself.

Such considerations led to a displacement of some basic modes of discourse, affecting in different ways nineteenth-century methods both of fiction and of persuasive writing—which in that time could also pass under the name of prophecy. At the same time certain familiar modes of speaking and thinking continued to emerge, even though their underpinning had disappeared. One notes, for instance, how the concept of

[28] Ibid. 324. The allusion is to *The Excursion*, IV. 94: 'For adoration thou endur'st . . .'.
[29] R *Works* xxxiv. 349.
[30] Preface to *Lyrical Ballads* (1800): WPrW i. 132.     [31] R *Works* v. 323.

'providence', even if used with the hint of a question mark, can still emerge almost unnoticed into the flow of contemporary writing. This is even more true of Ruskin, whose ideas of the providential proved notably persistent despite his responsiveness to the implications of current debates. At 26, describing the sublimity of Mont Blanc in terms that recall Coleridge and Shelley, he made a telling comparison:

> So stands the Providence
> Of God around us: mystery of Love!
> Obscure, unchanging, darkness and defence . . .[32]

Often in his writings he would take its presence for granted. He shared the concern of writers such as Dickens and George Eliot with those who could invoke it too readily, being particularly critical of those who argued that people should 'be content with the station in which Providence has placed them': that was, he maintained, a maxim 'peculiarly for home use'.[33] It led too easily to the 'lies about Providence' against which he inveighed in *Fors Clavigera*.[34] 'It is not likely,' he wrote in *Sesame and Lilies*, 'that the more accurate methods of recent mental education will now long permit young people to grow up in the persuasion that, in any danger or distress, they may expect themselves to be saved by the providence of God, while those around them are lost by their improvidence.'[35] Yet he was also quite sure that the purposes of providence could be divined, as when he asserted that it could sometimes bestow greater powers only that we might be humiliated by their failure, or appalled by their annihilation;[36] or that the just point between poverty and profusion had been fixed for us accurately by its wise laws.[37] It was the shallowness of the contemporary view he was questioning, not its ultimate basis. In *Proserpina* he would complain that for twelve years the idea of any providence for anything had been warred against as if it were a dangerous and painful error, and declare that he had neither time nor patience to say anything there in its defence,[38] but just over a year before, in *The Bible of Amiens*, he had written a little more elaborately:

[32] *R Works* ii. 287.
[33] 'Unto this Last', *R Works* xvii. 112; cf. xvi. 400, xvii. 320, xviii. 422.
[34] *R Works* xxviii. 636.      [35] Ibid. xviii. 41.      [36] Ibid. xiv. 111.
[37] Ibid. xvi. 61.      [38] Ibid. xxv. 507.

. . . you have the broadly philosophic history, which proves to you that there is no evidence whatever of any overruling Providence in human affairs. . . . Meantime, the two ignored powers—the providence of Heaven, and the virtues of men—have ruled, and rule, the world, not invisibly; and they are the only powers of which history has ever to tell any profitable truth.[39]

The current scepticism concerning providence, that is, sprang in his eyes from an inability to understand it properly—which was for Ruskin a very different matter from its being non-existent. 'God's *laws*', he wrote to Elizabeth Barrett Browning, 'you can trace. His Providence never.'[40] In the lectures he gave at Oxford in 1870 and published under the title *Aratra Pentelici*, he gave the matter larger consideration than elsewhere, relating it primarily to Prometheus. He continued to contest what he saw as a common misconception:

But, so far as we use the word 'Providence' as an attribute of the Maker and Giver of all things, it does not mean that in a shipwreck He takes care of the passengers who are to be saved, and takes none of those who are to be drowned; but it *does* mean that every race of creatures is born into the world under circumstances of approximate adaptation to its necessities; and, beyond all others, the ingenious and observant race of man is surrounded with elements naturally good for his food, pleasant to his sight, and suitable for the subjects of his ingenuity;—the stone, metal, and clay of the earth he walks upon lending themselves at once to his hand, for all manner of workmanship.[41]

With this ingenious version of current ideas of adaptation he goes back to and develops the ideas of Paley, whose conception of providence, as we saw, was linked with attempts to exhibit the ways in which nature was adapted to man's needs. Ruskin gave the discussion a new direction by looking at the gifts of nature in a more specialized manner, urging that an artist's sensitivity to providence was shown by a willingness to use the particular gifts of a locality—to work in flint in a flint country, for example, or marble in a marble country.

The adeptness with which Ruskin could steer his readers through difficult waters was not lost on George Eliot. She described him early on as 'the finest writer living'[42] and stated her

[39] Ibid. xxxiii. 38.     [40] Letter of 1861: ibid. xxxi. 364.
[41] Ch. v: ibid. xx. 306.
[42] Letter to Barbara Leigh Smith of 13 June 1856: *GEL* ii. 255.

belief that his 'absurdities on practical points' did no harm, while he was to be venerated for 'the grand doctrines of truth and sincerity in art, and the nobleness and solemnity of our human life, which he teaches with the inspiration of a Hebrew prophet'. His best work was 'strongly akin to the sublimest parts of Wordsworth'.[43] 'The truth of infinite value that he teaches is *realism*,' she asserted in reviewing the third volume of *Modern Painters*, modifying this judgement only by an indulgent aside:

When he announces to the world in his Preface, that he is incapable of falling into an illogical deduction—that, whatever other mistakes he may commit, he cannot possibly draw an inconsequent conclusion, we are not indignant, but amused . . .[44]

How far George Eliot would have been willing to go in supporting her attendant claim that 'he sometimes glides from a just argument into a fallacious one' is not clear, but her highlighting of his confidence in his own logical powers was shrewd. A marked feature of his work is an apparent blindness when larger internal contradictions were involved: it is as if he could deal readily with logical structures provided they operated within a limited sphere, but sometimes failed to perceive wider inconsistencies—perhaps because he could not admit that his own underlying principles might in any way contradict one another. He could not for instance acknowledge that the new principles of vitalism which were coming into prominence with the rise of the biological sciences might clash with the claims of conventional morality. No man could better express either the sensuousness of nature or the stern claims of the old morality; no man could less readily admit that they might ultimately be in conflict. Believing as he did in both, he allowed logical systems based on these competing principles to exist side by side in the depths of his mind like great tectonic plates; the patterns of his thought cannot be understood indeed without awareness of their coexistence, since at times their subterranean movements threaten to create an earthquake at the surface far above. The existence of such unexamined contradictions may provide a means of accounting for his episodes of what was commonly described as

[43] Letter to Sara Sophia Hennell of 17 Jan. 1858: *GEL* ii. 422–3.
[44] *Westminster Review*, 65 (Apr. 1856), 626.

'brain-fever'. They were certainly crucial to his dealings with Rose La Touche, the young woman whom he loved with such passion and frustration during many years.

They may also help to explain a feature of Ruskin's work that must strike many readers. One's first impression is of confidence and authority, as of one drawing on a great body of principles in the manner he so admired in Wordsworth. On closer examination, however, he emerges as a less coherent thinker—though one of great energy—constantly finding new ways of organizing his ideas and moving through his intellectual space in successive orientations, each of which is presented as if firm and even final. He moves and thrusts according to the side of his thought that is uppermost at the time. This emerges, for instance, in his attitude to Blake, who, he declares, in expressing conditions of glaring and flickering light is greater than Rembrandt,[45] yet elsewhere mentions as a poet who wrote 'a pretty song about a tiger'.[46]

Sometimes the working of his affirmative powers leaves one conscious of fissures in his writing only when considered in retrospect. In the third volume of *Modern Painters*, for instance (the one George Eliot was reviewing when she made her remark), Ruskin turns to survey the Greek attitude to nature and by implication to devalue that of his contemporaries:

With us, observe, the idea of the Divinity is apt to get separated from the life of nature; and imagining our God upon a cloudy throne, far above the earth, and not in the flowers or waters, we approach those visible things with a theory that they are dead; governed by physical laws, and so forth. But coming to them, we find the theory fail; that they are not dead; that, say what we choose about them, the instinctive sense of their being alive is too strong for us; and in scorn of all physical law, the wilful fountain sings, and the kindly flowers rejoice.[47]

The alert reader notes an absence: Ruskin gives no clear indication of the attitude he would think proper for the modern observer. The existence of the gap seems due to doubts set up by the recent advances of science. It was a fine thing to set one's sights on the ancient rocks as guarantors of the stability of the

---

[45] *R Works* xv. 223.    [46] Ibid. xix. 56.
[47] *Modern Painters*, IV. xiii. 13: *R Works* v. 231.

universe—until they proved to be the site of views that questioned further stabilities. His comment to a friend in 1851 is well known—at least in its first part:

If only the geologists would let me alone, I could do very well, but those dreadful Hammers! I hear the clink of them at the end of every cadence of the Bible verses—and on the other side, these unhappy blinking Puseyisms; men trying to do right and losing their very Humanity.[48]

As often, Ruskin sets his position between equally unacceptable extremes: the challenge from the geologists is matched by that from the Puseyites, trying desperately to keep alive the ancient authority of the Church. He went on to maintain that the present task was to examine the true roots of humanity before the axe was laid to it. As with some other Victorians, his most common strategy when faced with the need for a positive attitude was to attempt a solution to the problem posed by apparent disparities between the view of nature emanating from contemporary science on the one hand and from traditional values and standards of morality on the other by expressing a belief in the existence of a 'higher' faculty in human beings, enabling them not only to recognize the presence of such contradictory forces in their own natures but to transcend them there.

Ruskin's favoured term for such a higher faculty was 'nobility'. By the 1860s, when the loss of a firm moral stay for civilization produced by acceptance of Darwin's theories was encouraging the development of an ideal of behaviour that might be held up independently as exemplary, the traditions of chivalry had come appropriately to the rescue. One of the great founding contemporary texts of the movement to revive its forms had been Kenelm Digby's *The Broad Stone of Honour*, first published many years before in 1822, and subtitled 'Rules for the Gentlemen of England'. In this book, Ruskin wrote, the reader would find 'every phase of nobleness illustrated'.[49] Mark Girouard's study provides a fascinating account of this cult in all its ramifications, ranging from the revival of courtly events or the building of pastiche castles to the promotion of chivalric

---

[48] Letter to Acland, 24 May 1851: *R Works* xxxvi. 115.
[49] *Modern Painters*, IX. vii. 23 n: *R Works* vii. 361 n.

behaviour.[50] The Eglinton Tournament of 1839, a Tory-supported event attended by 100,000 spectators, where the proceedings were at first delayed by the problems of organizing the procession and then, at the moment of combat, washed out by torrential rain, became a laughing-stock to the irreverent; to others it remained an inspiration.

By the 1860s, literal-minded revivals had been overtaken by the desire to make the ideals they embodied relevant to the social problems of the time. Ruskin saw the cultivation of them as a means of satisfying the need to 'undo the French Revolution and all the issues of it', acknowledging that 'the Loyalty and love of Kinghood and "Noblesse" (the word in French still sounds more real than in any other tongue) which it was an insane reaction from,—was indeed a beautiful thing in itself:—but then—the nobles had no care to preserve it by giving it just grounds . . .'.[51] He was less interested in reviving the outward forms of medieval chivalry than in finding ways to meet the demands of everyday nineteenth-century life by translating its values into modern terms. His creation of the Guild of St George represented his own attempt at an answer.

Yet in spite of this central social ideal individual behaviour remained the key. Even more than for Myers, the relentless cultivation of noble conduct was for Ruskin a source of positive values that could be left to bear the weight of the age's problems and provide a sense of hope. When Tennyson insisted that the key to Shakespeare's Sonnets was that they were 'noble' it is evident that he had equally in mind his own ideals, including his expressions of affection for Arthur Hallam in *In Memoriam*;[52] and Ruskin was upholding the same ideal when he inaugurated his Guild as a body to guide the bewildered young of his time. The first article of its creed began 'I trust in the Living God, . . . the kindness of his law and the goodness of his work', the second 'I trust in the nobleness of human nature, in the majesty of its faculties, the fulness of its mercy and the joy of its love . . .'[53]

---

[50] *The Return to Camelot* (1981). Chapter v is devoted to Digby's book and its influence.

[51] Letter to Mrs Cowper, 6 June 1869: *RLMT* 208. Ruskin's account of honour as an ideal is continued in the next letter: *RLMT* 210–11.

[52] See Christopher Ricks's notes and discussion in his edition of Tennyson's *Poems* (1969), 860–1.      [53] *R Works* xxviii. 419.

For Ruskin the true sign of nobleness was to be found less in rightness of moral conduct than in the cultivation of sensitivity.[54] His ideal of intellectual education was that it should develop the faculties of admiration, hope, and love, through 'the site and history of noble persons and the setting forth of noble objects of action'.[55] It was only when it came to art that the existence of limitations was suggested: 'the law of nobleness in music and poetry is that both are necessary and natural expression of pure and virtuous human joy or sorrow'.[56] A moral requirement had intervened, shading off at its extreme into a demand for innocence that figured also in the general view of love among his contemporaries.

Such demands had intensified even since the time of Wordsworth, who had been readier to respond, for example, to the strong physical frankness of Burns's writings: Ruskin respected Burns (he kept his grandfather's copy) but no more; for his father's favourite Byron, on the other hand, he had more time, on the grounds that he had the greater heart.[57]

The appeal of Byron stopped there, nevertheless. The contradictions of the period were nowhere more evident than in the pressure that could be brought to bear on love between the sexes when the demands of nature and the human heart were confronted by those of conventional morality. As in the case of Frederic Myers and Annie Marshall love could readily grow up through a shared responsiveness to the subtler beauties of nature, yet at the same time provoke sharp underlying conflicts between a physical desire that followed the demands of natural instinct and the spiritual possibilities inherent in a relationship between individuals. Claims that the sexual desires of human beings were both natural and irresistible were likely to be rejected in favour of a conservative insistence on the overriding claims of morality, yet to those who were trying to solve the problems of Darwinism by appealing to the 'higher nature' of humankind there was an appealing attractiveness in the idea that the sexual instincts might be chastened and subsumed into a new idealism. In the latter case it could be held that human love was the one area of experience which opened a window of

---

[54] *Modern Painters*, IX. VII. 6: R *Works* vii. 346.     [55] R *Works* xxviii. 656.
[56] Ibid. xxxi. 107.     [57] See the many tributes in *Praeterita*.

hope for the betterment of humanity, since qualities of selflessness were there displayed that offered the potentiality—if only
they could be universalized—of a general improvement in
human affairs. And the concomitant growth of individualism
meant that such love relationships might assume a quite unprec-
edented prominence—even more if they were thought of as
providential. Myers, as we have seen, gave himself intensely to
his Platonic ideal, believing that the high form of love described
in the *Symposium* transcended other kinds, taking them up into
itself and transmuting them in the process. Ruskin's view was
not dissimilar. In his 1877 letters to the author of a pamphlet
entitled *The Science of Life* he affirmed that 'there is no con-
queror of Lust but Love' and spoke contemptuously of 'this
beautifully scientific day of the British nation, in which you have
no God to love any more, but only an omnipotent coagulation
and copulation'. He challenged the view that lust was 'the
normal condition of sexual feeling': 'the great relation of the
sexes is Love, not Lust; that is the relation in which "male and
female created he them"; putting into them, indeed, to be distinctly restrained to the office of fruitfulness, the brutal passion
of Lust: but giving them the spiritual power of Love.'[58]

Even with the best will in the world the strains produced by
such a mixture of aspiration with subordination of physical
instinct might in the end prove intolerable. Frederic Myers's love
for Annie Marshall narrowly escaped that fate, while hers for
him did not, resulting in her case in a kind of noble madness.
Ruskin's love for Rose La Touche provides an equally tragic
example, in which both lovers were involved.

Given the insistence on the need for purity and innocence it
was a logical conclusion (even if at first sight a paradoxical one)
that the ideal relationship for such a male lover might be with a
much younger girl, in whom might be discerned more clearly
and purely qualities that answered to one's ideal. It was not
unknown for an individual to educate a young woman from her
earliest years in the hope of shaping her qualities into those of
a perfect wife. In the Romantic period a man might even discern
in a young child the ideal qualities that were to be loved and
nurtured as if by an actual lover. An extreme instance was the

---

[58] R *Works* xxxiv. 527, 530.

nympholepsy which De Quincey describes as having overtaken
his love for little Catherine Wordsworth after her death, causing
him frequently to visit her grave at night and to prostrate
himself on it;[59] another, less dramatic version is that which
appears to have existed between the Reverend Charles Dodgson,
*alias* Lewis Carroll, and Alice Liddell.[60] In the latter case a
young girl who had led a sheltered life and might not even
have had the experience of mingling with others of her age at
school was receiving the attentions of a man who bestowed a
quite unusual degree of affection. From one point of view, this
extension of the best kind of fatherly or avuncular love would be
overwhelmingly attractive; yet the later projection of such an
emotion into full love and even a proposal of marriage could
seem insidious—and even, in its own way, perverted—in the
way that it drew strength from the power-balance naturally
belonging to a relationship between intimates and excluded
the kind of love created by two people growing together in an
equal relationship and in successive alignments of alienation and
discovery.

In the case of John Ruskin and Rose La Touche the story
was originally begun in outline in the manuscript draft of his
autobiography—according to his own account against the advice of some 'wise and prettily mannered, people' who had
advised him that he 'shouldn't say anything about Rosie at all'.[61]
It has been told at some length on several occasions since, but
usually as part of some other enterprise.[62] During and after his
lifetime most of the letters that passed between the lovers themselves were burnt, so that the central running thread in the
relationship was obscured, but since at the same time he wrote

---

[59] *DQW* ii. 443.

[60] See A. L. Taylor, *The White Knight: A Study of C. L. Dodgson—Lewis Carroll*
(Edinburgh, 1952).

[61] *Praeterita*, III, ch. ii: R *Works* xxxv. 529.

[62] Fine and tactful accounts can be found, for example, in the biographies by
Leon, Wilenski, and Abse (see Abbreviations), while the introduction to Van Akin
Burd's edition of Rose La Touche's diaries, which is particularly full up to 1867,
takes account of material published after the first two wrote. I draw also on the
published Mount-Temple and Norton Letters, as well as unpublished material in the
Myers collection and letters in the John Rylands Library (extracts from which have
been printed in articles in the Library *Bulletin* and in Margaret Spence's book). By
drawing on the full range of these sources the following account acquires, I hope, a
uniqueness of its own.

compulsively to some intimate friends about its progress a number of discussions and descriptions survived. Out of this tessellated range of sources it is possible to piece together much of the story—which in consequence reads at times more like an epistolary novel; yet in spite of the successive accounts, each of which in any case has needed to be modified in view of new sources that appeared after it, it is still not easy to unravel all the events, or to discriminate the issues fully.

Ruskin's first connection with the La Touche household came in 1858, when Rose was only 10 years old and had been drawn to Ruskin's attention by her mother, who considered her artistic gifts unusual. There followed a return visit by her family to see his pictures at Denmark Hill, in the house where he lived with his parents. In the years following he cultivated the family further, becoming a great friend of Mrs La Touche, who shared his artistic interests. It was, however, the time when the impact of Darwin's work was at its most powerful ('tidal', to use Myers's word). Ruskin's religious doubts pressed hard. 'The great questions about Nature and God and man have come upon me in forms so strange and frightful,' he wrote to Carlyle in the summer of 1861.[63] Mrs La Touche, who was devoutly religious, became alarmed by what he told her of his changing views and persuaded him not to publish them for ten years.[64]

Meanwhile he found himself increasingly enchanted by Rose, with whom he exchanged letters each week that were full of observation and affectionate banter. During September he suggested that she should learn Greek and shortly afterwards she set to work, mastering the alphabet in a remarkably short time. During a visit by him to their house at Harristown in Ireland they also discussed various aspects of religion: 'she walked like a little white statue through the twilight woods talking solemnly'.[65] Soon afterwards, Rose showed some signs of illness, which were to recur at regular intervals for the rest of her life. Ruskin's parents wondered whether he was putting her under too much mental strain; his father also enquired shrewdly whether her illness might have anything to do with his attentions to her, to which he replied

---

[63] *R Works* xxxvi. 382.    [64] Burd, *RLT* 60–1.
[65] Letter to his father of 2 Sept. 1861, quoted Burd, *RLT* 61–2.

Rosie's illness has assuredly *nothing* to do with any regard she may have for me. She [likes] me to pet her; but is in no manner of trouble when I go [aw]ay. Her affection takes much more the form of a desire to please *me* and make me happy in any way she can, than of any want for herself, either of my letters or my company.[66]

Her natural beauty was evident: 'Rosie is very bright, bare-headed in the Irish sunshine—(purest wild rose-colour, with threads of gold—literally if one had to paint her hair it would have to be done as Perugino used—with real gold here and there).'[67] Many years later he would remember how her eyes were 'rather deep blue at that time, and fuller and softer than afterwards. Lips perfectly lovely in profile:— . . . the hair, perhaps, more graceful in that curl round the forehead.'[68] That was when she was 13; her beauty may have been irregular in its visitations, particularly as she passed into adolescence, but it was never to be lost.

Up to this time the La Touches had been happy to encourage the friendship with Ruskin and in the spring of 1862 went so far as to offer him a small cottage-house near theirs where he would be able to see her each day as she went to the village school to help with the teaching. A month later, however, the offer was dropped and it became clear that the La Touches wished to discourage his visits. Their underlying motives are by no means clear; the whole phase is indeed one of the most obscure in the affair. It is quite possible that they had begun to be worried about the effects on Rose of such a relationship. If she was affected by strains at this time, on the other hand, they were more likely to have come from the religious tensions in her own household. While Mrs La Touche retained allegiance to the established Church her husband, who for some time had been swayed by the preaching of Charles Spurgeon, was increasingly drawn to the Baptist faith and would be baptized in 1863. His wife did not share his views; Rose, who was deeply attached to him, followed the firmness of his conviction and from now on clung increasingly to Evangelical Christian doctrines as a stable source for her beliefs and conduct.

Rose herself was a complex individual. R. H. Wilenski de-

---

[66] Letter of 15 Nov. 1861: Burd, *RLT* 66 (also *variatim* R *Works* xxxvi. 386).
[67] Letter to Mrs John Simon, 2 Sept. 1861, quoted Burd, *RLT* 62.
[68] *Praeterita*: R *Works* xxxv. 525.

scribed her as 'precocious, subject to melancholy, a neurotic who continually brooded on religion',[69] Derrick Leon as 'always balanced upon the edge of physical and psychic ill health',[70]— though he also mentioned her exuberance. These and other accounts, based on the extraordinary vacillations of her behaviour at times, were written before all the evidence was available, including the diaries kept by her in the years 1861 and 1867, which allowed the young girl she had then been to speak for herself more fully. The first diaries show her as a lively and intelligent 13-year-old, unusual in her ability to judge the landscapes and works of art that she was seeing during a continental tour. The very lively responsiveness and wit make it unlikely that anyone reading them in isolation would regard them as neurotic; they are full of life, intelligence, and whimsy, with occasional side-references to Ruskin that exhibit her affection. If one had no other record one would assume that she was growing into a very normal young lady of the time. He himself was charmed by her letters and later reproduced extracts in the drafts for *Praeterita*, commenting on the utter selflessness and sympathy for him they displayed.[71] Their flavour is best gained from a full reading but a typical pair of sentences shows her drawing on a phrase of Coleridge's (ironically, one that he would have used for the first coming of love[72]) in order to describe the experience of waiting to see the sunrise from their train:

So we watched & suddenly there rose (popped w$^d$ be a better word) such a sun—'nor dim nor red' (you know the verse) & then dipped back again below the hills. It was so beautiful—But I shocked Mama by saying 'Jack in the box' which awoke Emily who declared of course she had been wide awake and had seen it all.[73]

There are, in fact, unfortunately few objective accounts by others of her development. At an early stage in the relationship, however, Georgiana Burne-Jones wrote to Ruskin that she saw a likeness in the portraits of him and Rose as children: 'both of them determined, don't let us say "obstinate"'.[74] Her later behaviour towards Ruskin was undoubtedly cruel in its effects, but

[69] Wilenski, *Ruskin*, 80–2.     [70] Leon, *Ruskin*, 390.
[71] *R Works* xxxv. 533.     [72] See above, p. 22.     [73] *R Works* xxxv. 531.
[74] Letter of 16 Dec. 1862, Pierpont Morgan Library, quoted Burd, *RLT* 82.

not intentionally so. Even Charles Eliot Norton, who commented, 'She has done you such harm & wrong that I who love
you find it hard to forgive her,' wrote of her still as 'the Lady of
perplexity and pain'.[75]

The most surprising account of Rose is one that appeared
more than thirty years after her death. Its anonymous author
described her as 'a very lovely girl, with deep blue eyes, flaxen
hair, exquisitely chiselled features, somewhat aquiline nose,
and mouth indicative of firmness. She had chosen all knowledge
for her province, and was an admirable scholar. She was
very brilliant in conversation, and had an encyclopaedic
memory. She was moreover an accomplished horsewoman. In
politics she was a convinced Radical.'[76] No other surviving
account comes near the richness and variety of this one, though
it is consistent with the intelligence shown in the early writings
already quoted. If one assumes that it refers to a time (perhaps
in the mid-1860s) before she felt the full strain of the relationship it suggests how much was lost through subsequent events
and pressures.

With this account we may compare a later one from Ruskin
himself:

Rose was tall and brightly fair, her face of the most delicately chiselled
beauty—too severe to be entirely delightful to all people—the eyes
gray, and when she was young, full of play; after the sad times came,
the face became nobly serene—and of a strange beauty—so that once
a stranger, seeing her for the first time, said 'she looked like a young
sister of Christ's.'[77]

Between the two accounts (with their striking resemblances)
falls the shadow of Rose's ill-health, beginning when, after the
ominous signs of 1862, she suffered what her mother called one
of her 'mysterious brain-attacks'.[78] In the account of the subsequent illness which she sent to Mrs MacDonald and to George
MacDonald the novelist, one of those who had become

---

[75] Letter of 4 May 1874: *RCEN* 315.
[76] A writer in the *Freeman's Journal*, 27 Nov. 1906, after the death of Rose's
mother, quoted in *R Works* xxxv. lxxvn.–lxxvin.
[77] From a memoir written at the end of 1884, quoted in 'John Ruskin in the
Eighties', *Outlook*, 21 Oct. 1899, p. 380.
[78] Letter from Mrs La Touche to George MacDonald postmarked 15 Oct. 1863,
quoted Burd, *RLT* 89.

interested in psychic phenomena, she commented on some of its more mysterious aspects:

(she) has had a really dreadful illness, so long and full of strange changes, the only thing that never changed was her vivid and happy faith, in God and in her mother. It was wonderful, and in my long watching I often thought of you for there were what the doctors called 'psychic phenomena' that you would have understood better than anyone I know. Being with her was like a Revelation to me. There was a sort of clairvoyance, both of spiritual and earthly things, which was startling. For the first fortnight of her illness she was able to tell beforehand every little thing that would befall her thro' the day, and always said that she was 'guided' in everything. The doctors were perfectly amazed and actually yielded against their judgment in allowing her to follow this 'guidance' which never once erred. I do believe It—whatever It was—spared her much suffering and saved her much 'treatment' but she became frightfully emaciated and weak at the end of four weeks in bed. Then came the most wonderful change. From a state of weakness so great that she could not sit up in bed, she suddenly after one night's sleep awoke perfectly strong in body, but with an infant's mind, an infant's playfulness, and an entire oblivion of all acquired knowledge, and of every person and thing not known to her eleven years ago. By degrees she grew out of this state and it was quite lovely to watch her growth, a beautiful ideal infancy and childhood liv'd thro' in a fortnight. She told me, in the prescience that was given her before, exactly how all this would be, and named the day and hour in which her strength would return and her mind fail. Thus I was *quite* untroubled, for she had spoken with authority, and had all thro' said, that she would recover perfectly from this illness, body, mind and all, but that the mind would be the last to recover. I was both pitied and laughed at for believing her, but everything came true. She is well now, except for a weakness in her brain which makes it painful for her to have any thought or idea suggested to her in words, unless she asks for it—so she is not able to see people at all, and cannot either read or be read to . . .[79]

In her own account of the illness Rose wrote entirely in religious terms, maintaining that she had resigned herself to the mercy of God and that the guidance she received had been a direct result of that. It was her mother, or perhaps the doctors, who made the connection with 'psychic phenomena', reflecting the recent widespread interest in Britain. Mrs La Touche's reference

[79] Letter to George MacDonald, 19 Nov. 1863, quoted Leon, *Ruskin*, 360.

suggests that she knew Mrs MacDonald to be interested in such matters; through their mutual friend Mrs Cowper, who had become drawn to spiritualism, they were in turn to be taken more seriously by Ruskin as time went by; the notion of being 'guided' would become particularly important to him. Equally interesting are the indications that after this illness Rose was, if not born again, at least totally renurtured: it was as if she was being remade *ab initio*. Such an experience was bound to leave its mark on her personality and may help to account for the subsequent firmness of her attitude in the midst of other shiftings. On this reading her religious belief had become closely linked with her instinct for survival.

Despite the submissiveness she showed during her illness, she was not a passive or quiescent creature. At the time of her 1863 collapse, it is true, she had to be kept in a quiet and darkened room, not being able to bear either 'a gleam of light or a whisper',[80] but by the spring of 1865 Mrs La Touche could write that her returning strength had brought problems of a different kind:

Rosie is quite well—the cold makes no difference to her, nor does rain or snow or the bitter white frost and fog of morning and evening. Anything to her is better than many happy hours indoors. . . . She is perfectly wild & how she is ever to be made a modern 'young lady' of, I can't imagine! She is out from dawn till dark, & it is utterly useless to put on her any raiment that would not suit a peasant, or to expect from her any observance of the restraints of civilization, such as wearing a bonnet under any circumstances whatsoever—or decently thin [!] boots. . . .

She is out always at early morn—in and out of every cottage, as if she was everybody's dog. . . . She is a wonderfully *available* little creature in all the saddest realities of life, and yet they never do her a bit of harm. I wish Mr MacDonald could put her into a book—with her cream-coloured pony and her huge dog, and her wonderfully independent ways. . . .

Rosie gets on with all the poor people better than I do. I am afraid of intruding. They have no servant at the door to say 'not at home' or 'particularly engaged'. But Rosie runs in and out of the cabins as a breeze of wind might do . . .[81]

[80]  Leon, *Ruskin* 359; Burd, *RLT* 89.
[81]  Letter from Mrs La Touche of 14 Mar. 1865, quoted MacDonald, *Reminiscences*, 105–6 and in part, with variations, Burd, *RLT* 93.

Only a month before Ruskin had described her in not dissimilar terms: 'You know,—the child's just like a wild fawn—and she likes me well enough—about as much as a nice squirrel would.'[82] In September, similarly, Mrs La Touche wrote again: 'the Wild Rose is very well, but wilder than ever' and that she was wondering whether Rose would ever be a civilized being:

She is out in the dew like Nebuchadnezzar at break of day—and all day long she is in and out, let the weather be what it may, and not one single thing that girls do does she do—except a *little* music when she pleases. She has the run of all the cottages and cabins about, gets fed from the labourers' dinners and is an exception to every rule and custom of society.[83]

Much of her wild charm was perhaps made possible by the very strength of her father's religious doctrines and her unquestioning allegiance to them, which in giving her an underlying stability allowed her, paradoxically, to indulge her natural instincts more freely. But within a few years the devotion to her father's views overtook the attractive wildness, causing the 'spirituality' that became so marked a feature for those who met her to harden into something more dogmatic. Her wildness was in any case not self-regarding, as is shown by her care for the villagers, including her attempts to patch their quarrels.[84] This side of her activities would be more prominent a few years later.

Ruskin himself wrote of her 'genius' and 'wild spiritual nature'[85]—a striking description which one would like to have seen filled out more. Torn by the intellectual struggles of the age and beaten down by the emotional struggles of his recent private life, he found in his developing love for her a strand of affection to which he could cling. A letter to MacDonald in 1864 contains one of his earliest references:

I can't love anybody except my Mouse-pet in Ireland, who nibbles me to the very sick-death with weariness to see her.[86]

[82] Letter of 13 Feb. 1865, quoted Burd, *RLT* 93.
[83] Letter of 25 Sept. 1865 at Yale: cited Burd, *RLT* 94 and quoted more fully Leon, *Ruskin*, 361.
[84] Letter of 14 Mar. 1865: MacDonald, *Reminiscences*, 106.
[85] Letter to Margaret Ruskin, 18 May 1868: *R Winnington*, 625–6.
[86] Letter of 8 Feb. 1864: MacDonald, *Reminiscences*, 109.

This language of petting and affection, typical of the age,
also indicates Ruskin's desire to find a mediating mode that
would fill the widening gap between the natural and the moral
demands in his society. The growing importance to him of
her affection was shown by the fact that in 1866, when she
was 18, he proposed marriage. In reply, she asked leave to delay
her reply for three years (when she would come of age).
Before this could happen, however, her parents, discovering the
situation, forbade her to communicate with him. Ruskin, his
love for her checked only by a firm insistence that she obey them
in all things, sought constantly to find ways of resolving the
situation; the parents, meanwhile, adamantly refused permission to meet.

Caught in this situation Ruskin made confidants of one or
two friends, discussing developments as they emerged and looking to them for support. Mrs Cowper, probably the most important, had in fact crossed his path more than twenty years before
in Rome, when she was Georgiana Tollemache and he had
reverenced her beauty from a distance, visiting the church of
Santa Maria in Aracoeli in the hope of seeing her there.[87] She
had married William Cowper in 1848. Once he grasped that
this was the same woman he had so admired in his youth, the
memory became a strong link between them: a later request to
help him with his love for Rose 'for Aracoeli sake'[88] suggests
that he not only made a conscious association between the two
loves but at times tried to perceive a nexus between them and
the world of spirits to which Mrs Cowper was introducing him.
He came to regard her as his 'Madonna and Stella Maris';[89] their
house at Broadlands, where she entertained with gracious hospitality, was for him on occasion a haven of peace and tranquil-
lity. In 1863 they had introduced him to the MacDonalds,
who would also on occasion act as intermediaries with the La
Touches.

---

[87] See his account in *Praeterita* II, chs. ii and vi: *R Works* xxx. 191–2. Elsewhere
he recalls her 'statuesque serenity with womanly sweetness joined' and refers to her
as 'the living Egeria of Aracoeli': *R Works* xxxv. 277, 349. See also his letter to
Blanche Atkinson of 13 July 1873: Bodleian MS Eng lett. c. 39 fo. 128.

[88] Letter of 19 Feb. 1866, *RLMT* 53. In 1870 he expressed a hope that she would
go and look into his study sometimes 'just that I may remember Aracoeli': *RLMT*
267.

[89] *RLMT* 65.

That Mrs Cowper should succeed in interesting Ruskin in the psychical phenomena to which she had become devoted was by no means predictable, given his tendency to take a hardheaded view of such things. Yet certain aspects of what was now being studied corresponded with feelings that he, like Wordsworth, had experienced in earliest childhood, so that he could remark 'I am not now more surprised at perceiving spiritual presence, than I have been, since I was a youth, at not perceiving it.'[90] He was passing through a hard time, following the death of his father in March 1864 and the interventions by the La Touches to prevent his seeing Rose. Despite a strong note of scepticism in the letters where he discussed séances at which he had been present, he was unwillingly impressed. The problem for him at this point was not so much that of accepting the facts that were being conveyed, as of tolerating their frequent triviality. Of one session he writes

On the whole I am much happier for it, and very anxious for next time, but there is something also profoundly pitiful, it seems to me, in all that we can conceive of spirits who can't lift a ring without more trouble than Aladdin took to carry his palace, and I suppose you felt that their artistic powers appear decidedly limited.[91]

Some of the evidence that came forward kept him fascinated, nevertheless. One of the messages evidently concerned his earlier admiration for Mrs Cowper; he writes to her, 'That bit about the Aracoeli is of course irresistible'.[92] Yet he continued to be troubled by the larger implications of such experiences. It was not just the undertones of banality in the manifestations themselves; still worse was the recognition that the spirits did not always behave in a way that supported his own ideals of nobility, leaving him with the sense of 'a wrongness and falseness somewhere':

It seems, in the *best* people, to mean some slight degree of nervous disease: while in most of the instances I have heard of—or seen—it has not been manifested at all to the best people,—or the wisest.

It was particularly galling to discover the spirits apparently very ready to visit S. C. Hall, who conversed about art in a 'harmful

---

[90] Letter of Apr. 1864, *RLMT* 31.    [91] Ibid.
[92] Letter of 19 Dec. 1864, *RLMT* 43.

and mistaken' manner, yet not interested in himself—in spite of
his claims to greater expertise.[93] Eventually, after some demonstrations in 1868, he was to turn against the spiritualists altogether for the time being, on the grounds that the behaviour of
the spirits was identifiable with that of the 'familiar spirits'
condemned in the Bible. He would urge the Cowpers to 'have
done with mediums', and to take a walk with him through the
streets of London instead.[94] His language suggests that he
was coming to regard the phenomena as dangerously close to
devilry.[95]

The relationship with Rose and her parents became meanwhile steadily more fraught. The problem was not altogether
dissimilar. Ruskin could not accept that someone who was
behaving in such a noble and irreproachable manner towards
her as he believed himself to be doing should be treated with so
little respect.[96] At the same time he remained confident that since
he and Rose understood one another at a deeper level than her
parents could possibly appreciate, their relationship must eventually be triumphant. One of the best early accounts of his
feelings was given to Mrs Cowper in a letter plausibly dated
early in 1866, where he argued, in opposition to Mr La
Touche's resistance to their growing intimacy, that their relationship could only enhance hers with her father. He then went
on to describe his own attitude:

For me it is not a question of pain and of healing. It is a question of
two kinds of life—spiritual or material: The love of her is a religion to
me—it wastes and parches me like the old enthusiasm of the wild
anchorites. I do not know how long I could bear it without dying—in
that waiting—I am not sure even—how far in its conceivable happiness, it might be endurable by me—it might kill me soon—if the least
pang of doubt or regret for her, mingled with it; But I can part with it,
and take up material life of a kind, among stones, and plants, and the
like—and not die—nay—not be unhappy I told her this; and it is
true.—I was really quite happy examining the angles of calcite, before

[93] Letter of 6 Aug. 1866, *RLMT* 79.
[94] MS Letter of 2 Apr. 1868 (27M/60 Broadlands Estate Documents), quoted by
Van Akin Burd in *Ruskin, Lady Mount-Temple and the Spiritualists: An Episode in
Broadlands History*, Guild of St George Lecture (1982), 19–20.
[95] Four years before he had reported Carlyle's view that spiritualism was 'real
witchcraft': *R Works* xxxvi. 464.
[96] See his letter of 22 Mar. 1866, *RLMT* 68–9.

she came this time—and I can be again,—but it is no question of time
or healing—it is of being a lower or higher creature, for ever—or for
such ever as God has made us for.[97]

Two striking features of this account are the straightforward
adoption of the contemporary belief in the distinction between
'higher' and the 'lower' natures in humanity and the fact that,
unlike Myers, Ruskin betrays so little sense of a 'Platonic' conception of love, his love for Rose being cast rather in ascetic and
medieval terms—in the older romance tradition, in fact. There
was a touch of self-abasement, shading off into a willingness to
relapse into the life of rocks and stones and trees if he could not
be allowed to behave as a human being of a 'higher' kind. This
was coupled with indifference to the idea of intellectual collabo-
ration with her. So far as the last is concerned—which might
be considered a surprising attitude in view of her gifts—he
explained to Mrs Cowper why he needed no feminine companionship in his work:

... in my *small* specialty, I know that no one can help me—nor is it
intellectual sympathy that I need. I have enough of it from men. I do
not care for it from women:—nor is it even love that I need. I have had
much given me: But I want *leave* to love: and the sense that the creature
whom I love is made happy by being loved: That is literally all I want.
But it seems to me indeed—all—that without that all else is nothing. I
don't care that Rosie should love *me*: I cannot conceive such a thing for
an instant—I only want her to be happy in being loved:—if she could
tread upon me all day—& be happy—because it was me she trod on:
it would be all I want.[98]

Six months later he was producing a more complicated version
of his self-subordination. A reference to Jacob's seven-year service as herdsman to Laban for the hand of his daughter Rachel[99]
suggested a grander conception of his love, to be followed by a
turn of imagery, first into that of the Prodigal Son in his wretch-
edness and then to Lazarus at the rich man's gate:

... let M^r La Touche take me for a herdsman—*at Harristown*—give
me a shed to sleep in—and the husks that the swine did eat, for food—
and see if I should tire! But as it is—I am so sick already for the sight
of her, that—if it were not that it would plague herself, I would go to

[97] *RLMT* 60.     [98] Letter of 16 Mar. 1866, *RLMT* 64.     [99] Gen. 29: 18.

Ireland now, and lie down at their gate—and let them do what they chose with me, but I would see her.[100]

It does not seem to have occurred to Ruskin at any point that his love deserved to end in anything but success, given his nobility of attitude. That it might have been against Rose's best physical interests (a consideration which clearly weighed more heavily with her mother) would have been hard for him to conceive. How could nature and nobility be at such odds?

She herself, meanwhile, was torn between the two. Her mother, furious with her in late October on discovering that she had been hiding some of Ruskin's letters, accused her of being hard and unloving, forbade her to come into her room and told her there would be no further affection between them. Rose wrote to Mrs Cowper in her distress, telling her how horrible it was to hear her parents describe Ruskin as 'dishonourable'.[101] Her mother made it up almost immediately, but within a few days renewed the hurt.[102] In the following year Rose wrote a spiritual autobiography in which she not only discussed her strivings to act with moral rightness throughout her life so far but recalled how impressed she had been at the age of 12 by Ruskin's social teaching.[103] A characteristic that stands out is her seriousness of mind, coupled with determination to pursue ideas to their logical conclusion. She recalls, for instance, how she became worried by the question of the proper day for celebration of the Sabbath, reflecting that if the Bible were to be interpreted exactly according to the Old Testament commandments, Christians should be observing the seventh day. Whether this is regarded as over-serious or positively neurotic, the main point for attention is that as a sensitive young woman with little experience of human affairs on a wide scale, she had become so obsessed by points of logical detail. In the conflict for possession of her mind between her father and Ruskin, Rose was pulled sometimes in the direction of orthodox religion, sometimes in that of Ruskin's social teaching. On her father's estates she was strongly conscious of the effects of poverty and did what she

---

[100] Letter to Mrs Cowper of 28 Sept. 1866, *RLMT* 87.
[101] Letter to Mrs Cowper of 29 Oct. 1866, in Van Akin Burd, 'More Letters from Rose La Touche', *Bulletin of the John Rylands Library*, 65 (1983), 63.
[102] Ibid. 65.    [103] Burd, *RLT* 159.

could to minister to the poor. One problem for her, however, was that while her father's interpretation of his religion explicitly included the claims of humanitarianism, Ruskin's teachings rejected the more extreme doctrines of the Evangelicals. She could, in other words, satisfy more of her nature by following her father than by following Ruskin. Yet it was not as simple a matter as that might seem, since what appealed most immediately to her in religion was the teaching of Jesus in the Gospels; and at this level she agreed with Ruskin, perceiving that the beliefs of those who surrounded her, benevolent as they might be, did not meet the radical social claims of the time. There Ruskin came demonstrably closer to some of the Gospel teachings.

Her mind was by no means uncritical, moreover. According to her later account,[104] efforts were made to keep from her the discussions of the Higher Criticism of the Bible which now dominated many theological debates but she overheard conversations which she understood better than she was meant to; much, of course, was made of the inconsistencies between various biblical accounts of the same events. When she also followed the view of her father that there was no need for a baptized believer to pass through any other test before attending the Lord's Supper she found herself in conflict with her mother, who insisted that she ought not to go until she had been confirmed. It was in fact after she had followed her father's beliefs on this occasion in 1863 that she suffered her first severe illness.

Her intellectual and emotional conflicts continued. In her susceptibility to them she was not unlike Ruskin himself, moreover, who might write of 'those accursed religious hot-mushroom-sauces of her poor little head'[105] but suffered just as severely from the subterranean effects of the self-contradictions he tried to keep in balance. Rose's precarious state of health was characterized by an unwillingness to eat: in medical terms she may well have been exhibiting (as Joan Abse supposes[106]) *anorexia nervosa*. The painful conflict of mind set up in her by

---

[104] Burd, *RLT* 160–2.
[105] Letter to Dr John Brown of 1864 in the National Library of Scotland, quoted Burd, *RLT* 92.
[106] Abse, *Ruskin*, 262–3.

Ruskin's persistent attentions must have been at once attractive and disturbing. Small wonder that she clung to a firm basis for her beliefs—a course of action in which she showed herself more straightforwardly logical than Ruskin himself. Since his opposition to Evangelical doctrines ran deep enough to have given pain to his own mother, he was not likely to give ground now on the issue, even if his own current beliefs owed much to them. Although his attitude to religion was self-consistent, it had evolved through a complex process—including an element of belief in his own rightness that would in itself be thought by some to conflict with traditional Christian teaching. It was natural for Rose to cling to the established beliefs held by the people with whom she was most intimate and which therefore constituted a more accessible form of reality.

There was a period of particular stress and confusion from early in 1867, when Ruskin besought John La Touche that he might see Rose's face once more; the reply was couched in 'such terms as—A Banker uses to his clerk, I suppose'.[107] Rose's parents, seeing their lack of success in discouraging her response to Ruskin's pleas, intensified their efforts, behaving as a result in ways that he felt to be morally wrong. In August he wrote to Charles Eliot Norton that his relationship with Mrs La Touche had become very like that of the Master of Ravenswood to Lady Ashton,[108] indicating his search for a narrative template against which to fit his experience while insisting on the nobility of his own behaviour; the fact that in *The Bride of Lammermoor* Providence was spoken of as preparing 'a dreadful requital' for the villain[109] would have been reassuring. Seizing on such a work of fiction facilitated demonization of the other participants in his own drama and helped press his reading of the whole situation to a point where what had happened might be seen as part of a larger struggle between good and evil.

Rose promised to send him a letter on Christmas Day, leaving him when she failed to do so in a frantically agonized state of mind.[110] She, meanwhile, had had a further illness and been sent to a nursing-home, where Lily Armstrong, one of Ruskin's young friends at Winnington, found her strapped down to her

[107] Letter to Mrs Cowper of 27 Feb. 1867, *RLMT* 109.
[108] Letter to Norton of 8 Aug. 1867: *RCEN* 104.
[109] *The Bride of Lammermoor* II, i.          [110] Leon, *Ruskin*, 391.

bed and wrote to him at the end of January expressing concern.[111] There appears to have been a meeting shortly afterwards, which led to an intense correspondence with Mrs
Cowper as Ruskin found himself unable fully to understand
what was going on. Rose, he reported, 'wished me to be Lover
and Friend to her always—no more':

She spoke fearlessly, as a woman in Shakespeare would have done—as
the purest women are always able to do, if left unspoiled. She thought
it was what I wished, as it had been so with my first wife. On my
refusal, she refused all that she *could* refuse. She cannot, my love nor
my sorrow.[112]

Although she was not due to come of age until the following
year Ruskin gained the impression soon after (rightly or
wrongly) that she had been given permision to correspond with
him; on 10 May he wrote: 'she has free leave to write now, what
she will'.[113] A mystifying message received from her next day
ran, 'There is nothing but this "cannot" to separate our life and
love.' This he thought could mean that Rose was herself incapable of consummating the marriage—in which case he felt that
gossip about the ending of his former marriage might be revived,
losing him all his power to do good by his teaching. Driven
almost frantic by the resulting uncertainty, he wrote for clarification to Rose's friend Lady Higginson, who he believed to be in
her confidence—which only made matters worse when Lady
Higginson proved less discreet than he had assumed: the matter
reached the ears of Rose's advisers.[114]

It is not unlikely that Rose's 'cannot' had to do with her most
recent illness, and that her doctors had been led to advise against
her marrying on the grounds of her health, without, however,
having their opinion conveyed to Ruskin. Alternatively, she may
have been referring to the dictates of her religious position.
Whatever the meaning, there now followed a series of waverings
in Rose's feelings which drove Ruskin almost to distraction.
Meanwhile her family, realizing that Ruskin's attentions were
not easily to be stopped and that in spite of all their efforts to
the contrary Rose was writing encouraging letters to him, decided to approach his former wife Effie Millais in the hope of

---

[111] Ibid.     [112] Letter of 4 Mar. 1868, quoted ibid. 392.
[113] *R Winnington* 618.     [114] Leon, *Ruskin*, 392.

obtaining evidence concerning their marriage. Although the most crucial letters have not survived, their effect was to confirm what the La Touches already no doubt believed or suspected, that the annulment had been granted on the grounds of impotence on Ruskin's part: they were thus able to present the information to Rose as conclusive against the marriage. In a letter of 21 May her mother thanked Effie for providing information 'that has saved her, and us all, from much misery'.[115]

Had Ruskin really been totally impotent, as was implied in the suit that ended the marriage, the La Touches would evidently have had good cause to intervene, but it is virtually certain that he was not. He himself denied it categorically to George MacDonald, maintaining that he had withheld consummation because he believed the sexual relationship to be sacred and had not grown to love Effie as he had hoped.[116] There was clearly an element of distaste on his part, however, and it may well be that something about the physicalities of sexual encounter had shocked his over-refined nature, at least in his early experiences.[117] At all events Effie now pointed out that if Ruskin and Rose were to publish banns of marriage, this would throw doubt on the grounds of nullity that had been crucial to the ending of marriage from her own point of view, and that she would therefore be forced to publicize them in self-defence. This again suggests the existence of doubt in the case, since otherwise evidence that could have been used before would still have been valid.

Yet in a larger sense, and for different reasons, Ruskin's case was compromised. His defence that he had been unwilling to consummate the marriage with someone he did not love, if true, meant that his behaviour had compounded nobility with falsehood in an unusual mélange. The fact that it was in his interest to allow the falsehood to stand meant, indeed, that an element of bad faith was involved. According to Derrick Leon, 'he told George Allen that he could have defended the suit (presumably on the grounds of his wife's frigidity and reluctance), but that had he done so he would have been "saddled with the woman for life"'.[118]

---

[115] Letter of 21 May 1868, quoted Lutyens 'Correspondence', 9 (Burd, *RLT* 112).
[116] MacDonald, *Reminiscences*, 100–1.          [117] Ibid. 115.
[118] Leon, *Ruskin*, 404.

The charge that Ruskin was impotent may or may not have been found devastating by Rose, who according to his account as quoted above had already digested the lack of intimacy in the previous marriage and resolved that she could accept such a situation. If she had not known of the alleged reasons for that lack she might well have had to take her parents' word on the matter and its likely consequences. Yet supposing that to have been all that was in question she might still have regarded it as a suitable occasion for self-sacrifice.

In the subsequent period the picture is more confused than it might otherwise have been by the fact that both parties were dealing with one another partly through intermediaries, each having to interpret the other by way of distortions. In these circumstances feelings of acrimony could easily accrue. In February 1870, for instance, Ruskin, embittered by a letter from Rose in which she enquired whether all was 'at peace' between them, replied telling her of the dedication he was planning to inscribe in the copy of his lectures he would be sending her:

> To the woman,
> Who bade me trust in God, and her,
> And taught me
> The cruelty of Religion
> And the vanity of Trust,
> This—my life's most earnest work
> Which—without her rough teaching,
> Would have been done in ignorance of these things
> Is justly dedicate.

Wounded by this letter Rose wrote a letter of remonstrance, requesting Mrs Cowper-Temple to send it to him if she thought fit. In the course of it she said

> I do not think it is much use my saying how bitterly untrue some of your letter is. One thing I am sure—it is utterly impossible for us to judge each other—you me, or I you. Certainly I *cannot* know you, or your circumstances and feelings, and every word you write shows that you have not the faintest idea of mine.
>
> I am influenced and must be influenced, and have had to be obedient and I have never known or had a chance of knowing for the last three years *what* was kind or right.

I haven't the least faith in my own judgment, but I *can* only do what seems to me least wrong. . . .[119]

Mrs Cowper-Temple did not pass on the letter, so that any effect it might have had was lost. Rose then wrote a further reply (possibly at her prompting) which was at once positive and straightforward:

I will trust you.

I do love you. I have loved you, though the shadows that have come between us could not but make me fear you and turn from you—I love you, & shall love you always, always—& you can make this mean what you will.

I have doubted your love. I have wished not to love you. I have thought you unworthy, yet surely as I believe God loves you, as surely as my trust is in His Love.

I love you—still, and always.

Do not doubt this any more.

I believe God meant us to love each other, yet life—and it seems God's will has divided us.

My father & mother forbid my writing to you, and I cannot continue to do so in secret. It seems to be God's will that we should be separated, and yet—'thou art ever with me.' If my love can be any sunshine to you—take—and keep it. And now—may I say God bless you? God, who is Love—lead—guide, & bless us both.[120]

Although almost all the correspondence was later destroyed this was probably the most crucial letter of all since, whatever its implications, it contained the assurance Ruskin most wanted. Overjoyed, he wrote to Mrs Cowper-Temple (as she was now called[121]),

She has come back to me. She will not leave me any more, 'If my love is any sunshine to you take it—& keep it.'

—I may not yet see her—not even write. But with you, and her both—loving me—I may be content—I think! I rather rejoice in the thought of the faraway—dream-worship I must render to you both.[122]

---

[119] Letter of 21 Feb., published Leon, *Ruskin*, 480.

[120] Letter received on 24 Feb. and transcribed into letter to Mrs Cowper of 20 Mar. 1870: *RLMT* 273–4.

[121] She and William Cowper called themselves Cowper-Temple from 1869 and became Lord and Lady Mount-Temple on his elevation to the peerage in 1880.

[122] Letter of 23 Feb. 1870: *RLMT* 268.

To George MacDonald also he wrote in March, saying that the 'great darkness' had ended for him.

R. has come back to me—and nothing now can take her from me—in heart—though if fate will have it so I may never see her—but she is mine—now. No one must know this, however—as it would cause her infinite grief and pain with her people—but she is in peace now—and I also—which is much. It is all too late—all vain and full of shadows. But not full of *bitterness* any more—and if my strength is spared to me—I can work now, perhaps none the worse in the sadness—or the dream, of the strange—distant—moonlight—than others could in the sun.[123]

Yet despite what might have seemed the establishment of a permanent basis and a *modus vivendi* for the future, the happier state of affairs did not last long. As Ruskin attempted to gain new clarification of his marital status in the hope of establishing once and for all that he was free to marry Rose, her parents, alarmed by what they were coming to learn of this new turn in her attitude (particularly since she had now, in any case, come of age) redoubled their efforts to gain evidence of Ruskin's behaviour to his former wife. In response to a further letter Effie Millais wrote a denunciation more scathing than before:

His conduct to me was impure in the highest degree, discreditable and so dishonourable that I submitted to it for years not knowing what else to do, although I would have often been thankful to have run away and envied the people sweeping the crossings. His mind is most inhuman; all that sympathy which he expects and gets from the female mind it is impossible for him to return except upon artistic subjects which have nothing to do with domestic life. . . . from his peculiar nature he is utterly incapable of making a woman happy. He is quite unnatural and in that one thing all the rest is embraced.[124]

Almost everything is left to innuendo here, and the reader can only surmise that if there is an element of factual truth behind the sentences it must be that Ruskin, while refusing to consummate the marriage, had found alternative methods of gaining sexual relief for himself which Effie came to know about. His earlier confessions concerning his boyhood sexuality and the practices in which he had indulged—'Have I not often told you

[123] Letter of 11 Mar. 1870, quoted Leon, *Ruskin*, 481.
[124] Lutyens, 'Correspondence', 13–14.

that I was another Rousseau?'[125]—together with his insistence that by the 1870s they were a thing of the past lend support to such a supposition. In defence of his actual behaviour towards Effie, Ruskin could have asserted that, so far from being 'unnatural', it had been in accord with his 'higher' nature; what might seem to most people a kind of perversion, therefore, had been in his own eyes the natural outcome of a noble attitude.

Such an interpretation, however one may judge Ruskin's behaviour, is compatible with his insistence that he was not impotent; nor is it inconsistent with the idea that his behaviour towards Rose, had she agreed to marry him, would have been different. One of the most striking pieces of evidence here is his dream in June 1873 that 'she was still hard and cruel in heart, but that she came to me—and gave herself to me—as sweetly in body as Cressid to Troilus'.[126] This evocation of a great erotic passage in medieval literature suggests the existence of sexual impulses towards her that were both strong and fulfillable.

Whatever the content of Effie's assertions, Rose was evidently swayed against Ruskin; her mother was able to report to Effie that she was now 'quite saved' and had promised her father to have no more to say to him.[127] At this point he began to find Rose's behaviour intolerable, and a note of impatience crept into his statements. Conscious of the effects on him of the repeated vacillations of recent years, her felt that he must now lose no more time, but put his work first. To William Cowper-Temple he wrote in the following summer,

It would indeed destroy both health and usefulness, if I allowed hopes to return such as I had once. I wish that they *could* return—if they were allowed—but I have been too often & too sorely betrayed to trust, or hope more; and even if all should be determined favourable, as regards the legal question, I shall only request that, with the Bishops aid and influence, you would undeceive Rose as to the points of unjust evilspeaking against me. I am very weary of life;—and will not ask her

[125] Letter to Mrs Cowper-Temple of 2 June 1868: Leon, *Ruskin*, 410, *RLMT* 167, Burd, *RLT* 116.
[126] *The Brantwood Diary of John Ruskin*, 353, quoted Burd, *RLT*, 127.
[127] Letter of 14 Oct.: Burd, *RLT* 122, citing Lutyens, 'Correspondence', 9, 10, 13, 15.

to come to me.—If she wants to come, she must say so to me,—nor *can* she yet—say so, wisely until she understands a little what sort of life she must in that case join. I have pledged myself now publicly to many things—in my own mind, I am resolved on many more. I will not in one jot interrupt my work for her.[128]

In accordance with his resolve he sought expert advice on his marital situation, with the aim first of being able to lay it before Rose and second of clearing his name of calumny. Meanwhile he found that he remained thwarted more than he expected, his work being so spoiled by the affair that he was driven to revise the common image of the biblical Dalilah:

I know now, quite, what she was. She *was* rather tall. She was very narrow-waisted—& very shy, and had the *trimmest* little sweet knot of golden hair at the back of her head. And she had grey eyes—and was *so* good—so very good—and always did as her people told her.

His impatience meant that the Samson metaphor could not be left there, moreover: 'I can't afford to be blinded of all things. I shall go off to Venice, with the gates of Gaza on my back . . .'[129]

The situation could not be solved quite so decisively, however, and his anxiety drove him just afterwards into illness. Meanwhile the opinion of Dr Tristram in the Temple that the decree annulling his marriage could not be impeached was conveyed to him by his cousin, W. G. Richardson: 'For all practical purposes you are free to marry again.'[130] Rose did not shift her ground. In reply to what he described as a 'civil Letter' from him, she returned a reply which 'for folly, insolence, and selfishness beat everything I yet have known produced by the accursed sect of religion she has been brought up in'.[131] At this point he resolved to end the relationship once and for all and to return all her letters; '. . . and the young lady shall never read written, nor hear spoken word of mine more'.[132]

But Rose's attitude to him was not as simple as he was maintaining, her strongly principled attitude towards him still

---

[128] Letter to William Cowper-Temple of 1 June 1871: *RLMT* 290.
[129] Letter to William Cowper-Temple of 23 June 1871: *RLMT* 296. Cf. Judges 16: 1–3.
[130] Letter from W. G. Richardson of 21 July 1871, quoted Burd, *RLT*, 123.
[131] Letter to William Cowper-Temple of 27 July 1871: *RLMT* 310 (cited Burd, *RLT* 123–4).    [132] Ibid.

being combined with great affection. She summed up her own tragic sense of the matter in a letter to Mrs MacDonald: 'If it could have been so that I might have kept the *friend* who has brought such pain & suffering & torture & division among so many hearts—if there had never been anything but friendship between us—how much might have been spared'.[133] If she had come to feel that his advances must be rejected, she could not easily live without him, either: devoid of his presence she found herself desolated. The following spring she tried to explain her plight in a letter to George MacDonald: 'Should we always consider that circumstances are God's Providence for us? Or does he teach us truths we are powerless to obey? And how are we to keep ourselves from being tortured with disquiet when this is so?'[134] Foremost in her mind was the sense that in spite of enjoying what most people would regard as total liberty she was in fact imprisoned:

I have nothing in the world to do from day to day but what I like. . . . my daily life is simply hour after hour of leisure for pondering, wishing, praying, enduring. To drive and walk, see one or two poor people, paint, read, play—and at the end of each day I feel like a child tired out after a long, lonely holiday.[135]

Her contact with the 'one or two poor people' merely exacerbated such feelings:

I have learnt to realize how full the world is of darkness and suffering—and how impossible it is to sit content in believing I am possessed of everlasting treasures—as well as this world's goods which I may not share with those that need. I go about among our poor people here and come back in despair sometimes. They lead a life so much more like Christ's than mine, and I go jingling off from their doors in the carriage with my ponies and bells, but with a sadder heartache than many of them could know. . . . I want to be more on an equality with them—to serve them, help them, learn from them. 'Be happy yourself—separate yrself from the world—& preach to those you can reach'—this is my father's religion, & he is *very* good—but it is a religion that I cannot feel is the whole of Christianity.[136]

---

[133] Letter to Mrs George MacDonald of 14, 15, 16 May 1871. MS at Yale: Burd, *RLT* 124.

[134] Letter of 20 Apr. 1872: MacDonald, *Reminiscences*, 111.

[135] Ibid.

[136] Letter postmarked 20 Apr. 1872: quoted MacDonald, *Reminiscences*, 11–12 and in part (from MS) Burd, *RLT* 124.

One reason that she could not feel this was of course the fact that she had absorbed so sympathetically those teachings of Ruskin that emphasized contemporary social injustices. When considered against her solitary yet indulged life in Ireland, they were bound to seem closer to the teachings of Christ himself. On the other hand the fact that Ruskin did not share her religious beliefs remained for her an insuperable obstacle, causing her in the course of thinking about how to live her life well to insert a stumbling parenthesis: 'as I shall not marry (unless indeed one alters utterly and completely and miraculously during life!) . . .'[137] The two-pronged tension set up by her love for him and her religious insistence preyed on her more and more, prompting her to write of the result: 'a child's love, growing on year after year deepening in silence and suffering, becomes a strong intense spiritual power and passion'.[138]

As a result of Rose's correspondence with him George MacDonald put Ruskin's case to her afresh. Although appalled to be shown in the meantime a letter he had written to an aunt of hers about his earlier sexual behaviour, she agreed to see him. Ruskin himself, now in Venice, remained firm that he could not allow his work to suffer any further through the affair and insisted that if there was to be a meeting the MacDonalds should bring her to Geneva: 'I will not allow any more doubtful measures in this thing: nor let my thoughts return to it, unless in absolute certainty of seeing her. Nor, even if she should see me, should I feel justified in leaving my work here at present.'[139] The trip did not materialize, but the MacDonalds still urged him to return to England. He eventually agreed, but in his own time; Rose was wanting him to defend himself against 'evil reports', but he could not understand what they might be and they would not tell him. Eventually, at the MacDonalds' further urging, he made more speed, arriving on 27 July, and Rose joined him at their house in Hammersmith in early August. Once again the immediate effect of seeing her was to soften his attitude, so much so on this occasion that he later described the visit as 'three days of heaven, which I would—for my own part and if I had not had work to do—have very thankfully bought with all

[137] Leon, *Ruskin*, 485.
[138] Letter of 16 July 1872, ibid. 493.
[139] Letter to MacDonald of 30 June 1872, Leon, *Ruskin*, 490.

the rest of my life'.[140] The scene was observed by their son, then sixteen, who was to remember it vividly:

I recall clearly Ruskin's grandeur of face, his searching blue eyes, and his adorable smile. . . . I remember the frail Rose, so amazingly thin yet with such high colour and her great eyes, with the tenderest of smiles possessing so readily her exquisitely red lips. I was astonished at her being alive, seeing that, I well remember, her dinner once consisted of three green peas, and the very next day, of one strawberry and half an Osborne biscuit.[141]

This meeting represented the particularly welcome departure for Ruskin that for the first time Rose had managed to break with her parents and their wishes. He was also reconciled again to the situation, recognizing how ill she had been made by the whole affair: 'I thought before I saw her, that she could never undo the evil she has done—but she brought me back into life, and put the past away as if it had not been—with the first full look of her eyes.'[142] His attitude was now changed and he could see her advent in his life as truly providential: 'Better all the pain, than to have gone on—as I might twelve years ago—with nothing to love—through life.'[143] Rejoining her with the Cowper-Temples at Broadlands on the 13th, where they were left alone most of the day he again found the experience blissful: 'she was so good and so grave, and so gay, and so terribly lovely—and so merciless and so kind—and so "ineffable"'. His favourite word sprang back into service: 'But the great good to me is finding how noble she is—she is worth all the worship . . .'[144] The point was reiterated next day to MacDonald: 'I am so thankful to find her so noble. It is not her fault but her glory, that she cannot

---

[140] Letter to MacDonald of 11 Aug. 1872, Leon, *Ruskin*, 494. MacDonald, *Reminiscences*, 120, omitted the important parenthesis; Burd, *RLT* 125, omitted both that and the word 'would'.

[141] MacDonald, *Reminiscences*, 120. His first attempt at a description, published eight years before, contained some interesting differences: 'I have vivid memories of him and the frail girl in those days. I was but sixteen, and yet saw something of the heaven into which the sorrowful world was now changed for them. Also I remember Ruskin's strength of face, his searching blue eyes, and his truthful smile . . . I remember too the shadowy Rose, so amazingly thin, with her high colour and great eyes, and such a tender sad smile on her strangely red lips.' *George MacDonald and his Wife* (1924), 417–18.

[142] Letter to MacDonald of 11 Aug. 1872, Leon, *Ruskin*, 494–5.

[143] Ibid.        [144] *RLMT* 328.

love me better. I only wonder she ever loved me at all.'[145] Things
went even better during the next day or two and he began to
hope that after all things would move in his favour. After going
off to stay with friends in Cheshire she sent asking him to visit
her there. He wrote to a friend, 'I am called down suddenly into
Cheshire. . . . I think you would not be pleased with me if I
did not tell you that I like going down into Cheshire. But I've
no right to speak—yet . . . about anything that makes me
happier than I was.'[146] He duly went to Toft in Cheshire,
and attended church with Rose, holding her prayer book, but
it did not turn out as he hoped. While recognizing her love
for him she still distinguished in her mind between that love and
her love for God, and gave preference to the latter. In a letter
sent to MacDonald next day he wrote, '*She* sent for me to
Cheshire— . . . but was fearfully cruel', a statement which he
explained further to a friend a fortnight later by saying that
Rose would not marry him because 'I don't love God better that
I do *her*.'[147] This in fact followed with exactitude the line
that Rose had taken in her earlier letters, but her explanation to
Mrs MacDonald contained a further clue to her attitude: 'I
cannot be to him what he wishes, or return the vehement love
which he gave me, which petrified and terrified me.'[148] It seems
that exposure for a period to Ruskin, even when allowed to
declare his love fully and in person, brought with it a recognition that for all his good qualities there was a forcefulness in him
that in the end she could not endure. She was, in any case, worn
out with attempts to reconcile conflicting demands.

Faced with the new situation, where the La Touches were no
longer playing the key part, Ruskin could not fall back on the
plot of Scott's *Bride* for his model, or even on that emblem of
good and evil, St George and the Dragon; instead he turned to
the neighbouring image he had seen in the Carpaccio chapel:
that of St Urban with the Basilisk.[149] That he should associate
Rose with that creature and then suggest that she might be
turning to stone suggests that she was beginning to pass into a

---

[145] Letter to MacDonald of 14 Aug. 1872: Leon, *Ruskin*, 495.
[146] Letter to 'Angie' Acland, 17 Aug. 1872: Burd, *RLT* 126.
[147] Letter to A. W. Hunt of 4 Sept. 1872, quoted Burd, *RLT*, 126.
[148] MacDonald, *Reminiscences*, 121.
[149] Letter of 19 Aug. 1872, *RLMT* 332. Ruskin queries whether it is St Urban.

depressed condition similar to that which was to be observed in Annie Marshall three years later.[150] Early in September Ruskin, going to church in Coniston, received at the door his latest letter to her, returned unopened. That night he wrote in his diary 'It is finished'.[151]

Convinced that all hope had gone, Ruskin now devoted himself more fully to his work. At the same time he found himself at last able to move towards a relationship with Rose that could be sustained with some equability on both sides. She resumed correspondence with him in September 1874, when he was returning from his period of study in Italy and delighted him by the tone of her writing. Mrs La Touche began writing to him again also. There was no longer an aggrieved tone on his part, nor any renewal of his hopes of marrying Rose; by now he was becoming convinced that she was insane.[152]

The question of madness had been on his mind for some time. He seems always to have been afraid that he might himself topple into such a condition, though he could write about the prospect with every appearance of rationality. In a letter of July 1870, when he had just been travelling through Europe during the Franco-Prussian War, he had written to Charles Eliot Norton,

I have been endeavouring this morning to define the limits of insanity. My experience is not yet wide enough. I have been entirely insane, as far as I know, only about Turner and Rose; and I'm tired; and have made out nothing satisfactory.[153]

It is hard to know at this distance in time whether Rose had not for some years been suffering from an organic mental disease, so closely shadowed by her conscious behaviour as to make that seem self-determined on her part. Whatever the truth, the growing evidences of mental disturbance became during the remaining months of her life one of the most painful factors in the situation. How could someone so apparently noble and truthful yet behave so differently?

I have had much talk with her, & perceive her whole being to be undermined. The insane *cunning* is the thing that thwarts me beyond

---

[150] See above, pp. 164, 165.
[151] Letter to Mrs MacDonald of 28 Sept. 1872; *RLMT* 335; *R Diaries* ii. 732.
[152] *RLMT* 335.          [153] *R Works* xxxvii. 13.

my power; her naturally keen and delicately truthful nature being turned exactly wrong side out—like a cyclamen leaf—Only that curls its right side out, the moment it's long enough,—but my poor briar-rose will only drop the blighted leaves, one by one.[154]

Although he did not write in more detail about the question, it is clear from this statement that a possible link between insanity and devilry was lurking in his mind—to return from time to time in years to come. Meanwhile the fidelity to her that had been renewed at the Hammersmith meeting kept him at hand to help as he could and he continued to see and correspond with her until her death. By that time he was evidently drained by the whole affair, including the effects of her mental collapse at the end, when she had turned against her own father.

However much he might at times deplore Rose's mental condition in the last days, her death changed his feelings completely, transfixing him with grief. His first reaction, sent to Joan Severn, was, 'Of course I have long been prepared for this—but it makes one giddy in the head at first.'[155] A few days later he was writing to her, 'I find this thing more terrible than I knew; the way it seems to possess and shadow me all through and through,—just as the happy letters were warmth & light to me.'[156] For months afterwards he would be trying to come to terms with his loss. Despite a superficial reluctance to discuss the affair with others he was, if pressed by a sympathetic respondent, loquacious. When his friend Mrs Talbot asked about it, his first reply was characteristically reticent:

All *natural* griefs, however great, fill, but don't break hearts; whatever *you* feel of sorrow, only makes you kinder *more*—capable of affection rather than less. But a quite horrible, unnatural sorrow—(that is to say not of the kind which human nature is meant to bear) like this of the death of my mistress in madness, does, where the heart has been wholly given, break it, wholly; so that there is no true life in it any more. I have plenty of sympathy & compassion left—but no love. I was very happy the other day, to be able to give a poor—(and quite ugly!) girl thirty francs, her family's savings for a month, which she had lost on the way to put into the bank—and was in an agony of distress such as one

---

[154] Letter to Joan Severn of 15 Dec. 1874, Bodleian MS Eng. lett. c. 51, quoted Burd, *RLT*, 130.
[155] Letter of 28 May 1875, Bembridge MSS: see Burd, *RLT* 133.
[156] Letter of June, Bembridge MSS: ibid. 133–4.

rarely sees—and I am very sorry for my gondolier who is ill, and I was profoundly grateful to *you* for your goodness to Downes.—But you can't help me with affection.—If the dead live, some day, also, I shall live again—but I am as dead as they, now.[157]

Mrs Talbot's sympathetic reply to this letter won further confidences, including one of his most comprehensive accounts of the affair as a whole:

I am indeed grateful for this loving & lovely letter, and will take the regard you have given me trustfully,—and lean on it, to do which is when I look into my mind, the worst of the difficulties in that hardness in me.—I never can believe that people really care for me, I fancy they don't know themselves and will change;—and that no love but one's mother's, or true mistress's—is to be trusted. This feeling has been chiefly fixed in me by the failure of Rosie's mother to me; she was my very dearest friend, while Rosie was young—and I loved her deeply—and went to her always for advice, and help—and amusement—and comfort—and when Rosie grew to be eighteen instead of eleven, and was brought to London to be 'brought out'—I drew back out of the way quite properly and never thought of or hoped anything.

—But the child didn't like it, and questioned my cousin about me, and then came forward herself—and asked me 'if I would stay just as we used to be for three years and then ask her; being ready *then* to receive yes, or no?' It may be a grave question whether I ought not at once to have refused and told her it was right that we should think no more of each other—with such hardness as might have made her think she could do as her parents wished without giving me much pain.

Were the time to return—I should do again just what I did—say that I was her servant in all things always. Then she was very happy—and that went on for a while; but I insisted that she should tell her Father— She knew that to do so would be to separate us at once—and hesitating—showed my letter to some 'friend'—who told the Father,—thus everything inducing him—himself a man of the strictest honour, though hard & selfish—to think *me* treacherous, and his daughter disobedient. His morals—and much more his pride—were alike offended—and to my utter horror—the mother failed me also

—They stopped all intercourse between us at once—Rosie did not care but said— 'Wait—and it will be all right'. That went on for a year and a half—Then, when the father and mother found they made no progress, and that Rose was just as steady to me as the first day, the

[157] Letter of 27 Nov. 1876: Rylands Eng. MS 1161/37 (plain text printed Spence, *Talbot*, 59).

mother got quite furious with rage—went to Perth, where the people connected with my former wife lived—got whatever they chose to say of me under their hand,—and brought all this to Rosie. The child had never been brought into any contact with evil or evil thoughts before:—she loved and trusted her mother—distrusted herself—and therefore at last, me—She gave me up—; but, (not the *sorrow*, but) the *horror* of it—effectually broke down her life. For a year she remained silent to me—then gradually by Mrs. Cowper Temple's steady friendship and effort (the Φίλη of Sesame and Lilies) she was restored to me; but not the same,—partly ashamed of *herself*—partly in agony of conscience at what was now direct and resolute disobedience to her parents in holding any communication with me—and partly in fits of unconquerable doubt of *me*—Her brain gradually gave way—and one of the last scenes between us was long and vain pleading on my part that she would not send a letter to her Father full of *frantic* reproach.

We had—altogether—about three happy days together, before she died—but I had one entirely happy week at Chamouni, when she was writing me joyful letters as I was coming home to her in 1874: and stopped to see my old Chamouni guide and the places where I used to be with my Father & Mother.

I have never heard of or read, a story of so bitter tragedy;—the bride of Lammermuir is like it, but Rosie was a much more perfect and holy creature than Lucy Ashton.

So you see, I have not much of my old self left—but what I am, is faithfully & gratefully yours:

J Ruskin[158]

*The Bride of Lammermoor* had resumed its station in his mind as a central narrative by which to interpret the events and judge the participants. Yet it is hard for the disinterested reader to find in what actually happened the story of demonic malice that he traced. Rose's father John La Touche behaved throughout like the upright banker that he was, content to rely on the firm spiritual assets that he had discovered in the preaching of Charles Spurgeon when he was converted in 1863,[159] without enquiring further into their implications or effects. Her mother, who had nursed her through her severe illnesses in adolescence, worked throughout for what she considered to be

---

[158] Letter of 15 Dec. 1876: Rylands Eng. MS 1161/38, quoted Spence, *Talbot*, 60–2.

[159] See Burd, *RLT*, esp. 31–5, 85–6.

her good, even if she also accused her unfairly of lack of affection for her parents. It was very natural for the parents to ask
Effie for information before consenting to the marriage of their
young daughter, given the shadow over the end of Ruskin's
marriage, and Effie's testimony, though no doubt imbued by the
bitterness of her memories, seems to have been given basically in
good faith, in the hope of rescuing Rose from an unhappiness
similar to which she herself had known. The most tragic irony of
Ruskin's situation was located, in fact, in his own actions: by
tacitly consenting to the acceptance of a falsehood in the interests of making things easier for his wife—which could be considered an instance of his nobility while at the same time resolving
his marital situation (an action, by his own testimony, of more
doubtful motivation) he had unwittingly poisoned the springs of
his future hopes. The effects of a rare occasion when the exercise
of nobility had also involved a lack of full candour had been to
undermine all those others where his nobility had been more
unequivocally sustained.

It is very difficult, certainly, to condemn Rose's behaviour.
Put in an impossible position by the contending demands of her
father and Ruskin, she had found herself under continuous
stress. Her letter of 1870, quoted above, had included the words
'I have never known or had a chance of knowing for the last
three years *what* was kind or right.'[160] Two years later she had
written in a similar strain to the MacDonalds when they asked
her whether she had been ruled by her parents or her own mind:
'I knew what you wd say—Perhaps I am acting wrongly to some
"external relation" but I have been put in positions where I have
not known right from wrong', and again, '*My* interpretation of
right and my Parents' all pull different ways to puzzle a brain
that cannot bear perplexity.'[161]

If a marriage with Ruskin had received her parents' consent,
how would it have turned out? It is hard to peer into the fate of
an event that never happened. Mary Lutyens writes (referring
presumably to herself), 'There is at least one Ruskin lover who
believes that he might have got bored with her as quickly as he

---

[160] Letter of 21 Feb. 1870, not transmitted to Ruskin: see above, at n. 119.
[161] Letter to George MacDonald of 15 May 1872, quoted MacDonald, *Reminiscences*, 112, and MS letter at Yale (of the same date, probably the same letter)
quoted Burd, *RLT* 124.

did with Effie—or—does one dare say it?—even more quickly.'[162] On the evidence that survives, however, it is hard to justify such confidence. There were certainly potential difficulties. His demands for obedience from the young women who joined the Guild of St George, for example, indicate a streak of authoritarianism which, if repeated to one of Rose's obstinacy, might swiftly have led both of them to an impasse. The conflict between Rose's strong Evangelical views and Ruskin's equally potent mixture of devoutness and scepticism had already set up an obvious stumbling block of the kind. Yet the powerful bond of straightforward affection between them, which emerges again and again, reconfirmed whenever there was a renewed meeting after absence and recrimination, might have proved, as he himself believed, even more durable.

Among factors to be taken into account in considering the relationship, one must consider (as with Annie Marshall, but in this case more crucially) an ambiguity as to whether Rose was to be thought of as woman or child. Just as Annie wrote to her aunt as 'Your loving Child',[163] so Rose could address Mrs MacDonald in 1872 as 'Dearest Mother-bird' and sign herself as 'Your still unfledged but loving nestling'.[164] Yet she had already tried to divest herself of the child-image by writing to Ruskin (in a letter he did not receive) that she could not resume her former position in relation to him: 'For however sweet it might be, I am not the little thing I was.'[165] As she came of age Ruskin recognized that legally she could now be dealt with as an adult, yet he would continue to describe her in his private correspondence as if she were not: in 1874 she was still 'an amusing child' or 'That child whom you cannot forgive'.[166] There may indeed have been a mental regression during her last months of life; in January 1875 he reported that she was living 'chiefly on soda water and plum cake'.[167] After her death a few months later he found

---

[162] Lutyens, 'Correspondence', 16.      [163] See above, p. 147.

[164] MacDonald, *Reminiscences*, 121. Ruskin wrote to George MacDonald the following month that 'the worst of the aconite the fledgling gives me is that it blinds me to any other world' (quoted Burd, *RLT* 126).

[165] Letter of 21 Feb. 1870, published Leon, *Ruskin*, 480–1.

[166] Letters of 6 and 9 Mar. 1874: see below, at nn. 176, 216.

[167] Letter to Blanche Atkinson of 5 Jan. 1875: Rylands Eng. MS 1162/70 (see Spence, *Talbot*, 41 n.). In the same month Ruskin informed the readers of *Fors Clavigera*, that 'the woman I hoped would have been my wife is dying': *R Works* xxviii. 246.

himself wanting to find out 'when that child's "wake" was'.[168] At the same time he would not only describe himself as her lover,[169] but her as his mistress[170]—a term which, however voided of sexual connotations,[171] still balanced the child image against that of a woman mature enough to be capable of acting responsibly towards him.

This ambiguous behaviour, in the course of which Ruskin himself adopts attitudes ranging from that of vassal to that of reverend teacher (taking in the avuncular and the paternal *en route*), is even more evident in some of his other relationships with women such as Blanche Atkinson, daughter of a prosperous Liverpool soap manufacturer, whom he first befriended at the time when his difficulties with Rose were at their height. Blanche came on the scene in 1873 as a result of the publication of *Fors Clavigera*, and its encouragement of reader-participation. Her own contributions to the correspondence column soon led to a fertile exchange of letters with Ruskin himself, in which she was treated sometimes as pupil of the master, sometimes as confidante of the aggrieved lover, sometimes as audience for the afflicted human being.

Blanche herself was one of the young women of the latter part of the century who felt unreasonably constrained by the conventions that forced her to remain uselessly at home. What her inner feelings were toward Ruskin cannot precisely be known,[172]

---

[168] Letter to Joan Severn of 31 May 1875, Burd, *RLT* 133.

[169] 'Poor Rose is entirely broken—like her lover—': letter to George MacDonald of 25 Feb. 1875, quoted Leon, *Ruskin*, 500.

[170] See letter to Mrs Talbot above, p. 275. Cf. 'last Friday about twelve o'clock at noon my mistress passed me and would not speak', letter to Richard Horn of 12 Jan. 1869: Leon, *Ruskin*, 478; 'When I lost my mistress, the girl for whom I wrote *Sesame and Lilies*...', letter to Ernest Chesneau of 3 Apr. 1883: *R Works* xxvii. 445.

[171] It is conceivable that the unnamed lady who said of Rose to Gladstone's daughter in the 1920s, 'Oh, she was one of his mistresses wasn't she?' (MacDonald, *Reminiscences*, 99) had been misled by coming across an example of this usage by him.

[172] It is not difficult to believe that she was secretly in love with him, though the actual state of affairs was probably more complex—perhaps not fully considered by herself, even. It may well have been that any feelings she allowed herself to entertain towards him were informed by an element of provisionality—that she lived on the assumption of being out of his range, yet knew that if at any time Ruskin should come to treat her as something more than an acquaintance, she would be all too willing to respond.

but she has left one of the best accounts of what it was like to encounter Ruskin for the first time:

. . . as the slight, stooping figure came towards me with both hands out, and my first glance rested on the curious eager face, with large mouth and bushy eyebrows, my heart sank. For the first moment I was startled. Could this be my hero? 'Is it really you?' I said with a little gasp. Yes, it's myself entirely was the answer with an amused laugh. Then when he had talked and talked—when I had seen the flash of those deep-set steel-blue eyes, which seemed to look through and through me, and the radiance of the smile, and the ever-changing play of expression, I thought his face fascinating in its strange power and charm. Somehow, I had expected quick, decisive speech   quick, impatient movements. Instead, the words came slowly and deliberately; the movements were slow and quiet . . .[173]

As one reads the correspondence as a whole, one is struck by a lack of perceptiveness in Ruskin, who evidently found it hard to judge the effects of his letters. On the one hand he won Blanche's sympathy by telling the unfolding story of his love for Rose; on the other he was dogmatic in his views of what Blanche should be doing in terms of her own education. Simple controversy or banter would sometimes be replaced by brusqueness, to the point of cruelty, as in the autumn of 1875, when Blanche revealed that she had been reading the work of John Stuart Mill. Ruskin wrote a letter that seemed to amount to a breaking off of relations: 'I simply feel more and more that I can do you no good and am wasting time on you.'[174] On receiving an anguished reply he wrote to say that she had misunderstood his intent and that the change in his style of writing had been due not to anger at her wasting her time in reading Mill but to a feeling that her doing so meant that he was after all being of no use to her. He tried to establish a distinction between anger and displeasure, the latter being the motive behind his 'ceasing to speak when I find my sayings unserviceable'.[175]

The most striking feature of the exchange is not so much the

---

[173] Account of their first meeting in 1874, Rylands Eng. MS 1162/48, quoted Margaret Spence, 'Ruskin's Correspondence with Miss Blanche Atkinson', *Bulletin of the John Rylands Library*, 42 (1959–60), 208–9.
[174] Undated letter, Rylands Eng. MS 1162/95, quoted ibid. 215.
[175] Letter of 27 Oct. 1875, Rylands Eng. MS 1162/96: quoted ibid. 215.

suggestion of a will to dominate (which might be the initial interpretation of what he did) as the evidence of his extraordinary ability to alternate between considerable warmth, with signs of affection, and a distancing, objectifying attitude of which he did not apparently perceive the potentially devastating effects. One might also consider the implications of a casual comment on his feeling for Rose made in March 1874 which contrasts interestingly with his experience on Skiddaw seven years earlier:

Crossing the hills, yesterday, I found myself about 1 o'clock in want of a sandwich. I happened to have one in my pocket—ate it and got on—if I hadn't had it, I couldn't have got on—it would have been no use for any pious person to tell me I was making a God of my sandwich—and that God would be jealous of its importance on my mind.

I simply needed my mutton and mustard.—or I couldn't have done my work.—I only look upon Rosie as a sandwich—but I can't get on without her. She is not the moon, nor is she an idol—but an amusing child—with grey eyes which happens to be precisely the thing that I can't do without—I *do* after a fashion but badly.[176]

His imagery here might be compared with that used when on first learning that Rose's family were opposed to her marrying him he treated it as if it were a failure of divine providence: 'if it was possible for me to go to my Father in that personal way—(which it is not—) the very first thing I should say to him would be—"What have you been teasing me like this for?—Were there *no* toys in the cupboard, you could have shown me—but the one I can't have?"'[177] This particularly telling example suggests the behaviour of an indulged child—a sign here less of parental irresponsibility than of failure to grow up into a sense of other people and their needs. The lack of empathy, particularly notable in view of his extraordinary capacity for tenderness, is characteristic of his behaviour elsewhere. Myers was to record how in his later illness several of his friends clubbed together at some expense to buy back for him one of his favourite Turner pictures, only to be taken aback when he reproached them for not instead showing their loyalty to him by committing them-

---

[176] Letter of 9 Mar. 1874. Rylands Eng. MS 1162/53.
[177] Letter to George MacDonald about February 1866, quoted Burd, *RLT* 106.

selves to the Guild of St George.[178] Here again there is inability
to take an objective view of a situation, evacuation of the
feelings one might have expected to be at the centre. Yet his love
was far from static; indeed as we have seen, Rose's remarks
about her final refusal in 1873 suggest that, however much she
might have come to accept his friends' assurances as to the
genuineness of Ruskin's love, his expressions of it had left with
her a residual fear of his 'vehemence'.

An important element in all this was Ruskin's fanatical devotion to his work, which had also been a telling factor in the
failure of his marriage to Effie Gray. Already recognizing it
before they married she had promised in one of their love letters
that she would not disturb him in his work—and indeed be
ready to mend his pens for him if necessary.[179] The reality of
their married life, however, which involved his going away for
long periods with his parents in order to pursue his studies
abroad, went further, being more impersonal than she could
have expected and at odds with the development of a full loving
relationship.

The failure not just of self-knowledge but of empathy at the
deepest level was evident also in his attitude to Plato. Although
a great admirer, with repeated recommendations ('one of five
men whose opinions must be studied'[180]) and acknowledgement
of the influence on his own thought ('The philosophy I teach is
Plato's and Bacon's'[181]) the idea of platonic love that governed
the minds of some Romantic writers meant little to him. He read
his work regularly, particularly in the years following Rose's
death, and praised his wisdom on the subject of the soul, but his
most frequent references were to the *Laws* and the *Republic*: in
his published works the Platonic view of love was not discussed.
Nor did he even mention the *Symposium*; on the contrary, he
explicitly repudiated any devotion to 'translucent' beauty of the

[178] F. W. H. Myers, 'Obituary Notice VI: John Ruskin': Myers, *FPP* 92.
[179] See her letter to him of 9 Feb. 1848, quoted M. Lutyens, *The Ruskins and the Grays* (1972), 85–6. Her flippant tone in writing about this is of a different character from Dora Spenlow's when she wanted to help David Copperfield by holding his pens while he was writing (in ch. xliv of Dickens's novel, published in the following year). Dora's desire to be called David's 'child-wife' is relevant to other matters in the present study.
[180] *R Works* xxvii 143 n., 314; cf. xv. 226, v. 425.
[181] Letter of 1880: *R Works* xxxiv. 547.

kind that was honoured in the poetry of Coleridge and Myers. When Mrs Talbot raised the possibility he retorted, 'I shall not get off on any of your finedrawn notions of shining through. I like girls wholly for their pink shells,—and curls—and sparklings and softenings—and not a bit for anything "shining through".'[182]

However firmly he excluded the factor of 'lust', his love for Rose was for her visible, physical form. Shortly before her death he wrote:

The worst of me is that the Desire of my *Eyes* is so much to me! Ever so much more than the desire of my mind. . . . So that the dim chance of those fine things in the next world does me no good, and though I've known some really nice girls, in my time, in this world, who wouldn't have been so hard on me as some people, none of them had a thin waist and a straight nose quite to my fancy.[183]

After Rose's death his belief in the possibility of an innocent sensuous love persisted, in his enjoyment of 'flirting' and his range of relationships with young women, coupled with his scrupulous respect for the boundaries of conventional morality.[184]

When considered in this way the love between John Ruskin and Rose La Touche may be related to the crisis in the appreciation of nature commented on earlier. Myers's love for Annie Marshall had been another in a series of such relationships that also included Wordsworth's Lucy. Rose, however, took the puzzlement a stage further. She was always at one level a child of nature; and Ruskin's attempts to understand her and find ways of dealing with her were akin to his assaults on the significance of nature herself. Caught between the mechanism of a Darwinian universe and the flummery of a Puseyite revival, between the logic of atheism and the attractive yet possibly dangerous beckonings of spiritualism, Ruskin pursued his belief that if one could only press one's investigations far enough

---

[182] Letter of 1 June 1886, Rylands Eng. MS 1161/342 (printed by Robin Skelton, 'John Ruskin: The Final Years, A Survey of the Ruskin Correspondence in the John Rylands Library', *Bulletin of the John Rylands Library*, 37 (1954–5), 581).

[183] *RLMT* 358.

[184] See e.g. the testimony reported by George MacDonald from Mary Drew, Gladstone's daughter: 'Make no mistake about this . . . he never so much as laid a hand on any of us.' MacDonald, *Reminiscences*, 99.

nature would be found to hold the key. The difficulty for him, as it had been for Wordsworth, was rather to discover that key in a form that would still preserve nature's nobility.

The personality working within Rose's stubbornness, meanwhile, showed something of the same variety as nature, including at least an effect of wantonness (however unintentional) in her resistance to his attempts to find a way of truly placing and holding her. The search for a more adequate imagery led him most immediately to the stability of vegetative form, to flowers. Her own naming was not originally an accidental choice,[185] and was made more conscious by the frequency of her mother's allusions; in addition to the instances already cited, she wrote on one occasion of Rose as 'not always a sweetness . . . or if she is, it's the sweetness of the wild fruit, and the thorn guarded flower—and so best'.[186] Rose enjoyed the game as much as anyone. Writing to Ruskin in 1861 about the family's tour in Europe, she despaired of describing the beauty of the Esterelle Pass: 'You the author of Modern-Painters c<sup>d</sup> describe it Irish roses can't.' She continued, 'But I can tell you how my cousins the moorland roses nodded at me as I passed and how they couldn't understand why Irish roses bloomed in July instead of March.'[187] Her playfulness sometimes went further, as in her teasing early assurance that 'a trail of thorny wild rose is not so easily untwined'[188] and her sending him cloth of an oriental pattern which, she said, represented 'a hearts-ease in the middle of a rose'.[189] But what might be pleasant wordplay for everyone so long as she was a blooming adolescent burgeoned in time on Ruskin's part into a search for more significant symbolism. With near-neurotic delight he noted that two letters of the title of his planned botanical book *Proserpine* represented the initials of

[185] Supposing it better to be a rose with thorns than the 'cold, passionless' camellia that she admired, she wrote, 'Mamma said long long ago that I was born in the depth of the winter & called Rose that I might brighten the winters': letter to Mrs Cowper of 31 Oct. 1866, in Van Akin Burd, 'More Letters from Rose La Touche', *Bulletin of the John Rylands Library*, 65 (1983), 64–5.

[186] Undated letter to Mrs MacDonald, quoted Leon, *Ruskin*, 390.

[187] Letter of March 1861 in *Praeterita* III: *R Works* xxxv. 531.

[188] Quoted by him in a letter of 14 July 1872 as having been written to him ten years before from Venice: MacDonald, *Reminiscences*, 119, reading 'a wreath of wild rose is not so easily disentangled'. See also Leon, *Ruskin*, 492. The earlier reading looks more authentic.

[189] Letter to Margaret Ruskin, 12 Oct. 1864: *R Winnington*, 518–19.

'pet' and 'rose',[190] and that if those letters were taken away one
was left with 'ros' and 'épine' (thorn). By 1870, when he bought
for her a rare manuscript of the *Roman de la Rose*,[191] he had cast
himself thoroughly into the role of medieval lover with unattain-
able beloved—even if a more sceptical undertow was already
setting in. In October 1874, during the last phase of their love,
he sent her a copy of his lectures inscribed 'To Briar-Rose | Fleur
de Lys'[192] and six weeks later wrote to a friend 'I fear there is no
hope of any help now, for poor Sweet-briar'.[193] After her death
on 26 May 1875 he wrote, 'I've just heard that my poor little
rose is gone where the hawthorn blossoms go'[194] and a week
later, 'I was away into the meadows . . . when the news came
that the little story of my wild Rose was ended, and the hawthorn blossoms this year would fall—over her.'[195] From that
time any traditional rose symbolism would recall her.

She herself found a way round her parents' interdiction on
writing to him by sending him, sometimes anonymously,
presents of flowers: a rose he received in the summer of 1867 he
regarded as a sign not to believe rumours of an engagement;[196]
the effect of a letter telling of the ban on their correspondence,
which arrived on the morning of his Dublin lecture in 1868, was
alleviated by the two accompanying rose leaves, and even more
teasingly followed at the end of the lecture by a floral present
brought by a messenger consisting of Erba della Madonna (a
plant strongly associated with him by the La Touches) and two
bouquets, 'one a rose half open, with lilies of the valley, and a
sweet scented geranium leaf, the other a pink, with lilies of the
valley, and a green and white geranium leaf'.[197] Her 1870 letter
declaring her trust and love was accompanied by a 'little red and
green and golden rose'.[198]

[190] *RLMT* 235.
[191] Burd, *RLT* 121. As his Diaries show, Ruskin in subsequent years worked a
good deal on this manuscript, which he may have either kept for Rose or reclaimed
from her.
[192] The copy was preserved at Bembridge: Burd, *RLT* 130n.
[193] Letter to Joan Severn of 15 Dec. 1874. MS typescript from Cook and
Wedderburn transcripts: Bodleian MS Eng. lett. c. 51, quoted Burd, *RLT* 130.
[194] Letter to Susan Beever of 28 May 1875, quoted Burd, *RLT* 133.
[195] Letter to Carlyle of 4 June 1875, quoted Leon, *Ruskin*, 500.
[196] *R Works* xxxvi. 531 (Burd, *RLT* 111).
[197] Letters of 13 and 14 May 1868: *RLMT* 155-7.
[198] *RLMT* 273.

Flowers provided a good language of nature in her benign and mediating forms; in the case of the rose emblem Ruskin could extend the allusiveness, since the adjective 'wild' mingled suggestions of the charming and the untamable with a reference to nature herself when untouched by human intervention. But giving Rose the nickname of 'Flint', as he sometimes did, particularly when writing to his cousin Joan, expressed more fully the intellectual dilemma raised by such invocation of nature. There was a touch of childish language about this (and even more about his companion nickname for her, 'Tuck-up', for 'stuck up'): at the most obvious level it commented shrewdly on her known obstinacy and its implications. It also had subtlety, which he was not, as with some of his other images, eager to explain further, simply leaving the word to lurk gnomically in his text. When Rose described herself as acting like a flint, however, he enlarged on it:

Alas, if only she *did* behave like a flint! My flints *comfort* me. When I've said all that's in my mind against religion generally, I shall settle myself quietly to write the 'history of flint'—long intended,—headed by the species, 'Achates Rosacea'—I gave her such a pretty piece of rose-quartz ages ago—little thinking—when I told her laughing—it was a type of her (which made her very angry, *then*) that she would ever say so with her own lips.[199]

In time he turned increasingly to his collection of flints for 'comfort'. An early enterprise after Rose's death was his promised study, *Deucalion*, in which he dwelt on their qualities: how the flint could either endure or dissolve to foster new life, and how 'in its noblest forms it is still imperfect, and in the meanest, still honourable'.[200] Remarks such as these indicate how far Ruskin was willing to go in pressing what might otherwise have been a light image into serious service. Whereas the rose joined his love of nature to his sense of the great symbolic tradition that had traditionally surrounded the emblem, the image of the flint took him towards a point where nature might resist interpretation in any terms beyond its own surd self. Wordsworth had

---

[199] *RLMT* 255.
[200] *R Works* xxvi. 167–8, quoted by William Arrowsmith in 'Ruskin's Fireflies', *The Ruskin Polygon*, ed. John Dixon Hunt and Faith M. Holland (Manchester, 1982), 206.

traced as the poles of his visionary universe the star and the glow-worm, centres of light that bound the lore of the furthest cosmos to the world of intimate and local nature, so suggesting in nature a common illumination that could be thought of as exhibited centrally in human beings.[201] Ruskin went further: like Blake, who organized the chaos of the world towards artistic form by pointing out the mercy that human beings could reach a Limit of Opacity and a Limit of Contraction, so that light need never be finally swallowed up in darkness, nor matter disintegrate into non-entity,[202] he sought to reconcile the extremes of objective nature in emblems that would suffice. For him, however, the polarity involved was greater still, operating between the basic integrity of the flint and the natural energy exhibited in the delightful yet maddeningly unorganizable dance of fireflies. The rose-quartz, with its crystalline beauty, was an apposite emblem of a Rose who, even in her most rocky mode, was still beautiful. Yet at the opposite extreme the dazzling fireflies imaged with fidelity his frustrated attempts to make her qualities—like those of nature herself—finally intelligible.

Charles Eliot Norton, constantly dismayed by Ruskin's behaviour and particularly appalled that he should find his potential destroyed by 'the woman to whom [his] heart had been given . . . through her insane conceits & fluctuations'[203] believed that he needed a 'wise, constant friend' near him, such as Leslie Stephen,

one of the most affectionate & most honest minded and most modest of men; not to be knocked by any blow from his equipoise of sense & imaginative sympathy; a sceptic without bitterness, a thinker without pretention; muscular physically & mentally without brutality; shy, sensitive, tender, manly; looking out very strait on the world, & neither hoping, caring, or fearing much in life.[204]

When Stephen did meet Ruskin two years later (perhaps through Norton's good offices) the result was not as the latter had hoped: a subsequent letter from Stephen to Norton contained the comment, 'Nobody indeed can talk to him without

---

[201] See above p. 37.

[202] Blake, *The Four Zoas* IV, p. 56, ll. 17–22; *Milton*, plate 13, ll. 18–21: *The Poetry and Prose of William Blake*, ed. David V. Erdman and Harold Bloom (Garden City, NY, 1965), 331, 106.

[203] Letter to Ruskin of 30 Oct. 1874: RCEN 345.          [204] Ibid.

seeing his genuine kindliness as well as genius, and yet it takes a more sympathetic person than I am not to be repelled by some of his crotchets.'[205]

Myers, with whom he enjoyed for a time a growing sympathy, was a person more suited to Ruskin's needs. There were obvious differences. Both took their loves to extremes, but whereas the love of Myers for Annie Marshall infringed the propriety of marital fidelity, that of Ruskin for Rose La Touche involved the affective advantage gained by an older man with constant access to a young girl while she was still well below the age of consent. In each case, nevertheless, the same central issue was that of honour. Annie, who had more obviously transgressed the spirit—though not the letter—of the moral law was driven to suicide; Rose, suffering the tensions of the conflict in the depths of her own psyche, and allowing them to consume her, reached the same end by slower means.

Given his belief in nobleness as the human quality that could transcend the contending demands of the time Ruskin was likely to feel an affinity with the ideas of a man such as Myers. The furtherance of their acquaintance came about partly by chance, however. On the assumption that their original meeting in Keswick was no more than a casual encounter, it might have been expected to be assisted by Myers's membership of the Marshall family, with their ownership of various local properties. James Stuart, the pioneer of adult education, whom Myers came to know in Cambridge, describes in his *Reminiscences* how he first met Ruskin in 1867 at Henry Marshall's house on Derwent Island,[206] a house that has already figured in the present book,[207] and we have seen that this was probably the occasion when Myers also met him.[208] The decisive event in fostering the friendship seems, however, to have been the unexpected advent of Prince Leopold, a son of Queen Victoria, who had been delicate in health from his earliest years and spent some time in Oxford from the autumn of 1872. When, shortly after his

---

[205] Ibid. 383 n.

[206] James Stuart, *Reminiscences* (1912), 211–12. Elsewhere (pp. 154, 228) Stuart describes how Henry and Theodosia Marshall helped his attempts (supported also by Myers) to promote the higher education of women in the north of England, entertaining him at Weetwood Hall on one occasion when the Trades Union Congress was meeting in Leeds.

[207] See above, pp. 145, 163, 234 n.     [208] See above, n. 3.

arrival, Ruskin received an invitation through one of his attendants he replied excusing himself:

> Corpus Christi College
> Oxford
> 26ᵗʰ Nov. 72.

My dear Sir

I must beg you to express for me to his Royal Highness my true sense
of the grace he does me—but also my hope that he will withdraw his
command, for I am under a sharp domestic grief at present which takes
away from ⟨me⟩ the power of availing myself of any such happy
privilege as he would grant me.

I trust that he will not less believe me his faithful Servant

> J Ruskin.[209]

Leopold, who had been tutored by R. H. Collins, a friend of
Myers, sent him a copy of the 1870 volume of Myers's *Poems*,
which Ruskin acknowledged in December:

> C.C.C. Oxford,
> Shortest Day. 1872.

Sir,—I have been in London during the last seven days, and though
your Royal Highness's kind letter came to me, there, I was afraid to
send for the book lest any mischance should come to it, and have only
been able to look at it today.

But now, much more than most books, I have looked at & learned
from it. I am very heartily glad to know that yʳ R[oyal] H[ighness] likes
it—but it seems strange to me—you are very happy in being enough
sad to enter into the feeling of these poems—already.

The 'John Baptist' seems to me entirely beautiful & right in its dream
of him. The Sᵗ. Paul is not according to my thought—but I am glad to
have my thought changed.

I wish the verses were less studiously alliterative, but the verbal art
of them is wonderful.

Some of the minor poems are the sweetest of their kind I ever read—
Wordsworth with a softer chime. I wish I had something adverse to
say, for this note must read to you as if I only wanted to say what
would please you. That is indeed true—but I should neither hope, nor
attempt, to do so by praising what I did not like.

I will venture, unless I receive your Royal Highness's command to

---

[209] TCL MS Myers 4⁷, hitherto unpublished. The mention of 'domestic grief'
refers to the death of Ruskin's mother in December 1871 and his consequent state
of depression, coupled with anxiety concerning Rose la Touche, who was on the
verge of mental breakdown.

the contrary, to keep the book until your return to Oxford, when I hope you will find some occasion of enabling me to show how truly I am your Royal Highness's very grateful and loyal servant

John Ruskin[210]

Something about Myers's 'St Paul' had evidently roused his disputing instincts, since in the course of a letter to Collins on 20 Feb. 1874 he remarked

I hope I may meet Mr Myers again. He failed me utterly—receding quite ignobly, I thought, from my Pauline Challenge—but to my great comfort, for I was not in fighting trim at all, even though the Prince gave me leave.—With faithful regards to him.[211]

This reflects an entry in his diary for the previous day:

Dine at Prince's; on his right, between him and Frederick Myers, but the talk at too careless a level for me, and I thoroughly uncomfortable.[212]

On 18 November, however, he wrote in a different vein:

... dine with the Prince, and heard from Mr Myers, things wonderful and most precious.[213]

Between the writing of these two entries there had intervened a visit of Myers and Edmund Gurney to Mrs Cowper-Temple, Gurney's aunt, at Broadlands (where she had arranged the meeting between Ruskin and Rose La Touche in August 1872[214]). In the course of this they had met and been impressed by the Reverend Stainton Moses,[215] and it was an account of his experiences that probably formed the core of what Myers relayed to Ruskin on this occasion, reawakening his interest in psychical research. His previous hostility, aroused by a reluctance to have dealings with the familiar spirits condemned in the Bible, may

---

[210] TCL MS Myers 4[15]. Published *variatim* in Myers, *FPP* 24–5 and in *R Works* xxxvii. 54.

[211] *R Works* xxxvii. 82. In the previous year he had written in a letter to Blanche Atkinson about 'the dark side of St Paul'—explaining, however, that though he entertained important reservations about him he still believed him to be a saint: Rylands Eng. MS 1162/21. Cf. Margaret Spence, 'Ruskin's Correspondence with Miss Blanche Atkinson', *Bulletin of the John Rylands Library*, 42 (1959–60), 202. There is also a reference in a letter to Collins of 21 May 1873: Bodleian MS Eng. lett. c. 39, fo. 94.

[212] *R Diaries* iii. 774.

[213] Ibid. 824.     [214] See above, p. 272.     [215] See above, p. 137.

also have reflected his impatience and despair that Rose La Touche should have set so much store by her belief in a future life where all would be made good. To Blanche Atkinson, who had shown sympathy with his predicament when he described it to her, he had written in the previous spring,

That child whom you cannot forgive has destroyed herself and me entirely by her trust in a future life. 'Wait—she always said—wait. All pain is good for you. We shall be perfectly happy in heaven.' An Indian dies in torment, in the same faith—and torments his enemy—as *she* did her lover.[216]

The death of Rose la Touche on 26 May 1875 removed the grounds for Ruskin's bitterness concerning her belief in a future life, replacing it with a hope of re-establishing contact with her by paranormal means; his further thought on this topic brought him and Myers more closely together. When in the following months, moreover, Prince Leopold fell ill with typhus, and came near to death, Ruskin engaged in conversations with him, some of which at least were heard and admired by Myers. The Prince accepted Ruskin as an important teacher; having also felt during his illness some assurance of a future life he later (without offering it public patronage) gave support to the newly founded Society for Psychical Research.[217]

To Mrs Talbot, who warned Ruskin against the current fashion for spiritualism, he wrote on 29 November,

I hear facts about spiritualism, and have seen some which gave me—and still give—the deepest anxiety to know more of the new dispensation under which we live—but the sorrow which has made that change upon me you saw,—is the very strongest guard I have against the danger. For I know that—if she *can* come to me, she will, without my dishonouring the love I bear her by impatience or mean methods of appeal; and if any *good* angel is to be sent to me,—*she* will be sent. And meantime, I am clear that it is no part of my duty, perhaps not even permitted ⟨to me⟩ enquiry, to follow out this frightful mystery that is tormenting or disturbing so many—I *know* that so far as I myself see, I see rightly; that what I recognize for noble and ignoble—for joy or sorrow,—is so, and may be shown to be so, to the good of all men.—

[216] Letter of 6 Mar. 1874; Rylands Eng. MS 1162/52. See Spence, *Talbot*, 39 n.
[217] Myers, 'Leopold, Duke of Albany:—In Memoriam', *Science and a Future Life* (2nd edn., 1901), 219–20; 231–3.

I seek no more than *all* may find—If God chooses to tell me, by dream—vision—or miracle—more than I yet know—He will do it at His own time ⟨and⟩ as ~~he~~ He sees best—and according to ~~my rights or~~ the degree in which I now obey what light ~~he~~ He has given me. I may be worn out—or broken—or blunted—or spoiled by earthly weakness and failure in Watching—or in temper of Prayer—but I shall not (I speak reverently)—be misled, or maddened, or betrayed by false fire . . .[218]

Perhaps in accordance with this guarded interest, he had set up further visits to the Cowper-Temples at Broadlands in August, making it a condition only that he should be undisturbed after six o'clock in the evening.[219] On 13 February 1876 he described to Mrs Talbot a current transformation:

. . . only a little while after I answered you—'If any message is to be brought to me, *one* spirit will come bearing it!', that *one* came—in the house of the lady named in the preface to Sesame and Lilies—Φίλη— (—~~with~~ beside whom the shade I looked for was first seen)—who had been ~~both our~~ the chief friend to both of us to whom we went in all saddest times.

Well—since that day—all things have more or less worked together for good for me . . .[220]

In December 1875, when he attended a séance there, a medium named Mrs Acworth[221] had told him that she saw the apparition of a tall, graceful, fair-haired young lady near him and Mrs Cowper-Temple on several occasions, and that she had looked particularly pained and sorrowful, with her hand to her head, when she heard Ruskin in discussion denigrating the loyalty of women compared with that of men.[222] He wrote in his journal,

Heard from Mrs Ackworth, in the drawing room where I was once so happy, the most overwhelming evidence of the other state of the world that has ever come to me; and am this morning like a flint stone suddenly changed into a fire fly, and ordered to flutter about—in a bramble thicket. Yet slept well and sound all night.[223]

---

[218] Rylands Eng. MS 1161/10 (plain text quoted Spence, *Talbot*, 38–9).

[219] Letter to Mrs Cowper-Temple of 10 Aug. 1875: *RLMT* 360.

[220] Letter of 13 Feb. 1876, Rylands Eng. MS 1161/11 (plain text in Spence, *Talbot*, 40).

[221] So spelt by William Cowper-Temple: TCL MS Myers 24[22].

[222] Abse, *Ruskin*, 276, citing Bembridge papers L40.      [223] *R Diaries* iii. 876.

The firefly readily represented for him the energized state in which he found himself, the thicket imagery that immediately followed signifying bewilderment at his inability to organize such experiences or know what to make of such phenomena. Yet the manifestations continued: Mrs Cowper-Temple's friend, he wrote, thrown into a trance by her, 'tells me all things that ever I did'.[224] A day or two later he was writing, 'Again, first through Φίλη and her friend, then, conclusively in evening talk after reading, the truth is shown to me, which, though blind, I have truly sought,—so long.'[225] He was no doubt particularly gratified when Mrs Acworth claimed to transmit a message from his dead mother that his religious doubts and questions, which had given her so much grief, had been helpful in rousing her from the narrowness of her old creed into a larger charity, enabling her to reach at once into a higher sphere than she would otherwise have attained.[226] He was not always quite so optimistic, however. Writing to Charles Eliot Norton on 13 January he once again depicted himself as living between two worlds:

Here in England, Atheism and Spiritualism mopping and mowing on either side of me. At Broadlands, either the most horrible lies were told me, without conceivable motive—or the ghost of R. was seen often beside Mrs.——or me.—Which is pleasantest of these things I know, but cannot intellectually say which is likeliest—and meantime, take to geology.[227]

In his fear of being deceived the flints were again proving a basic comfort, but evidence favouring the authenticity of psychic phenomena remained welcome: on 30 January, an entry dated from Broadlands ran 'Much nice talk in evening with Myers and Clifford',[228] and two days later he recalled with pleasure how just after the shade of Rose was asserted to have been seen at his side there he had recovered the most precious of the letters she

---

[224] *R Diaries* iii. 876. Cf. the comment of the woman of Samaria about Jesus: John 4: 29.

[225] Ibid., 877. For more on the spiritualism of the time and Ruskin's dealings with it see Leon, *Ruskin*, 505–8.

[226] Abse, *Ruskin*, 276 n.

[227] *R Works* xxxvii. 189.

[228] *R Diaries* iii. 883. Edward Clifford was a portrait painter according to *R Diaries*.

ever wrote to him.[229] His belief in the providential, thus reinforced, remained active—for example, in a revived habit of opening the Bible at random to see which text came into view[230]—and was now evident in the comfort he found in coincidences, and the superadded symbolic significance of certain elements in their relationship—such as her Christian name.

Myers's love for Annie Marshall gave scope for a closer bond. As it happened, the time of their greatest happiness began a few months after the 'three days of heaven' that Ruskin spent with Rose at the MacDonalds' in August 1872. The two relationships have points of strong correspondence—particularly the aspirations towards nobility. Ruskin's love, however, took to a further extreme the tensions inherent in Myers's. The childlike nature of the two women involved a point of difference. Writing to her aunt, Myers's mother, Annie might present herself in the persona of a 'child' but this was inevitably a pose: as a mature woman and a mother, she was forced to exercise adult judgement. In a setting where reality was constituted by the demands of home and parents on the other hand, Rose, deprived of any means of development, was likely to find a greater sense of security than could be provided by her lover with his call to an idealized behaviour.

After Rose's death the understanding between the two men naturally deepened. Ruskin, as we saw, had been particularly impressed by Myers's poem 'John the Baptist' when the 1870 *Poems* were sent to him by Prince Leopold in 1872. Writing to him four years later with recent events in mind, he was able to take comfort from what the poem had had to say about mortality:

Corpus Christi College
Oxford
15th March 1876.

Dear M[r] Myers

I cannot tell you how grateful I am for the writing of that noble poem;—though I cannot understand how you could have known so

---

[229] Letter to Norton, 1 Feb. 1876: *R Works* xxxvii. 190; *RCEN* 377. The editors of *RCEN* think this was the 'Star-letter' of Christmas 1861, printed in Burd, *RLT* 71–3, but do not give conclusive evidence. It might equally, for example, have been the letter of late Feb. 1870 in which she protested her love for him: see above, p. 266.

[230] Derrick Leon dates this practice to the period of 1866: *Ruskin*, 387.

much of Death—and of the power of its approach, in your fervid youth.—and though I, in spite of all, you, and other very dear friends have taught me, feel too fatally the terror, still.—But it is partly a help to know that one does not walk in the shadow alone.

Yes, I can come to Cambridge at the time you ask me—being on the last day of this month.—staying over the Sunday. I have been greatly pained by reading some of Miss ~~Anna Blackwell's~~ 'Spiritism'—and need some help from nobler hands.

Ever affectionately yours,

John Ruskin[231]

Although it is not clear which part of the poem had struck home with such force it seems likely that the lines were those that urged the need for 'patient hope and dumb humility' in confronting the refusal of the invisible to make itself fully manifest, and went on to describe the fear of insanity:

> Yea Lord, I know it, teach me yet anew
> With what a fierce and patient purity
> I must confront the horror of the world.
> For very little space on either hand
> Parts the sane mind from madness; very soon
> By the intenser pressure of one thought
> Or clearer vision of one agony
> The soothfast reason trembles, all things fade
> In blackness, and the demon enters in . . .[232]

Ruskin duly visited Cambridge, arriving on 31 March, and wrote in his journal next morning 'Pleasant talk with Myers last night'.[233] Having stayed two more nights (concerning which his Diary records are somewhat mixed) he wrote later in the month,

---

[231] TCL MS Myers 4⁸. Published *variatim* in Myers, *FPP* 23 and in *R Works* xxxvii. 184–5 (deletion evidently made by a later editor: Bodleian MS Eng. lett. xi fo. 46).

[232] Myers, *Poems* (1870), 62–3. In the copy that Mary Gladstone passed to him Ruskin wrote above the poem 'J. R., with deep thanks', describing it to her as one 'which had taught and helped me in the highest ways'. *R Works* xxxvii. 239.

[233] *R Diaries* iii. 891. See also his letter of 10 May 1876 to Prince Leopold: 'I had a happy time at Cambridge with Mr Myers: I cannot enough thank your Royal Highness for giving me that friend.' *R Works* xxxvii. 199. The only other mention of Myers in the *Diaries* is on 10 July 1877 (iii. 965) when he writes that he is 'at Grosvenor with Φίλη [Mrs Cowper-Temple], Myers, Mr and Mrs Gurney' (the latter being not, as the editors suppose, Mr and Mrs Russell Gurney but Edmund Gurney and his wife Kate, whom he had married on 5 June). Myers also mentions this meeting in his journal for 9 July.

Oxford,
11<sup>th</sup> April. 76

My dear Myers,

I am *very* grateful—for infinitely surprised—by your letter. It is a comfort and strength to me in extreme weakness of soul—The surprise being that in this weakness, I am able to give you the pleasure you tell me of. My own feeling is always that the things of which I try to show the force are open to every one who will look at them—& that my own work is merely a dog's *quartering* a field—and that the very *game* I put up is not for me—and I don't expect anybody to care for me, ever, & I mean—that being sure there is a spiritual world—I am so poor-hearted & cold that I never think I shall get to it; but I may show the path. It makes me hope better of myself—ever so much, that you were happy with me. I ought to have written to have thanked you for all things and to be remembered to all the friends that showed themselves so friendly—very especially to M<sup>r</sup> Stewart—very earnestly to all.

It is late—and I am weary and cannot say what I would but I am ever affectionately yours,

J Ruskin[234]

That being the summer of Annie Marshall's decline into her last depression and her death, Myers presumably told Ruskin the story of his love for her and of its tragic conclusion. By the end of the year Ruskin was in Venice, where during the period over Christmas he passed through a time of considerable, if obscure excitement involving both moral self-examination and supposed signs, some of them associated with Rose by way of St Ursula, a saint who particularly intrigued him since she had not been willing to accept her suitor until he became converted to Christianity and at 15 (like Rose at 18) had asked him to wait three years before she would marry him. She provided a link with the veneration for Catholicism that had grown as a result of his experiences in Umbria. In Venice he became fascinated by Carpaccio's series of paintings on her life and persuaded the authorities of the Accademia to bring down one of them, 'The Dream of St Ursula', so that he could spend days in examining it closely. As he became gradually persuaded that he was being 'guided' by Rose, everything assumed providential significance. The gift of a pot of dianthus from Lady Castletown, linked with

---

[234] TCL MS Myers 4<sup>9(1)</sup>. Published *variatim* in Myers, *FPP* 23–4 and in *R Works* xxxvii. 185. The 'Mr Stewart' he mentions is probably to be identified with the James Stuart of Ch. 5, n. 85, and nn. 3 and 206 above.

the painting of one by Carpaccio on the sill of St Ursula's bedroom, could be regarded as a gift from the saint, as he recorded in *Fors*.[235] On the last day of the year he wrote to Myers,

> Venice.
> Eleven; Sunday morning
> 31st December, 1876.
>
> My dear friend,
>
> Do not think me heartless in beginning, with this orderly date to tell you how precious your letter is to me.
>
> The date, when you hear what has been happening to myself this last week, will be of importance to yourself also. What you have written is for us both; and for us both in almost precisely alike states of mind, and trial: except only that *your* letter comes to me as the close of a series of comforts, while this of mine cannot be of complete use for the moment to you,—till you hear how we are both being guided;—I can only tell you—for I want this to be written in instant answer, that the especial virtue of your help to me is in what you now have told me of the madness of noble souls: the one mystery that still bitterly troubled me.
>
> I cannot write more to day. Accept all you would have of my life, for any help it can be to you—and believe me your grateful and faithful
>
> John Ruskin[236]

The reference to his 'being guided' is not only a reminder of his providential thinking but takes us back to Rose's use of that word at the time of her early illness, when she was showing uncanny powers.[237]

In a short space of time, however, he was in a less confident mood, writing to Mrs Talbot,

> you are a very inconsistent mama, to be anxious now because you think I have no clear sense of Rosie's being near me, when you said all you could to keep me from trusting to the only evidence I had of her being so! One reason that it fails from me is that I am never quite sure how far it is right to be still dependent on selfish affection or hope. But in the Christmas teaching, it was nearly all St Ursula and very little of Rosie—and I do wonder why she leaves me so long without sign.[238]

---

[235] *Fors Clavigera*, letter 74, Christmas Day 1875: *R Works* xxix. 30.
[236] TCL MS Myers 4[11]. Published Burd, *Christmas Story*, 224 n.
[237] See the letter quoted above at n. 79.
[238] Letter of 18 Feb. 1877: Rylands Eng. MS 1161/42. (Spence, *Talbot*, 64–5).

His accompanying puzzlement about the whole affair may well have been caused not only by a residual scepticism concerning the credibility of such phenomena but by a feeling of the ultimate uselessness of any renewed contact with Rose that did not bring her back in the body, physically. Two years before, while Rose was still alive, he had written to Susan Beever concerning her refusal to see him, 'I wanted my Rosie *here*. In heaven I mean to go and talk to Pythagoras and Socrates and Valerius Publicus.'[239] He remained intrigued by the possibilities opened up by his recent experiences, but without exhibiting the clerkly scepticism that enabled Myers to balance an ardour for discovery in psychical research against recognition that he might after all be dealing with an illusion. In his own case ardour and scepticism excluded one another more absolutely.

Although for the time being ardour was in the ascendant, the quest for signs soon assumed a more disturbing form. A severe attack of brain-fever just over a year later included the vivid belief that Rose was walking up the aisle of a church, while he as bridegroom waited for her at the altar steps, his dog barking for joy nearby.[240] So complete was the delusion that he wrote off inviting his friends to rejoice with him at the new turn of events, causing them deep worry and concern that he be brought under medical care. The breakdown, which began at the end of February, lasted through the spring. It was not until 7 April that he was able to get down to his study again, 'after illness such as I never thought to know'.[241] A subsequent letter to Myers gave a vivid account:

> Brantwood,
> Coniston Lancashire,
> 14th May 1878.

Dear Myers,
   *Very* thankful am I for your dear little note. I shall have much to tell you of the illness—a terrific and abasing one—sifting me, like—*blighted* wheat.—and full of astonishment to me. its immediate result being however, to show me that I must—do just what I like!—for this

---

[239] *Hortus Inclusus* (Orpington, 1887), 18, repr. in R *Works* xxxvii. 117.
[240] Leon, *Ruskin*, 509–10.
[241] R *Diaries* 18 June 1878, iii. 976. Myers's journal for 5 Apr. has an entry that reads 'Ruskin better'. A further note on 20 July reads 'Ruskin at Cowper-Temples'. He also met him there on 26 Oct. 1879: see TCL MS Myers 3[71].

summer which will be botany & mineralogy.—and I must not think! nor—but with extreme fear, feel!

—But I *do* think I'm going to be of a little use, yet.—only, I am stunned just now—and feel ~~a good deal~~ as if I had been putting hand to the Ark like Uzzah—and had been struck all *but* dead, therefore.— But I must not go on—about the illness. It has left me weak, but I believe my wits are coming back to me, one by one—I may have to sweep the barn diligently before I find the last of them, perhaps; or get rid of the last devil—A good seven I think must have got into me since the last garnishing.

A lady writes to me (about S^t George) with a pretty name— 'Anne S^t Amand Newbery' 23 Sussex Place Kensington Gate, W.

I've some notion theres a Lady N. or Hon^l. or something—would you kindly find out and address enclosed rightly for me.

Much love to E. G. & his treasure.

Ever yours JR.[242]

A description to George Richmond two weeks later of the illness that had overtaken him brought out its lighter aspects as well:

The dream itself, though full of *merest* fantasy and madness in many respects, was on the *whole* a sifting examination of me, by myself, on all the dark sides and in all the dark places; coupled with some passages of bright conceit enough; and others of great beauty and bright jest.[243]

The providential 'guiding', which had turned out to be, as he reported to Myers, that he should do just what he liked, was honoured by dedicating more time to his geological and mineralogical studies, where he could engage with nature in her most organizable form. In further episodes of madness, which would in turn be interpreted again in terms of their providential messages, there would be less wrestling with the intractable problems of nature and her moral significance and a devotion to what came more easily. Even in coming to terms with the memory of Rose he would simply do what he could. A letter to Charles Eliot Norton of 26 April 1881 includes the record 'got in my own evening thoughts into a steady try if I couldn't get Rosie's ghost at least alive by me, if not the body of

---

[242] TCL MS Myers 4^{12(1)}. Hitherto unpublished. The envelope is addressed to Frederick W. H. Myers, 9 Bolton Row, Mayfair, W. London. The story of Uzzah, who was killed by God for touching the ark in order to steady it, is in 2 Sam. 6: 6– 7 and 1 Chron. 13: 9–10. 'E. G. & his treasure' refers to Edmund Gurney and his wife: see p. 218 and n. 233 above.

[243] Letter to George Richmond of 31 May 1878, *R Works* xxxvii. 246–7.

her'.[244] The mention of her *body* echoed his remark to Susan Beever: it was all that would really satisfy him, associated with contemporary attempts to establish material realizations of the dead which were sometimes persuasive at the time, even if they later ended in the discovery of fraud.[245] It was a somewhat desperate enterprise, and Ruskin's general sense of things no doubt told him so. But without any further sign from Rose such attempts at least had the simplicity to which he was now increasingly devoting himself in other spheres.

This urge to simplicity, taken up into the economy of his psyche, may even have assisted the insurgence of further delusions on his own account, involving a tendency to demonize. In 1883 he wrote to Norton,

... last year, at this very time, I saw the stars rushing at each other— and thought the lamps of London were gliding through the night into a World Collision.—took my pretty Devonshire farm-girl Nurse for a Black Vision of Judgment . . .[246]

This was still for him a matter of being 'guided': at the end of March 1881 he had written to Norton about his recent bout of madness,

The two fits of whatever you like to call them are both parts of the same course of teaching, and I've been more gently whipped this time and have learned more but I must be very cautious in using my brains yet awhile.[247]

A few days later he wrote to Dr Brown that this illness had been more definite in its dreaming than the last:

It taught me much, as these serious dreams do always, and I hope to manage myself better, and not go Argonauting any more. But *both* these illnesses have been part of one and the same constant thought, far out of sight to the people about me, and of course, getting more and more separated from them as *they* go back to live with my Father and my Mother and my Nurse, and one more,—all waiting for me in the Land of the Leal.[248]

As they continued the delusions became harder to interpret sensibly. One, in which the shrieking of a peacock outside was

---

[244] *R Works* xxxvii. 355.    [245] See e.g. Gauld, *Founders*, 104–14.
[246] *RCEN* 461–2.
[247] Letter to Norton of 24 Mar. 1881: *R Works* xxxvii. 345.
[248] Letter to Dr Brown of 29 Mar. 1881: *R Works* xxxvii. 347–8.

heard as the voice of the Evil One, bidding him commit some hideous wrong, and a large black cat that jumped into the room was seized and dashed against the floor in consequence, marked an intensification of the demonizing tendency that had distorted his relationship with the La Touches. It was hardly compensated for by other experiences in which his room shone with an unearthly radiance and his Turner drawings were translated into pictures out of heaven.[249]

All this contributed to his resolve to follow a saner guidance. An 'Advice by Mr Ruskin' printed at the beginning of George Allen's List of his Works in July 1882 and in subsequent issues, counselled his readers that it was 'a prettier attention to an old man, to read what he wishes to say, and can say without effort, than to require him to answer vexing questions on general subjects, or to add to his days' appointed labour the burden of accidental and unnecessary correspondence'.[250] This asseveration, which amused some of his readers, was another result of his 'teaching', a decision to do what he could do 'without effort' and so avoid being bound back on the wheel of attempting to deal with the age's contradictions through efforts to resolve his own.

One might have expected the result to be the retirement of a doting old man into a sealed world of his memories and an end to his writing; instead, he began to write out those memories. It may be that attempts to call the past to life in this way were a compensation for the failure of his efforts to revive Rose by psychical means.[251] Certainly his interest in those matters dropped away.[252] When he resumed contact with Myers in 1883 it was by way of replying to an invitation from his wife Eveleen, whom Myers had married in the meantime. Her sister Dolly Tennant, as a promising artist, wanted to talk to, and be advised by him; such an appeal from a young woman rarely left him untouched.

---

[249] See Wilenski, *Ruskin*, 145 and n., quoting an article in the *British Medical Journal* for 27 Jan. 1900 repr. in *R Works* xxxviii. 172–3.

[250] *R Works* xxxiv. 652.

[251] The short unpublished section devoted to her in the original MS of *Praeterita* is reproduced in *R Works* xxxv. 525–34.

[252] Myers commented in his *FIL* MS 'There was about Ruskin in his later years something of impatience and waywardness w[h] prevented him from thoroughly studying the subject': TCL MS Myers 26[63(74)].

Oxford 25<sup>th</sup> Nov. 83

Dear M<sup>rs</sup> Myers

I am ashamed to find your kind note yet unans<sup>d</sup>. but have been a mere straw in the wind lately. never able to say—where next:—and now—I must get home by tomorrows train—and have no hope of seeing you or Dolly till January.—but January will be here—like tomorrow and then I *must* see Dolly at any rate for I want her to help me to make Miss Greenaway 'serious'—If only I could get those two shuffled a little in head and heart! and re-dealt.—fairly!

Dear love to your husband and I am ever your faithful Serv<sup>t</sup>.

John Ruskin[253]

His interest in psychical research continued to be inhibited by the nature of some of its results. It was a disappointment to some of the leading members of the Society for Psychical Research, such as Henry Sidgwick, that when the phenomena being investigated showed signs of authenticity they were often unaccompanied by endorsement of noble behaviour—a frustration which, as we have seen, Ruskin shared to the full, particularly when questions of art were involved. In 1884 he was put out by the poor quality of the drawings that had been used for some experiments in thought transference:

Brantwood,
Coniston Lancashire,
3<sup>rd</sup> Aug. 1884.

My dearest Myers

I don't know a more curious proof of the non-naturalness of spiritual phenomena, than that the Society should have been beguiled into the publication of those beastly drawings. You really must not go on with that sort of thing. Get somebody to draw who *can*, for this *first* drawing ~~and~~ then let the spirits caricature ⟨or bungle⟩ as they like. but

---

[253] TCL MS Myers 4<sup>19(?)</sup>. Hitherto unpublished. Dolly Tennant was, like her sister, painted by Millais: see Myers's letter to Caroline Jebb of 21 Jan. 1880: Bobbitt, *Dearest Love*, 155; she married H. M. Stanley the explorer in 1890. (Fifteen years earlier Stanley had applied for permission to bring into England a pirated edition of Ruskin's works which he was planning to take with him to Africa. Ruskin had refused the request, commenting that 'he had better not burden himself with stolen property on his Missionary expedition. He shall certainly not do so with permission of mine' (Rylands Eng. MS 1254/86, unpublished).) The comment on Kate Greenaway's lack of seriousness matches one in a letter to H. S. Marks of 1879: 'I want her to make more serious use of her talent': *R Works* xxxvii. 303.

don't publish such *'originals'* any more. They *have* their value, as Fors has ordered them—but don't give *any more*.

Ever your loving, JR.[254]

The testiness displayed in this letter had become an increasingly regular feature of his behaviour. On another occasion he responded to an invitation from Eveleen Myers's mother Mrs Tennant with a pungent note on the futility of trying to summarize his thought:

Dear M^rs^ Tennant

I will come to lunch on Friday; but Dorothy can no more 'hear' my views on Art over a mutton chop, than she could hear Scott's novels in the same period—But novelists are not asked to relate their novels over again—while I find myself—being now old and weary, continually asked to repeat, in half an hour what I have taken forty years to learn—and ten at least—to write.

Dorothy ought to have gone to Florence—not to have stayed in Paris. The time she has spent in Paris—(not to say London), has not only *lost* ground for her at present—but undermined it for the future—Ever faithfully Yrs

J Ruskin.[255]

The note of weary despair spread across many fields. His demands for social justice narrowed into a suspicion of proposals for change, particularly on a local scale. Like Wordsworth and Myers he found himself opposing the extension of the railways in the Lake District, in his case protesting against a proposal to build a line between Windermere and Keswick.[256]

Yet the larger questions, including that of the providential, remained, being so closely implicated in the Victorian modes of discourse he had inherited. When Carlyle, for example, wrote 'the old Eternal Powers do live forever; nor do their laws know any change, however we in our poor wigs and church-tippets may attempt to read their laws',[257] he displayed belief in a

---

[254] TCL MS Myers 4[14(1)] (referred to, Gauld, *Founders*, 140n). Examples of the drawings used at this time can be found in the *Proceedings of the Society for Psychical Research* (Nov. and June 1883–4) ii. 33–42 and 208–12. When not simple diagrams they were of a simple 'cartoon' quality, not likely to appeal to Ruskin.

[255] TCL MS Myers 4[16]. Hitherto unpublished.

[256] 'The Extension of Railways in the Lake District: A Protest': 1876, repr. in *On the Old Road, R Works* xxxiv. 133–43.

[257] Ch. viii, 'Coleridge', in *The Life of John Sterling* (1851), 79.

controlling order which, though not to be read by the methods
of conventional religion was still inexorable in its operation. It
was a foreshadowing of Ruskin's assertion that the difficulty of
tracing the exact workings of providence should not be made a
reason for doubting its existence as such.

The conviction was closely caught up with the expectations of
contemporary readers who hoped, especially in their fiction, for
happy endings that were congruent with poetic justice. Ruskin,
an advocate, as we have seen, of such justice in art found
elsewhere that in his teaching the two modes could clash. The
resulting tension is evident in his 1884 lectures 'The Storm-
Cloud of the Nineteenth Century', where he finds himself torn
between reading the new weather conditions that he has been
observing simply as an effect of the new industrialism or as a
sign of Divine Judgement:

> Blanched Sun,—blighted grass—blinded man.—If, in conclusion,
> you ask me for any conceivable cause or meaning of these things—I can
> tell you none, according to your modern beliefs; but I can tell you what
> meaning it would have borne to the men of old time. Remember, for
> the last twenty years, England, and all foreign nations, either tempting
> her, or following her, have blasphemed the name of God deliberately
> and openly; and have done iniquity by proclamation, every man doing
> as much injustice to his brother as it is in his power to do. . . . Of states
> in such moral gloom every seer of old predicted the physical gloom,
> saying, 'The light shall be darkened in the heavens thereof, and the
> stars shall withdraw their shining.'

He goes on to press the moral—but always at one remove. He
cannot bring himself to declare that the bad weather is directly
due to the iniquity of Europe; instead, he ends by saying,
'Whether you can affect the signs of the sky or not, you can the
signs of the times. Whether you can bring the sun back or not,
you can assuredly bring back your own cheerfulness, and your
own honesty.' There is, in other words, a turn to inward meaning, a contenting of himself with the reaffirmation that cultivating righteousness will bring about a kind of inner sunshine. But
the suggestion that it might bring about an improvement in the
weather as well is not totally excluded.

This fissure between the natural and moral strains in his
thinking is accompanied by a continuing belief in the providential which was not shared by most of his contemporaries; yet

many would continue to use the word lightly, as if the matter were not one of the greatest consequence. This is so even in the writings of Henry Sidgwick, who might have been expected to guard his use of the word more firmly. He himself was to relate how after a lesson at school in which it was pointed out that at the very time when Tacitus was expressing his gloomy indignation at the corruption of his times the founder of Christianity was at work he went away 'startled into a reverent appreciation of the providential scheme of human history which was not soon to be forgotten'.[258] The word remained ready to hand for the rest of his life, whether to be used jocularly[259] or with an element, at least, of seriousness. With some sceptical writers of the time one might simply assume the presence of mental inverted commas around the word, but in a thinker of such scrupulousness as Sidgwick one cannot let the frequency of his usage slip by so easily. In a man who agonized so much over moral choices there evidently remained an area of unexamined confidence in the purposes of the universe, assisted perhaps by his work as a psychical researcher. To that extent, perhaps, Myers had won him over from scepticism. In the same vein, serious rather than otherwise, Gurney wrote to William James, 'I ... cannot be too thankful to Providence for bringing me across you, both as philosopher and ... friend.'[260]

Other contemporaries, facing such implications, emphasized their controlling and overriding sense of destiny. In his morality tale 'Lord Arthur Savile's Crime' Oscar Wilde portrayed a man who found that his attempts to control his own destiny served only to fulfil it. Or the issue might be treated more lightly.

---

[258] *Sidgwick Memoir*, 10.

[259] Hearing that two of his philosophic friends at Cambridge were to be married, he 'bowed to the decrees of Providence' (Ibid. 161 (cf. 170, 214)).

[260] Writing to Myers in 1871 about the cause of women's education, Sidgwick declared, 'I feel with Luther that if Providence has the cause of Female Education at heart, now is the time for some manifest intervention.' (Letter of 20 Dec. 1871, TCL MS Add. c. 100[222].) Those who, like himself, hoped for reform in Cambridge in 1873 were, he said, 'partly waiting on Providence and Gladstone'; he hoped to visit his mother the following year but 'Providence ... ordered otherwise'; in 1886 he was confident that he would complete his work shortly—'if Providence allows me time'; ten years later he and his wife, having escaped influenza and other calamities were feeling themselves 'the favourites of Providence'. *Sidgwick Memoir*, 276, 287, 455, 513.) Gurney's use of the word is from the letter of 15 February 1883 quoted by G. Ebberson, *The Mind of Edmund Gurney* (1997), 52.

When in this play Lady Windermere replied to the charge of tempting providence with the words 'surely Providence can resist temptation by this time' the natural and moral elements in the situation as it stood danced in an ingenious play of language. As for the more serious Ruskin, unable to resolve the dilemma so either in a direct acceptance of fate or in a witticism, the attempt to bridge the gap instead by advocacy of noble conduct leaves the reader with a disturbing sense of looming madness.

This was (for whatever reasons) the actual outcome; indeed, as a result of Ruskin's extraordinary articulacy we have in his subsequent writings some of the best accounts of madness from the patient's point of view that have ever appeared.[261] After one of them he declared that he had for the first time understood the meaning of the phrase 'beside myself', having been 'a double, or even treble, creature through a great part of the dream'.[262] To an unusual degree his delusionary episodes were accompanied by the activity of a watchful eye that at a different level was still trying to study and make sense. In the worst of times all he could do was confer some kind of rational shape on his delusions, allowing them to pursue their own crazy logic— which at least betrayed the continuing presence of the stifled rational powers. His direst attacks of brain-fever were still accompanied by intense attempts to reduce them to a responsible account. He could abandon neither his ideal of nobility nor the belief that it must be possible to establish the existence of its close relationship to nature. Inasmuch as an interpretation of the human condition in these terms remained challenged by the workings of human instinct, he continued to rely for success on demonstrating that human beings had an innate power of subduing their ignoble urges; his thought was still aligned with Tennyson's

> Arise and fly
> The reeling Faun, the sensual feast;
> Move upward, working out the beast,
> And let the ape and tiger die.[263]

---

[261] Wilenski, *Ruskin*, provides some of the best accounts, though some of his interpretations are open to debate.

[262] Letter to Mrs John Simon of 15 May 1878, quoted ibid. 156.

[263] *In Memoriam* CXVIII. 25–8: Tennyson, *Poems*, ed C. Ricks (1969), 970.

Detection of a quixotic element in all this would not have been rejected outright, for it was a critique already entertained and partly accepted. In an acute comment on his own nature he wrote to Charles Eliot Norton about his reading of Cervantes's masterpiece,

It always affected me *throughout* with tears, not laughter—It was always, *throughout*—*real* chivalry to me; and it is precisely because the most touching valour and tenderness are rendered vain by madness, and because, thus vain, they are made a subject of laughter to vulgar & shallow persons; and because *all* true chivalry is thus by implication accused of madness, and involved in shame—that I call the book so deadly . . .[264]

Future developments were to show that the 'vulgar and shallow' people who thought of the revival of chivalry as a form of eccentricity bordering on madness were not without justification. The writer now coming into his own was Thomas Hardy, not the straightforwardly anti-providential writer he might at first seem but a novelist continually questioning the underlying optimism that allowed his contemporaries to continue using the word, lightly or otherwise, in a manner that seemed to take for granted a benevolent guiding hand. By the turn of the century he was beginning to carry his point. As late as 1896, Edmund Gosse had shown how little he appreciated it when, reviewing *Jude the Obscure*, he enquired, 'What has Providence done to Mr Hardy that he should rise up in the arable land of Wessex and shake his fist at his Creator?'[265] It was not long before the gibe seemed less urbane. In 1903, when Hardy published *The Dynasts* and provided for his epic-drama to be presided over by a 'group of intelligences', he insisted that they were merely 'contrivances of the fancy', commenting

---

[264] Letter to C. E. Norton of 9 Aug. 1870, *RCEN* 202–3. The editor draws attention to similar judgements in 1853 (*R Works* xii. 55–6) and in *Praeterita* i, ch. iii (ibid. xxxv. 61) as well as his self-description as 'the Don Quixote of Denmark Hill' (ibid. xxx. 110).

[265] Review in *Cosmopolis, An International Review* (Jan. 1896). Gosse himself was increasingly an admirer of Hardy's work: Ann Thwaite, *Edmund Gosse: A Literary Landscape 1849–1928* (London, 1984), 388. Seventy years later Lois Deacon, assisted by Terry Coleman, attempted a literal answer to his question in *Providence and Mr Hardy* (1966), suggesting that much of Hardy's dark view of life was due to the fact that he was unable to marry his cousin Tryphena Sparks.

The wide prevalence of the Monistic theory of the Universe forbade, in this twentieth century, the importation of Divine personages from any antique Mythology as ready-made sources or channels of Causation, even in verse, and excluded the celestial machinery of, say *Paradise Lost*, as peremptorily as that of the *Iliad* or the *Eddas*.[266]

In the processes of that sweeping elimination the fact that, along with all such machinery, the sense of providence itself was also disappearing could pass almost unnoticed.

Ruskin's death in January 1900, which preceded by only a few months those of Sidgwick and of Myers (the latter of whom still had time to write for the Society for Psychical Research an obituary including the memory of their first encounter with which this chapter opened) coincided with the beginning of a century that would see the nations of Europe each invoking ideals of nobility as they plunged into a conflict that would be dominated by the success of nineteenth-century technology in developing the metallurgy of cannon, the sweeping accuracy of machine-guns and the chemistry of poison gases. Ruskin's admonition concerning the great manufacturing towns, 'we manufacture everything there except men'[267] would receive the grimmest of endorsements. As the participants fulfilled humanitarian fears concerning the consequences of industrialism they would invoke ideals of 'gallantry' with a blindness and intensity that could quite properly be described as mad.[268] For the rest of the century men and women in Europe would be haunted by the waste of so many noble actions in the mammoth futility of prolonged battles that turned into a kind of consuming machinery.[269] While one might contemplate the fate of individuals such as John Ruskin and Rose La Touche simply as personal tragedies, events on this scale threw the issues on to a giant screen, as it were, provoking questions about the sanity of the

---

[266] Preface to *The Dynasts*.

[267] *The Stones of Venice* VI. i. 16: R *Works* x. 196.

[268] R. H. Wilenski contends spiritedly that although the War fulfilled so many of Ruskin's forebodings and in spite of his pacifist urgings in some places, he would, had it happened during his lifetime, have been overcome by patriotic fervour: Wilenski, *Ruskin*, 40–1.

[269] The concurrence between the development of killing by industrial methods in slaughter-houses and the growth of industrialized warfare has been explored by Daniel Pick in *War Machine: The Rationalisation of Slaughter in the Modern Age* (New Haven, 1993).

human race generally. When the obstinate adherence to noble principle that had destroyed the love between these two became a motive force in the conduct of nations at large international relations were turned over to the politics of the madhouse. By the time that the effects could be surveyed in retrospect, ideas of a providential order watching over human fates had for thoughtful people not simply moved into the distance but passed out of sight.

The strong survival of such thinking in the nineteenth century demonstrates that Myers was far from alone in seeing the cultivation of honour and nobility as the course of action that might fill most satisfactorily the gap left between the old codes of conventional religion and the new regard for scientific truth. Indeed he had not been the most predictable proponent of such an attitude, given the versatility of his own personality: on one occasion he affirmed it as his belief that he contained within himself every potentiality of human behaviour, for good or ill.[270] Ruskin's cultivation of nobility was, by comparison, more deeply ingrained. His enthusiastic reading of Scott's novels provided an accessible code of conduct and a mode of discourse he never abandoned. 'Noble' was always a prime word of approval (just as 'pretty' was never far from his vocabulary in more patronizing moods), while Nature remained his touchstone. The strands remained inexorably locked in tension. As late as 1885, when *On the Old Road* appeared, he could write—still, apparently, despite all his experiences to the contrary, with no hint of questioning—'Nature and her laws recognize only the noble.'[271]

In the midst of the prophetic frustrations of his later years, however, Ruskin had made a discovery that helped him face them creatively. Just as Rose, in the depths of her 1863 illness, had touched springs of ultimate resilience that allowed her to deal with her disorder by following the dictates of her own 'wild spiritual nature', until she recovered in a way that seemed miraculous to her watching mother, so now Ruskin, having worked and suffered his way through the formidable self-contradictions of his career, discovered a guiding mode that allowed him to mingle strenuousness with relaxation. It was the

---

[270] Mentioned Gauld, *Founders*, 102.     [271] R *Works* xxxiv. 354.

same guiding power that had revealed to him how his best course in future would be to do 'just what he liked'. What he liked, he had found, was to recall the best memories of his earlier years; evoking them into prose enabled him to pour his powers of eloquence, easily and single-mindedly, into rhapsodic pages of autobiography. The marvellous and unlooked for outcome was *Praeterita*, the work that allowed him to meditate at length on the great themes of his life while reproducing in vivid detail the upbringing with his 'Father and Mother and Nurse', and even to include an account (though abortive) of his love for Rose. The book culminated in a passage in which the destructive rushing stars of his recent nightmares were replaced by a vision of dancing fireflies outside Siena as he remembered them from earlier years—a vision now given the place of honour. If there was a providence in the world, it seemed, its work was to be sought and found in the subconscious resources of the human psyche itself; and to recognize this justified looking back over one's own lifetime in an attempt to perceive the patterns at work. The last paragraph of *Praeterita* begins with the words 'How things bind and blend themselves together!'

It was in the human psyche too, and perhaps only there, that the truth of nobility could in the last resort be justified. To grasp that was to recognize also the survival of the Wordsworth whose statement, long before, in his pamphlet on the Convention of Cintra, could have served as a point of departure for much of Ruskin's thinking also:

The true sorrow of humanity consists in this;—not that the mind of man fails; but that the course and demands of action and of life so rarely correspond with the dignity and intensity of human desires: and hence that, which is slow to languish, is too easily turned aside and abused.[272]

By this time community in their sense of loss had abolished enmity between Ruskin and the La Touches,[273] leaving him to reassert the providentiality of his love for Rose and confront his own Romanticism more steadily. In spite of his overt impatience with some aspects of Wordsworth he could now, from the hardgained position of his late years, see still further into the

---

[272] *WPrW* i. 339.
[273] Mrs La Touche visited him in the summer of 1881: *RLMT* 379.

kinds of experience on which the poet's thinking had drawn. If he now reasserted his obstinate belief in an indissoluble link between nature and human nobility he could do so most convincingly by way of a more complex observation:

The only *real* sorrow is the thought of pain given long ago; the rest is loss, not pain, and even a certain gain of nobleness in bearing loss. But the Difference, yes, immeasurable.[274]

It was in one sense no more than an expansion of Wordsworth's reflection on the death of Lucy. And since such 'Difference' could be measured, if at all, only in time it followed that in the face of lost love the most reliable Providence (thought of by Ruskin, like Wordsworth, as beautiful more often than otherwise) was, once again, the providence that showed itself in memory, which could restore with wonderful freshness experiences of upspringing vitality, constantly renewed in nature and humanity alike.

[274] Letter to Dr John Brown of 5 June ?1880: *R Works* xxxvii. 317.

# Appendix

## Identifying Lucy?

The problem of dating a possible Lakeland love for Wordsworth during this period is complicated by the existence of the poem 'I travelled among unknown men . . .' This, it will be recalled, refers to a visit abroad, during which Wordsworth discovered the full depth of his own love for England. It also records a resolution that he would not again leave the country in which he had loved Lucy and where she had died. The supposed date of this foreign visit and resolve is not easy to determine, however. He went abroad at least three times during the years leading up to the composition of the poem: to France in 1790 and 1791–2 (possibly again in 1793); and then, after several years in Britain, to Germany in 1798–9. The poem might record a resolution made earlier in France, or it might be based on a current reaction to his German surroundings, reflecting more directly his sense of alienation during the winter of that stay. In either case the resolution may have had to do with the aftermath of his love for Annette Vallon and have borne in on his reasons for not returning to marry her. But however one reads this element in the poem it throws little direct light on the dating of an association with Lucy.

If one believes that Wordsworth visited a particular 'beloved Maid' during at least some part of the period as a whole it is natural to turn from clues in the text and look at the poetry he was writing, since although little of it was published in his own lifetime much survived in manuscript. There is a small quarto notebook, for example, which contains a number of pieces, including some love poems. Once again, however, this trail, despite initial promise, leads to no definite conclusions; the most striking feature of the poems is that when a girl is named, her name is normally Mary. In the first, an imitation of Anacreon inscribed 'Hawkshead, August 7th, 1786' in which he invokes Sir Joshua Reynolds as the artist most appropriate to paint his love, no name is given; the lines of description begin

> Waving in the wanton air
> Black and shining paint her hair;

> Could with Life the canvass bloom
> Thou mightst bid it breathe perfume
> Let her forehead smooth and clear
> Through her shading ~~face~~ locks appear,
> As ~~the wandering~~ \<at eve the\> shepherd sees
> The silver crescent through the trees . . .

The description continues with 'the roses hue' for the lip, a 'tint of snow' for the neck, and a 'snowy mantle',

> As silver'd by the morning beam
> The white mist curls on Grasmere's stream,
> Which like a Veil of flowing light
> Hides half the landskip from the sight . . .

It ends with a vision of

> The pathway winding through the dale,
> The cot, the seat of Peace and Love,
> Peeping through the tufted grove.[1]

Another poem, the fragmentary ode 'Beauty and Moonlight', begins

> High o'er the silver rocks I rov'd
> To wander from the form I lov'd.
> In hopes fond Fancy would be kind
> And steal my Mary from my mind.
>         'Twas Twilight and the lunar beam
> Sail'd slowly o'er Winander's stream.
> As down its sides the water stray'd
> Bright on a rock the moonbeam play'd.
> It shone half shelter'd from the view
> By pendent boughs of tressy yew.
> True time to love but false to rest
> So fancy whisper'd to my breast
> So shines her forehead smooth and fair
> Gleaming through her sable hair.[2]

This vision of a Mary who is characterized by a contrast between black hair and white skin is unlike any of the young women described later in Wordsworth's poetry; whether or not it is an actual person who is being described, moreover, the poetic language is driven by sentiment and fantasy. The lines just quoted have their own attractiveness; and eventually Wordsworth made a present of them to Coleridge, who

---

[1] Cf. *WPW* i. 261–2.       [2] Ibid. i. 263–4. From MS.

changed the young woman's name to 'Lewti' and published them under his own name.[3] Had they had any strong link with a real woman in his memory he might not have been so ready to relinquish them: they are more the stuff of adolescent fantasy, enjoying an easy relationship with the facts of real life (and perhaps superannuated for him by real relationships with 'Lucy' and Annette). The same is true of a Gothic poem (titled 'A Ballad' by de Selincourt) which was written in March 1787, when he was still 16. This concerned a young woman named Mary who was betrayed by a young man named William and died. In her despair,

> . . . oft she roam'd at dark midnight
> Among the silent graves
> Or sat on steep Winander's rock
> To hear the weltering waves.[4]

These verses are all set in the region between Hawkshead and Grasmere. If there was a real woman behind any of them, it is likely that she was called Mary, and had a complexion of dark hair and white skin, unlike Mary Hutchinson[5] or any other Mary we know of in Wordsworth's career. F. W. Bateson projected a 'Mary of Esthwaite Water' to fit the verses of this time and speculated about the story that might lie behind them.[6] But he was forced to confess the difficulty of reaching any conclusions, the line between realism and fantasy being hard to draw in verses that were so clearly following current taste.

There is among the early verse, however, another poem, not discussed by Bateson, which raises similar questions in an intricate, yet at the same time more interesting form. In the manuscript it is entitled 'Septimi, Gades', and a reference in it to a stay 'once' by the Rhône— which he had actually visited in the summer of 1790—suggests that they must have been written later than that, though how much later is not clear:[7]

[3] *CPW* (EHC) i. 253–5. The successive drafts showing the gradual move from the original can be studied ibid. ii. 1049–52.

[4] *WPW* i. 265–7.

[5] 'Like twilight's, too, her dusky hair': 'She was a Phantom of delight . . .', l. 6: *WPW* ii. 213.

[6] Bateson, *Wordsworth*, 65–70.

[7] Mark Reed, who looks at the question in *W Chronology EY*, considers that the lines might have been written in late 1790, since he does not think it likely that Wordsworth would have written such lines once he had met Annette Vallon. On the other hand the use of the word 'once' for the visit to the Rhône suggests a lapse of time longer than a few months. The notebook in which they are found belongs to the 'Windy Brow' period around 1794.

### 1

Oh thou whose fixed bewildered eye
In strange and dreary vacancy
Of tenderness severe
With fear unnamed my bosom chilled
While thus thy farewell accents thrilled
Or seemed to thrill mine ear

### 2

Think not from me my friend to roam
Thy arms shall be my only home
My only bed thy breast;
No separate path our lives shall know
But where thou goest I shall go,
And there my bones shall rest.

### 3

Oh! might we seek that humble shed
Which sheltered once my pilgrim head
Where down the mountains thrown
A streamlet seeks through forest glooms
Through viny glades and orchard blooms
Below the solemn Rhone.

### 4

But if the wayward fates deny
Those purple slopes, that azure sky
My willing voice shall hail
The lone grey cots and pastoral steeps
That shine inverted in the deeps
Of Grasmere's quiet vale.

### 5

To him who faint and heartless stands
On pale Arabia's thirsty sands
How fair that fountain seems
Where last, beneath the palmy shade
In bowers of rose and jasmine laid
He quaffed the living streams.

### 6

As fair in Memory's eye appear,
Sweet scene of peace thy waters clear
Thy turf and folding groves
On gales perfumed by every flower
Of mountain-top or mead or bower
Thy honey people roves.

7

What finny myriads twinkle bright
Along thy streams—how pure and white
The flocks thy shepherds fold!
What brimming pails thy milkmaids bear!
—Nor wants the jolly Autumn there
His crown of waving gold.

8

Yes Nature on those vivid meads
Those [   ] slopes and mountain-heads
Has shower'd her various wealth
There Temperance and Truth abide
And Toil with Leisure at his side
And Chearfulness and Health.

9

No spot does parting Phoebus greet
With farewell smile more fond and sweet
Than those sequestered hills
While as composing shades invest
With purple gloom the waters breast
The grove its music stills.

10

When shouts and sheepfold bells and sound
Of flocks and herds and streams rebound
Along the ringing dale
How beauteous round that gleaming Tide
The silvery morning vapours glide
And half the landscape veil.

11

Methinks that morning scene displays
A lovely emblem of our days
Unobvious and serene
So shall our still lives half betrayed
Shew charms more touching from their shade
Though veiled yet not unseen.

12

Yes, Mary, to some lowly door
In that delicious spot obscure
Our happy feet shall tend
And there for many a golden year
Fair Hope shall steal thy voice to chear
Thy poet & thy friend—

13
Though loudly roar the wintry flood
And Tempest shake the midnight wood
And rock our little nest
Love with his tenderest kiss shall dry
Thy human tear and still the sigh
That heaves thy gentle breast.[8]

This poem is one of Wordsworth's most enigmatic. Its most notable feature is that while it employs the very kind of poetic diction that Wordsworth was to deplore in the *Lyrical Ballads* Preface it also gives a strong sense, particularly in the opening, that, by comparison with the others we have looked at, it is about a real, closely observed woman. The mention of her 'fixed bewildered eye | In strange and dreary vacancy | Of tenderness severe' is particularly striking. It might have been written to the original of Lucy (in which case it would suggest that her real name was Mary); it might have been written to another Mary—or even some other young woman altogether. One cannot dismiss the possibility that it was addressed to Mary Hutchinson, in which case it would show that an expectation of future marriage was in their minds on at least some occasions during the 1790s.[9]

From the scattered and disparate pieces of evidence examined both here and in the main text it is not easy to construct a chronological narrative that will be faithful to the implications of each and every one. Continuing the assumption that an actual Lucy existed, a putative chronology might place significant encounters with her (whenever they originally began) during the first summer vacations of Wordsworth's university career (1788, 1789), and see the relationship ripening (following the 1790 visit to France) in the summer of 1791. After his return from the second and longer visit to France, on the other hand, the intervening love affair with Annette Vallon and the birth of Caroline on 15 December 1792 would necessarily have been upper-

---

[8] ? 1791, ? 1794 *WPW* i. 296–8. From MS.

[9] See my n. 68 to Ch. 2 above, however. In this connection it may be mentioned that the Spedding family at Armathwaite Hall, with whom Wordsworth sometimes stayed in the 1790s, having known their son at school, had two beautiful daughters, Mary and Margaret. In a letter of 21 Apr. 1794 Dorothy mentions that William had been staying with the family before he went to Halifax and comments on the charm of the daughters: 'They are women whose acquaintance I am very desirous of cultivating. They have read much and are amiable and engaging in their manners': *WL* (1787–1805) 115; cf. 118 and 299. There is no positive evidence of an attachment on Wordsworth's part, however, whereas the poem under consideration here suggests something more than a passing flirtation.

most in his mind. It is on the face of it unlikely that any serious commitment to the original Lucy would have survived those events, given that Wordsworth not only could not have presented himself on his return as a faithful lover but that his having fathered a child had set up new responsibilities: at that time he may well have believed that if he was going to marry anyone it should be Annette. If there was a break, on the other hand, it need not have been acrimonious. It is quite possible to imagine that after his return he remained on good terms with such a young woman as friend, both parties accepting, tacitly or explicitly, that there would in any case have been no immediate prospect of marriage. The precariousness of his financial situation in the 1790s has already been mentioned. The long lawsuit with the Lonsdale family was to drag on for many years, not being settled until 1802, and during this period he had nothing to live on except the small but crucial legacy from Raisley Calvert early in 1795 and such sums as were allowed him by his relatives. Above all things he was conscious of a long-standing dedication to poetry—a poetry, moreover, in which he would be attentive to current social ills.[10] This in itself would have explained his reluctance to marry and his decision to set up house with Dorothy, who, understanding and sympathizing with his poetic aspirations, was willing to share the meagre standard of living they entailed.

THE TOPOGRAPHICAL QUESTION

I have already argued the case for supposing that the most likely area for Lucy to have lived and been visited by Wordsworth was the upper part of the Duddon Valley, in or around Seathwaite. In examining this possibility further it is natural to ask how he became familiar with the inhabitants of Donnerdale in the first place. How did he come to enjoy hearing about their 'merry pranks', or—if this is indeed where he came across them—to meet the 'frank-hearted maids'? Did he simply walk in without introduction?

At this point attention may be drawn to a skein of evidence which, though tenuous, is worth pursuing on account of the tantalizing possibility towards which it points. It was mentioned earlier that his enthusiasm for the area was first aroused by Hugh Tyson, husband of his nurse, who found his way from there to Hawkshead and became a Sandys Charity boy at the Grammar School.[11] Hugh later set up a joinery business which by 1717 was employing three men but afterwards declined; in later years he worked largely on his own behalf,

[10] *W Prel* (1805) IV. 341-4.
[11] T. W. Thompson, *Wordsworth's Hawkshead*, ed. Robert Woof (1970), 6.

serving on occasion as a local undertaker.[12] He died at Colthouse on 28 February 1784,[13] when Wordsworth was 13, and is buried at Hawkshead; at the time of his death, according to the records, he was 70 years of age. Efforts to trace his forebears had failed when T. W. Thompson wrote his study of the district, but my own wider examination of the local registers reveals that a Hugh Tyson, son of Richard Tyson, was born at Bootle on the coast of Cumberland in 1715. In years when records were not kept very strictly a discrepancy of one year in the record of his age at death would not be very significant; and since this appearance of Hugh as Christian name for a Tyson seems unique in the registers of north-west England at that time (I have found no other instance) it is fair to assume that this was the same person. Bootle is within walking distance of the Duddon Valley, 10 miles away across the fells, so that the identification falls in readily with what is known of his later enthusiasm for the area. We may suppose that he found his way in early life over the fells to the Valley, later going on to Hawkshead.

Little more is known about Hugh's activities apart from one small incident, in which, as it happens, the Duddon Valley again figures. On one of the few occasions when his name appears in the local records, in 1748, he was a witness in a local court case dealing with an appeal from the Overseer of the Poor at Hawkshead that the care of a certain widow Caddy should fall to the churchwardens at Haverbrack near Milnthorpe in south Westmoreland rather than to his own district. To gain the evidence he needed, the overseer, John Hodgson, travelled to 'Bolton and Seathwaite'; when the appeal was heard his supporters were named as Hugh and Daniel Tyson. The 'Bolton' he visited must have been Bolton-le-Sands, on the coast of Lancashire, since it was there, one learns (again from parish records), that in 1733 a William Caddy married a Jane Holton, who evidently became the widow in question. The fact that the overseer also went to Seathwaite in the Duddon Valley suggests that Jane had some connection there also, and the calling of Hugh and Daniel Tyson as witnesses implies that one or both were in a position to provide evidence concerning it. (Caddy is a name that occurs in the valley.[14]) This suggests in turn that the Daniel Tyson who accompanied Hugh was called into service because he knew Seathwaite—and probably that he was still living there. The relevance of this to our present concerns lies in the fact that if there was in the area a branch of Hugh's family with whom he had remained in

[12] T. W. Thompson, *Wordsworth's Hawkshead*, ed. Robert Woof (1970), 7–12, 18–22.

[13] Moorman, *Wordsworth*, i. 84.

[14] According to the parish register of Ulpha a Henry Caddy of Loggan Bank was buried there on 20 Jan. 1723/4.

contact, this would have provided a natural nucleus of acquaintances for Wordsworth to have cultivated when he revisited the valley as a young man.

More than one Daniel Tyson lived at Seathwaite during this time. One who catches the eye lived at Wallowbarrow and married Sarah Walker of Mosshouse on 22 December 1737; since the date suggests that he was a coeval with Hugh, who would have been 22 at the time, he might well be the Daniel Tyson who accompanied him as witness in the Caddy case. Three children (Joseph, Elizabeth, and Leonard) were born to a father named as Daniel Tyson of Mosshouse between 1738 and 1743. After this, presumably because an additional house was built, Mosshouse disappears from the registers; it is replaced by two houses, Highmosshouse and Lowmosshouse. These houses still stand beyond the village of Seathwaite, a little way off the road that continues up the valley and near a house or homestead called 'Hollinhouse', which also appears regularly in the record. Later in the same register Daniel Tyson of Highmosshouse in Donnerdale is recorded as having married Elizabeth Sawrey of Wallowbarrow (born at Seathwaite in 1745) at Seathwaite church in April 1768. This might have been either the same Daniel Tyson, marrying again after the death of his first wife, or a relation of his. A child, Anne, was born to Daniel Tyson and his wife at 'Holehouse Dunerdale' in March 1772. This would appear to have been Hollinhouse (sometimes known also as Hollinghouse); it may have been the name both of a house and of a farmstead comprising more than one habitation, to judge from the frequency with which its name recurs in the register against various people's names. If we suppose that the Daniel Tyson who lived at 'Holehouse' was indeed related to Hugh Tyson, and that when Wordsworth went to the Duddon Valley in his adolescence he was encouraged by his old nurse to visit surviving members of the family, it is not difficult to imagine how pleasing it would have been to discover there a girl less than two years younger than himself—particularly if she turned out to be a 'gentle maid' who

> though her years ran parallel with mine
> Did then converse with objects of the sense
> In loftier style . . .[15]

The location fits the poems well. As the road passes up the valley from Seathwaite a broad track leads off to the right, opening out after a short distance into a plain on which a number of separated properties stand, including High Moss House, Low Moss House, and Hollin House (as it is now called), reached by ways even now unfrequented

[15] *W Prel* 441 n.

in an area that could without exaggeration be described as a 'lonely heath' and through which small streams run down to a large tributary that joins the main Duddon just past Seathwaite. A girl who spent her childhood here, among these untrodden ways and beside streams providing further springs for the Duddon, would, like Lucy Gray, have known 'the spirit of solitude' and, like the child Lucy of the poems, have lived close to nature. Her dwelling-place would also have been sufficiently far up the valley to make it advisable for a potential lover coming from its far end to visit her on horseback.

If Anne Tyson was indeed the original young woman of Wordsworth's elegiac poems, the fact that she had a name almost identical with that of his old nurse Ann Tyson would have given him a more than usually strong incentive to find another when he wanted to express his especial feelings for her. I have already suggested that the poem 'Moon-light', published during Wordsworth's first year at Cambridge and known to have been read by him, offered a very suitable one. Her real name, meanwhile, being monosyllabic, would have fitted the metre and diction of the lines about the 'one beloved maid' in drafts for *The Prelude* where, I have suggested above, one may well have originally appeared before the alteration to 'And':

> **And** blessed are your days
> That such delights are yours.[16]

Anne Tyson also fits my tentative hypothesis in another crucial respect. According to the same parish records of Seathwaite, where the population was very sparse indeed during this time, an unmarried woman of that name died on 18 February 1797, the place of her residence being then given in the register as 'Nook in Ulpha'. Although it is obviously impossible in the present state of the evidence to identify her conclusively as Wordsworth's Lucy, it must be acknowledged that everything we know about her fits well.[17] 'Nook' lies some way above Ulpha church, in that part of the valley where it has broadened into more open country below Seathwaite (where Daniel and Elizabeth Tyson lived). A small house of that name still stands there. The nature

---

[16] It is not at all clear from the state of the MS what word might have been there, except that there are no traces of ascenders or descenders at that point. It could be—as I have tentatively read above, in the interests of the sceptical—'Then', or some other such word.

[17] The other conceivable candidate would be Mary Fleming of Hollinhouse, who was baptized on 6 June 1774, married John Bowness, a slate-getter, on 4 Feb. 1795 and died at Lowmosshouse on 24 Jan. 1798. She must have known Anne Tyson and no doubt attended Robert Walker's school, forming another member of the Donnersdale community whom Wordsworth could have known; but by 1798 she was by definition no longer a 'maid'.

of the nearby landscape, dominated by a sweeping hayfield, is such that if this was the house where Anne Tyson died, and if Wordsworth had seen it or heard it described, the view from it would aptly have fitted his depiction of 'the last green field | That Lucy's eyes survey'd'.

In that case another question arises. From early in 1795 to mid-September 1798 Wordsworth was continuously in the south and west of England, after which he sailed for Germany. If his former love, and surviving friendship, was indeed for a young woman who lived in the Duddon Valley and died there early in 1797 how could news of her death have reached him at that time, given the obscurity of her dwelling-place?

There is, as it happens, at least one possible channel of communication by which he could have heard. Among the circle of his acquaintance in the Furness area during his university vacations was the family of Dr Roger Baldwin, which included a college acquaintance of his named John Baldwin and his sister Cecilia, who in time married John's friend James Losh. After having met Cecilia and James near Bristol on several occasions in 1798, Wordsworth caught up with John Baldwin that autumn at the beginning of his German tour, staying with him for a brief time in Hamburg.[18] If we suppose that, as seems likely, the Baldwins also had been Wordsworth's companions on some of the excursions into the Duddon Valley, we find a possible channel by which Wordsworth, arriving in Germany in the later months of 1798, might have learned there about the death of his former love. And if the news reached him just as he had reached a strange land where he would spend several months in a growing sense of alienation, the unexpected strength of his reaction would have been all the more understandable. The fact that while he was drafting lines in appreciation of her feeling for nature she had been, unknown to him, lying already in her grave, a victim of nature's indifferent workings, would have been almost unbearably poignant.[19]

The more general irony involved could hardly have escaped him, moreover. Only the previous summer he had been writing lines to Dorothy that included the assurance, 'Nature never did betray the heart that loved her'; now he had to wrestle with the fact that even as he wrote them the young woman who for him had best demonstrated the bond between Nature and the human heart was already dying or dead; if his assurance was to be rescued at all it could

---

[18] *W Chronology EY* 249; *WL* (1787–1805), 229; *CL* i. 433.

[19] It may even be the case that the words 'Long time' in the lines 'Long time before her head lay low | Dead to the world was she' in the last stanza of 'My love was one from cities far', which he described as being 'injurious to the sense', in fact represent a displacement of his dismay on learning how long she had been dead without his knowing.

be only by an appeal to the larger universe that continues to roll us all round, after every death, as part of the sublime process laid bare by Newton—a process the knowledge of which mortifies and consoles us by turns.

After his return to England in 1798 it was some time before Wordsworth is known to have returned to the Duddon Valley, though he visited the general area. When he and Coleridge undertook their first northern tour late in 1798 they stayed at an alehouse at Wasdale Head kept by a Thomas Tyson.[20] Coleridge returned to the area in 1802 and stayed again at Thomas Tyson's, where he was welcomed and given advice about the climbing of nearby mountains,[21] which he followed before going on to drop into the Duddon Valley and sleep at Ulpha. Setting out on another walking-tour two years later (the one when Dorothy referred to the 'Rocks, hills, bushes and trees' of the vale[22]) William and Dorothy stayed again with Thomas Tyson on their way to the valley: Dorothy wrote to Lady Beaumont that they were 'very hospitably entertained at the house of a *statesman* at Wasdale head, for there is no Inn there, and the next day we went to his Cousin's who keeps an alehouse at Seathwaite.' She goes on to comment, '. . . We were received by the good people of the publick house with the same hospitality as by their kinsfolk in Wasdale.' The experience provoked reflections that staying in the place enabled them to see how the natives of that part of the country used to be before it was much visited by tourists.[23]

This devotion to Tysons and the Duddon Valley may, obviously, represent no more than a series of coincidences, particularly given the fact that the name is by no means uncommon in Lakeland.[24] A further reference in September 1808, however, when Coleridge and Sara Hutchinson, with Wordsworth, visited the same limited region, in a trip described by Coleridge as 'a literary Engagement, involving a small Tour on the Duddon',[25] (after which the party went on once again to stay with Thomas Tyson at Wasdale[26]) brings one up short. An entry Coleridge made on this occasion in his notebook, where it appeared in the midst of reflections on his agonizing love for Sara, is especially notable in view of all that has been said above:

[20] *CL* ii. 839; *CN* i. 535 n., 540 n., 541.

[21] *CL* ii. 839–40; *CN* i. 1214 n., 1217, 1219 n.

[22] See above, p. 79.

[23] *WL* (1787–1805), 507.

[24] It may be pointed out, nevertheless, that Wordsworth showed some further interest in people of the name. He recorded—apparently when collecting information about Robert Walker—some details about 'Henry Tyson now living in Nether Wasdale, aged 81', who had 14 children: see *W Chronology MY* 674.

[25] Letter to Eliza Nevins of 16 Sept. 1808, *CL* iii. 123.     [26] *CN* iii. 3384.

Seathwaite Vale, 19 Sept. 1808—
W. Wordsworth, Sara, & I—the Cottage, Hollingshouse!! all, all/[27]

Why did they visit this particular cottage—which must have been the same as the 'Hollinhouse' mentioned above—in such an out of the way place? And what was it that made such an impression on Coleridge when they did so? Had Coleridge and Sara Hutchinson asked Wordsworth to show them the original cottage where he had visited Lucy? And did Wordsworth agree to do so, while asking them to preserve his confidentiality on this sensitive subject? Did Coleridge now feel that he could understand 'all, all'[28] about the events behind those poems and their relation to his friend's earlier career? At this point any readers who up to now may have believed that we are dealing with, at best, nothing more than coincidence and its notoriously long arm must surely feel less secure.

For readers in general the journey towards identification may well be found more profitable than any likely arrival. Trying to fit the surviving evidence to an actual narrative and to such records as survive can produce an effect like that of reading a French *roman nouveau*, where the attempt to reconstruct an original course of events produces a narrative effect which, passing into enigma, causes one to focus on the actual scene described ever more vividly. Whether or not it produces a firm conclusion about Lucy, the effect of the searching and teasing involved is to make the reader more aware of the actualities ineluctably evoked by the poems: the shape and positioning of Lakeland cottages, the rhythms of horse riding, the magic of luminescence in darkness, the potentialities of living alone in nature. In such circumstances the experiences of searching for the original Lucy and of reading and rereading the poems about her can work together in an unexpectedly profitable way. The journey will be valued for its own sake.

If my investigations here have been fruitful, nevertheless, one has the added bonus that they can after all lead to single and identifiable ends:

---

[27] *CN* iii. 3376. It is worth recording that I noticed this entry, with its significant implications for this study, *after* I had followed the trail recorded in this appendix and reached most of my conclusions.

[28] The phrase 'All, all,' occurs twice in variant lines for the first stanza of the poem 'Love' (*CPW* (EHC) i. 330), which in the original runs

> All thoughts, all passions, all delights,
> Whatever stirs this mortal frame,
> All the but ministers of Love,
> And feed his sacred flame.

See *CPW* (EHC) ii. 1054. In the third line the first variant reads, 'All, all are ministers of Love,'; the second reads, in the second line, 'All, all that stirs this mortal frame': *CPW* (EHC) ii. 1054.

to a cottage at Hollinhouse, among the untrodden ways above Seathwaite, where Lucy's original may have grown up close to the rocks and trees of a nature she loved and was taught to know better by the local priest and schoolmaster, and to another, a few miles away at Nook in Ulpha, where she perhaps looked across green English fields for the last time.

# Index